שָׁעַר to esteem
שַׁעַר gate
שֹׁעֵר porter
שִׂיב vb
שֻׁדַּד shudder
שַׂעַר hair
שַׂעַר fear

בְּיוֹם

bard
bird
beard
aboard
brod
braed
bred
treed
brood
abrood
brood

52 +3 con

INTRODUCTORY HEBREW
METHOD AND MANUAL

WILLIAM R. HARPER'S

Introductory Hebrew
METHOD AND MANUAL

REVISED BY
J. M. POWIS SMITH

THE UNIVERSITY OF CHICAGO PRESS
CHICAGO & LONDON

THE UNIVERSITY OF CHICAGO PRESS, CHICAGO 60637
The University of Chicago Press, Ltd., London, W.C. 1

Published 1959. Fourth Impression 1969.
Printed in the United States of America

FOREWORD

At last students can again obtain William Rainey Harper's *Introductory Hebrew Method and Manual* and *Elements of Hebrew*, textbooks which for generations have been used with great success in the teaching of biblical Hebrew. It was with regret that we saw them withdrawn and it is with enthusiasm that we welcome their return. No other textbooks have been able to win the respect and popularity that the Harper books have always had. Pupils and teachers alike can testify that they furnish an excellent and enduring means for gaining a knowledge of Hebrew.

The inductive method employed by Professor Harper is based on sound educational principles. From the very first lesson the student has the incentive of a feeling of definite accomplishment. The constant repetition of the biblical material both establishes and fortifies the student's knowledge of the Hebrew language.

The grammar, as presented in the *Elements of Hebrew*, is neither oversimplified nor belabored with involved and wordy complexity. Essential principles are enunciated briefly, clearly, and soundly, with ample illustration. They can be grasped and retained easily.

The aids to instruction incorporated in the *Introductory Hebrew Method and Manual*, used in conjunction with the *Elements*, are a teacher's delight. In addition to the discussion of the biblical words in the reading lesson, there are exercises that are distinctive for establishing a real appreciation of Hebrew style and syntax. The volume also contains the vocalized text of Genesis I–VIII for reading purposes, the unvocalized text of Genesis I–IV for practice in vocalizing, and the transliterated text of Genesis I to afford the student a check on his work during the early lessons. In addition to the usual vocabularies necessary for the lessons, the *Manual* also contains the frequency lists developed by Professor Harper to help the student master vocabulary rapidly and efficiently by learning first the words most frequently used in the Bible. Such accessories are valuable aids to the teacher, for they make possible greater flexibility in method so that materials can be adapted to the needs of the class.

These books were written long ago by Professor Harper, the first president of the University of Chicago, on the basis of his successful experience both with classes and with his famous correspondence courses. They have met the test of time and are surprisingly modern. As his employment of the educationally sound inductive method and his development of frequency lists in vocabulary demonstrate, Professor Harper could be said to be ahead of his time. Judiciously and carefully revised by Professor J. M. P. Smith, these books are regarded by many as still the best tools for the learning and teaching of biblical Hebrew. While it is true that Hebrew studies have progressed in the interim and that consequently at some points minor improvements might be made if and when a revision is undertaken, there is no serious obstacle to the use of these volumes as now reproduced.

With the present increasing interest in biblical Hebrew, the reintroduction of these fine textbooks will afford an opportunity for increasing numbers of students to learn Hebrew quickly and well, whether in class or privately.

RAYMOND A. BOWMAN

UNIVERSITY OF CHICAGO

PREFACE

The *Method and Manual* of the late President William Rainey Harper first appeared as *A Hebrew Manual* in 1883. Since the 2nd edition in 1885, several reprints have been made, but the text of that edition has stood practically without change. The Inductive approach to the study of Hebrew represented by the Harper text-books has commended itself to a wide circle of teachers and has yielded satisfactory results in arousing and maintaining the interest of large numbers of students. The fact that since its first presentation more American students have studied Hebrew by this method than by all other methods combined, and that notwithstanding the need of revision in the text-books, the method has held its own in a field where competition is keen, warrants the effort to bring the *Method and Manual* into line with advancing knowledge. The scope of the revision has been determined by the New Edition of the *Elements of Hebrew* (1921) with which the *Method and Manual* should be used.

The student mind is confronted by an ever-increasing variety of subjects, each with its own special appeal and many of them offering an apparently short and easy route to a desired goal. It is inevitable that Hebrew should suffer some loss of adherents; and it is well that such as have no special aptitude for linguistic study should expend their energies in fields that are for them more productive. But as long as the Old Testament remains one of the great historical documents of the Jewish and Christian faiths, there will ever be many who will seek to obtain a scholar's control of the literary sources of their historic beliefs. As the prologue to the Wisdom of Sirach says, "When things spoken in Hebrew are translated into another tongue they have not quite the same meaning; and not only these things (i. e. the following chapters), but the Law itself and the

Prophecies and the rest of the books, convey a different meaning when spoken in their original [language]." All who would enter into the inner sanctuary of the Hebrew spirit must first equip themselves with the linguistic key. The chambers to which it furnishes access are spacious and splendid to a degree that can never be appreciated by one who has not seen them. The Hebrew mind must remain largely *terra incognita* to him who does not know its native language. That the first steps in the learning of that language may be made simple and may represent actual progress in the mastery of the Old Testament in its own idiom is sufficient reason for sending out the Harper *Method and Manual* in a new edition.

To my colleague Professor Ira Maurice Price who guided me in my first journey through the *Introductory Hebrew Method and Manual*, and has aided in the making of this edition by reading both copy and proof, I gratefully acknowledge my indebtedness. To teachers long familiar with this book in its old form, I offer no apologies for changes. Every true teacher rejoices in the progress of knowledge, even when that progress is at his cost. New editions teach new duties. The best teachers are always themselves eager learners.

J. M. POWIS SMITH

THE UNIVERSITY OF CHICAGO

PREFACE TO THE SECOND EDITION

The student of a language must acquire three things: (1) a working vocabulary of the language, (2) a knowledge of the grammatical principles of the language, (3) an ability to use this vocabulary and to apply these principles, so as to gain the best results, whether for a literary or an exegetical purpose.

While all agree as to the end desired, the method of attaining this end is a question in dispute. According to one view, the student is first to learn the principles as they are laid down in the grammars, and then apply them to selected words, or short sentences. And after a short preliminary training of this sort, he is plunged headlong into a text without notes of any kind, and expected to make progress, and to enjoy the study. His vocabulary is to be learned by looking up the words in the Lexicon, until they become familiar. Different phases of this method are in use among teachers of Hebrew; but all follow practically the same order, (1) study of grammar; (2) application of grammar.

It is the purpose of this volume to furnish a text-book, which shall assist in acquiring the Hebrew language by a different method. The method employed may be called an inductive one. The order of work which it advocates is, *first*, to gain an accurate and thorough knowledge of some of the "facts" of the language; *secondly*, to learn from these facts the principles which they illustrate, and by which they are regulated; *thirdly*, to apply these principles in the further progress of the work. A few words of explanation are needed at this point:—

(1) The method is *an* inductive, not *the* inductive method; and while, upon the whole, it is rigidly employed throughout the course, a slight departure is made at times, in order to make more complete the treatment of a subject, for some detail of which an example has not occurred.

(2) The term "facts," as used, includes data from whatever source gathered; not merely the grammatical forms found in the passages studied, but also the paradigms which contain these and other forms systematically arranged.

(3) It is not to be supposed that a long time must elapse before

the beginner is ready to take hold of principles. On the contrary, he is taught important principles, and that, too, inductively, during the first hour's work. The three processes are all the while going on together. He is increasing the store of "facts" at his command, and, at the same time, learning from the facts thus acquired new principles, and applying these principles to the new forms continually coming to his notice. Great care must be exercised, however, that the correct order be followed. Let him attempt to learn no principle of which he has not had several illustrations. Let him be required to apply no principle the application of which he has not already learned from familiar cases.

(4) The memorizing of the "facts" of a language, before a knowledge of the principles has been acquired is, indeed, a piece of drudgery; yet not so great as is the memorizing of grammar without a knowledge of the "facts." Nor will it long remain drudgery; for very soon, the student will begin to see analogies, to compare this word with that, and, in short, to make his own grammar. From this time, there will be developed such an interest in the work, that all thought of drudgery will pass away.

The question is frequently asked, How is the first lesson given? A brief statement must suffice:—

The first word of Genesis I. 1 is written on the board, and the English equivalent of each consonant and vowel-sound indicated to the student. The word, as a whole, is then pronounced, and its meaning given. The student is called upon to pronounce it, and to give its meaning. The second word is taken up and treated in the same manner. Then the two words are pronounced together, and their meaning given. After this, each remaining word is considered, and with each new word a review of all the preceding words is made. When he has learned thus to pronounce the entire verse, and to give a Hebrew word when its English equivalent is named, the student is shown the "Notes" (see pages 3–4) of the "METHOD," where, for his private study, he will find, for substance, the aid already given orally. His attention is also directed to the "Observations," with most of which he has been made familiar by the previous work. He is now informed that at the following recitation he will be expected (1) to pronounce the verse without hesitation from the pointed Hebrew (2) to pronounce it, and write it on the board, from the English translation; (3) to pronounce it, and write it on the board from the unpointed text; (4) to write the transliteration of it, as given in the "Notes" or in the *Manual*. The absolute mastery of the verse is, therefore, the first thing. There will remain to be taken up, (1) the "Notes," for all of which the student is held responsible; (2) the "Observations," which he is expected to recall, at the suggestion of the word on which the observation is based; (3) the "Word-Lesson," which, at first, includes few words not contained in the verse or verses of the Lesson, and which is to be learned in such a manner that when the English word is pronounced, the Hebrew equivalent will be given; (4) the "Exercises," which are to be written on paper beforehand, copied on the board in the class-room, criticised by instructor and class, and corrected by each student on his paper.

The "Topics for Study" are intended to furnish a resume of the more important points touched upon in the Lesson. By their use, a rapid and helpful review of the hour's work is accomplished.

In subsequent "Lessons," a "Grammar-Lesson" is assigned. In every case, however, the instructor should read and explain each reference to the class before asking them to prepare it.

The "Lessons" cover chapters I-VIII. of Genesis, and include a formal study of almost every important portion of the grammar, except the Accents, the Euphony of Vowels, the Euphony of Consonants, the Verb with Suffixes, the Irregular Nouns, and the Inflection of Feminine Nouns, to all of which, however, numerous allusions and references are made in the "Notes."

All the help possible is given the student in the first fifteen "Lessons." But from this point he is led gradually to rely more and more upon himself. The "Lessons" will be found to contain more, perhaps, than some classes can prepare for a single recitation, although this will depend largely upon the character of the class and the number of recitations during a week. It was deemed best, however, to make them thus, since it is an easy matter for the instructor to indicate that a certain portion of the exercises may be omitted. The author himself will feel inclined to require everything in the "Lessons."

Special attention is invited to the "Review-Lessons," in the study of each of which two or more recitations may profitably be spent.

The "Method" is understood to include also the "MANUAL," although the latter, for a sufficient reason, is paged separately, and given a title-page and preface of its own.

For the material contained in these Lessons, and for its arrangement, the author is indebted to no one. The book, as it now appears, presents the results of five years' experience, during which it has been his privilege to teach not less than five hundred men their first lesson in Hebrew.

Many valuable hints have been received from Mr. Frederick J. Gurney, by whom great assistance has been received in the work of the Correspondence School of Hebrew. He has also kindly helped in the preparation of manuscript for the printer, and in revising the proof-sheets. For similar service the author is indebted to Mr. C. E. Crandall, and to Rev. John W. Payne. To the latter credit is also due for his painstaking care in the typographical work of the book.

With a faith in the Inductive Method, which grows stronger every year, and with the hope that the time may soon come when many others shall have an equally strong faith in it, the author commits the "METHOD" to its friends.

W. R. H.

MORGAN PARK, September 1, 1885.

TABLE OF CONTENTS

INTRODUCTORY METHOD.

		Page
Lesson I	Genesis I. 1	3– 6
Lesson II	Genesis I. 2a	6– 10
Lesson III	Genesis I. 2b, 3	10– 13
Lesson IV	Genesis I. 4	13– 17
Lesson V	Genesis I. 5	17– 20
Lesson VI	Genesis I. 6	21– 24
Lesson VII	Genesis I. 7, 8	24– 27
Lesson VIII	Genesis I. 9	27– 30
Lesson IX	Genesis I. 10, 11	31– 34
Lesson X	Genesis I. 12, 13	34– 36
Lesson XI	Genesis I. 14, 15	36– 39
Lesson XII	Genesis I. 16, 17	39– 43
Lesson XIII	Genesis I. 18–20	43– 45
Lesson XIV	Genesis I. 21–23	45– 50
Lesson XV	Genesis I. 24–26	50– 53
Lesson XVI	Genesis I. 27–29	54– 57
Lesson XVII	Genesis I. 30, 31	58– 60
Lesson XVIII	Review	60– 63
Lesson XIX	Genesis II. 1-3	63– 67
Lesson XX	Genesis II. 4-6	67– 72
Lesson XXI	Genesis II. 7-9	72– 76
Lesson XXII	Genesis II. 10-12	76– 80
Lesson XXIII	Genesis II. 13, 14	80– 83
Lesson XXIV	Genesis II. 15, 16	83– 86
Lesson XXV	Genesis II. 17, 18	86– 88
Lesson XXVI	Genesis II. 19–21	88– 91
Lesson XXVII	Genesis II 21, 22	91– 95
Lesson XXVIII	Genesis II. 23	95– 97
Lesson XXIX	Genesis II. 24, 25	98–101
Lesson XXX	Review	102–104
Lesson XXXI	Genesis III. 1, 2	104–108

TABLE OF CONTENTS.

		Page
Lesson XXXII	Genesis III. 3-5	108–112
Lesson XXXIII	Genesis III. 6-8	112–115
Lesson XXXIV	Genesis III. 9-11	116–119
Lesson XXXV	Genesis III. 12-14	119–122
Lesson XXXVI	Genesis III. 15-17	122–127
Lesson XXXVII	Genesis III. 18-21	127–130
Lesson XXXVIII	Genesis III. 22-24	130–134
Lesson XXXIX	Genesis IV. 1-4	134–136
Lesson XL	Genesis IV. 5-8	136–139
Lesson XLI	Genesis IV. 9-12	139–141
Lesson XLII	Genesis IV. 13-17	141–144
Lesson XLIII	Genesis IV. 18-22	144–146
Lesson XLIV	Genesis IV. 23-26	147–149
Lesson XLV	Review	150–151
Lesson XLVI	Genesis V. 1-16	152–154
Lesson XLVII	Genesis V. 17-32	155–157
Lesson XLVIII	Genesis VI. 1-8	158–160
Lesson XLIX	Genesis VI. 9-15	161–163
Lesson L	Genesis VI. 16-22	163–165
Lesson LI	Genesis VII. 1-8	166–168
Lesson LII	Genesis VII. 9-16	168–170
Lesson LIII	Genesis VII. 17-24	171–173
Lesson LIV	Genesis VIII. 1-7	173–175
Lesson LV	Genesis VIII 8-14	176–178

MANUAL.

		Page
I.	The Hebrew Text of Genesis Chaps. I.-IV	181–191
II.	A Literal Translation of Genesis Chaps. I.-IV	192–202
III.	The Unpointed Hebrew Text of Genesis Chaps. I.-IV	203–212
IV.	Transliteration of Genesis Chap. I	213–215
V.	The Hebrew Text of Genesis Chaps. V.-VIII	217–226
VI.	Hebrew-English Vocabulary of Genesis Chaps. I.-VIII	229–250
VII.	English-Hebrew Vocabulary of Genesis Chaps. I.-VIII	251–256
VIII.	Word Lists—Hebrew	257–263
IX.	Word Lists—Translation	264–269

INTRODUCTORY HEBREW METHOD

LESSON I.—GENESIS I. 1.[1]

[*To the student* :—Let it be understood from the outset that nothing short of complete mastery, and that, of everything in the Lesson, will accomplish the end in view. Not a needless word or statement has been inserted. Let it be a matter of principle to do just what is assigned,—no more, no less.]

1. NOTES

1. בְּרֵאשִׁית—bᵉrē'-šîθ (two syllables)—*In-beginning:*

   a. *Six letters:*—בּ (b); ר (r); א, called 'ălĕf,[2] not pronounced, but represented by '; שׁ (š = sh); י (y), here silent after ֵ ; ת (θ = th, as in *thin*).

   b. *Three vowel-sounds:*— ְ (ᵉ) under בּ , pron. like *e* in *below*, see § 5. 6. a ;[3] ֵ (ē), like *ey* in *they;* י ִ (î), like *i* in *machine*.

2. בָּרָא—bâ-râ' (two syllables)—(he)-*created:*

   a. *Three letters:*— בּ (b); ר (r); א (') called 'ălĕf,[2] see 1 a.[4]

   b. *Two vowel-sounds:*—Both ָ (â), like *â* in *all*.

3. אֱלֹהִים—'ᵉlô-hîm (two syllables)— *God* (literally *Gods*):

   a. *Five letters:*— א ('); ל (l); ה (h); י (y), silent after ֹ ; ם (m).

   b. *Three-vowel-sounds:*— ֱ (ᵉ), like *e* in *met*, quickly uttered, § 5. 6. c; ֹ (ô), like *ô* in *note;* י ִ (î), see 1. b.

   c. The accent ֽ with ֱ , marks this word as the middle of the verse.

4. אֵת—'ēθ—not translated, but represented in translation by)(.

5. הַשָּׁמַיִם—hăš-šâ-mă'-yĭm (four syllables)—*the-heavens:*

   a. *Five letters:*— ה (h); שׁ (š = sh), but שּׁ (with a dot in its bosom) is š doubled; מ (m), written so at beginning or in the middle of a word; י (y), not silent as before but like *y* in *year;* ם (m), written so at end of a word, § 3. 2.

---

[1] The text of Gen. 1:1 will be found on page 181; the transliteration, on page 213; the translation, on page 192.
[2] This word is pronounced with ă like a in all, law, etc.
[3] References preceded by § are to the "Elements of Hebrew," 1921 edition (reprinted 1959).
[4] References without § mark are to preceding Notes in these Lessons.

b. *Four vowel-sounds:*— ◌ָ (ă), like *a* in *hatter*, § 5. 1; ◌ָ , see 2 *b;*
◌ֲ (ă); ◌ִ (ĭ), like *i* in *pin*, § 5. 2

c. The sign ◌ְ under מ is used arbitrarily in these Lessons to indicate the position of the accent when as in this word, it is not on the last vowel.

d. The ĭ of the last syllable is only of secondary importance.

6. וְאֵת —wᵉʼēθ (one syllable)—*and*-)(, see 4:
a. *Three letters:*—ו (w), like *w* in *water;* א (ʼ); ת (θ).
b. *Two vowel-sounds:*— ◌ְ (ᵉ), see 1. *b;* ◌ֵ (ē), see 1. *b.*

7. הָאָרֶץ: —hâ-ʼâ´-reṣ (three syllables)—*the-earth:*
a. *Four letters:*—ה (h); א (ʼ); ר (r); ץ (ṣ), a sharp hissing sound, § 2. 7.
b. *Three vowel-sounds:*— ◌ָ (å); ◌ָ (å); ◌ֶ (ĕ), like *e* in *met.*
c. The last vowel is of secondary character, as in 5 *d.*
d. The accent ◌ֽ , under א, marks this word as the end of the verse; the ׃ is equivalent to a period.

2. OBSERVATIONS.

1. The letters in this verse are:—(1) א, (2) ב, (3) ה, (4) ו, (5) י, (6) ל, (7) מ, (8) ם, (9) ץ, (10) ר, (11) שׁ, (12) שׂ, (13) ת.

2. The vowel sounds:—(1) ◌ָ , (2) ◌ֵ , (3) ◌ִ , (4) ◌ְ , (5), ◌ֲ , (6) ◌ֶ , (7) י◌ִ , (8) ◌ֵ , (9) ◌ְ .

3. To be carefully distinguished in pronunciation are:—
(1) ◌ְ (ᵉ), ◌ִ (ᵉ), ◌ֱ (ĕ), ◌ֵ (ē); (2) ◌ַ (ă), ◌ָ (å); (3) ◌ִ (ĭ), י◌ִ (î).

4. *Above* the line, a dot is ô (as in *note*); below the line, it is î [(as in *pin*).

5. The Hebrew is written from right to left.

6. The plural ending of masc. nouns is ים◌ִ (îm), as in אֱלֹהִים (lit., *Gods*); cf. the Hebrew words that have been Anglicized, *cherub*-im, and *seraph*-im.

7. אֵת (ʼēθ), not translatable, is a sign placed before the object of a verb, when that object is both direct and *definite.*

8. The preposition *in*, בְּ, and the conjunction *and*, וְ, are never written separately, being always *prefixed to the* following *word*.

9. When it is desired to pronounce a letter *twice in succession*, that letter is written but *once*, and a dot inserted (see שׁ) in its bosom.

10. The letter of the Definite Article (*the*) is ה (h).

11. Most words are accented on the last vowel; those which are accented elsewhere mark the place of the accent in this book, by the sign ֖.

12. Every syllable begins with a consonant. The vowel-sounds ְ and ֱ cannot alone carry a syllable.

3. WORD-LESSON.

(1) אֱלֹהִים God   (5) בְּ *in*   (9) מָשַׁל[1] *he-ruled*
(2) אָמַר[1] *he-said*   (6) בָּרָא[1] *he-created* (10) רֵאשִׁית *beginning*
(3) הָאָרֶץ *the-earth* (7) הַ, הָ *the*   (11) שָׁמַיִם *heavens*
(4) אֵת)((8) וְ *and*   (12) שָׁמַר[1] *he-kept*

4. EXERCISES

1. To be translated into Hebrew:—(1) *And-beginning;* (2) *And-heavens;* (3) *He-created*)(*the-earth and-*)(*the-heavens;* (4) *God kept* (Hebrew order: *kept God*))(*the-heavens;* (5) *God* (*is*)[2] *in-heavens;* (6) *God ruled* (Hebrew order: *ruled God*); (7) *In-beginning God said;* (8) *The* (הָ)-*beginning;* (9) *the* (הָ-*God;* (10) *And-the-earth*.

2. To be translated into English:— (1) וְהַשָּׁמַיִם; (2) שָׁמַר; (3) אֱלֹהִים אֵת הָאָרֶץ; (4) מָשַׁל אֱלֹהִים בְּשָׁמַיִם; (5) וּבְרֵאשִׁית; אָמַר הָאֱלֹהִים.

---

[1] A verb in the past tense 3d person singular masculine.
[2] Parentheses ( ) enclose words which are not to be rendered into Hebrew.

3. To be written in English letters: — (1) שָׁמַר, (2) אָמַר, (3) אֱלֹהִים (9) וְאֵת (8) בָּרָא, (7) הַשָּׁמַיִם (6) וְ, (5) בְּ, (4) מָשָׁל, (10) הָאָרֶץ.

4. To be written in Hebrew letters:—(1) lā, (2) lāš, (3) hĭl, (4) bĕ, (5) rå, (6) yĭm, (7) îm, (8) lᵉ, (9) hᵉ, (10) lē.

5. TOPICS FOR STUDY.

(1) The sounds represented by the letter *e* as variously printed.
(2) The plural ending; the preposition *in;* the conjunction *and*.
(3) The sign אֵת; the method employed to indicate the doubling of a letter.
(4) The article; the usual place of the accent; the difference between מ and ם.

LESSON II.—GENESIS I. 2a.

1. NOTES.

8. וְהָאָרֶץ—wᵉhā-'å'-reṣ—*and-the-earth:* see 7, preceding Lesson.

9. הָיְתָה—hā-yᵉθå(h) (two syllables)—(she) *was:*

a. 1st syllable, הָ (hå), ends in a vowel and is said to be *open*, § 26. 1.
b. 2d syllable, יְתָה yᵉθå(h); the final ה is silent, as always at the end of a word; the ָ is not a full vowel, and goes with what follows.
c. The sign ָ with ְ indicates a secondary accent, § 18.

10. תֹהוּ—θō'-hû (two syllables)—(a)-*desolation:*

a. 1st syl., תֹ (θ), ֹ ō, (not ô), ends in a vowel i. e. is *open* § 26. 1.
b. 2d syl., ה (h), וּ (û), like *oo* in *tool*, is open, § 26. 1.

11. וָבֹהוּ—wā-vō'hû (three syllables)—*and-*(a)-*waste:*

a. ב is not *b* (בּ), but *v* as in *vote*.

b. Each syllable is open, § **26.** 1.

12. וְחֹ֖שֶׁךְ—wᵉḥō'-šĕx (two syllables)—*and-darkness:*

a. ו (w); ח (ḥ), a harsh *h*-sound, § **2.** 3; שׁ (š=*sh*); ךְ (x), like German ch (weak).

b. ֶ (ᵉ); the ֹ over שׁ serves also for the vowel ō; ֶ (ĕ).

c. The ֶ in ךְ must be written, when final, but it has no sound.

d. The final vowel here is of secondary character; see 5.*d* and 7.*c.*

13. עַל־פְּנֵי—'ăl+pᵉnê (two syllables)—*upon+faces-of:*

a. ע ('), practically unpronounceable for us, called 'ă'-yĭn, § **2.** 2; ל (l); פ (p); נ (n).

b. The י after ֵ (ê) is silent, as was that after ִ (î), see 1. *b.*

c. The sign ־ is the Hebrew hyphen, represented in transliteration by +.

d. These two words, *upon* and *faces-of*, are pronounced as if one.

14. תְהוֹם—θᵉhôm (one syllable)—*abyss:*

a. A syllable beginning with two consonants, but between them is the short *e*-sound described in § **5.** 6.*a.*

b. The syllable ends in a consonant,—it is *closed*, § **26.** 2.

c. As י is silent after ֵ or ִ, so ו is silent under ֹ (ô).

d. ְ, see 3.*c*, preceding Lesson.

2. *LETTERS AND VOWELS PROMISCUOUSLY ARRANGED.*

י	ה	בּ	ח	ֵ	ָ	ַ
ה	ךְ	ם	נ	ֻ	ָ	ִ
ב	נ	א	י	ֶ	ֻ	ֳ
ע	ר	ץ	פּ	ָ	ִ	ִי
שׁ	ת	ו	בּ	ֶ		וֹ
ל	פ	מ	ה	וּ	ַ	ָ

Suggestion.—Study this table until every sign has been mastered. It contains sixteen out of the twenty-two letters, and eleven out of the fifteen vowel-signs in Hebrew.

3. OBSERVATIONS.

13. New letters: (1) ב, (2) ה, (3) ך, (4) ע, (5) פ, (6) נ.

14. New vowels: (1) וֹ, (2) ִי, (3) וּ; but ִי and וֹ (ê and ô) are pronounced just like ֵ and ֹ (ē and ō), the former having what is termed a *fuller* writing.

15. ְ, called Šᵉwâ, is the least vowel-sound and cannot carry a syllable.

16. While the conjunction *and* (וְ) is usually written with Šᵉwâ (thus: וְ), it is once written in this lesson וָ (wâ).

17. Syllables ending in a vowel are called *open;* ending in a consonant, they are called *closed*.

18. Observe the difference between בּ (b) and ב (v); ח (ḥ) and ה (h); א (') and ע ('); ו (w) and (û).

19. Observe that י is silent after ֵ or ִ ; ו, under ֹ or with a dot in it (וּ); ה, at the end of a word.

20. The Hebrew verbal inflection distinguishes *gender*.

21. While most Hebrew words are accented on the last vowel, see Obs. 11, *four* words in this Lesson, out of *seven*, have the accent elsewhere, as shown by the position of the sign ֔ .

22. The Hebrew says: *faces-of abyss*, not *faces of-abyss;* that is, the *first* of two words in the genitive relation suffers change; this order is never changed.

4. GRAMMAR-LESSON.

Learn in the "Elements of Hebrew" the following sections:—
1. § **2.** 1—3,6,8,   The pronunciation of א, ה, ע, ח, שׁ, ו.
2. § **3.** 1,   Order of writing; extended letters.
3. § **9.** 1, and § **5.** 6.*a*,   Šᵉwâ, its representation and pronunciation.

4. § **26**. 1, 2,   Open and Closed Syllables.
5. § **49**. 1,   The ordinary writing of the conjunction *and* (וְ).

5. WORD-LESSON.

(13) בֹּהוּ *waste*   (16) חֹשֶׁךְ *darkness*   (19) פָּנִים *faces*
(14) הָיָה *he-was*   (17) עַל *upon*   (20) תֹּהוּ *desolation*
(15) הָיְתָה *she-was*   (18) פְּנֵי *faces-of*   (21) תְּהוֹם *abyss*

Note.—The word for *waste*, when it stands by itself, is בֹּהוּ (bō'-hû), not בְהוּ (vō'-hû); so we say תֹּהוּ (tō'-hû) *desolation*, not תְהוּ (θō'-hû), and תְּהוֹם not תהום.

6. EXERCISES.

1. To be translated into Hebrew:—(1) *In-beginning was* (f.) *the-earth;* (2) *Darkness was upon+the-earth;* (3) *Desolation* (תֹּהוּ, not תְהוּ) *was* (m.) *upon+faces-of the-heavens;* (4) *Faces;* (5) *Faces-of abyss;* (6) *God ruled in-*(= *over*)- *darkness;* (7) *God-of* (אֱלֹהֵי) *the-heavens;* (8) *God was in-beginning;* (9) *He-created*)(*the-earth and-*)(*the-heavens;* (10) *The-earth was* (f.).

2. To be translated into English:—

(1) חֹשֶׁךְ הָיָה עַל־פְּנֵי הָאָרֶץ וְעַל־פְּנֵי הַשָּׁמַיִם

(2) הָיְתָה הָאָרֶץ בְּחֹשֶׁךְ וְחֹשֶׁךְ הָיָה עַל־פְּנֵי תְהוֹם

3. To be written in English letters:—(1) פָּנִים, (2) הָיָה, (3) אֱלֹהֵי, (4) הָיְתָה, (5) תְּהוֹם, (6) תהום, (7) תְהוּ, (8) תֹּהוּ, (9) בְהוּ, (10) בֹּהוּ.

4. To be written in Hebrew letters:—(1) hâ, (2) hû, (3) hă, (4) hō, (5) hî, (6) ḥō, (7) ḥâ, (8) nîm, (9) 'ăl, (10) šex, (11) pâ, (12) šă.

7. TOPICS FOR STUDY.

(1) Two ways of writing *and*. (2) The circumstances under which ‍ו and ‍ו are silent. (3) New letters and vowels. (4) Open and closed syllables. (5) The sign ‍ָ ; its representation and pronunciation. (6) Extended letters. (7) Words in the genitive relation.

LESSON III.—GENESIS I. 2b, 3.

1. NOTES.

15. וְרוּחַ—wᵉrû(ă)ḥ (one syllable)—*and-spirit-of:*

a. *Three consonants:*—ו (w), ר (r), ח (ḥ) the harsh *h*-sound.

b. The conjunction *and* (ו) written with Sᵉwâ, §49. 1; ו = û, as *oo* in *fool;* the ‍ָ (ă) to be pronounced *before* the ח, and not after it.

c. This word is treated as having but one syllable, the ᵉ and ă not counting as full vowels.

d. The ‍ָ is slipped in between the û and the ḥ in order to form a transition sound between these two sounds of such different physiological formation.

16. מְרַחֶפֶת—mᵉră(ḥ)-ḥĕ′-fĕθ (three syllables)—*brooding:*

a. פ = *f*, while פּ is *p*; cf. ב = *v* and בּ *b*, § **12.** 1. N. 1.

b. The final unaccented vowel is of secondary origin, cf. 5.*d*, 7.*c*, and 12.*d*.

c. מְ indicates that the form is a participle; ת, that it is feminine.

17. הַמָּיִם:—hăm-mâ′-yĭm (three syllables)—*the-waters:*

a. מ = m, מּ = mm: a point in a letter preceded by a full vowel indicates doubling, and is called Dâğĕš-fŏrtē, § **13.** 1, cf שׁ (5. *a*).

b. The י here precedes ‍ָ and so is sounded (as *y* in *year*).

c. The article *the* is ה, with ‍ָ under it and Dâğĕš-fŏrtē in the following consonant; cf. הַשָּׁמַיִם (5), § **45.** 1.

d. The ĭ is an unaccented secondary vowel; cf. 5.*d*, 7.*c*, 12.*d*, and 16.*b*.

e. The accent ֑ indicates the end of the verse; ׃ always follows this accent.

18. וַיֹּ֫אמֶר—wăy-yô′′-mĕr—(three syllables)—*and*-(he)-*said*, §§ **26.** 1, 2, Note 1; **13.** 1:

a. The perf. 3rd. p. masc. is אָמַר ('ă-măr) *he-said*.
b. The prefixed וְ indicates the imperfect, יֹאמֶר
c. The conjunction (וַ) connects this sentence with the preceding, and also makes the imperfect equivalent to a *perfect* (*and-he-said*). This seeming anomaly will be taken up later; it is sufficient here to learn that אָמַר = *he said;* וַיֹּאמֶר = *and-he-said*.

19. יְהִי־—yᵉhî+—*shall-be* (or *let-be*), §§ **10.** 1; **26.** 1; **17.** 1:

a. The first יְ indicates the imperfect as in יֹאמֶר.
b. The ְ being a šᵉwâ vowel, this word has but one syllable, § **27.** 1.
c. הָיָה *he-was;* cf. הָיְתָה (9) *she-was*.

20. אוֹר—'ôr—*light*, §§ **5.** 5; **26.** 2:

a. א has no sound, but is represented by ', § **2.** 1.
b. ו, with a point over it, unites with the point, as in תְהוֹם (14).

21. וַיְהִי־—wăy-hî+—*and-*(there)*-was*, § **17.** 1:

a. The conjunction here, as in וַיֹּאמֶר (18), not merely *connects*, but *converts* the imperfect (*shall be*) into a perfect (*was*).
b. The conjunction in וַיֹּאמֶר was וַ, but here it is וְ, the Dağēš-fōrtē having been rejected.
c. The sign (֮) with ־ indicates a secondary accent, cf. 9. *c*, § **18.** 1.
d. י forms a diphthong with preceding ă; cf. § **10.** 2 *a*.

2. *WORDS ARRANGED PROMISCUOUSLY FOR EXAMINATION.*[1]

מַיִם	אֱלֹהִים	בֹהוּ	תְהוֹם	וַיְהִי־	הָיְתָה
הַמַּיִם	הַשָּׁמַיִם	רוּחַ	אוֹר	בָּרָא	יֹאמֶר
מְרַחֶפֶת	פְּנֵי	תֹהוּ	עַל	וַיֹּאמֶר
בְּרֵאשִׁית	וְהָאָרֶץ	חֹשֶׁךְ	אֵת	יְהִי

[1] Examine, pronounce aloud, translate, and *master* these words.

3. OBSERVATIONS.

23. A sign of the feminine gender is the letter ת.

24. פ = p, but פ = f; ב = b, but ב = v.

25. A syllable closing with Dāḡēš-fŏrtē is called *sharpened*. All *sharpened* syllables are, of course, *closed* syllables.

26. The prefix י marks the *imperfect* (3 masc. sing.).

27. ו connects, but וְ, a stronger form, connects and *converts*.

28. Roots have *three* letters (see אָמַר *he said*, בָּרָא *he created*), all other letters are prefixes or suffixes.

29. The laryngeals א, ה, ח, ע, ר, causing many seeming irregularities in the forms of words, deserve special attention. [vowel.

30. Dāḡēš-fŏrtē[1] is in every case immediately preceded by a

31. The vowel of *open* syllables is long, of *closed*, short; of accented syllables it may be either long or short.

32. The letter of the article is ה; its vowel is regularly ◌ַ; it usually has D. f.[2] in the first letter of the word to which it is prefixed. But note הָ, in הָאָרֶץ.

4. GRAMMAR-LESSON.

Learn in the "Elements of Hebrew" the following sections:—

1. Under § 4. 1, The laryngeals א, ה, ח, ע, and ר, cf. Obs. 29.
2. § 13. 1, Dāḡēš-fŏrtē, cf. Obs. 30.
3. § 28. 1, 2, Quantity of vowels in syllables, cf. Obs. 31.
4. § 47. 1, The writing of the preposition בְּ (*in*).

5. WORD-LESSON.

(22) אוֹר *light*   (25) וַיֹּאמֶר *and-he-said*   (28) מְרַחֶפֶת *brooding*
(23) אִישׁ *man*   (26) וַיְהִי *and-(there)-was*   (29) רָאָה *he-saw*
(24) מַיִם *waters*   (27) יְהִי *let-(there)-be*   (30) רוּחַ *spirit, wind*

---

[1] The *a* in this word is pronounced as *a* in *all*; the *e* like *ey* in *they*. The main accent is on the syllable ğĕš.

[2] D. f. = Dāḡēš-fŏrtē.

Notes.—(1) אוֹר means *light* or *light-of;* אִישׁ, *man* or *man-of;* רוּחַ, *spirit* or *spirit-of;* (2) The word for *waters* is מַיִם, but at the *end* of the verse, where the voice rests upon the word, it is written מָיִם.

6. EXERCISES.

1. To be translated into Hebrew:—(1) *Darkness* (was)[1] *upon*+ *the-waters, and-upon*+(*the*)*-faces-of the-earth;* (2) *In-beginning* (the) *spirit-of God* (was) *brooding upon the-waters;* (3) *God saw*)(*the-heavens, and-*)(*the-waters;* (4) (*The*)*-man-of God,* (the)*-light-of the-heavens;* (5) *And-he-said, he-said; he-was, she-was, let-*(there)*-be, and-*(there)*-was;* (6) *he-saw, he-created, he-was.*

2. To be translated into English:—(1) הַפָּנִים; (2) בְּאוֹר; (3) מַיִם (8) וְרוּחַ (7) וְאִישׁ (6) הָאֱלֹהִים (5) הָאִישׁ (4) ;הָאָרֶץ (9), וְהָאוֹר (11) הָאוֹר, (10) הַמַּיִם.

3. To be written in English letters:—(1) רָאָה, (2) אִישׁ, (3) יְהִי, וַיְהִי (8), אוֹר (7), וְרוּחַ (6), פַּת (5), מַיִם (4).

4. To be written in Hebrew letters:—(1) šiṯ, (2) rû, (3) nê, (4) yīm, (5) 'iš, (6) mᵉrâ, (7) mᵉră, (8) šăl, (9) măr, (10) hăm.

7. TOPICS FOR STUDY.

(1) Prep. בְּ. (2) Laryngeals. (3) Quantity of vowels in syllables. (4) Dāgēš-fŏrtē. (5) Sign of the feminine. (6) Sign of the participle. (7) Writing of the article. (8) Sign of the imperfect. (9) Root. (10) וְ and וַ-. (11) Sharpened syllable.

LESSON IV.—GENESIS 1. 4.

1. NOTES.

22. וַיַּרְא—wăy-yăr' (two syllables)—*and-*(he)*-saw*, cf. 18. *c*, 21. *a:*
a. The conjunction וַ-, forming, with י, a sharpened syllable, § **26.** Note 1.
b. The letter י indicates the imperfect, יִרְא, cf. 18. *b.*

---

[1] Words in parentheses are not to be rendered in Hebrew.

c. šᵉwâ under ר silent, § 11.; א here without force, § 43. 1. R. 1.

23. אֶת־הָאוֹר—'ĕθ+hă-'ôr (three syllables)—)(+*the-light:*

a. In v. 1 אֵת is an *accented* closed syl.; here *un*-accented, because joined by Măkkēf to following word, § 17. 1. 2.; hence short ĕ appears in the unaccented syllable, § 29. 4. *a*.

b. Article here is הָ, as in הָאָרֶץ; but cf. הַ- in הַשָּׁמַיִם, הַמַּיִם.

c. 1st syl. unaccented closed; 2d, unac. open; 3d, accented closed, § 28. 1, 2.

d. The o is ô, not ō, same sound, but different value, § 7. 4.

24. כִּי־טוֹב—kî+ṭôv (two syllables) —*that+good:*

a. Three consonants: כ (k), cf. כ (x); ט (ṭ), cf. ת; ב (v).

b. Two unchangeable vowels: ִי (î), וֹ (ô), § 30. 2. *b*., 6. *c*.

c. On the use of letters to indicate vowel-sounds, § 6. 2, 3.

25. וַיַּבְדֵּל—wăy-yăv-dēl—*and-(he)-caused-a-division,* § 28. 1,2:

a. ד (d) a new letter; without the dot (ד), it is d̄ (= *th* in *this*).

b. 1st and 2d syl.'s unaccented closed (*short* vowel); 3d, accented closed (*long* vowel).

c. šᵉwâ under ב is silent.

26. בֵּין—bên—*between,* §§ 3. 2; 5. 3; 6. 3; 12. 1:

a. The letter *n* at the *end* of a word is written ן, not נ.

b. Both ê (ֵי) and ē (ֵ) are pronounced as *ey* in *they*.

c. The vowel here is unchangeable (ê), not changeable (ē).

d. There is a dot in ב, as there was in ב of בְּרֵאשִׁית

27. וּבֵין—û-vên—*and-between,* §§ 12. 1; 49. 2:

a. Before the labial ב, the word for *and* is written וּ

b. Note that *between* is bên, *and-between* is û-vên.

28. הַחֹשֶׁךְ—hă(ḥ)-ḥō'-šĕx—*the-darkness;* (cf. 12. *a, b, c*):

a. The article in this case is הַ; not הָ., nor הָ.

b. The accent falls on the vowel ō, the final ĕ being only a secondary vowel; cf. 5.*d*, 7.*c*, 12.*d*.

Lesson 4.

c. Note that ה appears to be an unaccented open syllable with a short vowel. However, in the case of a strong laryngeal like ḥ a doubling is implied after the article. Cf. the same usage in 16.

2. THE OCCURRENCE OF SPIRANTS IN GENESIS I. 1—4.

בְּרֵאשִׁית	בּ	(*b*, not *v*) follows nothing; ת (θ) follows î.
בָּרָא	בּ	(*b*, not *v*) follows ת of the preceding word.
אֵת	ת	(θ, not *t*) follows the vowel-sound ē.
הָיְתָה	ת	(θ, not *t*) follows the vowel-sound ָ.
תֹהוּ וָבֹהוּ	ת	(θ) follows å of preceding word; ב (*v*) follows å.
עַל־פְּנֵי	פ	(*p*) follows the consonant ל.
תְהוֹם	ת	(θ) follows the vowel-sound ê of preceding word.
מְרַחֶפֶת	פ	(*f* not *p*) follows ĕ; ת (θ) follows ē.
כִּי־טוֹב	כ	(*k*, not χ) follows ר; ב (*v*) follows ô.
וַיַּבְדֵּל	ב	(*v*) follows ă; ד (*d*, not d) follows the consonant ב
בֵּין	בּ	(*b*) follows the preceding consonant ם.
וּבֵין חֹשֶׁךְ	ב	(*v*) follows the vowel וּ; ך (χ) fol. ĕ.

3. OBSERVATIONS.

33. Six letters, called *spirants*, have two sounds: בּ *b*, ב *v*, ג[1] *g*, ğ (as in German *Tage*), ד *d*, ד[d] χ, כּ *k*, כ χ, פּ *p*, פ *f*, תּ *t*, ת θ.

34. Their smooth or hard sound, *b*, *g*, *d*, *k*, *p*, *t*, was indicated by a point called Dåğēš-lēnē.

35. These letters receive this point **whenever they do not immediately follow a vowel-sound**, i. e., a vowel or vocal Šᵉwâ.

36. This lesson has two new letters: ט (ṭ), pronounced practically like ת; and ד (*d*).

4. GRAMMAR-LESSON.

Learn in the "Elements of Hebrew," the following sections:
1. § **12.** 1, and Note,   Spirants and Dåğēš-lēnē.

---
[1] This letter is introduced here, in order to complete the list.

LESSON 4.

2. § 17. 1, 2,   Măkkēf and short vowel.
3. § 45. 1,   The usual form of the Article.
4. Under § 4. 1,   The letters פ, מ, ו, ב.

5. WORD-LESSON.

(31) בֵּין between (34) וַיַּרְא and-he-saw (37) לָמַד he-learned
(32) וְ and (35) כִּי that (38) נָתַן he-gave
(33) וַיַּבְדֵּל and-he-caused-a-division (36) טוֹב good (39) שֵׁם name

Note.—The root of וַיַּבְדֵּל is בָּדַל be-separate; the root of וַיַּרְא is רָאָה see; שֵׁם = either name, or name-of.

6. EXERCISES.

1. To be translated into Hebrew:—(1) *And-saw God)(the-heavens and-)(the-earth and-)(the-waters;* (2) *The-light the-good* (= the good light); (3) *Good light* (in Heb., *light good*) *was upon the-earth;* (4) *In-beginning* (was) *darkness; God created light; and-he-caused-a-division between light and-between darkness;* (5) *God gave)(+the-light;* (6) *He-gave the-light the-good* (= *the good light*); (7) *Name, the-name,* (the) *name-of God;* (8) *Between the-heavens and-between the-earth;* (9) *He-learned that the-light* (was) *good* (Heb. order, *He learned the light that good*).

2. To be translated into English:—(1) הַשֵּׁם; (2) הָאוֹר הַטּוֹב; (3) הַטּוֹב; (4) הַחֹשֶׁךְ וְהָאוֹר; (5) הָאֱלֹהִים הַטּוֹב; (6) בְּשֵׁם הָאֱלֹהִים; (7) וַיַּרְא אֶת־הָאָרֶץ, נָתַן אֱלֹהִים אֶת־הַמַּיִם.

3. To be written in English letters:—(1) לָמַד, (2) שֵׁם, (3) נָתַן, (4) וּבֵין, (5) הַטּוֹב, (6) בְּשֵׁם, (7) וַיַּבְדֵּל, (8) בֵּין.

4. To be written in Hebrew letters:—(1) bēn, (2) dēl, (3) bēn, (4) dēl, (5) ṭôv, (6) hō, (7) θōʹhû, (8) ʼôr, (9) bōʹhû, (10) vēn, (11) ḡēl, (12) χî.

7. TOPICS FOR STUDY.

(1) Three ways of writing *and*. (2) Three ways of writing *the*. (3) Măkkēf. (4) Laryngeals. (5) Labials. (6) Dăğĕš-lēnē. (7) Spirants (8) Sign of feminine, of participle. (9) Open, closed, and sharpened syllables. (10) Difference between ō and ô, ē and ê. (11) -וְ. (12) Plural ending.

LESSON V.—GENESIS I. 5.

1. NOTES.

29. וַיִּקְרָא—wăy-yĭḳ-rå'—*And-(he)-called*, § **26.** 1. 2, N. 1.:
a. On וְ, see 18. *c*; on יִ see 18. *b*; wăy, a sharpened syl.
b. ק (ḳ), a new consonant pronounced practically like כּ (k), § **2.** 4.
c. The ְ under ק is silent, § **11.** 1.
d. יִקְרָא *he-will-call*; קָרָא *he-called*, cf. בָּרָא *he-created*.

30. לָאוֹר—lå-'ôr—*to-the-light*, § **28.** 1, 2:
a. לְ the preposition *to*, with ָ, the vowel of article, § **47.** 4.
b. וֹ is ô, not ō.
c. *Light* = אוֹר ; *the-light* = הָאוֹר ; *to-the-light* = (not לְהָאוֹר) לָאוֹר, ה of the article being dropped out, § **45.** R. 3.

31. יוֹם—yôm—*day;* ô not ō.

32. וְלַחֹשֶׁךְ—wᵉlă(h)-ḥṓ-šĕχ—*and-to-the-darkness:*
a. Four words: (1) וְ *and*, (2) לְ *to*, (3) ה *the*, (4) חֹשֶׁךְ *darkness*.
b. ה of article elided and its vowel (ă) given to לְ, § **45.** R. 3.
c. First syl. (wᵉlă(h)) is unaccented and apparently open, but with a *short* vowel, contrary to § **28.** 1. The fact is D. f. is understood in ח, which, being a *laryngeal*, cannot receive it, § **14.** 3. N. 1.

33. קָרָא—ḳå-rå'—*he-called*, § **55.** 1. 2:
a. This is the simple stem or root of the verb.
b. א, as always at the end of a word, is quiescent, § **43.** 1, a.
c. This word would regularly be accented on the ultima. It is

קָרָא here because of the acc. syl. לְ immediately following.

34. לַיְלָה—lâ'-y⁽ᵉ⁾lâ(h)—*night*, § **24.** 2, and N. 1:

a. ה is not a consonant, but used merely to represent the prec. ָ, § **6.** 1.

b. י and its š⁽ᵉ⁾wâ belong to the second syl.; the ַ is *initial*, § **10. 1**

c. Both ָ 's are *tone*-long (â), not naturally long (â).

35. וַיְהִי־עֶרֶב—wăy-hî 'ĕ-rĕv—*and*-(there)-*was*+*evening:*

a. The first syl. (wăy) is unaccented and ends with a diphthong; there should be a D. f. in י, but it has been lost, § **26.** 2. and N. 2; § **28.** 4; § **14.** 2.

b. The vertical line with ֽ is called Méθĕğ; it is a secondary accent written upon the second syl. before the principal accent, § **18.** 1.

c. The ֶ under ע though short is accented, and the final ĕ is secondary.

36. וַיְהִי־בֹקֶר—wăy-hî+vṓ-ḳĕr—*and*-(there)-*was*+*morning:*

a. On the syl. *wăy* and on Méθĕğ see 35. *a*, *b*.

b. On the connective Măḳḳēf represented by +, § **17.** 1.

c. The ֹ is ō (tone-long), not ô (naturally long), § **31.** 3. *b*.

d. The final ĕ is secondary.

37. אֶחָד—'ĕ(h)-hâd—*one:*

a. The ֶ is short ĕ, d. f. being understood in ח; cf. 32 *c*.

b. The ד is đ, like *th* in *the*, not d, which would be דּ.

2. TABLE OF WORDS CONTAINING LONG VOWELS.

1. Words with tone-long â: יִקְרָא, קָרָא, לַיְלָה, בָּרָא, etc.

2. Words with tone-long ē: יַבְדֵּל, אֵת.

3. Words with naturally long ê: פְּנֵי, בֵּין.

4. Words with tone-long ō: תֹּהוּ, חֹשֶׁךְ, בֹּקֶר, בֹּהוּ.

5. Words with naturally long ô: יוֹם, טוֹב, אוֹר.

R. The *o* of וַיֹּאמֶר and of אֱלֹהִים is ŏ, not ō, although not written וֹ.

3. OBSERVATIONS.

37. Tone-long vowels are vowels which are long because of their proximity to the tone; i. e., being originally short, they have become long through the influence of the accent.

38. Naturally long vowels are vowels which are long, generally, because of the contraction of two distinct elements, e. g., $ă+w = ô$, or $ă+y = ê$.

39. Tone-long vowels are, generally, indicated only by the vowel-sign.

40. Naturally long vowels are generally, but not always, indicated by a vowel-sign and also by a vowel-letter, e. g., ō is ֹ , but ô is וֹ; ē is ֵ , but ê is ֵי.

41. Tone-long vowels, if the tone changes, are liable to change; but naturally long vowels are unchangeable.

42. The short accented ĕ, which always comes from ă, is especially worthy of note.

4. GRAMMAR-LESSON.

1. § 8.	The names of the vowels.
2. §§ 45. R. 3; 47. 4.	The article after a preposition.
3. § 55. 1, 2,	The root of a verb.
4. § 58. 1.	The simple verb-stem; its name.
5. § 30. (opening words), also Notes 1 and 2 under § 30. 7,	The naturally long-vowels,—(1) their origin, (2) their writing, (3) their character.
6. § 31. (opening words), also Note 1 under 3.	The tone-long vowels, (1) their origin, (2) their number, (3) their writing, (4) their character.

5. WORD-LESSON.

(40) אֶחָד one   (43) וַיִּקְרָא and-he-called   (46) עֶרֶב evening

(41) בֹּקֶר morning   (44) יָשַׁב he-sat, dwelt   (47) קוֹל voice

(42) יוֹם day   (45) לַיְלָה night   (48) קָרָא he-called

Note.—The word for *night* is לַיְלָה, but in the middle of the verse it is written and pronounced לָיְלָה.

6. EXERCISES.

1. To be translated into Hebrew:—(1) *To-(the)-beginning-of the-day God called morning; to-(the)-beginning-of the-night God called evening;* (2) *In-day one God created)(the-light;* (3) *God created)(the-light and-he-called to-the-light day;* (4) *The good day* (Heb., *the-day the-good*); (5) *(The)-name-of the-light* (is) *day, and-(the)-name-of the-darkness* (is) *night;* (6) *Heavens, the-heavens, to-the-heavens, in-the-heavens;* (7) *Earth, the-earth, in-the-earth, to-the-earth, and-to-the-earth;* (8) *(The)-voice-of God;* (9) *Day and-night;* (10) *The-waters, in-the-waters.*

2. To be translated into English:—(1) בְּקוֹל; (2) לְאוֹר; (3) בֵּין הַיּוֹם; (4) לְאִישׁ; (5) בָּאָרֶץ; (6) לַשָּׁמַיִם; (7) בַּיּוֹם; (8) וּלְאוֹר; (9) יָשַׁב אֱלֹהִים בַּשָּׁמַיִם וּבֵין הַלַּיְלָה.

3. To be written in English letters:—(1) קוֹל, (2) יָשַׁב, (3) יוֹם, (4) קָרָא, (5) אֶחָד, (6) עֶרֶב, (7) אוֹר, (8) בֵּין.

4. To be written in Hebrew letters:—(1) lăm, (2) lâm, (3) lĕm, (4) lôm, (5) lōm, (6) lēm, (7) lêm, (8) yĭḳ, (9) bên, (10) rĕv, (11) yᵉlå.

7. TOPICS FOR STUDY.

(1) Root. (2) Simple verb-stem. (3) Names of vowel-signs. (4) Article after a preposition. (5) Naturally long vowels. (6) Tone-long vowels. (7) Laryngeals and labials. (8) Dăğēš-lēnē.

LESSON VI.—GENESIS I. 6.
1. *NOTES.*

38. וַיֹּאמֶר—wăy-yō'-mĕr—*and*-(he)-*said* (see N. 18):
a. Syllables: (1) sharpened, (2) open, (3) closed.
b. Vowels: (1) Păṯăḥ, (2) Ḥōlĕm, (3) Sᵉğôl.
c. א, though a letter, has here no consonantal force; hence it has no Šᵉwâ under it; it is quiescent, § **11.** R.

39. אֱלֹהִים—'ᵉlō-hîm—*God* (see N. 3):
a. Only two syllables: (1) open, (2) closed.
b. Vowels: (1) Ḥōlĕm; (2) Ḥîrĕḳ; Ḥăṭēf-Sᵉğôl (ֱ), though a vowel-sound, is not a full vowel.
c. While ְ is *simple* Šᵉwâ, ֱ is a *compound* Šᵉwâ, § **9.** 1, 2.
d. Šᵉwâs do not form syllables, § **27.** 1.

40. רָקִיעַ—râ-ḳî(ă)'—*expanse;* cf. רוּחַ *spirit* (15):
a. Syl's: (1) open, (2) closed; vowels: (1) Ḳămēṣ, (2) Ḥîrĕḳ.
b. The ַ under ע is *not treated as a vowel;* it is called Păṯăḥ-*furtive*, because in pronunciation it *steals* in before its consonant, cf. רוּחַ = rû(ă)ḥ, not rû-ḥă. Though pronounced, it is merely a transition-sound from the labial *û* to the laryngeal consonant ʻ, and is inserted for euphony, §§ **27.** 1; **42.** 2. *d*.

41. בְּתוֹךְ—bᵉṯôx—*in-midst-of,* §§ **12.** 1; **11.** 2. *a*:
a. בּ has Dăğēš-lēnē but ךְ has none.
b. The full vowel וֹ (= ô), is unchangeable.
c. This word means *in-midst-of,* not *in-midst.*

42. הַמָּיִם—hăm-mă'-yîm—*the-waters,*§§ **13.** 1; **26.** 1. 2. N. 1. **45.** 1:
a. The ִ being unaccented and in a closed syl. must be ĭ, not ī, § **28.** 2.
b. Here ָ (1) indicates that the second vowel is accented, and also (2) marks the end of the clause, § **24.** 2.

43. וִיהִי—wî-hî—*and-let-*(it)-*be:*

a. *Let-*(it)*-be* = יְהִי; *and* = וְ; but we have וִיהִי in place of וְיְהִי, since (1) when two Sᵉwâs would stand together at the beginning of a word, the first is represented by ִ ; and (2) ִ (ĭ) under וְ fol. by י (ĭy) = î, § **49.** 4. N. 1; cf. the very different וַיְהִי = *and-*(there)*-was* (21).

b. On the origin of ַ see § **36.** 8. *a*.

44. מַבְדִּיל—măv-dîl—*causing-a-division* or *dividing:*

a. A participle (shown by מ) from same root as וַיַּבְדֵּל (25).

b. Vowels: (1) Păθăḥ, (2) Ḥîrĕḳ; but ִ is silent.

c. ב (preceded by ־ֵ) *without,* דּ (preced. by בְּ) with Dăğēš lēnē.

45. מַיִם לָמָיִם—mă'-yĭm lă-mă'-yĭm—*waters to-waters:*

a. Vowel under מ in first word, ă; in second, â; because the second word is the last in the verse, and so the voice *rests* upon it and strengthens the vowel. Such a word is said to be *in pause*, § **38.** 2.

b. The prepositions sometimes take a tone-long â, instead of ַ , when they are directly before the accented syllable, § **47.** 5.

c. לָמַיִם = *to-waters;* not *to-the-waters,* which would be לַמָּיִם; the stroke over מ̄ emphasizes the absence of Dăğēš-fŏrtē, § **16.** 2.

2. WORDS WITHOUT POINTS OR VOWEL-SIGNS. GEN. I. 1—6

קרא,	פני	כי, ל	יאמר	ה	ב	אור
ראשית		לילה	ויבדל	היתה	בהו	אחד
	רקיע	יהי, יום	מבדיל	ו	בין	אלהים
	שמים	מים	יקרא	חשך	בקר	ארץ
	תהו	על, ערב	וירא	טוב	ברא	את

3. OBSERVATIONS.

43. This verse has *twenty-two* syllables,[1] of which twelve are closed, ten open; of the closed, two are *sharpened.*

44. This verse has twenty-six vowel-sounds: twenty-two full

---

[1] Let the student count the syllables and thus verify this statement.

vowels, three Šᵉwâs (two simple, one compound), one Páṭăḥ-furtive.

45. This verse has *forty-four* letters, of which *nine* are silent; of these nine, seven are י, one ו and one א.

46. This verse has two silent Šᵉwâs.

47. The accent ־ֿ ('Aṯnâḥ) is written only in the *middle* of a verse.

48. The accent ־ֽ (Sillûḳ) is written only at the *end* of a verse.

4. GRAMMAR-LESSON.

1. § 6. 1,2, 3, and Notes 1—4,   The Vowel-letters.
2. § 14. 3, and Notes 1, 2,   Omission of D. f. from laryngeals.
3. § 9. 1, 2,   Simple and Compound Šᵉwâ.
4. § 11. 1, 2. *a*, and Remark,   Silent Šᵉwâ.

5. WORD-LESSON.

(49) מַבְדִּיל *dividing*   (50) מַיִם *waters*   (51) רָקִיעַ *expanse*

6. EXERCISES.

1. To be translated into Hebrew:—(1) *Between the-waters and-between the-waters;* (2) *Between the-waters to-the-waters;* (3) *Between waters to-waters;* (4) *Waters, waters* (in pause), *to-the-waters* (in pause), *to-waters* (in pause); (5) *Let-*(there)*-be, and-let-*(there)*-be, and-*(there)*-was;* (6) *Expanse and-spirit;* (7) *Expanse, the-expanse, to-the-expanse.*

2. To be translated into English:—(1) חֹשֶׁךְ (2) אוֹר בַּיּוֹם; (3) יְהִי אוֹר וַיְהִי; (4) טוֹב הָאוֹר; (5) הַמַּיִם עַל פְּנֵי הָאָרֶץ; (3) בַּלַּיְלָה, לָמַיִם, בָּרָקִיעַ; (6) רָקִיעַ וִיהִי מַבְדִּיל.

3. To be written in English letters:—(1) חֹשֶׁךְ, (2) עֶרֶב, (3) יַבְדֵּל, (5) מַבְדִּיל, (6) רָקִיעַ, (4) בְּתוֹךְ.

4. To be written in Hebrew letters:—(1) 'ăl, (2) mă'-yĭm, (3) wî-hî, (4) dăl, (5) dēl, (6) dêl, (7) hăd, (8) dîl.

7. TOPICS FOR STUDY.

(1) Vowel-sounds rep. by ו. (2) Vowel-sounds rep. by י. (3) D. f. rejected from laryngeals. (4) D. f. implied. (5) Compound Šᵉwâ. (6) Silent Šᵉwâ. (7) Simple verb-stem. (8) Laryngeals and labials. (9) Dăḡēš-lēnē, (10) Sharpened syllables. (12) Naturally long and tone-long vowels. (13) Măķķêf. (14) Quantity of vowels in syllables.

LESSON VII.—GENESIS I. 7, 8.

1. NOTES.

46. וַיַּעַשׂ—wăy-yă-'ăś—*and-*(he)*-made:*

a. שׂ (ś) is to be distinguished from שׁ (š), § **2. 6**.

b. The וַ is the same as in וַיֹּאמֶר (18), וַיִּקְרָא (21), וַיַּרְא (22).

c. The root is עָשָׂה *he-made;* the imperfect is יַעֲשֶׂה, a shorter form is used with וַ.

d. The last ă is a helping-vowel.

47. הָרָקִיעַ—hā-rā-ḳî(ă)'—*the-expanse:*

a. The ָ is Păθăḥ-furtive, cf. רוּחַ (rû(ă)ḥ); see 40. *b.*

b. The article is הַ, hence *the-expanse* should be הַרָקִיעַ; but ר rejects D. f., and the preceding (short) ַ now standing in an open syllable becomes ָ, §§ **14. 3**; **36. 1** *b;* **28. 1**.

c. The secondary accent is written on the second syllable before the tone, § **18. 1**.

d. The accent ֥ above ק and ע marks the end of a section; it is used only when the verse has *three sections,* § **24. 3**.

48. אֲשֶׁר—'ăšĕr (one syllable)—*which,* §§ **9. 2**; **27. 1**:

a. The ֲ is the compound Šᵉwâ of the A-class (cf. ֱ, of the I-class); it is pronounced like ă, but with much less voice. It is **not a full vowel, and does not form a syllable**.

b. The Relative particle does not vary for gender or number, § **53. 1.** *a*.

LESSON 7.

49. מִתַּחַת—mĭt-tă-ḥăθ—*from-under* (for מִן תַּחַת), § **48.** 1:
a. The final letter (n) of מִן is assimilated, § **39.** 1.
b. A letter thus assimilated is represented by D. f., § **39.** N.
c. The point in תּ is D. f., because it follows a vowel, § **13.** 1.
d. In this case the point is *also* Dăḡēš-lēnē, since the sound doubled is *t*, not θ, § **13.** 2. N. 1.

50. לָרָקִיעַ—lā-rā-ḳî(ă)'—*to-the-expanse*, § **45.** R. 3:
a. רָקִיעַ *expanse;* הָרָקִיעַ *the-expanse;* לָרָקִיעַ *to-the-expanse;* וְלָרָקִיעַ *and-to-the-expanse.*

51. מֵעַל—mē-'ăl—*from-upon:*
a. מִן (*from*) assimilates its final consonant, see 49. *a; but*
b. ע refuses D. f., and ִ is lowered to ֵ, § **48.** 2.

52. וַיְהִי־כֵן—wăy-hî+χēn—*and-(it)-was+so:*
a. ָ with ִ is Méθĕḡ, second syllable before tone, § **18.** 1.
b. ֵ with ־ Sillûḳ, marking end of verse, § **24.** 1. N.

53. שָׁמָיִם—šā-mā'-yĭm—*heavens,* cf. שָׁמַיִם of v. 1:
a. There is ָ under מ, instead of ַ, because *in pause*, § **38.** 2; the Aθnâḥ (⌄) is, next to Sillûḳ (־), the strongest accent.

54. שֵׁנִי—šē-nî—*second:* tone-long, ē, not ê.

2. FORMS FOR SPECIAL STUDY.

(7) הָרָקִיעַ	(3) אוֹר	(7) מִן	(5) לָאוֹר	(2)¹ רוּחַ
(7) לָרָקִיעַ	(4) טוֹב	(7) מִתַּחַת	(5) לַחֹשֶׁךְ	(6) רָקִיעַ
(7) וַיְהִי־כֵן	(5) יוֹם	(7) מֵעַל	(8) לָרָקִיעַ	(8) לִרְקִיעַ

3. OBSERVATIONS.

49. Păθăḥ-furtive, a mere transition-sound, does not form a syl.

---
¹ These numerals refer to the verse containing the word cited.

Lesson 7.

50. The ה of the article is elided after the preposition ל (also בְּ).

51. The prep. *from* is *min*, but the *n* is often assimilated and represented by D. f.; if the following letter refuses D. f., the ĭ is lowered to ē.

52. The naturally long ô, generally וֹ, in Hebrew does not change.

53. Where a verse has two sections, the end of the *first* is marked by ־ֽ ; the end of the *second* by ־ֿ. If the verse has *three* sections, the end of the *third* is marked by Sᵉğôltâ (־֒). In the use of the accents, we commence at the *end* of the verse, not at the beginning.

4. GRAMMAR-LESSON.

1. § 45. 2, 3,   The article before strong and weak laryngeals.
2. § 106. 1, 2. c, 3—5, Affixes for gender and number.
3. § 107. (opening), 1, 2, The absolute and construct states.
4. § 24. 1—3,   The three most important accents.

5. WORD-LESSON.

(52) אֲשֶׁר *who, which*   (55) כֵּן *so*   (58) שָׁלַח *he-sent*
(53) וַיַּעַשׂ *and-he-made* (56) מִן *from*   (59) שֵׁנִי *second*
(54) יָם *sea*   (57) עָשָׂה *he-made* (60) תַּחַת *under*

6. EXERCISES.

(1) To be translated into Hebrew:—*In-the-waters which God made;* (2) *God* (is) *in-the-heavens and-upon the-earth;* (3) *The-waters* (are) *in-the-sea;* (4) *The-earth* (is) *beneath* (in Heb., *from-under to*) *the-sea;* (5) (A) *second day*[1]; (6) *The-day the-second*[1] (=the second day); (7) *God sent*)(*the light and-*)(*the darkness;* (8) *From*+*the-heavens to-the-earth;* (9) *Between the-sea and-between the-earth;* (10) *And-*(it)-*was*+*so.*

---

[1] The adjective, when attributive, follows its noun; and, if the noun is definite, the adjective receives the article.

2. To be translated into English:—(1) הָרֵאשִׁית; (2) מֵעַל לָאָרֶץ; (3) מִן־הָאָרֶץ; (4) וּבַיָּם; (5) הַמַּיִם אֲשֶׁר בַּיָּם; (6) הָאוֹר הַשֵּׁנִי; (7) לַשָּׁמַיִם; (8) בַּבֹּקֶר וּבָעֶרֶב; (9) שָׁלַח אֶת־הַמַּיִם עַל־הָאָרֶץ. עָשָׂה אֶת־הָרָקִיעַ.

3. To be written in English letters:—(1) שָׁלַח, (2) כֵּן, (3) כֵּן, (4) יָם, (5) עָשָׂה, (6) בֵּין, (7) פְּנֵי, (8) שֵׁנִי, (9) מֵעַל.

4. To be written in Hebrew letters:—(1) kēn, (2) bên, (3) 'ôr, (4) bṓ-hû, (5) măḥ, (6) 'ăl, (7) 'ăl, (8) 'ăs, (9) mē, (10) bēn.

7. TOPICS FOR STUDY.

(1) The three important accents. (2) The article before laryngeals. (3) The preposition (לְ and בְּ) before the article. (4) The preposition *from*. (5) Assimilation. (6) The position of the attributive adjective. (7) The vowels ē and ê. (8) The vowels ō and ô. (9) Secondary accent. (10) Păθăḥ-furtive. (11) Labials. (12) D. f. in a spirant. (13) Laryngeals and D. f. (14) Sillûḳ and Méθĕǧ. (15) Măḳḳēf.

LESSON VIII.—GENESIS I. 9.
1. *NOTES.*

55. יִקָּווּ—yĭḳ-ḳā-wû—*Let-*(or, *shall*)*-be-collected:*

a. The ו indicates the *imperfect;* וּ is the *plural-*ending of verbs.

b. The D. f. in ק is for an assimilated נ, which is the characteristic of a *passive* verb-stem; the ā under ק is pretonic.

56. הַמַּיִם—hăm-mă-yĭm—*the-waters,* see 17:

a. מ has ־ֲ, not ־ָ as in v. 2, since it is not *in pause*.

b. The article, written regularly with ă and D. f., § 45. 1.

57. אֶל־—'ĕl+—*unto,* with which compare לְ *to.*

58. מָקוֹם—mā-ḳôm—*place:*

a. Tone-long ā, but naturally long ô; the former changeable, the latter unchangeable.

LESSON 8.

b. The root is קוּם ; מ is a prefix often used in noun-formation.

59. וְתֵרָאֶה—wᵉθē-rā-'é(h)—*and-(she)-shall-be-seen:*

a. **Five** letters, of which the root can have but *three*, § 55. 1; וְ = *and;* ת (= *she*) is a prefix of the *imperfect*, like י, which = *he.*

b. הֵרָאֶה should be תֵּרָאֶה (with the same D. f. and â which are in יָקוּם (55) above), for it is *passive;* but ר refuses D. f., and I under ת becomes ē, as in מֵעַל (51), § 48. 2.

c. Cf. closely the following forms:—

3 masc. sg.	יָקוּם	יִרְאֶה	*he-will-be* etc.
3 fem. sg.	תָּקוּם	תִּרְאֶה	*she-will-be* etc.
3 masc. pl.	יָקוּמוּ	יִרְאוּ	*they-will-be* etc.

d. This is the first case of ה ֶ = *ê* (h).

60. הַיַּבָּשָׁה—hăy-yăb-bâ-šâ(h)—*the-dry* (land):

a. Four syllables,—two sharpened, two open, § 26. 1. N. 1.

b. Point in בּ is D. f. yet also Dâğēš-lēnē, § 13. 2, and N. 1.

c. The final ה stands for the preceding â, just as י stands for î, or ו for ô; cf. אֱלֹהִים and יוֹם.

2. HEBREW-ENGLISH WORD-REVIEW.*†

⁴²רָקִיעַ	³²מַיִם	²¹יְהִי	¹¹בֹּקֶר	¹אוֹר
⁴³שָׁמַיִם	³³מִן, מִי, מֶ	²²יוֹם	¹²בָּרָא	²אֶחָד
⁴⁴שֵׁנִי	³⁴מָקוֹם	²³יַעַשׂ	¹³הַ־, הָ	³אֶל
⁴⁵תֹּהוּ	³⁵מְרַחֶפֶת	²⁴יִקָּווּ	¹⁴הָיְתָה	⁴אֱלֹהִים
⁴⁶תְּהוֹם	³⁶עַל	²⁵יִקְרָא	¹⁵וְ, וָ, וּ	⁵אֶרֶץ

* Every word is accented on the last vowel, unless the sign ֶ indicates that it is accented elsewhere.

† Omitting the prepositions and the relative particle (eleven words in all), those that remain in this list, together with their related grammatical forms, occur in the Bible about 27000 times. This would make about one hundred and thirty pages, or about one tenth of the entire Old Testament.

Lesson 8.

⁶אֲשֶׁר	¹⁶חֹשֶׁךְ	²⁶יֵרָא	³⁷עֶרֶב	⁴⁷תּוֹךְ
⁷אֶת־, אֵת	¹⁷טוֹב	²⁷כִּי, ²⁸לְ	³⁸פְּנֵי	⁴⁸תַּחַת
⁸בְּ	¹⁸יֹאמֶר	²⁹כֵּן	³⁹קָרָא	⁴⁹תֵּרָאֶה
⁹כֹּהוּ	¹⁹יַבְדֵּל	³⁰לַיְלָה	⁴⁰רֵאשִׁית	
¹⁰בֵּין	²⁰יַבָּשָׁה	³¹מַבְדִּיל	⁴¹רוּחַ	

3. ENGLISH-HEBREW WORD-REVIEW.

46abyss	12created, he	38faces-of	30night	13the
15and	16darkness	33from	2one	28to
21let be	22day	4God	34place	48under
40beginning	45desolation	17good	18say, he will	3unto
10between	19divide, he will	43heavens	44second	36upon
35brooding	31dividing	8in	26see, he will	6which
25call, he will	20dry (land)	1light	49seen, let be	14was, she
39called, he	5earth	47midst-of	29so	9waste
24collected, let be	37evening	11morning	41spirit-of	32waters
	42expanse	23make, he will	27that	7(sign of object)

4. WORD-LESSON.

(61) אֶל־ unto

(62) יַבָּשָׁה dry (land)

(63) יִקָּווּ they-shall-be-collected

(64) מָקוֹם place

(65) תֵּרָאֶה she-shall-be-seen

5. GRAMMAR-LESSON

1. § 18. 1, Méθĕğ, on second syllable before tone.
2. § 27. 1, 2, 3, Syllabification.

Review.—§§ 5; 6; 9; 11. 2. *a* and Rem.; 12. 1; 13. 1; 14. 1, 2, 3;

17. 1, 2; **24.** 1—3; **26.** 1, 2; **28.** 1 2; **30.** (opening words), 7, N. 1, 2; **31.** (opening words), 3, N. 1; **45.** 1, 2, 3. and Rem. 3; **47.** 1, 4, 5; **49.** 1, 2; **55.** 1. 2; **58.** 1, 2. and N. 1; **106.** 1, 2. *c*, 3—5; **107.** 1, 2.

Note.—The stem seen in בָּרָא, קָרָא, מָשַׁל, etc., is the simple active verb-stem, called Ḳăl, § **58.** 1; the stem seen in יִקָּווּ and וְתֵרָאֶה is the simple *passive*-stem, called Nĭf-'ăl § **58.** 2.

6. *EXERCISES.*

1. To be translated into Hebrew:—(1) *In-the-place which* (is) *between heavens and-between earth;* (2) *God will-be-seen upon*+ *the-earth;* (3) *The-waters will-be-seen in-the-sea;* (4) *The-earth* (f.) *will-be-seen beneath* (= *from-under to*) *the-heavens;* (5) *The-waters shall-be-collected unto*+*place one;* (6) *In-the-waters;* (7) *God created*)(*the-dry* (land).

2. To be translated into English:—(1) יִקָּווּ הַמַּיִם עַל־הָאָרֶץ; יֵרָאֶה הָאִישׁ (6); וּמָקוֹם (5); וּבַמָּקוֹם (4); וּלְאוֹר (3); וְלַמָּקוֹם (2); וּמֵעַל, מֵעַל, עַל (8); יֵרָאוּ הַשָּׁמַיִם (7).

3. To be written in English letters:—(1) עֶרֶב, (2) אֶרֶץ, (3) יִקָּוֶה (6) וּבַמָּקוֹם (5) אֶחָד, (4) תֵּרָאֶה.

7. *TOPICS FOR STUDY*

(1) The sign of masc. sing. future, of fem. sing. future, of masc. pl. fut. (2) The characteristic of the *passive*-stem. (3) A use of Méθĕǧ. (4) Final ה. (5) Use of מ in formation of nouns. (6) Various forms of ו conjunctive. (7) The words for *sea* and *day*. (8) The position of the adjective when attributive. (9) The plural affixes of nouns. (10) The feminine affixes.

LESSON IX.—GENESIS I. 10-11.

1. NOTE-REVIEW.

אֲשֶׁר (48); (4) הָאָרֶץ (7); (3) אֱלֹהִים (3); (2) (18); וַיֹּאמֶר (1)
וַיְהִי־כֵן (52); (6) וַיְהִי־עֶרֶב (35); (7) וַיְהִי־בֹקֶר (36); (8) יוֹם (31). (5)

2. NOTES.

61. לַיַּבָּשָׁה—lăy-yăb-bå-šå(h)—*to-the-dry* (land), § **45.** R. 3.

62. אֶרֶץ—'é-réṣ—*earth*,—with article הָאָרֶץ, § **45.** R. 2.
a. another case of a helping-vowel; like עֶרֶב (35).

63. וּלְמִקְוֵה—û-lᵉmĭḳ-wê(h)—*and-to-collection-of:*
a. And is here written וּ, § **49.** 2; *to* is written, as usually, לְ.
b. The root is קָוָה, whence the passive future 3rd plural יָקוּוּ (55).
c. The מ is the prefix used in noun-formation, cf. מָקוֹם (58. *b*).
d. This noun (= *collection-of*) is in the construct state, § **107.** 2.

64. יַמִּים—yăm-mîm—*seas:*
a. The sing. is יָם from which the plural differs in that a D. f. appears in מ, and ă appears instead of å.
b. יָמִים (= yåm-mîm) would be an impossible form, § **28.** 2, 3; just as, on the other hand, מָקוֹם (= mă-ḳôm) would be impossible, § **28.** 1.

65. תַּדְשֵׁא—tăd-šē'—(she)-*shall-cause-to-spring-forth:*
a. תּ, as in תֵּרָאֶה (59), = *she*, being the feminine prefix.
b. The ־ under דּ is silent, § **11.** 1.
c. ד, שׁ, and א are the three root-letters; דֶּשֶׁא, cf. קָרָא, בָּרָא.
d. This stem is neither the simple nor the passive verb-stem, but a *causative* stem. It generally has ־ under the preformative, i. e., under the letter which is prefixed to the root to designate person or gender; cf. יַבְדֵּל (25), which has ־ under י, and means *he-causes-a-division.*

66. דֶּ֫שֶׁא—dḗ-šĕ'—*grass*, cf. the preceding root דְּשָׁא (65. c):

a. דּ (preceded by ֵי) = d; but ד (preceded by ־ֱ) = ḍ.

b. This word, like אֶ֫רֶץ, עֶ֫רֶב, and others, has a secondary, or helping vowel.

67. עֵ֫שֶׂב—'ḗ-śĕv—*herb*: ב = v; שׂ = ś, not š (sh).

a. The secondary ĕ being only a helping vowel is not accented.

68. מַזְרִיעַ—măz-rî(ă)'—*causing-to-seed*, root זָרַע:

a. A new letter ז z; Păṯăḥ-furtive under ע.

b. A participle, as shown by מ, cf. מַבְדִּיל, (44), מְרַחֶ֫פֶת (16)

c. A causative form, as shown by ־ִ under the preformative.

69. זֶ֫רַע—zĕ́-răʻ—*seed*,—from the root זָרַע:

a. This word, like אֶ֫רֶץ, עֶ֫רֶב, דֶּ֫שֶׁא and עֵ֫שֶׂב has an unaccented helping vowel.

70. עֵץ—'ēṣ—*tree-of*; פְּרִי—pᵉrî—*fruit*.

71. עֹ֫שֶׂה פְּרִי—'ō-śé(h) pᵉrî—*making fruit*:

a. The ô, here written over the right arm of שׂ (ś), is naturally long.

b. The ה ־ֶ, like that in תִּרְאֶה, is ê.

c. The point in פ is D. f., being preceded by a full vowel (ê); it therefore joins the two words together and is called D. f. conjunctive, § **15**. 3.

d. עֹשֶׂה accented on penult because closely followed by a monosyllable, § **21**. 1.

e. עֹשֶׂה is a participle from עָשָׂה *he-made*.

72. לְמִינוֹ—lᵉmî-nô—*to-kind-his*:

a. The prep. לְ, the noun מִין, and the suffix וֹ (= *his*).

73. זַרְעוֹ־בוֹ—zăr-ʻô+vô—*seed-his+in-him*:

a. זֶ֫רַע *seed*, but זַרְעוֹ *his-seed*, the ־ֶ being silent.

b. וֹ is a pronominal suffix meaning *his* or *him*.

c. בוֹ is made up of בְּ the prep. *in*. and וֹ the suffix *him*.

d. It is בוֹ (vô) not בּוֹ. because of the preceding וֹ.

e. בוֹ .... אֲשֶׁר = which....in-him; this is the idiom for in which.

3. FORMS FOR SPECIAL STUDY.

תַּרְשֵׁא,	in wh.	תּ=she	and—under תּ	indic. a causative idea
מַבְדִּיל,	"	מ indic. a part. and—under מ	"	"	"
יַבְדֵּל,	"	י=he	and—under י	"	"	"
מַזְרִיעַ,	"	מ indic. a part. and—under מ	"	"	"

4. OBSERVATIONS.

54. There are in Hebrew (1) a *simple* verb-stem, (2) a *passive* verb-stem, and also (3) a *causative* verb-stem.

55. The characteristic of the passive stem is the letter נ, or a D. f. in the first radical representing נ assimilated.

56. The causative stem may be known by the ־ַ which always occurs under its preformative (י, תּ or מ).

57. The name of the simple stem is Ḳăl, of the passive stem, Nif'ăl, of the causative stem, Hif'îl.

58. The letter י prefixed to verbal forms means *he*, the letter תּ means *she*, while מ so prefixed indicates a participle.

5. GRAMMAR-LESSON.

1. § **1.** The names of the Hebrew letters.
2. § **13.** 2. and N. 1, Dăgēš-förtē in spirants.
3. § **57.** 1—3, Inflection.

6. WORD-LESSON.

(66) יַמִּים *seas* (69) דֶּשֶׁא *grass* (72) עֵץ *tree*
(67) מִקְוֶה *collection* (70) זֶרַע *seed* (73) תַּרְשֵׁא (see N. **65**)
(68) מִקְוֵה *collection-of* (71) מִין *kind, species*

7. EXERCISES.

1. To be translated into Hebrew:—(1) *To-the-tree making fruit* (there is) *seed* (according)-*to-its-kind;* (2) *The-seed which+in-it* (= in which) (is) *fruit;* (3) *The-day which+in-it* (is) *light;* (4) *The-earth shall-cause-to-spring-forth*)(*the-grass and-*)(*the seed;* (5) *The-fruit* (is) *in-the-seed, and-the-seed* (is) *in-the-earth.*

2. To be translated into English:— (1) הַיָּם אֲשֶׁר מַיִם בּוֹ; (2) עֵץ הַפְּרִי; (3) הַלַּיְלָה אֲשֶׁר חֹשֶׁךְ בּוֹ; (4) וַיְהִי־דֶשֶׁא; (5) זַרְעוֹ בָאָרֶץ.

3. To be written in English letters:—(1) תַּדְשֵׁא, (2) דֶּשֶׁא, (3) עָשָׂה, (6) עֵץ, (5) בֵּין, (4) פְּרִי.

4. To be written in Hebrew letters:—(1) zé-răʻ, (2) dé-šĕʼ, (3) rû(ă)ḥ, (4) χēn, (5) 'ô-śêʼ(h), (6) tôṣēʼ, (7) vô, (8) wăy-hî.

8. TOPICS FOR STUDY.

(1) The characteristic of the Nifʻäl stem. (2) The characteristic of the Hifʻîl stem. (3) The origin and character of tone-long and naturally long vowels. (4) The sign of the participle. (5) The 3 sg. masc. pron. suffix. (6) The character of ָ in עָשָׂה. (7) The D. f. Conjunctive. (8) What inflection includes. (9) The names of the Hebrew letters.

LESSON X.—GENESIS I. 12, 13.

1. NOTE-REVIEW.

(1) וַיֹּאמֶר (18); (2) וְרוּחַ (15); (3) אֶת־ (23); (4) יָמִים (64); (5) תַּדְשֵׁא (65).

2. NOTES.

74. וַתּוֹצֵא—wăt-tô-ṣēʼ—*and-*(she)-*caused-to-go-forth:*

a. Wâw Conversive וַ, and the feminine prefix תּ (= *she*).

Lesson 10

b. The וֹ is a contraction of וְ‏ַ (aw); hence תוֹצֵא is for תַוְצֵא, which, like תַדְשֵׁא, has ־ַ under the pref. and is *causative*.

c. The root is יָצָא, which is for וָצָא, *he-went-forth*.

75. לְמִינֵהוּ —l°mî-nê-hû—*to-kind-his:*

a. An uncontracted form, with same meaning as לְמִינוֹ.

b. הוּ is the full form of suffix meaning *his* or *him;* ־ֵ may, for convenience, be called a connecting vowel.

76. שְׁלִישִׁי —š°lî-šî—*third;* cf. שֵׁנִי *second.*

3. FORMS FOR SPECIAL STUDY.

מַזְרִיעַ	וְתִרְאֶה	הַמַּיִם	בֹּקֶר
לְמִינֵהוּ	וַתּוֹצֵא	מַבְדִּיל	בָּהוּ
זַרְעוֹ	עֵשֶׂב	הַמָּקוֹם	מְרַחֶפֶת

4. OBSERVATIONS.

59. The full form of the pronom. suffix 3rd p. sg. masc. is הוּ, the short form is וֹ.

60. There are many nouns that take a supplementary helping-vowel, usually ě, under certain circumstances ă, which is never accented.

5. GRAMMAR-LESSON.

1. § 47. 1, 2, 4, 5.   The Inseparable Prepositions.
2. § 49. 1, 2.   The Wâw Conjunctive.
3. § 45.   The Article.

6. WORD-LESSON

(74) תוֹצֵא (see N. 74)   (77) עֵשֶׂב *herb*   (80) שְׁלִישִׁי *third*

(75) מַזְרִיעַ *yielding seed*   (78) עֹשֶׂה *making*

(76) יָצָא *he went-forth*   (79) פְּרִי *fruit*

7. EXERCISES.

1. To be translated into Hebrew:—(1) *The-day the-third* (= the

third day). (2) *The-earth shall-cause-to-go-forth*)(*the-herb and-*)(*the-tree.* (3) *Let-(there)-be* (a) *place between the seas and-the-land.* (4) *And-she-caused-to-go-forth*)(*the-spirit upon+the-waters.* (5) *And-created God*)(*-the-light and-*)(*the-darkness in-day one.* (6) *Day and-seas and-waters.*

2. (1) הַיּוֹם אֲשֶׁר אוֹרוֹ־בוֹ טוֹב, (2) וַיַּבְדֵּל בֵּין הַיָּם לָאָרֶץ,
(3) וַיִּבְרָא אֶת הָרָקִיעַ בַּיּוֹם (4) וַתּוֹצֵא הָאָרֶץ אֶת־הַדֶּשֶׁא,
(5) וַיַּעַשׂ אֱלֹהִים אֶת הַיַּבָּשָׁה וְאֵת מִקְוֵה הַמַּיִם, הַשֵּׁנִי.

3. To be written in English letters:— (1) לָרָקִיעַ, (2) וְלַחֹשֶׁךְ
(3) מִתַּחַת, (4) מַזְרִיעַ (5) זַרְעוֹ־בוֹ (6) וַיַּרְא.

4. To be written in Hebrew letters:—(1) yĭḳ-ḳâ-wû, (2) bᵉθόχ, (3) 'ĕl+mâ-ḳôm, (4) lᵉmî-nô, (5) 'ēṣ, (6) 'ăšĕr, (7) zăr-'ô+vô, (8) šᵉlîšî.

8. *TOPICS FOR STUDY.*

(1) The helping vowel. (2) The syllable. (3) Păθăḥ furtive. (4) The forms of the conjunction *and*. (5) The origin of î under wॱ in וִיהִי (6) The use of the imperfect with wâw conversive. (7) The sign of the definite object, its forms and usage. (8) The influence of laryngeals upon neighbouring vowels.

LESSON XI.—GENESIS I. 14, 15.

1. *NOTE-REVIEW.*

(1) יְהִי (19); (2) הַשָּׁמַיִם (5); (3) בֵּין (26); (4) יוֹם (31);
(5) לַיְלָה (34); (6) וַיְהִי־כֵן (52).

2. *NOTES.*

77. מְאֹרֹת—mᵉʼô-rôθ—*luminaries:*

a. Sing., מָאוֹר (like מָקוֹם *place*); but when the plur. ending ôθ is added the tone moves one syllable, and the original ă is reduced to ְ, § 109. 1. *a.*

b. Both ô's are naturally long, though written defectively, § 6. 4 N. 2.

c. אוֹר = *light*, but מָאוֹר = *luminary;* on this use of מְ, see 63.*c*.

78. בִּרְקִיעַ—bĭr-ḳî(ă)'—*in-expanse-of:*

a. Abs. רָקִיעַ (40); const. רְקִיעַ, the original ā being reduced to ְ, §109. 3. *a*.

b. Before ר the prep. בְּ takes ִ instead of ְ, § 47. 2.

c. The syl. בִּר (bĭr) is closed, § 26. N. 2.

d. The šᵉwâ under ר is silent, § 10. 2.

79. לְהַבְדִּיל—lᵉhăv-dîl—*to-cause-a-division:*

a. An infinitive; the prefix ה shows it to be *causative* (Hif'îl).

b. D. l. in ד because it does not immediately follow a vowel-sound.

80. וְהָיוּ—wᵉhå-yû—*and-they-shall-be:*

a. הָיָה = *he-was;* הָיְתָה = *she-was;* הָיוּ = *they-were.*

b. But וְ connects this with what precedes, and likewise carries on to the perfect the time-sense of the preceding context; cf. with this the form of the conjunction (וַ) which gives the *imperfect* the time-sense of the preceding context, see 18.

81. לְאֹתֹת—lᵉ'ô-θθ—*for-signs:*

a. Sing. אֹת or אוֹת; plur. אֹתֹת, by the addition of ôθ, § 106. 3.

b. Both vowels are naturally long (ô), written defectively.

82. וּלְמוֹעֲדִים—û-lᵉmô-'ăđîm—*and-for-seasons:*

a. The conjunction, before a consonant with šᵉwâ, is written וּ § 49. 2.

b. The וּ is ô, not ŏ; Mé̄θeğ is written before comp. šᵉwâ, § 18. 3.

c. ע, being a laryngeal, takes a *compound* šᵉwâ, § 42. 3.

d. The noun is in the plur. masc., as shown by îm.

83. וּלְיָמִים—û-lᵉyă-mîm—*and-for-days:*

a. Another case of וּ, instead of וְ, before a consonant with šᵉwâ, see 82. *a*.

b. This is an *irregular plural form from* יוֹם *day.*

84. וְשָׁנִים—wᵉšå-nîm—*and-years:*

a. A masc. pl. ending with a noun (שָׁנָה) which has feminine sg. ending, § **106.** 4. N.

85. לִמְאוֹרֹת—līm-'ô-rôθ—*for-luminaries:*
a. What was said in 78. *b, c,* concerning bĭr, applies to līm.
b. Here the first ô is written *fully*, the second defectively, § **6.** 4. N. 2.

86. לְהָאִיר—lᵉhā-'îr—*to-cause-to-shine;* cf. אוֹר *light:*
a. Another *causative infinitive* (cf. הַבְדִּיל), but with ־ָ under ה instead of ־ַ, because it is in an *open* syllable, § **28.** 1.

3. FORMS FOR SPECIAL STUDY.

עֶרֶב	מְאֹרֹת	יְהִי	וְשָׁנִים
אֶרֶץ	אֹתֹת	מְאֹרֹת	וּבֵין
דֶּשֶׁא	יָמִים	בִּרְקִיעַ	וּלְמוֹעֲדִים
זֶרַע	שָׁנִים	לִמְאוֹרֹת	וּלְיָמִים

4. OBSERVATIONS

61. The *fem.* plur. ending is ôθ, the *masc.*, îm.
62. For the initial and so-called medial šᵉwâ, see § **10.** 1, 2.
63. *And* is usually written וְ, but before labials and before consonants with šᵉwâ it is written וּ.

5. GRAMMAR-LESSON.

1. § **47.** 1, 2, 4, 5, The Inseparable Prepositions.
2. § **49.** 1, 2, The Wâw Conjunctive.
3. § **10.** 1, 2, Initial and (so-called) Medial Šᵉwâ.
4. § **7.** 1— 4, Classification of Vowel-sounds.

6. WORD-LESSON.

(81) אוֹת *sign*   (83) מָאוֹר *luminary*   (85) שֶׁמֶשׁ *sun*

(82) יָרֵחַ *moon*   (84) מוֹעֵד *season*   (86) שָׁנָה *year*

7. EXERCISES.

1. To be translated into Hebrew:—(1) *The-sign, the-moon, the sun, the-year, the-season;* (2) *The-sun will-be-seen in-the-heavens;* (3) *Signs and-luminaries and-seasons and-years;* (4) *The-sun shall-be* (יִהְיֶה) *in-expanse-of the-heavens;* (5) *For-seasons and-for-luminaries;* (6) *To-cause-a-division between the-day and-between the-night;* (7) *Seas and-waters;* (8) *Days and-seas;* (9) *The-luminary, the-luminaries.*

2. To be translated into English:— (1) הַמְּאֹרֹת מֵעַל לָאָרֶץ; (2) וַיַּבְדֵּל בֵּין הַשָּׁמַיִם וּבֵין הָאָרֶץ; (3) הַמָּאוֹר הַשֵּׁנִי; (4) בִּרְקִיעַ, בִּרְקִיעַ, בִּרְקִיעַ; (5) בָּרָא אֱלֹהִים אֶת־הַשֶּׁמֶשׁ; (6) הָרָקִיעַ אֲשֶׁר הַשֶּׁמֶשׁ בּוֹ; (7) לַמְּאוֹרֹת, לִמְאוֹרֹת.

3. To be written in English letters:— (1) יָרֵחַ, (2) מוֹעֵד, (3) יַבְדֵּל, (4) מוֹעֲדִים, (5) שָׁנָה, (6) שֶׁמֶשׁ.

4. To be written in Hebrew letters:—(1) hâ-'îr, (2) 'ô-θôθ, (3) yôm, (4) yâ-mîm, (5) bĭr-ḳî(ä)'.

8. TOPICS FOR STUDY.

(1) Change of ָ to ַ. (2) Prepositions בְּ and לְ with î. (3) Wâw Conversive with the past tense. (4.) Various forms of the verb הָיָה *he-was.* (5) וְ and וָ. (6) ־ים and ־וֹת. (7) Difference between הִבְדִּיל and הֵאִיר. (8) Nouns with helping vowels. (9) Initial and so-called Medial Šᵉwâ. (10) Classification of vowel-sounds according to formation, quantity, nature, value.

LESSON XII.—GENESIS I. 16, 17.

1. NOTE-REVIEW.

(1) מְאֹרֹת (77); (2) הַמַּיִם (56); (3) מָקוֹם (58); (4) בִּרְקִיעַ (78); (5) לְהָאִיר (86); (6) הַחֹשֶׁךְ (28); (7) וַיִּרְא (22); (8) וַיִּקְרָא (29).

2. NOTES.

87. וַיַּעַשׂ—wăy-yă-'ăś—*and-(he)-made*, see 46:

a. Like יְהִי, a short form of the *imperfect*, root עָשָׂה.

b. Third syllable, has an unaccented helping or secondary vowel.

88. שְׁנֵי—šᵉnê—*two-of*; *cf.* פְּנֵי *faces-of*:

a. The construct state of the numeral שְׁנַיִם, of which ַיִם is the *dual* ending, §§ **106.** 5; **107.** 6.

b. The word has but one syllable, ְ not being a full vowel.

89. הַגְּדֹלִים—hăg-gᵉdô-lîm—*the-great* (ones):

a. The article written regularly with ַ and D. f., § **45.** 1.

b. An adjective in the plur. (note the ending ִים) from גָּדוֹל.

c. The ֹ is ô, though in the plural form written defectively.

d. The ָ and ְ under גּ in the sing. and plur. respectively, both arise from an original ă. In the singular this ă is in an open syl. immediately before the tone and therefore is rounded to â; in the plural the tone has moved away upon the addition of îm, and so original ă is reduced to šᵉwâ; cf. sg. m. גָּדוֹל, but sg. f. גְּדוֹלָה, pl. m. גְּדוֹלִים, pl. f. גְּדוֹלוֹת, in which, by the addition of an affix, the tone is changed. This change of a full vowel to šᵉwâ is called reduction, § **36.** 2. *b.*

90. הַמָּאוֹר הַגָּדֹל—hăm-mâ-'ôr hăg-gâ-dôl—*the-luminary the-great* (one):

a. Both words have a tone-long â, and a naturally long ô, although in the adjective the ô is written defectively.

b. Both words have the article in its usual form.

91. לְמֶמְשֶׁלֶת—lᵉmĕm-šĕ-lĕθ—*for-dominion-of*:

a. Two unaccented closed syllables, one accented open.

b. The final ĕ is a helping vowel.

c. לְ is the prep.; מ, the formative prefix, cf. 58. *b;* ת, the fem. ending; the root being מָשַׁל.

LESSON 12.

92. הַקָּטֹן—hăk-ḳå-ṭōn—*the-small;* with tone-long ō.

93. הַכּוֹכָבִים—hăk-kô-ẋå-vîm—*the stars:*

a. The ־ under כ is Méθĕǧ, § **18. 1**; under בּ it is Sillûḳ.

b. Cf. כּוֹכָב *star,* כּוֹכָבִים *stars,* הַכּוֹכָבִים *the-stars.*

94. וַיִּתֵּן—wăy-yĭt-tēn—*and-(he)-gave:*

a. יִתֵּן *he-will-give* is the Ḳăl Imperfect from נָתַן *he-gave.* With Wåw Conversive (cf. 18) it has the force of a Perfect (past).

b. The D. f. in תּ is for the first radical נ, which has been assimilated; cf. מִתַּחַת for מִן תַּחַת, see 49, § **39**. 1.

95. אֹתָם—'ô-θåm—)(-*them:* the pronominal suffix ָם with אֵת, another way of writing the sign of def. obj., § **51. 2**.

3. FORMS FOR SPECIAL STUDY.

הַמְּאֹרֹת הַגְּדֹלִים—*the-luminaries the-great*=the great luminaries.

הַמָּאוֹר הַגָּדֹל—*the-luminary the-great* = the great luminary.

הַמָּאוֹר הַקָּטֹן—*the-luminary the-small* = the small luminary.

4. OBSERVATIONS.

64. In the words cited above, the noun stands first, the **adjective**, second.

65. The noun is masculine,[1] the adjective is masculine.

66. When the noun is sing., the adjective is sing.; when the noun is plur., the adjective is plur.

67. The noun has the article, and so has the adjective.

68. The following is, therefore, the rule governing the position and agreement of an attributive adjective: *The adjective, when attributive, follows its noun, and agrees with it in gender, number and definiteness.*

---

[1] The noun מָאוֹר is *masculine,* although in the plural it has a feminine form.

5. GRAMMAR-LESSON.

1. § **57**. Notes 1, 2,   Tenses and Moods.
2. § **58**. 1.   The Simple Verb-stem, Ḳăl.
3. § **14**. 1—3,   Omission of Dăğĕš-fŏrtē.
4. § **11**. 2. a, b,   Šᵉwâ under final consonants.

6. WORD-LESSON.

(87) אוֹר *to shine*   (89) כּוֹכָב *star*   (92) רְבִיעִי *fourth*
(88) גָּדוֹל *great*   (90) מֶמְשָׁלָה *ruling*   (93) שְׁנַיִם *two*
                          (91) קָטֹן *small*

7. EXERCISES.

1. To be translated into Hebrew:—(1) *The great day;* (2) *In the great day;* (3) *And in the great day;* (4) *The great stars;* (5) *The small star;* (6) *The good God;* (7) *He-gave, he-ruled;* (8) *God gave)(the-luminaries for-(the)-ruling-of the-day and-for-(the)-ruling-of the-night;* (9) *The great luminary* (is) *the-sun; the small luminary, the-moon;* (10) *The-sun and-the-moon* (are) *in-(the)-expanse-of the-heavens;* (11) *God will-give)(the-day.*

2. To be translated into English:— (1) עָשָׂה אֶת־הַמָּאוֹר הַגָּדֹל;
(2) הַכּוֹכָב הַטּוֹב; (3) מוֹעֵד אֶחָד; (4) הַשָּׁנָה הַשְּׁלִישִׁית; (5)
הַמָּאוֹר הַקָּטֹן הַשֵּׁנִי; (7) הַמָּאוֹר הַשֵּׁנִי; (6) יְהִי כוֹכָבִים בַּלַּיְלָה; (8)
הָעֵץ אֲשֶׁר (10); עֵץ הַפְּרִי; (9) וַיַּבְדֵּל בֵּין מְאֹרֹת לִמְאֹרֹת
בּוֹ זֶרַע.

3. To be written in English letters: — (1) יִתֵּן, (2) יַעַשׂ, (3)
מְאֹרֹת, (8) לִמְשֹׁל, (7) בָּרְקִיעַ, (6) אַתֶּם, (5) כּוֹכָב, (4) מֶמְשֶׁלֶת,
(9) הַיּוֹם.

4. To be written in Hebrew letters:—yôm, (2) yôm, (3) šĕx,
(4) lēx, (5) 'ătt, (6) țălt, (7) yēšt, (8) hå-'ôr.

8. TOPICS FOR STUDY.

(1) Affixes of the feminine. (2) Affixes of the masculine plural and dual, in absolute and construct. (3) Change of ָ to ַ. (4)

The construction of the attributive adjective. (5) Mĕθĕġ and Sĭllûḳ. (6) Assimilation of נ. (7) The infinitive of the root מָשַׁל. (8) The conjunction before a labial. (9) The ordinals meaning *second, third, fourth*. (10) Tenses and moods in Hebrew. (11) The form of the simple verb-stem (Ḳal). (12) Omission of Dåġĕš-fŏrtē. (13) Šᵉwâ under final consonants.

LESSON XIII.—GENESIS I. 18—20.
1. NOTE-REVIEW.

(89); הַגְּדֹלִים (40); (4) רָקִיעַ (3); (7) הָאָרֶץ (2); (17); הַמָּיִם (1)
(5) אֲשֶׁר (48); (6) לְמִינֵהוּ (75); (7) וַיַּרְא (22).

2. NOTES.

96. וְלִמְשֹׁל—wᵉlĭm-šōl—*and-to-rule:*
a. Conjunction וְ; prep. לְ with ־ֹ, § **47.** 2; the ־ under מ silent.
b. An infinitive from the root מָשַׁל, cf. **91**; tone-long ō.

97. בַּיּוֹם וּבַלַּיְלָה—băy-yôm û-văl-lăy-lă(h)—*in-the-day and-in-the-night,* §§ **45.** 4. R. 3; **47.** 4; **49.** 2.

98. וּלְהַבְדִּיל—û-lᵃhăv-dîl—*and-to-cause-a-division.*
a. וְ, § **49.** 2; לְ, § **32.** 3. *c*; הַבְדִּיל, see **79.**
b. The root is בָּדַל (pronounced bâ-dăl).

99. רְבִיעִי—rᵉvî-'î—*fourth;* cf. שְׁלִישִׁי *third.*

100. יִשְׁרְצוּ—yĭš-rᵉṣû—(they) *shall-swarm:*
a. Ḳăl Imperfect 3 pers. plur. masc. from שָׁרַץ *he-swarmed;* יִשְׁרֹץ *he-will-swarm;* יִשְׁרְצוּ *they-will-swarm.*
b. Two šᵉwâs—first, silent; second, vocal, § **11.** 3. N. 1, 2.
c. The Imperfect tense represents an action as unfinished, incomplete, whether in past, present or future time.

101. שֶׁרֶץ—šĕ'-rĕṣ—*swarm,* or, collectively, *swarms:*

a. Like עֶרֶב, אֶרֶץ, דֶּשֶׁא, זֶרַע and עֵשֶׂב; these nouns have but one essential vowel, viz., the first, since the second is inserted merely for euphony. They are called *Seğolates*.

b. The essential vowel in all these cases, except עֵשֶׂב, was originally ă, which has been deflected to ĕ, § **89.** 1. The essential vowel of עֵשֶׂב was originally ĭ.

102. נֶפֶשׁ —nĕ'-fĕš—*soul-of:* Another Seğolate, of which the primary form was נַפְשׁ; cf. the primary form of זֶרַע, viz., זַרְע, which appears before the suffix in זַרְעוֹ, see 73.

103. חַיָּה —ḥăy-yà(h)—*life:* Feminine, as shown by ־ָה.

104. וְעוֹף —wᵉ'ôf—*and-fowl:*

a. The Wāw Conjunctive pointed regularly with šᵉwâ.

b. A case of naturally long ô; the *final* form of פ (Pē).

105. יְעוֹפֵף —yᵉ'ô-fēf—(he) *shall-fly:*

a. An Imperfect from the root עוּף *to-fly.*

b. Unchangeable ô; both פ's are spirants.

3. FORMS FOR SPECIAL STUDY.

נֶפֶשׁ	לִמְשֹׁל	יִשְׁרֹץ
זֶרַע	הַבְדִּיל	יִשְׁרְצוּ

4. OBSERVATIONS.

69. The Imperfect Ḳăl has a preformative in the 3d masc. the letter י, written with ĭ.

70. In forming the plural of the Ḳăl perf., the vowel of the second radical becomes vocal šᵉwâ.

5. GRAMMAR-LESSON.

1 § **50.** 1,   The regular forms of the Personal Pronoun.
2. § **50.** 2, 3.   Pausal forms and Remarks (*to be read only*).

6. WORD-LESSON.

(94) חַיָּה *life* (96) עוּף *to-fly* (98) שֶׁרֶץ *swarm*
(95) נֶפֶשׁ *soul* (97) עוֹף *fowl*

7. EXERCISES.

1. To be translated into Hebrew:—(1) *The-waters shall-swarm;* (2) *God created*)(*the-earth, and-he-made*)(*the-heavens;* (3) *And-saw God*)(*the-earth which he-had-created, and-*(it)*-was+good;* (4) *I* (am) *God who created*)(*the-light;* (5) *Thou* (art) *in-the-heavens and-I* (am) *upon+the-earth;* (6) *We* (are) *great;* (7) *Thou* (m.) (art) *small;* (8) *Thou* (f.) (art) *good;* (9) *Ye* (are) (the) *light-of the-earth.*

2. To be translated into English:—(1) אָנֹכִי וְהוּא, (2) אֵת בָּרָא (5); גְּדֹלִים הַשָּׁמַיִם (4); יִקְרְאוּ לַמַּיִם יָמִים (3); גָּדְלָה הָעוֹף (6); אֱלֹהִים אֶת־הַנֶּפֶשׁ.

3. To be written in English letters:—(1) שֶׁרֶץ, (2) וְלִמְשֹׁל, (3) עוֹף, (4) נֶפֶשׁ, (5) נַפְשׁוֹ, (6) וּלְהַבְדִּיל.

4. To be written in Hebrew letters:—(1) ḳôl, (2) nĕ'-fĕš, (3) mᵉ'ô-rōθ, (4) 'â-nô-χî, (5) 'ătt, (6) 'ăt-tĕm, (7) năḥ'-nû.

8. TOPICS FOR STUDY.

(1) Force of the Imperfect. (2) Seğolates. (3) The vowel ĕ, as derived from ⁻. (4) The vowel ŏ. (5) The various ways of writing the article. (6) The forms of the Personal Pronoun. (7) The simple verb-stem. (8) The Passive. (9) The Causative.

LESSON XIV.—GENESIS I. 21—23.

1. NOTE-REVIEW.

(1) נֶפֶשׁ, 74 (4), וַתּוֹצֵא (3), 18ˋ (2), וַיֹּאמֶר (42), הַמַּיִם (1)
חַיָּה (102. 103); (5) וַיַּעַשׂ (46).

2. NOTES.

106. וַיִּבְרָא—wăy-yĭv-rā'—*and*-(he)-*created:*

a. יִבְרָא *he-will-create*, but with וְ the force of the tense is changed.

b. Compare (1) קְרָא and וַיִּקְרָא with (2) בָּרָא and וַיִּבְרָא.

107. הַתַּנִּינִם—hăt-tăn-nî-nîm—*the-sea-monsters:*

a. Points in ת and נ are D. f., because preceded by vowels.

b. The ִ under נ is î written defectively, § **6**. 3. N. and 4. N. 2.

c. (1) Article ‎ הַ, (2) noun תַּנִּין, (3) plural ending ‎ ִים.

108. כָּל־נֶפֶשׁ—kŏl+něʹ-fĕš—*every+soul-of:*

a. כָּל־ is an unaccented closed syllable, for the word before Măḳ-ḳēf *always* loses its accent, § **17**. 1, 2.

b. An *unaccented* closed syllable must have a short vowel, § **28**. 2; but is ָ a short vowel? *It is.* In this word we have for the first time ŏ, or Ḳāmĕṣ-ḥāṭûf, which is represented by the same sign[1] (ָ) as ā, § **5**. 5.

109. הַחַיָּה—hă(ḥ)-ḥăy-yă(h)—*the-life:* The article with its D. f. implied, § **45**. 2; Méθĕǧ, second syllable before tone, § **18**. 1.

110. הָרֹמֶשֶׂת—hā-rô-měʹ-śĕθ—*the-*(one)*-creeping:*

a. The article with D. f. rejected and ַ rounded to ָ, § **45**. 3.

b. A participle (although without מ) fem. (ת) sg. from רָמַשׂ.

c. Observe that the ֹ is ô, not ō, although defectively written.

111. שָׁרְצוּ—šā-rᵉṣû—(they) *swarmed:*

a. *He-swarmed* שָׁרַץ, *they-swarmed* שָׁרְצוּ; cf. יִשְׁרַץ *he-will-swarm*, יִשְׁרְצוּ *they-will-swarm;* and so בָּרָא *he-created,* בָּרְאוּ *they-created;* קָרָא *he-called*, קָרְאוּ *they-called;* נָתַן *he-gave,* נָתְנוּ *they-gave.*

b. Ḳăl Perf. 3 m. pl., as shown by the ending וּ.

---

[1] There is practically no difference in pronunciation between ָ = ā and ָ = ŏ; but in this book they are transliterated differently in order to emphasize the difference in their origin.

112. לְמִינֵהֶם—lᵉmî-nê-hĕm—*to-kinds-their*:

a. הֶם is pron. suf. 3 m. pl., as used with plur. nouns, § **51. 1.** *c*.
b. ֵ (= ê) is a defective writing for יִ the plur. const. ending.

113. כָּנָף—kâ-nâf—*wing*:

a. The first ָ is â, because *before* the tone and in an open syllable: the second is â because under the tone, § **31. 1.** *a*. (1), *c*.
b. Const. sing. would be כְּנַף; *dual* would be כְּנָפַיִם.

114. וַיְבָרֶךְ—wăy-vâ'-rĕx—*and-(he)-blessed*:

a. Root is בָּרַךְ, יְ being sign of Impf., and וְ the conjunction.
b. D. f. of יְ omitted from יְ, which has only a Šᵉwâ, § **14. 2.**
c. The final ךְ has, as always, a Šᵉwâ, § **11. 2.** *a*.
d. In the syllable וַיְ ay forms a diphthong, hence the following ב is a spirant.
e. This stem is not at all like either (1) the simple verb-stem, as seen in יִקְרָא, or (2) the passive-stem, as seen in יָקוּם, or (3) the causative-stem, as seen in מַבְדִּיל, יַבְדֵּל. It is a *new* stem, viz., the *intensive*. The form would regularly be יְבָרֵךְ, but ר rejects the D. f., and the preceding ֵ becomes ָ, while, by a change of tone, ָ yields to ֶ; cf. אֵת, but אֶת־ (**23**).
f. The characteristic of the intensive-stem is Dâğĕš-fŏrtē in the second radical, not, as in יָקוּם (**55**), in the first.

115. לֵאמֹר—lê'-mōr—*to-say*, generally translated *saying*:

a. Inf. const. of אָמַר *say* is אֱמֹר; cf. מְשֹׁל (**96**) from מָשַׁל.
b. Before 'א, the prep. לְ takes ֵ, giving לֵאמֹר, § **47. 3.**
c. א being weak, finally quiesces, carrying ְ along with it, and in compensation ְ becomes ê.

116. פְּרוּ—pᵉrû—*be-ye-fruitful*: A Ḳăl Imperative plural.

117. וּרְבוּ—û-rᵉvû—*and-multiply-ye*: Ḳăl Imperative plur. with Wâw Conjunctive, here וּ before a consonant with Šᵉwâ, § **49. 2.**

118. וּמִלְאוּ—û-mĭl-'û—*and-fill-ye*:

a. Wâw Conjunctive before a labial is written וּ, § **49.** 2.
b. Š^ewâ is silent, §§ **10.** 2. *b*; **26.** 4. N. 2; **28.** 4.
c. Ḳâl Imperative plural of מָלֵא, וּ indicating the plural.

119. בַּיַּמִּים—băy-yăm-mîm—*in-the-seas:*

a. יָם *sea,* יָמִים *seas,* הַיָּמִים *the-seas,* בַּיָּמִים *in-the-seas.*
b. Cf. יוֹם *day,* יָמִים *days,* הַיָּמִים *the-days,* בַּיָּמִים *in-the-days.*

120. וְהָעוֹף—w^ehâ-'ôf—*and-the-fowl,* §§ **49.** 1; **45.** 3.

121. יִרֶב—yĭ'-rĕv—*let-*(him)-*multiply:*

a. Ḳâl Impf., short form, from same root as רָבוּ (**117**).
b. י is the pref. of the Impf.; ר and בּ, radicals; third radical lacking.
c. ֶ is a helping vowel.

122. חֲמִישִׁי—ḥamî-šî—*fifth,* § **9.** 2.

3. FORMS FOR SPECIAL STUDY.

הַמַּיִם	מְרַחֶפֶת	יִקְרָא – קָרָא
הַחַיָּה	מֶמְשֶׁלֶת	יִבְרָא – בָּרָא
הָרְמֶשֶׂת	רֹמֶשֶׂת	יִשְׁרְצוּ – שָׁרְצוּ

4. OBSERVATIONS.

71. Upon the addition of וּ in the Impf. as well as in the Perf. the vowel of the second radical becomes vocal Š^ewâ.

72. The feminine ending ת is often preceded by an unaccented ֶ, inserted for euphony.

73. The article is ♦הַ; while ה (also חַ) takes the D. f. by implication, ר (also ע and א) entirely rejects it.

74. The quiescense of a consonant is usually compensated for by the strengthening of the preceding vowel.

5. GRAMMAR-LESSON.

1. § **106.** 2. *b*, The fem. ending ת attached to a stem by means of ֶ .
2. § **106.** 2. *c*, The fem. ending ת changed to הָ .
3. § **42.** 1. 3[1] The peculiarities of laryngeals.

6. WORD-LESSON.

(99) כָּל־ *all, every*   (102) תַּנִּין *sea-monster*
(100) כָּנָף *wing*   (103) בֵּרֵךְ *he-blessed*
(101) רָמַשׂ *he-crept*   (104) מָלֵא *he-filled*

7. EXERCISES.

1. To be translated into Hebrew:—(1) *God said, "Let-there-be (an)-expanse" and-he-created)(+ the-heavens.* (2) *And-he-made)(+the-great stars* (lit. *the-stars the-great*). (3) *Fill-ye the-waters and-multiply-ye in-the-seas.* (4) *And-blessed God every winged fowl* (lit. *every+fowl-of wing*). (5) *Let-multiply the-fowl upon+the-earth.* (6) *God blessed)(every + living-thing that creeps* (lit.)(*every soul-of the-life the-creeping*); (7) *The-waters swarmed according-to-their-kinds.*

2. To be translated into English: — (1) וַיִּבְרָא אֱלֹהִים אֶת־ (2) הַתַּנִּינִים בַּיּוֹם הַחֲמִישִׁי, (3) וַיִּשְׁרְצוּ הַמַּיִם לְמִינֵהֶם, (4) בֵּרֵךְ אֹתָם אֱלֹהִים לֵאמֹר (5) יִרֶב הָעוֹף עַל־הָאָרֶץ, נָתַן אֹתָם אֱלֹהִים בַּיַּמִּים וְעַל־הָאָרֶץ.

3. To be written in English letters: — אָדָם, יְבָרֵךְ, שִׁרְצוּ, הַגְּדֹלִים, הַתַּנִּינִים, וּרְבוּ, חֲמִישִׁי.

4. To be written in Hebrew letters:—(1) kōl, (2) kŏl+, (3) yī'-rĕv, (4) šĕ'-rĕṣ, (5) hă(h)-hāy-yâ(h), (6) năf-šô, (7) šᵉnê.

---

[1] Learn only the general statement, not the sub-sections marked *a*, *b*, *c*, etc.

8. *TOPICS FOR STUDY.*

(1) The plural (masc.) of verbal forms. (2) The feminine ending ה. (3) The dual ending. (4) The intensive stem. (5) The peculiarities of laryngeals. (6) Compensatory strengthening of vowels.

LESSON XV.—GENESIS I. 24—26.

1. *NOTE-REVIEW.*

(1) לְהָאִיר (108); (2) וְלִמְשֹׁל (96); (3) וּבַלַּיְלָה (97); (4) כָּל־ 86; (5) אֶת־הָאוֹר (23); (6) וִיהִי (43).

2. *NOTES.*

123. תּוֹצֵא—tô-ṣē'—*Let-(her)-cause-to-go-forth:*

a. וֹ (ô) is contracted from וְ_; תּוֹצֵא is like תַּדְשֵׁא (65).
b. Hif'îl Impf. 3 fem. sg. from the root יָצָא *he-went-forth.*

124. לְמִינָהּ—lᵉmî-nâh—*to-kind-her:*

a. לְ *to,* מִין *kind,* הָ_ *her;* cf. לְמִינוּ, לְמִינֵהוּ.
b. The point in הּ is neither D. f. nor D. l.; it is inserted to show that הּ has a consonantal force and is *not* silent, for ה at the end of a word is always silent unless it has this point, called Măppîḳ, § **16.** 1.

125. בְּהֵמָה—bᵉhē-mā(h)—*cattle:*

a. ה, having no Măppîḳ, is silent; the noun is fem., § **106.** 2. c.

126. וָרֶמֶשׂ—wă-rĕ'-mĕś—*and-creeper:*

a. Wâw Conj. before the tone-syl. receives ָ, § **49.** 4; cf. וָבֹהוּ (11).
b. רֶמֶשׂ is a Seğolate noun from the same root as רֹמֶשֶׂת (110).
c. The secondary, helping vowel is not accented.

127. וְחַיְתוֹ־אֶרֶץ—wᵉḥăy-ṭô+'ĕ'-rĕṣ—*and-beast-of +earth:*

a. חַיָּה (absolute) = *life* or *beast;* חַיַּת is construct, § **107.** 2, 4.
b. וֹ is an old ending, now obsolete, § **105.** 1. Rem.

c. חַיְתוֹ is for חַיָּתוֹ, but ־ under י has become silent ־ְ, D. f. in י being dropped, and וֹ_ forms a diphthong; hence ת is spirant.

128. חַיַּת—ḥay-yăṯ—*beast-of:* with the same meaning as the preceding *archaic* form חַיְתוֹ; here D. f. remains.

129. הָאֲדָמָה—hā-'ăḏā-mā(h)—*the-ground:*
a. The article before a weak laryngeal has ־ָ, § 45. 3.
b. The vowel before a compound šᵉwâ always has Méṯĕǧ, § 18. 3.
c. א, a laryngeal, takes compound rather than simple šᵉwâ, § 9. 2.
d. ה, having no Măppīḳ (§ 16. 1), is silent; the word is feminine, § 106. 2. c.

130. נַעֲשֶׂה—nă'-ăśé(h)—*we-will-make,* or, *let-us-make:*
a. Of these four consonants only *three* can be radicals; the root is עָשָׂה.
b. The נ, from pronoun אֲנוּ *we,* indicates 1 p. pl., *we,* just as י indicates 3 m. sg., *he,* and ה, 3 fem. sg., *she.*
c. The laryngeal ע takes *compound* šᵉwâ, § 9. 2.
d. Méṯĕǧ, as always, before a compound šᵉwâ, § 18. 3.
e. The vowel ה_ is *ê,* cf. same vowel in וְתֵרָאֶה (59) and עָשֶׂה (71).
f. To the first syl. ᵃ is an overhanging sound helping in the transition from the laryngeal to the following sibilant.

131. אָדָם—'ā-ḏām—*man:* both vowels changeable.

132. בְּצַלְמֵנוּ—bᵉṣăl-mē'-nû—*in-image-our:*
a. Prep. בְּ; noun צֶלֶם; connecting-vowel ־ֵ; suffix נוּ.
b. The accent ־ֵ is disjunctive, separating the word from what follows.

133. כִּדְמוּתֵנוּ—kĭḏ-mû-ṯē'-nû—*according-to-likeness-our:*
a. כּ has D. l. because of preceding disjunctive accent, § 12. 3.
b. The šᵉwâ becomes silent, as in לִמְשֹׁל (96), after the inseparable preposition.
c. The noun is דְּמוּת, the suf. and connecting-vowel being ־ֵנוּ.

134. וְיִרְדּוּ—wᵉyīr-dû—*and-they-shall-have-dominion:*

a. וְ = *and;* י indicates Impf. וְ, plural; radicals, ר and ד.

135. בִּדְנַת—vĭđ-ğăθ—*in-fish-of:*

a. The stroke over בּ is Râfê, § **16.** 2.
b. Prep., before a consonant with šᵉwâ, takes ִ, § **47.** 2.
c. On ğ, see §§ **10.** 2, *d.* and **28.** 4.
d. Noun in abs., דָּגָה; in const., דְּנַת, § **106.** 2. *a.* (2).

136. הָרֶמֶשׂ הָרֹמֵשׂ—hâ-rĕ'-mĕš hâ-rô-mĕš—*the-creeper the-creeping:* the noun and the participle, both with article.

3. FORMS FOR SPECIAL STUDY.

וָבֹהוּ	פְּרוּ	חַיָּה	לֶאֱמֹר *for* לֵאמֹר
וָרֶמֶשׂ	רְבוּ	חַיַּת	תּוֹצֵא *for* תּוֹצֵא
לַמַּיִם	מִלְאוּ	חַיָּתוֹ	לְמִינָה *for* לְמִינָהּ

4. OBSERVATIONS.

75. Contractions are common; thus וָ (ăw) becomes ô; הָ (â-hâ) becomes הָ (âh). The result is always a naturally long vowel.

76. The original fem. ending, was ת, which is retained in the construct, but in the absolute the ת is lost and the preceding ַ becomes ָ.

77. The Imperative has only a second person.

78. Before a tone-syllable Wâw Conjunctive and the inseparable prepositions *may* take a tone-long ָ.

5. GRAMMAR-LESSON.

1. § **51.** 1. *a—c,*   Pronominal Suffixes,—separate forms.
2. § **51.** 2,   Pronominal Suffixes with אֵת.

Lesson 15.

6. WORD-LESSON.

(105) אֲדָמָה ground
(106) בְּהֵמָה cattle
(107) פָּרָה he-was-fruitful
(108) רָבָה he-multiplied
(109) רֶמֶשׂ creeper

7. EXERCISES.

1. To be translated into Hebrew:—(1) *God created)(-them;* (2) *He-said to-the-sea-monsters, Fill-ye)(+the-seas;* (3) *The-fowl multiplied upon+the-earth;* (4) *The-day the-fifth;* (5) *(The) beast-of the-earth was (fem.) upon+the-ground;* (6) *To-kind-his, and-to-kind-her, and-to-kinds-their;* (7) *His-day, my-day, her-day;* (8) *God made)(+the-creeper upon+the-ground;* (9) *The-cattle the-good (f.);* (10) *The good beast;* (11) *And-saw God all+that he-had-created, and-(it)-was +good;* (12) *The-waters (are) in-the-seas and-upon+the-earth.*

2. To be translated into English:—(1) וְהָעוֹף יְעוֹפֵף; (2) וַתּוֹצֵא, (3) הָאָרֶץ דֶּשֶׁא וְעֵשֶׂב וָעֵץ וַתּוֹצֵא הָאָרֶץ אֶת־הַבְּהֵמָה וְאֶת־ (4) הָרֶמֶשׂ וְאֵת חַיַּת הָאָרֶץ; וַיְבָרֶךְ אֶת־כָּל־רֶמֶשׂ הָאֲדָמָה.

3. To be written in English letters: — (1) מָלֵא, (2) רָבָה, (3) בָּרַךְ, (4) בְּהֵמָה, (5) לְמִינָהּ, (6) לֵאמֹר, (7) תּוֹצֵא.

4. To be written in Hebrew letters:—(1) kōl, (2) kŏl+, (3) bēn, (4) bēn, (5) bĕn+, (6) rĕ'-mĕś, (7) hay-ŧô, (8) băy-yăm-mîm, (9) 'ᵃšĕr, (10) rēx, (11) vå'-rēx.

8. TOPICS FOR STUDY.

(1) The Intensive-stem. (2) Omission of D. f. (3) Inf. const. of אָמַר with prep. לְ. (4) Difference between the words for *sea, seas* and *day, days.* (5) The ordinals 2d to 5th. (6) Pron. suf. of 3d per. fem. (7) Mappîḳ. (8) Relation between the fem. affixes ָה and ת. (9) Pronominal suffixes,—separate forms. (10) Pronominal suffixes with אֵת.

LESSON XVI.—GENESIS I. 27—29.

1. NOTE-REVIEW.

וַיִּבְרָא (1); וְעוֹף (104); (2) בְּהֵמָה (125); (3) וָרֶמֶשׂ (126); (4) וּרְבוּ (106); (5) אֹתָם (95); (6) וַיְבָרֶךְ (114); (7) פְּרוּ (116); (8) הָרֹמֶשֶׂת (110). (11) חַיָּה (103); (10) וּמִלְאוּ (118); (9) (117).

2. NOTES.

137. בְּצַלְמוֹ—b°ṣăl-mô—*in-image-his*:

a. בְּ *in*; צֶלֶם, see 132. *a*; וֹ *his*, as in לְמִינוֹ (72), זַרְעוֹ (73).

b. The accent over מ is disjunctive, cf. ־ֶ (132. *b*).

138. בְּצֶלֶם—b°ṣĕ'-lĕm—*in-image-of*:

a. בְּ has D. l. because of preceding disjunctive accent, § **12. 3**.

b. This is the usual form of the noun, but צַלְמ (137. *a*) is the *primary* form, to which suffixes are attached. Cf. זֶרַע, but זַרְעוֹ (73); and so אֶרֶץ, but אַרְצוֹ, עֶרֶב, but עַרְבוֹ, נֶפֶשׁ, but נַפְשׁוֹ, etc., § **109. 4.** *a*, *b*.

139. אֹתוֹ—'ō-θô—)(-*him*, § **51. 2**.

140. זָכָר וּנְקֵבָה—zā-xăr û-n°ḵē-vă(h)—*male and-female*:

a. זָכָר is a noun like אָדָם, with two tone-long vowels which were originally short, § **90. 1.** *a*.

b. Wăw Conj., before a consonant with š°wâ, is וּ § **49. 2**.

c. The ending ־ָה is the feminine affix, § **106. 2.** *c*.

141. לָהֶם—lā-hĕm—*to-them*, §§ **47. 5; 51. 3.** *b.* and N.

142. וְכִבְשֻׁהָ—w°xĭv-šû'-hā—*and-subdue-ye-her*:

a. וְ *and*; כִּבְשׁוּ for כִּבְשׁוּ [cf. מִלְאוּ (118)] *subdue-ye* הָ *her*; the root being כָּבַשׁ.

b. ֻ is usually ŭ, but here a defective writing for וּ (û), the sign of the plural; ŭ is sounded as *u* in *put*, but û as *oo* in *tool*.

143. וּרְדוּ—û-r°ḏû—*and-have-ye-dominion*:

Lesson 16.

a. On וֹ see § **49.** 2; the accent ֪ over ד is disjunctive.

144. בְּדְגַת—bĭd-ğăθ—*in-fish-of;* cf. בְּדְגַת (135):

a. בְּ has D. l., because of preceding disjunctive accent, § **12.** 2, 3.

145. הִנֵּה—hĭn-nē(h)—*behold!* an interjectional adverb.

146. נָתַתִּי—nă-θăt′-tî—*I-have-given:*

a. D. f. in תִּ is for נ assimilated, נָתַנְתִּי = נָתַתִּי; root נָתַן.
b. The ending תִּי =*I;* cf. אָמַרְתִּי *he-said,* אָמַרְתִּי *I-said;* יָדַע *he-knew,* יָדַעְתִּי *I-knew;* מָשַׁל *he-ruled,* מָשַׁלְתִּי *I-ruled.*

147. לָכֶם—lă-xĕm—*to-you* (m.):

a. Prep. has ָ, cf. לָמִים (45), לָהֶם (141).
b. כֶם is the pronominal suffix for the 2d. pl. masc.

148. זֹרֵעַ זַרְעַ—zô-rē(ă)ʻ ză′-răʻ—*seeding seed:*

a. זֹרֵעַ is the active participle of the Ḳăl stem—note the ô.
b. On ־ under ע read § **42.** 2. *d.*
c. זַרְעַ is for זֶרַע (69), on account of the accent (֔), § **38.** 2.

149. יִהְיֶה—yĭh-yê(h)—*he-(i. e., it)-shall-be:*

a. Observe the Mêθêğ with ־ and that the Šᵉwâ is silent, § **18.** 5.
b. Root, הָיָה; י indicates Impf. cf. shortened form יְהִי (19).

150. לְאָכְלָה—lᵉʼŏx-lă(h)—*for-food:*

a. The ־ under א, in an unaccented closed syl. is ŏ, not ā.
b. The root is plainly אָכַל *he-ate;* ה ָ indicates fem.

3. FORMS FOR SPECIAL STUDY.

בְּצֶלֶם	בְּצַלְמוֹ	צֶלֶם	צַלְמֵנוּ	אֹתָם	כִּבְשָׁהּ
וּרְדוּ בִדְגַת	צַלְמוֹ	אֹתוֹ	לָהֶם	כִּבְשָׁהּ		

4. OBSERVATIONS.

79. When a disjunctive accent stands between a spirant and the preceding vowel, the spirant does not *immediately* follow the vowel, and hence takes Dåğēš-lēnē.

80. Seḡolates before suffixes take what is called their primary form, i. e., the original form of the noun, which had but one vowel, that vowel standing under the first radical.

81. The suffix meaning *him* is וֹ, *them* הֶם or ם.

82. The personal *pre*-fix 1 p. pl. meaning *we* is the letter נ; the pronominal *suf*-fix *our* is נוּ; *her* is הָ.

83. Syllables ending with laryngeals and having a short vowel followed by a compound šᵉwâ are loosely closed; the šᵉwâ eases the transition between the laryngeal and the following consonant.

5. GRAMMAR-LESSON.

1. § **52.** 1. *a*, *b*, *c*, and 2,   The Demonstrative Pronouns.
2. § **53.** 1. *a*. *b*,   The Relative Particle.
3. § **54.** 1, 2. *a—d*,   The Interrogative Pronouns.

6. WORD-LESSON.

(110) אָדָם *man*   (113) זָכָר *male*   (116) צֶלֶם *image*
(111) דָּגָה *fish*   (114) כָּבַשׁ *he-subdued* (117) רָדָה *he-subdued*
(112) דְּמוּת *likeness* (115) נְקֵבָה *female*   (had-dominion)

7. PRINCIPLES OF SYNTAX.—THE ARTICLE.

הַמָּאוֹר הַגָּדֹל = *the-luminary the-great* = the great luminary.
הַמָּאוֹר הַקָּטֹן = *the-luminary the-small* = the small luminary.

Principle 1.—The adjective, when attributive, follows its noun, and, if the noun is definite, receives the article.

הַיּוֹם הַזֶּה = *the-day the-this*   = this day.
הָאָרֶץ הַזֹּאת = *the-earth the-this* (f.) = this earth.
הַשָּׁמַיִם הָאֵלֶּה = *the-heavens the-these* = these heavens.

Principle 2.—The demonstrative pronoun, when attributive, follows its noun, *both noun and demonstrative receiving the article.*

8. EXERCISES.

1. To be translated into Hebrew:[1]—(1) *The great place;* (2) *The great heavens;* (3) *The good seed;* (4) *The good luminaries;* (5) *This male and this female;* (6) *These luminaries which* (are) *in the heavens;* (7) *This good place;*[2] (8) *These great luminaries;* (9) *This spirit* (f.), (10) *Who created man in his image?* (11) *Who made this light?* (12) *To whom* (are) *these heavens and this earth?* (13) *What did God create in beginning?*

2. To be translated into English: — (1) הָאֲדָמָה הַזֹּאת; (2) מַה־ (3) הַשָּׁנִים הָאֵלֶּה; (4) הַפְּרִי הַטּוֹב הַזֶּה; (5) הַיּוֹם הַגָּדֹל; (6) נָתַן אֱלֹהִים לָהֶם; (7) מַה־קָּרָא לַיַּבָּשָׁה; (8) וְהַיָּרֵחַ; לְמִי הַשֶּׁמֶשׁ אֱלֹהִים אֲשֶׁר הָאָרֶץ לוֹ.

3. To be written in English letters:—(1) זֶה, (2) זֹאת, (3) אֵלֶּה, (4) אֲשֶׁר, (5) מִי, (6) מָה, (7) זָכָר, (8) נְקֵבָה.

4. To be written in Hebrew letters:—(1) dᵉmûθ, (2) ğăθ, (3) dă-ğă(h), (4) lă-hĕm, (5) 'ô-θô.

9. TOPICS FOR STUDY.

(1) Laryngeals with compound šᵉwâ. (2) The vowel הָ. (3) Accents ⸱, ⸳, ⸴. (4) Loosely closed syllables. (5) Medial šᵉwâ. (6) D. l. after a disjunctive accent. (7) Râfê. (8) Primary form of Segolates. (9) אֵת, אֶת־, אֵת. (10) The vowel ⸱. (11) Demonstratives. (12) Relative. (13) Interrogatives. (14) Rule for attributive adjectives. (15) Rule for attributive demonstrative.

---

[1] In this and in following exercises, words making in Hebrew *one* word will not be joined together by hyphens.

[2] The order will be: (1) noun, (2) adjective, (3) demonstrative, the article being written with each word.

LESSON XVII—GENESIS I. 30, 31.

1. NOTE-REVIEW.

(1) עֵ֫שֶׂב (67); (2) זֶ֫רַע (69); (3) אֲשֶׁר־בּוֹ (73. e); (4) חַיַּת (128); (5) נֶ֫פֶשׁ חַיָּה (102,103); (6) וַיְהִי־בֹ֫קֶר (22); (7) וַיַּרְא (36).

2. NOTES.

151. רֹמֵשׂ—rô-mēś—*creeper* (literally, *creeping*):

a. Naturally long ô, tone-long ē; Ḳăl act. part., cf. זֶ֫רַע (148).

b. This ô (in Ḳăl act. part.) is seldom written fully, as here.

152. אֶת־כָּל־יֶ֫רֶק—'ĕθ+kŏl+yĕ'-rĕk—)(+*every*+*greenness-of*:

a. On the short vowels ֶ and ֶ see § **17.** 2.

b. יֶ֫רֶק, like אֶ֫רֶץ and many others, is an *a*-class Segolate.

153. עָשָׂה—'ā-śā(h)—*he-made*:

a. Ḳăl Perf. 3 m. sg.,—the *root-form* from which came וַיַּ֫עַשׂ (46), and עֹשֶׂה (71).

154. מְאֹד—mᵉ'ôđ—*exceedingly:* an adverb.

155. הַשִּׁשִּׁי—hăš-šĭš--šî—*the-sixth*.

3. FORMS FOR SPECIAL STUDY.

נָתַ֫תִּי (*I*)	וּלְכָל־חַיַּת	אֶת־כָּל־עֵ֫שֶׂב
לָכֶם (*you*)	וּלְכָל־עוֹף	אֶת־כָּל־יֶ֫רֶק
בּוֹ (*him*)	וּלְכֹל רוֹמֵשׂ	אֶת־כָּל־אֲשֶׁר

4. OBSERVATIONS.

84. Note, in cases cited above, how ֶ and ֵ give place to ֶ and ֶ (ŏ), when, as when the word is joined by Măḳḳēf to the following word, the tone has passed away from them.

85. The conjunction וְ is written וּ before a consonant with Šᵉwâ.

86. תִּי = *I*; כֶם = *you*; וְ for הוּ = *him*.

Lesson 17.

5. GRAMMAR-LESSON.

1.	§ **2.** 4, 5, 7,	Pronunciation of צ, ט, ק.
2.	§ **3.** 2, 3,	Letters with double forms, and with similar forms.
3.	§ **4.** 1, 2.	Classification of Letters.
4.	§ **12.** 2, 3,	Spirants with šᵉwâ preceding, with disjunctive accent preceding.
5.	§ **15.** 1, 3,	Dâḡēš-fŏrtē compensative and conjunctive.
6.	§ **16.** 1, 2,	Măppîḳ and Râfē.
7.	§ **26.** 2, N. 1.	Sharpened syllables.

6. WORD-LESSON.

(118) אָכְלָה *food* (120) נָתַן *he-gave* (122) מְאֹד *exceedingly*

(119) הִנֵּה *behold* (121) יֶרֶק *greenness* (123) שִׁשִּׁי *sixth*

7. PRINCIPLES OF SYNTAX.—THE ARTICLE.

עַל־פְּנֵי הַמָּיִם = *upon+faces-of the-waters* = upon the face[s] of the waters.

רוּחַ אֱלֹהִים = *spirit-of God* = the spirit of God.

לְמִקְוֵה הַמַּיִם = *to-collection-of the-waters* = to the collection of waters.

כָּל־נֶפֶשׁ הַחַיָּה = *all+soul(s)-of the-life* = all the souls of life.

בִּדְגַת הַיָּם = *in-fish-of the-sea* = in the fish of the sea.

Principle 3.—The article cannot be prefixed to a noun in the construct state; if the article is needed, it is given to the noun following.

Principle 4.—If the second of the nouns in the construct relation is definite, because it is a proper noun, or because it has the article, the first noun is also to be regarded as *definite*.

8. EXERCISES.

1. To be translated into Hebrew:—(1) *I know that thou* (m.) (art) *good;* (2) *I gave to the cattle and to the beast(s) of the earth grass and herb(s) for food;* (3) *The tree yielded* (Heb., *made*) *good fruit;* (4) *God gave to the fowl of the heavens the seed of the earth for food;* (5) (*There*) *was fruit in all the earth;* (6) *All that God made was exceedingly good.*

2. To be translated into English:—(1) בְּיוֹם אֶחָד עָשָׂה אֱלֹהִים אֶת־הָאוֹר; (2) בְּיוֹם הַשֵּׁנִי עָשָׂה אֶת־הָרָקִיעַ; (3) בַּיּוֹם הַשְּׁלִישִׁי (4) הָיְתָה הַיַּבָּשָׁה וַתּוֹצֵא עֵשֶׂב וָעֵץ; בַּיּוֹם הָרְבִיעִי נָתַן בָּרָקִיעַ (5) הַשָּׁמַיִם אֶת־הַמְּאֹרֹת; בַּיּוֹם הַחֲמִישִׁי בָּרָא אֱלֹהִים אֶת־עוֹף (6) הַשָּׁמַיִם וְאֶת דְּגַת הַיָּם; בַּיּוֹם הַשִּׁשִּׁי עָשָׂה אֶת־הַבְּהֵמָה, וַיִּבְרָא אֶת־הָאָדָם בְּצֶלֶם אֱלֹהִים.

3. To be written in English letters:—(1) אָכְלָה, (2) יֶרֶק, (3) זֶרַע, (4) יוֹם, (5) בֹּקֶר, (6) כֵּן, (7) בֵּין.

4. To be written in Hebrew letters:—(1) hû, (2) xĕm, (3) hā, (4) hᵃmî, (5) xā, (6) nû, (7) 'ēllê.

LESSON XVIII.—REVIEW.

[*To the student:*—This lesson is a review of all that have preceded it. Nothing is so necessary, in the acquisition of a language, as constant and thorough review. One should carry forward with him at least nine-tenths of what he has learned. The first chapter of Genesis contains one hundred and two different words, and about four hundred and fifty different forms. The most common, and most important principles of the language have been considered. Many additional principles might have been brought forward in connection with this chapter, but it has been deemed wise to hold them in reserve. It is understood that in no case will the student proceed to take up Lesson XIX., until this Lesson with all which it includes has been learned. Let every word, every verse, every principle be mastered absolutely.]

1. WORD-REVIEW.

[In this list of words, the superior figures indicate the verse in which the word, or its derivative, is found. In the case of nouns, the singular absolute is given, in the case of verbs, the root. The student is expected to compare with each word as here given, the various forms of that word which occur in the chapter, e. g., with הָיָה, he will compare הָיְתָה *she was,* יְהִי *let-*(there)*-be,* וִיהִי *and-let-*(there)*-be,* וַיְהִי *and-*(there)*-was,* וְהָיוּ *and-they-shall-be,* יִהְיֶה *it-shall-be.*]

1. VERBS.

רָדָה²⁶	קָוָה⁹	נָתַן¹⁷	יָצָא¹²	בָּרַךְ²²	אוֹר*¹⁵
רָחַף²	קָרָא⁵	עוּף*²⁰	כָּבַשׁ²⁸	דָּשָׁא¹¹	אָמַר³
רָמַשׂ²¹	רָאָה⁴	עָשָׂה⁷	מָלֵא²²	הָיָה²	בָּדַל⁴
שָׁרַץ²¹	רָבָה²²	פָּרָה²²	מָשַׁל¹⁸	זָרַע¹¹	בָּרָא¹

* The Infinitive form, see § 55, 3.

Lesson 18.

2. NOUNS, PARTICLES, ETC.

⁶רָקִיעַ	²⁰עוֹף	⁵לְ	²³חֲמִישִׁי	²⁴בְּהֵמָה	²⁶אָדָם
¹³שְׁלִישִׁי	²עַל	⁵לַיְלָה	²חֹשֶׁךְ	⁴בֵּין	²⁵אֲדָמָה
¹שָׁמַיִם	¹¹עֵץ	³¹מְאֹד	⁴טוֹב	⁵בֹּקֶר	³אוֹר
¹⁴שָׁנָה	⁵עֶרֶב	¹⁴מָאוֹר	¹⁹יַבָּשָׁה	¹⁶גָּדוֹל	¹⁴אוֹת
⁸שֵׁנִי	¹¹עֵשֶׂב	¹⁴מוֹעֵד	⁵יוֹם	²⁶דָּגָה	⁵אֶחָד
¹⁶שְׁנַיִם	²פָּנִים	²מַיִם	¹⁰יָם	²⁶דְּמוּת	²⁹אָכְלָה
²⁰שֶׁרֶץ	¹¹פְּרִי	¹¹מִין	³⁰יֶרֶק	¹¹דֶּשֶׁא	⁹אֵל
³¹שִׁשִּׁי	²⁶צֶלֶם	¹⁶מֶמְשָׁלָה	²⁶כְּ	¹הֲ ·	¹אֱלֹהִים
²תֹּהוּ	¹⁶קָטֹן	⁷מִן	¹⁶כּוֹכָב	²⁹הִנֵּה	¹אֶרֶץ
²תְּהוֹם	¹רֵאשִׁית	¹⁰מִקְוֶה	⁴כִּי	¹וְ	⁷אֲשֶׁר
⁶תָּוֶךְ	¹⁹רְבִיעִי	⁹מָקוֹם	²¹כֹּל	²⁷זָכָר	¹אֵת
⁷תַּחַת	²רוּחַ	²⁰נֶפֶשׁ	⁷כֵּן	¹¹זֶרַע	¹בְּ
²¹תַּנִּין	²⁴רֶמֶשׂ	²⁷נְקֵבָה	²¹כָּנָף	²⁰חַיָּה	²בֹּהוּ

2. VERSE-REVIEW.

1. Pronounce the pointed text of each verse until it can be read aloud rapidly and without hesitation (see p. 181).

2. Write out on paper the unpointed text, one verse at a time, and then, without the aid of either pointed text or translation, insert the necessary points and vowel-signs. Compare the result with the pointed text, and note the mistakes; repeat the exercise till each verse can be pointed without mistake (see p. 203).

3. Write the Hebrew of the chapter, verse by verse, with only the English translation before the eye. Here also correct the result each time by the pointed text (see p. 192).

4. Write the Hebrew of the chapter, verse by verse, from the transliteration, noting with care, in the case of each word, the exact English equivalent for each sign or character in the Hebrew (p. 213).

3. *GRAMMAR-REVIEW.*

1. The alphabet, § **1.** 1-3.
2. Pron. of א, ע, ח, ק, § **2.** 1-4.
3. Pron. of ט, שׁ, צ, ו, § **2.** 5-8.
4. Extended, final, and similar letters, § **3.** 1-3.
5. Classification of letters, § **4.** 1, 2.
6. Pronunciation of ־ָ § **5.** 1.
7. Pron. of ־ֳ, § **5.** 6. *a.*
8. Vowel-letters, א, ו, י, § **6.** 1, 2, 3, and Notes 1-4.
9. Classificat'n of vowel-sounds, § **7.** 1-4.
10. Names of vowels, § **8.**
11. Simple šᵉwâ, § **9.** 1.
12. Compound šᵉwâ, § **9.** 2.
13. Initial šᵉwâ, § **10.** 1, 2.
14. Silent šᵉwâ, § **11.**
15. Dåğēš-lēnē, § **12.** 1, and N. 1.
16. D. l. after a šᵉwâ, § **12.** 2.
17. D. l. after a disj. acc., § **12.** 3.
18. Dåğēš-fŏrtē, § **13.** 1, 2, and Note 1.
19. Omission of D. f., § **14.** 1-3. Notes 1, 2.
20. D. f. compensative and conjunctive, § **15.** 1, 3.
21. Măppîḳ and Råfê, § **16.** 1, 2.
22. Use of Măḳḳēf, § **17.** 1-2.
23. Méθĕğ, § **18.** 1.
24. More common accents, § **24.** 1-3.
25. Kinds of syllables, § **26.** 1, 2. N. 1. 2.
26. Syllabification, § **27.** 1-3.
27. Quantity of vowels in syllables, § **28.** 1-4.
28. Naturally long vowels, § **30.** (opening words) and Notes 1, 2, under § **30.** 7.
29. Tone-long vowels, § **31.** (opening words) and Notes 1, 2, under **31.** 3.
30. Peculiarities of laryngeals § **42.** 1-3.
31. The article, § **45.** 1, 2, 3, & R. 3.
32. Inseparable prepositions, §**47.** 1-5.
33. Wåw conjunctive, § **49.** 1-4.
34. Personal pron., § **50.** 1-3.
35. Pronominal suffixes, § **51.** 1. *a-c,* 2.
36. Demonstrative pronoun, § **52.** 1. *a-c,* 2.
37. Relative particle, § **53.** 1. *a, b.*
38. Interrogative pronouns, § **54.** 1, 2. *a-d.*
39. Roots, § **55.** 1, 2.
40. Inflection, § **57.** 1-3.
41. Tenses and Moods, § **57.** 3. Notes 1, 2.
42. Simple verb-stem, § **58.** 1, 2. *a-c.*
43. Gender of nouns, § **106.** 1, 2, *a, b.*
44. Number of nouns, § **106.** 3-5.
45. States of nouns, § **107.** 1, 2.

4. *EXERCISE.**

To be translated into Hebrew:—

1. *The name of the light is day, and the name of the darkness is night.*
2. *Waters, to waters, the waters, to the waters.*
3. *The earth will be seen beneath the heavens.*
4. *The day, in which is light.*
5. *The fruit, in which is seed.*
6. *The fruit is in the seed, and the seed is in the earth.*
7. *The sun will be seen in the heavens.*
8. *To cause-a-division between the day and the night.*
9. *And in the great day. The great stars.*
10. *The great luminary is the sun; the small luminary is the moon.*
11. *The sun and the moon are in the expanse of the heavens.*
12. *Thou art in the heavens, and I am upon the earth.*
13. *And God saw all which he had created, and it was good.*
14. *God created the earth, and he created the heavens.*
15. *The waters are in the seas and upon the earth.*
16. *His day, her day, my day.*
17. *The beast of the earth was upon the ground.*
18. *This good place.*
19. *These great luminaries.*
20. *God gave to the fowl of the heavens the seed of the earth for food.*

LESSON XIX.—GENESIS II. 1-3.

1. *NOTE-REVIEW.*

(1) אֹתָם (4); (153) עָשָׂה (3); (8) וְהָאָרֶץ (2); (5) הַשָּׁמַיִם (1);
(48) אֲשֶׁר (7); (73) בּוֹ (6); (24) כִּי (5); (95).

---

* These sentences are selected from preceding exercises.

2. NOTES.

156. וַיְכֻלּוּ—*and-(they)-were-finished;* cf.[1] וַיְבָרֶךְ (114), יָקוּ (55):

a. D. f. omitted from וּ, § 14. 2; וּ indicates the plural number.

b. The ֻ, in verbal forms, always marks the *passive;* under the first radical it indicates the Pŭ'äl (intensive passive) stem, § 58. 4. *a. c.*

c. Root is כָּלָה, meaning in Pī'ēl, *finish,* in Pŭ'äl, *be-finished.*

157. וְכָל־צְבָאָם—*and-all+host-their;* cf. אֶת־גְּדֹלִים (89. *d*):

a. וְ acc. to § 49. 1; ָ is ŏ, because in a closed syllable which has lost its tone, § 29. 5.

b. צָבָא host, *but* צְבָאָם *host-their;* the original ַ which became ָ in an open syl. before the tone, is reduced to ְ when the tone moves farther away, § 36. 2. *b.*

c. ָם is the pron. suf. of the 3 masc. plur., § 51. 1.

158. וַיְבָרֶךְ—*and-(he)-finished;* cf. וַיְכֻלּוּ, וַיְכַל:

a. Shorter form for וַיְכַלֶּה, the Pī'ēl of כָּלָה (156. *c*).

b. Two D. f.'s omitted: one from י because without a full vowel, one from ל because final, § 14. 1, 2.

159. בַּיּוֹם הַשְּׁבִיעִי—*in-the-day the-seventh:*

a. The accent ֔ over הַשְּׁבִיעִי marks the end of a *secondary section.* It is called Zâḳēf ḳâṭōn, i. e., little Zâḳēf, § 24. 4.

160. מְלַאכְתּוֹ—*work-his;* cf. רֵאשִׁית, זַרְעוֹ:

a. Abs. sg. מְלָאכָה; א has lost its consonantal force.

b. The original ַ of ל is retained unchanged because it is in a closed unaccented syl., § 29. 1. *a.;* in the abs. form ַ is rounded to ָ, being in an open, pretone syl.

c. The abs. has ָה, but the form with suf. has ְתּ, § 106. 2. *a.*

161. וַיִּשְׁבֹּת—*and-he-rested;* cf. וַיִּקְרָא, וַיִּבְרָא:

---

[1] Every old word, suggested for comparison with the new word under consideration, has at least *one* important point in common with that new word.

a. This is the regular form of the Ķăl Impf., the ֶ in יִקְרָא and יִבְרָא being due to the presence of the weak letter א.
b. The ֹ in this word is ō (tone-long), not ô.
c. The root is plainly שָׁבַת *he-rested*, see below, 163.

162. וַיְקַדֵּשׁ—*and-he-sanctified;* cf. וַיְבָרֶךְ, וַיְכַל:
a. D. f. omitted from י, as in וַיְהִי, וַיְבָרֶךְ, וַיְכֻלּוּ, וַיְכַל.
b. The root is קָדַשׁ, meaning, as a verbal form, *he-was-holy*.
c. The first radical has ַ, the second radical, D. f.; these indicate a Pï'ēl form; read §§ 58. 3.; 65. 2. *a. b.*
d. Compare each vowel-sound in יְקַדֵּשׁ and יְבָרֶךְ, and note that the latter has ְ instead of ַ, because ר refuses D. f., and ֶ instead of ֵ, because the accent is on the penult.
e. The root means *be-holy;* the Pï'ēl, here intensive or causative, means *make-holy, sanctify,* § 58. 3. *c.*

163. שָׁבַת—*he-rested;* cf. בָּרָא, קָרָא, עָשָׂה:
a. Ķăl Perf. 3 masc. sing. of the strong verb שָׁבַת.

164. לַעֲשׂוֹת—*to-make, i. e., in-making*.
a. The prep. לְ with ַ, because of following laryngeal, § 47. 3.
b. עֲשׂוֹת is a Ķăl Inf. const. of עָשָׂה.
c. Further information concerning this form will be given later.

3. FORMS FOR SPECIAL STUDY.

יְבָרֶךְ *but* יָבֵרֵךְ	מְאֹרֹת *but* מָאוֹר	יִשְׁבֹּת
מְלַאכְתּוֹ *but* מְלָאכָה	גְּדֹלִים *but* גָּדֹל	יָקֻוּוּ
כָּל־ *but* כֹּל	אֲדָמָה *but* אָדָם	יְקַדֵּשׁ
אֶת־ *but* אֵת	צְבָאָם *but* צָבָא	יְכֻלּוּ
זַרְעוֹ *but* זֶרַע	כְּנָפַיִם *but* כָּנָף	יַבְדֵּל

4. OBSERVATIONS

87. Short vowels are retained in *closed* unaccented syllables.

88. In *open* unaccented syllables, short vowels give away to Šᵉwâ. This change is called *reduction*.

89. The Ḳăl Impf. has no special characteristic; unless one of the radicals is a weak letter, it generally has ō for the vowel of its second radical.

90. The Nĭf'ăl Impf. has D. f. in and ִ under the first radical, while the other *passive* stem (Pŭ'ăl) has ֻ under the first radical and D. f. in the second.

91. The Pĭ'ēl Impf. has (besides D. f. in the second radical) ְ under the first radical; the Hĭf'îl Impf. has ַ under the preformative.

5. GRAMMAR-LESSON.

1. § **58.** 1.   Simple verb-stem, Ḳăl.
2. § **60.** (& p. 195)   Tabular view, Inflection of the Ḳăl Perfect.
3. § **60.** 1—3.   Remarks on inflection.
4. § **36.** 2. *a*.   Reduction of an ultimate vowel in verbal inflection.
5. § **36.** 2. N. 2.   [This covers the reduction to ְ in the forms וְקָטַלְתֶּן ,קְטַלְתֶּם.

6. WORD-LESSON.

1. Learn from the Hebrew word-lists under List I., verbs occurring 500 to 5,000 times, those words numbered 1-10.
2. Make a list of the new words in Gen. II. 1-3.

7. EXERCISES.

1. To be translated into Hebrew:—(1) *I said, we said, she said, thou* (f.) *didst say, they said, ye* (m.) *said;* (2) *She ruled, they*

ruled, ye (f.) *ruled, I ruled, we ruled, thou* (m.) *ruledst;* (3) *They gave, we gave, I gave, she gave, thou* (m.) *gavest, he gave;* (4) *I knew, she knew, we knew, they knew, thou* (m.) *didst know.*

2. To be translated into Hebrew:—(1) *The heavens will be finished;* (2) *The waters will be collected;* (3) *God will sanctify the seventh day;* (4) *God rested in the seventh day;* (5) *He created the heavens and all their host;* (6) *He made the great luminaries;* (7) *He will rest in this day;* (8) *We rested, she rested, ye* (m.) *rested, they rested.*

3. To be translated into English:—(1) מִי שָׁבַת מִכָּל־מְלַאכְתּוֹ; (2) זֶה (4) שָׁבַתִּי בַּיּוֹם הַשְּׁבִיעִי; (3) מִי יִשְׁבֹּת בַּיּוֹם הַשְּׁבִיעִי הַיּוֹם הַשְּׁבִיעִי אֲשֶׁר־בּוֹ שָׁבַת אֱלֹהִים.

4. To be written in English letters:—*The first three verses of Genesis II., from the pointed text.*

5. To be written with points and vowel-signs:—*The first three verses of Genesis II., from the unpointed text.*

8. TOPICS FOR STUDY.

(1) Omission of D. f. (2) Characteristics of Pŭ‘ăl stem. (3) Reduction of a penultimate vowel, of an ultimate vowel. (4) The Ḳăl Imperfect. (5) The Pī‘ēl Imperfect. (6) Retention of short vowels. (7) Difference between the vowels of שָׁבַת and בָּרָא, וַיְקַדֵּשׁ and וַיְבָרֶךְ. (8) Original form of the simple verb-stem. (9) Form in use. (10) Its inflection. (11) Forms of the Ḳăl Perf. containing Sᵉwâ. (12) The various personal termination and their origin.

LESSON XX.—GENESIS II., 4-6.

1. NOTE-REVIEW.

(1) אֶרֶץ (62); (2) יִהְיֶה (149); (3) הָאֲדָמָה (129); (4) פְּנֵי (13).

2. NOTES.

165. אֵלֶּה—*these;* cf. זֶה (m.), זֹאת (f.).

166. מוֹעֲדִים, תּוֹלְדוֹת—*generations-of;* cf. מְאֹרֹת:

a. Plur. fem., never found in sing.; two syllables.

b. Absence of D. l. in ד because preceding šᵉwâ is vocal, § **12. 2.**

c. Three spirants; both o's are ô, not ō.

167. צְבָאָם, יָקוּ: בְּהִבָּרְאָם—*in-being-created-their;* cf.

a. בְּ pointed with šᵉwâ; ם ָ same as in צְבָאָם (157).

b. It is קְטָל, but קְטָלָה; so הִבָּרֵא, but הִבָּרְאָם, i. e., the ultimate vowel is reduced when ם ָ is added, § **36. 2. a.**

c. הִבָּרֵא has D. f. *in* and ִ *under* the *first* radical, the characteristics of the Nif'ăl or passive stem, § **72.** R. 2.

d. This is an Inf. const. governed by the prep. בְּ.

e. The small ה written above the line is a traditional writing handed down by the Massoretic Editors (§ **19.**).

168. עֲשׂוֹת—*to-make,* or *making-of:* see 164.

169. יְהֹוָה—Written *Jehovah* in the Revised English Bible. But this pronunciation is due to an error dating as far back as the 14th. century A. D. The present vocalization of the Hebrew name is due to the later Jewish reverence for the ancient name of their God, which made them fear to pronounce it. The original pronunciation seems to have been יַהְוֶה. For this, the later Jews regularly substituted אֲדֹנָי, *Lord.* In order to remind themselves of this change, they regularly point יְהוָה not with its own vowels, but with those of אֲדֹנָי, (*Lord*) as here, thus indicating that אֲדֹנָי should be pronounced, and not יְהֹוָה.

170. שִׂיחַ—*shrub-of:* one syllable, § **27.** 1; cf. רוּחַ.

171. הַשָּׂדֶה—*the-field;* cf. יִהְיֶה, עָשָׂה:

a. The accent ֑ over הַשָּׂדֶה, like ֑ over הַשְּׁבִיעִי (159. *a*), marks a secondary section. It is called Rᵉvî(ă)', § **24.** 5. *b*.

172. טֶרֶם—tĕ′-rĕm—*not-yet*: an adverb.

173. יִצְמָח—(he) *will-sprout-forth*; cf. וַיִּשְׁבֹּת׃

a. Ḳăl Impf. 3 m. sg. of צָמַח *he-sprouted-forth*.

b. The ָ under מ is pausal for ַ, § **38.** 2.

c. This verb has ַ (in pause ָ) rather than ִ, as seen in וַיִּשְׁבֹּת, because of the laryngeal ח, § **42.** 2. *b*.

174. לֹא—lô'—*not*; cf. זֹאת, יֹאמֶר.

175. הִמְטִיר—(he) *had-caused-to-rain*; cf. הַבְדִּיל, מַבְדִּיל׃

a. Here are three radicals, making מָטַר *he-rained*.

b. The prefix הִ (originally הַ) indicates the Hif'îl Perfect, § **58.** 5. *a. b;* and § **59.** 3.

c. Cf. the vowel of the preformative in the forms תַּדְשֵׁא, יַבְדֵּל, מַזְרִיעַ, מַבְדִּיל, with that in הִמְטִיר, הַבְדִּיל, § **72.** R. 6.

176. אֵין—a noun meaning *nothing*, but always used as a predicate, *there is not, there was not;* hence the phrase means *and man was not*, or *and there was no man*.

177. לַעֲבֹד—*to-serve*; cf. לִמְשֹׁל, לַעֲשׂוֹת׃

a. The עֲבֹד is Ḳăl Inf. const. of עָבַד *he-served;* but ע has ֲ, where מ of מְשֹׁל, a similar form, has ְ, because it is a laryngeal, § **42.** 3. *a*.

b. The prep. ל takes ַ, as in לַעֲשׂוֹת, according to § **47.** 3.

178. וְאֵד—wᵉ'-êd—*and-(a)-mist*.

179. יַעֲלֶה—(he) *will-go-up*, or (he) *used-to-go-up;* cf. יִהְיֶה׃

a. י is the pref. of the Impf.; the root is עָלָה *he-went-up*.

b. The vowel under י in יִשְׁבֹּת and יִצְמָח is ִ, but in this word it is ַ, because of the following ע, § **42.** 2. *a*.

c. Just as an original ַ is retained under the preformative of all Hif'îl forms except the Perfect, where it has been *attenuated* (§ **36.** 3) to ִ (cf. הִמְטִיר), so an original ַ has been retained under the performative of the Ḳâl Impf. *before laryngeals*, where otherwise it is attenuated to ִ .

d. In יִשְׁבֹּת the first rad. has ְ , but in יַעֲלֶה it has ֲ , § **42**. 3. *b*.

e. The Imperfect here expresses customary action in past time.

180. מִן—*from*: so written only before the article; cf. מִ , מֵ , § **48**. 1, 2.

181. וְהִשְׁקָה—*and-used-to-cause-to-drink*; cf. הִמְטִיר :

a. Another Hif'îl Perf., as indicated by הִ ; root שָׁקָה .

b. The וְ here is Wâw Conv., and gives to the verb the force possessed by יַעֲלֶה, which preceded it, § **70**. 1. *b*, 2. *b*.

3. FORMS FOR SPECIAL STUDY.

רוּחַ	יִקְרָא	הִמְטִיר	עֲשׂוֹת
רָקִיעַ	יִשְׁבֹּת	הִשְׁקָה	לַעֲבֹד
מַזְרִיעַ	יִצְמַח	יַבְדֵּל	יַעֲלֶה
שִׂיחַ	יַעֲלֶה	תַּדְשֵׁא	יִצְמַח

4. OBSERVATIONS.

92. A laryngeal will take (1) *under* it a compound instead of a simple Sʰwâ; and (2) *before* it the vowel ֲ rather than ְ or ִ .

93. The Hif'îl stem has, under the preformative, the vowel ַ except in the Perfect, where it has been *attenuated* to ִ (cf. Latin *facilis*, but *difficilis*).

94. The vowel of the preformative in the Ḳâl Imperfect was originally ַ , but this has been retained only before laryngeals, being elsewhere attenuated to ִ .

95. The Ḳâl Imperfect may have for its stem-vowel either ō, or ă. In the cases cited above, note how ַ before א and in pause has been rounded to ָ , while before ה it has become ĕ.

96. Păθăḥ-furtive creeps in under the final laryngeals ע, ה, ח, when they are preceded by any long vowel except ָ.

5. GRAMMAR-LESSON.

1. § 58. 3. a, b, c.   Origin and use of the Pī'ēl stem.
2. § 58. 4, a, b, c.   Origin and use of the Pŭ'ăl stem.
3. § 58. 7 a, b, c.   Origin and use of the Hīθpă'ēl st.
4. § 62. 1. b, 2. a, b, (& pp. Inflection of these stems in Perf.
   194, 195)
5. § 36. 3. a, b.   Attenuation of ַ to ִ

6. WORD-LESSON.

1. In the Word-Lists, under List I., the verbs numbered 11—20.
2. Make a list of the new words in Genesis II. 4—6.

7. EXERCISES.

1. To be translated into Hebrew:—(1) *He sanctified* (קְדֵשׁ, Pī), *we sanctified, they sanctified, I sanctified, ye* (m.) *sanctified;* (2) *She spoke* (דבר *in* Pī'ēl), *I spoke, we spoke, they spoke, thou* (f.) *didst speak, ye* (m.) *did speak;* (3) *He was sanctified* (Pŭ'ăl), *I was sanctified, we were sanctified, they were sanctified;* (4) *She purified herself* (קְדֵשׁ *in* Hīθpă'ēl), *we purified ourselves, they purified themselves, I purified myself.*

2. To be translated into Hebrew:—(1) *Yahweh God sanctified this day and this place;* (2) *This* (is) *the day which God sanctified;* (3) *These* (are) *the heavens and the earth which God created;* (4) *The shrub and the herb will be in the field;* (5) *There was no man upon the earth in those days;* (6) *God did not cause it to rain upon the dry* (land); (7) *The herb will sprout forth upon the field;* (8) *These generations;* (9) *This earth;* (10) *This day.*

3. To be translated into English:—(1) קִדַּשְׁתִּי אֶת־הַיּוֹם; (2)

(3) הִמְשִׁיל אֱלֹהִים אֶת־הָאָדָם; נָתַתִּ לוֹ אֶת הָאָרֶץ הַזֹּאת (4) בָּרָא אֶת־הָאָדָם; בְּדִגְנַת הַיָּם וּבְעוֹף הַשָּׁמַיִם וּבְכָל־הָאָרֶץ לַעֲבֹד אֶת־הָאֲדָמָה.

4. To be written in English letters:—*Verses 4—6 of chapter II. from the pointed text.*

5. To be written with points and vowel-signs:—*Verses 4—6 of chapter II. from the unpointed text.*

8. TOPICS FOR STUDY.

(1) Forms of the Dem. pron. (2) Use of D. l. (3) Reduction of an ultimate vowel in verbal forms. (4) Characteristics of the Nif'ăl. (5) The word יהוה. (6) Pâθâḥ-*furtive*. (7) The difference in pointing between יִשְׁבֹּת and יִצְמַח, between יִשְׁבַּת and יִקְרָא, between יִשְׁבַּת and יַעֲלֶה. (8) Attenuation of ־ַ to ־ִ. (9) Hif'îl Perfect. (10) אֵין, לֹא and טֶרֶם. (11) Difference between עָבַד and מָשַׁל. (12) Force of the tense in יַעֲלֶה. (13) Peculiarities of laryngeals. (14) The origin, use, and inflection of the three intensive stems. (15) The form קָטְלָה. (16) The form קְטַלְתֶּם. (17) Rounding of vowels. (18) The Personal pronoun.

LESSON XXI.—GENESIS II. 7-9.

1. *NOTE-REVIEW.*

(1) יְהוָֹה (169); (2) מִן (180); (3) נֶפֶשׁ חַיָּה (102,103); (4) כָּל־ (108); (5) בְּתוֹךְ (41); (6) עֵץ (70); (7) טוֹב (24).

2. *NOTES.*

182. וַיִּיצֶר—*and-*(he)-*formed;* cf. וַיֹּאמֶר:

a. The first י is the preformative, the second, the radical.

Lesson 21.

b. Ḳāl Impf. 3 m. sg. of the root יָצַר *he-formed.*

c. The ִ under צ is ĕ; consideration of it may be postponed.

183. עָפָר—*dust:* with the article it would be הֶעָפָר, § **45. 4.**

184. וַיִּפַּח—*and-he-breathed;* cf. מִתַּחַת, יִצְמָח:

a. For יִנְפַּח, the נ being assimilated; root נָפַח.

b. On ִ instead of ִ before ח see § **42. 2. *b.***

185. בְּאַפָּיו—*bᵉ'ăp-pâw—in nostrils-his:*

a. אַף *nose;* אַפִּים *nostrils;* אַפָּיו *his-nostrils.*

b. Learn that יו_ָ, pronounced âw (the ו having no force), is the form of 3 masc. sg. suf. when attached to plural or dual nouns.

c. The D. f. in פ stands for נ, the original form being אַנְפּ.

186. נִשְׁמַת—nĭš-măθ—*breath-of;* cf. דְּנַת, חַיַּת:

a. Abs. sg. is נְשָׁמָה, but in const. ה_ַ goes back to the orig. ת_ַ; the other changes will come up later.

187. חַיִּים—*lives;* cf. חַיָּה *life, beast.*

188. וַיִּטַּע—*and-(he)-planted;* cf. יִפַּח:

a. So far as concerns vowels and form, the same as וַיִּפַּח (184); from the root נָטַע *he-planted.*

189. גַּן—*garden;* cf. below in v. 9 הַגָּן *in pause.*

190. מִקֶּדֶם—mĭḳ-ḳĕ'-đĕm—*from-east;* cf. עֶרֶב:

a. The prep. מִן with נ assimilated, § **48. 1.**

b. An *a*-class Seğolate, primary form קַדְם, § **89. 1. *a.***

191. וַיָּשֶׂם—*and-he-put:* learn (1) this form, (2) its meaning, (3) its root שִׂים *to-put.*

192. שָׁם—*there:* an adverb.

193. יָצַר—*he-formed,* or *he-had-formed;* cf. וַיִּיצֶר:

a. Pausal for יָצַר, the root form, see 182. *b.*

194. וַיַּצְמַח—*and-(he)-caused-to-sprout-forth;* cf. וַיַּבְדֵּל:

a. Cf. with Ḳāl יִצְמָח (173), which has ִ under י instead of ַ.

b. The ֲ under the preformative is the indication of the Hif'îl (except in Perf.).

c. יַבְדֵּל has ֵ under 2d rad., but יִצְמַח has ַ; why? § **42.** 2. *b.*

d. Hîf. Impf. 3 m. sg. of the root צָמַח *he-sprouted*.

195. נֶחְמָד—nĕḥ-mād—*desirable*, or *desired:*

a. The Šᵉwâ, though under a laryngeal, is silent.

b. The root is חָמַד, נ indicating a Nif'ăl.

c. On the vowel ֶ see § **42.** 2. c; on ָ, § **68.** 2.

196. לְמַרְאֶה ... לְמַאֲכָל—*for-sight ... for-food:*

a. Two nouns formed by the prefix מ; cf. מִקְוֶה, מָקוֹם; § **96.**

b. The roots are רָאָה *he-saw*, אָכַל *he-ate*.

197. הַחַיִּים—hă(ḥ)-ḥăy-yîm—*the-lives;* cf. הַחֹשֶׁךְ:

a. The D. f. of the article is implied in ה, §§ **42.** 1. *b;* **45.** 2.

b. Mé͟θĕğ on the second syllable before the tone.

198. הַדַּעַת—*the-knowing* — a verbal noun from יָדַע *he-knew*, with the article pointed as usual; it has here a direct object.

b. A one-vowel noun originally; the final ă is a helping vowel.

199. וָרָע—wā-rā'—*and-evil;* cf. וָבֹהוּ:

a. Wāw Conj., before a tone-syllable, takes sometimes ָ, § **49.** 4.

b. רָע, instead of רַע, because in pause, § **38.** 2.

---

3. FORMS FOR SPECIAL STUDY.

בֹּקֶר	עֵשֶׂב	דֶּשֶׁא	אֶרֶץ	נֶפֶשׁ
חֹשֶׁךְ	עֵדֶן	שֶׁרֶץ	עֶרֶב	קֶדֶם

---

4. OBSERVATIONS.

97. Nouns with two vowels, and having an accented ֶ as their first vowel, are *always* a-class Segolates, the ĕ being a deflection of an original ă.

98. Nouns with two vowels, and having an accented ֵ as their

first vowel, are *always* i-class Seğolates, the ē coming from an original ĭ.

99. Nouns with two vowels and having an accented ָ for their first vowel, are *always* u-class Seğolates, the ō coming from an original ŭ.

100. The final unaccented ֶ in all these nouns is merely an inserted helping-vowel (§ 37. 2).

5. GRAMMAR-LESSON.

1. § 58. 5a. b. c,   Origin and use of the Hifʿîl stem.
2. § 62. 2. c,   Inflection of this stem (cf. p. 184.)
3. § 89. 1,   Origin of Seğolates.
4. § 36. 2a. b. N. 1, Changes of ă, ĭ, ŭ, due to the tone.

6. WORD-LESSON.

1. In the Word-Lists, Lists I. and II., the verbs numbered 21—30.
2. Make out a list of the new words in Genesis II. 7—9.

7. EXERCISES.

1. To be translated into Hebrew:—(1) *He caused to rain, they caused to rain, I caused to rain, we caused to rain;* (2) *He caused to kill, she caused to kill, they caused to kill, ye* (m.) *caused to kill;* (3) *He divided* (Hif. of בָּדַל), *she divided, they divided, I divided, we divided.*

2. To be translated into Hebrew:—(1) *And God breathed into his nostrils;* (2) *In the garden which God planted in Eden was fruit;* (3) *This fruit was good for food;* (4) *The good fruit;* (5) *The evil fruit;* (6) *The good tree and the evil tree;* (7) *And he caused to sprout forth grass and herb*(s) *and tree*(s).

3. To be translated into English:— (1) הִבְדִּיל אֱלֹהִים בֵּין הָעֵץ אֲשֶׁר בְּתוֹךְ הַגָּן עֵץ הַחַיִּים; (2) הַטּוֹב וּבֵין הָרָע

(3) נָתַן אֱלֹהִים אֶת־הָאָדָם בַּגַּן אֲשֶׁר (4) ;נָטַע אֶת־הָעֵץ בַּגָּן הִבְדִּילָה, (5) ;נָטַע וַאֲשֶׁר־בּוֹ הַצְּמִיחַ כָּל־עֵץ נֶחְמָד לְמַרְאֶה הִבְדַּלְתֶּם, הִבְדַּלְנוּ, הִבְדִּילוּ.

4. To be written in English letters:—*Verses 7—9 of chapter II., from the pointed text.*

5. To be written with points and vowel-signs:—*Verses 7—9 of chapter II., from the unpointed text.*

8. TOPICS FOR STUDY.

(1) Assimilation. (2) The vowels ִ and ֵ in the stem of the Ḳăl Imperfect. (3) Pronunciation and meaning of the affix יןָ. (4) The root *to-put*, the form *and-he-put*. (5) Difference between יַבְדֵּל and יַצְמִחַ. (6) מ as a prefix in the formation of nouns. (7) A-class Segŏlates. (8) I-class Segŏlates. (9) U-class Segŏlates. (10) Origin, use and inflection of the Hĭf'îl stem. (11) Effect of tone upon vowels. (12) The helping-vowel ĕ.

LESSON XXII.—GENESIS II. 10-12.

1. *NOTE-REVIEW.*

(1) מְלַאכְתּוֹ (160); (2) וַיִּשְׁבֹּת (161); (3) תּוֹלְדוֹת (166); (4) יַצְמִחַ (173); (5) יַעֲלֶה (179).

2. *NOTES.*

200. וְנָהָר—*and-*(a)*-river;* cf. כָּנָף, אָדָם:

a. This noun belongs to a large class, formed from the root by means of two primary short vowels, both of which, the one *before,* and the other *under,* the tone, have undergone change, § **90.** 1. *a.*

201. יֹצֵא—yô-ṣē'—*going-forth,=goes-forth;* cf. רֹמֵשׂ:

a. The active participle of Ḳăl, used, as often, for a present tense.

b. The first vowel is ô, not ō; the root, יָצָא *he-went-forth.*

202. מֵעֵדֶן—*from-Eden;* cf. מֵעַל, § **48.** 2; עֵשֶׂב, § **89.** 1. *b:*

a. Note the Zâḳêf-ḳâṭōn (⸣); it marks the end of a secondary section and also the accent of מֵעֵדֶן, cf.. 159. *a.*

203. לְהַשְׁקוֹת—*to-cause-to-drink,* i. e., *to-water;* cf. עֲשׂוֹת, הַבְדִּיל:

a. Like הַבְדִּיל, this word has the pref. הַ; it is Hîf. Inf. const.
b. Like עֲשׂוֹת, it ends in וֹת.
c. Cf. also the Hîf. Perf. 3 m. sg. הִשְׁקָה (181).

204. וּמִשָּׁם—*and-from-there;* cf. מִתַּחַת, וּבֵין.

205. יִפָּרֵד—*it-will-be-divided,* or *it-divides-itself:*

a. D. f. in and â under פ indicate at once the Nîf'ăl.
b. The root is פָּרַד; Nîf. Perf., נִפְרַד; cf. יָקוּו (55).

206. לְאַרְבָּעָה—*for-four;* cf. רְבִיעִי, *fourth.*

207. רָאשִׁים—râ(')šîm—*heads:* an irregular plural from רֹאשׁ.

a. א here is silent, as always after a vowel.

208. שֵׁם—šēm—*name:* same as the proper name *Shem.*

209. הַסֹּבֵב—*the-*(one)*-surrounding;* cf. רֹמֵשׂ, יֹצֵא:

a. On ⸣ see 171. *a.*

210. הַחֲוִילָה—hă(ḥ)-ʰwî-lâ(h)—*the-Havilah:*

a. The *article* here belongs really to אֶרֶץ, the phrase = *all the land of Havilah,* not *all land of the Havilah,* see Principle 3 (p. 69).

211. אֲשֶׁר־שָׁם—*which+there,=* where; cf. אֲשֶׁר־בּוֹ = *in which.*

212. זָהָב—*gold:* A noun like אָדָם, נָהָר, כָּנָף, § **90.** 1. *a.*

213. וּזֲהַב—û-zʰhăv—*and-gold-of:*

a. The Wâw, before a consonant with šᵉwâ is וּ, § **49.** 2.
b. Comp'd šᵉwâ, under וּ, preceding a laryngeal, § **32.** 3. *c.*
c. Méθěğ with וּ before compound šᵉwâ, § **18.** 3.
d. זֲהַב differs from זָהָב in that the form is treated as if the

accent had passed from it to the following word. This is virtually true, for the noun is in the construct state, § **107.** (opening words); § **109.** 3. *a*, *b*. The ground-form of the noun is זָהָב. In the absolute, both vowels are rounded to â, because of tonal influence, one being under the tone and the other in an open syl. before the tone. In the construct, the final ă remains unchanged, being in a closed, unaccented syl. but the preceding ă is reduced to šᵉwâ, being in an open unaccented syl.

e. Cf. נָהָר abs., *but* נְהַר const.; כָּנָף abs., *but* כְּנַף const.

214. הַהוּא—hă(h)-hî' (*not* hă(h)-hîw')—the-that; cf. הַחֹשֶׁךְ:

a. הוּא is archaic for הִיא, § **50.** 3. *a;* here used as a Demonstrative, § **52.** 2.

b. The Demonstrative follows its noun, *and has the article.*

c. ה being a laryngeal implies the doubling; hence ă of the article is only *apparently* in an open syl.

215. הַבְּדֹלַח—hăb-bᵉdō'-lăḥ—*the-bdellium.*

216. אֶבֶן הַשֹּׁהַם—'ĕ'-vĕn hăš-šō'-hăm—*stone-of the-onyx:*

a. Two Segolates,—one *a*-class, one *u*-class.

b. Helping-vowel in first is ֶ, in second, after ה, ַ, § **37.** 2. *a.*

3. *FORMS FOR SPECIAL STUDY.*

יֵצֵא	הָאֶחָד	חַיָּה abs., but	חַיַּת const.
סָבַב	וְזָהָב	נְשָׁמָה abs., but	נִשְׁמַת const.

4. *OBSERVATIONS.*

101. The *o* of the Ḳăl active Participle is ô, not ō.

102. Note, in the words cited above, Mếṭĕğ written (1) on second syl. before the tone, (2) with a vowel before compound šᵉwâ.

103. The original fem. ending in Hebrew was ת ; but this has been weakened to ָה, except where something closely following protects it. On account of the following noun, it is preserved in the construct state.

5. *GRAMMAR-LESSON.*

1. § **72.** Table,   General view of the Verb-stems.
2. § **72.** R's 1—7,   Changes from original vowels.
3. § **58.** 2. *a, b, c.* Origin and use of the Nĭfăl stem.
4. § **58.** 6. *a, b, c.* Origin and use of the Hŏfăl stem.
5. § **62.** 1. *a, c.*   Inflection of the Nĭfăl and Hŏfăl perfects.

6. *WORD-LESSON.*

1. In the Word-Lists, under List II., verbs numbered 31—40.
2. Make out a list of the new words in Genesis II. 10—12.

7. *EXERCISES.*

1. To be translated into Hebrew:—(1) *Thou* (m.) *wast caused to divide, I was caused to kill, we were caused to kill;* (2) *He was killed, they were killed, she was killed;* (3) *Thou* (m.) *wast sanctified* (Nif.), *ye* (f.) *were sanctified, they were sanctified;* (4) *We were kept, thou* (f.) *wast kept, she was kept.*

2. To be translated into Hebrew:—(1) (The) *river of that land is* (a) *great river;* (2) (The) *name of that river is Pishon;* (3) *The river which goes forth from Eden will be divided;* (4) (The) *gold of* (the) *land of Havilah is good gold;* (5) *Thou shalt call the river which surrounds* (=the one surrounding) *that land Pishon.*

3. To be translated into English:—(1) כּוֹכָב קָטֹן אֶחָד; (2) נָהָר גָּדֹל; (3) שֵׁם הַגָּן הוּא עֵדֶן; (4) יָצַרְתָּ אֶת־הָאָדָם עָפָר; (5) סָבַב אֶת־הָאָרֶץ אֲשֶׁר־שָׁם זָהָב לֹא יָדַעְתִּי הַמָּקוֹם אֲשֶׁר; (6) שָׁם הוּא עֵדֶן תִּשְׁבַּתִּי בַּיּוֹם הַשְּׁבִיעִי.

4. To be written in English letters:—*Verses* 10—12 *of chapter II., from the pointed text.*

5. To be written with points and vowel-signs:—*Verses* 10—12 *of chapter II., from the unpointed text.*

6. To be written:—(1) The verbs שָׁמַר, פָּרַד, and מָשַׁל in the perf. 3 m. sg. of the Nifäl; (2) the verbs מָלַךְ, שָׁמַר, and לָמַד in the perf. 1st p. plur. of the Hŏfäl.

8. TOPICS FOR STUDY.

(1) Nouns formed by prefixing מ. (2) Nouns which had originally two short vowels. (3) A-class, I-class and U-class Seḡolates. (4) The vowels of the Ḳal Part. act. (5) A comparison of הַשְׁקוֹת with הַבְדִּיל and עֲשׂוֹת. (6) The word meaning *he-was-divided*. (7) The construct state of nouns like נָהָר, זָהָב, etc. (8) The construct state of Seḡolates. (9) The two forms of the fem. ending הָ_, and ת_ּ. (10) Méθěḡ. (11) The original forms of the various Perfect stems.

LESSON XXIII.—GENESIS II. 13-14.

1. NOTE-REVIEW.

(1) יַעֲלֶה (202); (2) לְמַאֲכָל (196); (3) יִצְמָח (173); (4) מֵעֵדֶן (179); (5) וַיִּשְׁבֹּת (171); (6) יִפָּרֵד (205).

2. NOTES.

217. חִדֶּקֶל—hĭd-dĕ'-ḳĕl—*Tigris*. This name is written *I-dig-lat* in the Assyrian inscriptions.

218. הַהֹלֵךְ—hă(h)-hô-lēx—*the-*(one)*-going;* cf. הַסֹּבֵב:
a. D. f. of article is implied in ה, cf. הַהוּא (214), § **45.** 2.
b. Ḳal act. Part. (ô, not ō) of הָלַךְ *he-went.*

219. קִדְמַת—ḳĭd-măθ—*eastward-of;* const. of קִדְמָה:
a. The original ת_ is retained in the const state, § **106.** 2. *a.* (3)

b. A fem. form related to קֶדֶם (190).

220. הוּא פְרָת—*is Euphrates.*

3. FORMS FOR SPECIAL STUDY.

| הוּא הַסֹּבֵב | קִדְמַת | שֵׁם ־ הַנָּהָר |
| הוּא הַהֹלֵךְ | הָרְבִיעִי | וְשֵׁם הַנָּהָר |

104. Note in words cited above, Mêθĕğ written (1) with a tonal vowel in a closed syl. before Maḳḳêf, (2) with Ḳâmĕṣ before a vocal šᵉwâ, (3) with a primary short vowel (ă) before a laryngeal with doubling implied.

105. Note that the participle often serves as the equivalent of a relative clause.

5. GRAMMAR-LESSON.

§ 63. Tabular View.	Inflection of Ḳăl Imperfect (active).
§ 63. R. 1.	Various prefixes and affixes used.
§ 63. R. 2.	Original Stem of the Ḳăl Imperfect.
§ 63. R. 3, 4.	The terminations ִי, וּ and נָה.

6. WORD-LESSON.

Make out a list of the new words in Genesis II, 13-14.

7. PRINCIPLES OF SYNTAX.—THE PERSONAL PRONOUN

הוּא הַסֹּבֵב He [or IT] (is) the (-one-) surrounding.

וּזְהַב הָאָרֶץ הַהוּא And the gold of THAT land.

וְהַנָּהָר הָרְבִיעִי הוּא פְרָת And the fourth river IS Euphrates.

Principle 5.—The personal pronoun besides (1) its ordinary use as a *personal* pronoun, may have (2) the force of a remote demonstrative pronoun (*that*), and (3) the force of a *copula*, i. e., to mark the relation between the subject and the predicate.

8. EXERCISES.

1. To be translated into Hebrew:—(1) *He will rest, I shall rest, we shall rest, they will rest, thou* (f.) *shalt rest;* (2) *They* (m.) *will swarm, he will swarm, she will swarm, they* (f.) *will swarm, ye* (m.) *shall swarm;* (3) *He will call, she will call, I shall call, we shall call, thou* (m.) *shalt call;* (4) *He will plant, I shall plant, thou* (m.) *shalt plant, she will plant, they will plant;* (5) *He will give, she will give, I shall give, we shall give, thou* (m.) *wilt give.*

2. To be translated into Hebrew:—(1) *The river which surrounds* (the) *land-of Cush is Gihon;* (2) *The river which goes eastward-of Assyria is Euphrates;* (3) (The) *name-of the great river is Tigris;* (4) *She will rest in* (the) *land-of Havilah;* (5) *We shall give that land.*

3. To be translated into English:—(1) הָאָרֶץ הַהוּא קִדְמַת (2) אַשּׁוּר; (3) הַנָּהָר הַהוּא הַסּוֹבֵב אֶת־כָּל־אֶרֶץ כּוּשׁ; (4) שָׁבַת אֱלֹהִים בַּיּוֹם הַהוּא יִשְׁרְצוּ הַמַּיִם שֶׁרֶץ נֶפֶשׁ; (5) חַיָּה יִפָּרֵד הַנָּהָר הַגָּדוֹל וְהָיָה לְאַרְבָּעָה רָאשִׁים.

4. To be written in English letters:—*Genesis II 13-14 from the pointed text.*

5. To be written with points and vowel-signs:—*Genesis II, 13-14, from the unpointed Hebrew text.*

6. To be written:—The verbs שָׁבַת and מָשַׁל in the Ḳāl Imperfect tense throughout.

9. TOPICS FOR STUDY.

(1) Inflection of the Ḳāl Imperfect (active). (2) Prefixes of the Imperfect. (3) Affixes of the Imperfect as compared with those of the Perfect. (4) The difference in the stem-vowels of יֵשֵׁב, יִטַּע, and יִקְרָא.

LESSON XXIV.—GENESIS II. 15-16.

1. *NOTE-REVIEW.*

הַדַּעַת (4) (190); מִקֶּדֶם (3) (115); לֵאמֹר (2) (184); וַיִּפַּח (1) (198); (5) וְרַע (199).

2. *NOTES.*

221. וַיִּקַּח, וַיִּטַּע—*and-*(he)*-took;* cf. וַיִּטַּע:

a. For וַיִּלְקַח, but ל is assimilated (like נ), § **39. 3**.

b. The laryngeal ח has ־ַ (ă) before it, rather than ō, § **42. 2.** *b*.

222. וַיַּנִּחֵהוּ—wăy-yăn-nî-ḥē-hû—*and-he-caused-to-rest-him:*

a. The וַ is Wâw Conver.; ־ֵהוּ is the pron. suf. of 3 m. sg.

b. The root is נוּחַ *to-rest;* the form is an *irreg.* Hîf'îl.

223. לְעָבְדָהּ וּלְשָׁמְרָהּ—l°ŏv-dâh ûl°šŏm-râh:

a. The translation of these words is: *to-serve-her and-to-keep-her.*

b. The insep. prepositions are as usual; ו before ל becomes וּ, § **49. 2**.

c. The final ה is a consonant, as indicated by Măppîḳ, § **16. 1**.

d. The ־ָ under ע and שׁ, if it were â, would have Mĕθĕğ, § **18. 2**.

e. ־ָהּ is a contraction of ־ָהָ; cf. וּ for הוּ, § **108. 1. R. 1**.

f. These forms are Ḳăl Inf's const. (cf. מְשֹׁל), and without suffixes would read עֲבֹד and שְׁמֹר (§ **70. 2**); but, before the suffix, a different form is used.

g. The syllables ŏv- and šŏm- being unaccented and having short vowels must be closed. Š°wâ is therefore silent. The absence of d. l. from ד is a survival from a period when there was a short vowel under ב (cf. §§ **10. 2.** *d;* **28. 4.**). This survival was aided by the fact that the spirant letter ב greatly facilitated the spirant articulation of the following

224. וַיְצַו—*and-*(he)*-commanded;* cf. וַיְכַל from כָּלָה:

a. Long form וַיְצַוֶּה, Pî'ēl Impf. of צִוָּה *he-commanded.*

b. D. f. omitted (1) from י and (2) from ן, § **14.** 1, 2.

c. The unfailing indication of the Pi'ēl is here, viz., ִ under 1st rad.

d. צִוָּה, in Pi'ēl, = *he-commanded;* so כִּלָּה, in Pi'ēl, = *he-finished.*

225. אֲכֹל—'ă-xōl—*to-eat,* or *eating:*

a. Ḳăl Inf. *absolute* of אָכַל *he-ate;* second vowel *unchangeable.*

b. Cf. with this the form of the Inf. const. אֱכֹל (cf. מְשֹׁל) = 'xōl, the *o* being *changeable,* § **67.** 1. *b,* 2.

c. Cf. מָשׁוֹל (ō) and מְשֹׁל (ŏ); שָׁמוֹר (ō) and שְׁמֹר (ŏ).

226. תֹּאכֵל—tô'-xēl—*thou-shalt-eat:*

a. תּ indicates the Impf. 2 m. sg. (*thou*), root אָכַל.

b. Cf. with this וַיֹּאמֶר *and-he-said,* from אָמַר.

3. FORMS FOR SPECIAL STUDY.

אָכֹל	יָקוּו	וַיַּבְדֵּל	וַיְקַדֵּשׁ	וַיִּקַּח
שָׁמְרָה	יִפְרֹד	וַיַּעֲמַח	וַיְצַו	וַיִּטַּע
עָבְדָה	תֵּרָאֶה	תַּדְשֵׁא	וַיְבָרֶךְ	וַיִּפַּח

4. OBSERVATIONS.

106. Verbs whose third radical is a laryngeal must have ַ for their stem-vowel in the Imperfect.

107. The Pi'ēl Impf. may always be distinguished by the ִ (or, if the second radical is a laryngeal, the ָ) which is under the first radical.

108. The Hif'îl Impf. may be distinguished by the ִ which is under the personal preformative.

109. The Nif'ăl Impf. may be distinguished by the **D. f.** *in* and the ָ *under* the first radical.

110. The *o* of the Inf. abs. is ô unchangeable; but the *o* of the Inf. const. is tonal ō, and varies with the position of the accent.

5. GRAMMAR-LESSON.

1. § **65.** 2. a, b,   The stem and inflection of the Pī'ēl Impf. (cf. p. 185)
2. § **65.** 3, a, b,   The stem and inflection of the Hĩθpă'ēl Impf. (cf. p. 184)
3. § **65.** 5. a, b,   The stem and inflection of the Hĭf'îl Impf. (cf. p. 184)

6. WORD-LESSON.

1. In the Word-Lists, under List II., verbs numbered 41—50.
2. Make out a list of the new words in Genesis II. 15—16.

7. EXERCISES.

1. To be translated into Hebrew:—(1) *He will keep, they will keep, we shall keep, thou* (f.) *shalt keep.* (2) *She will sanctify, I shall sanctify, ye will sanctify, they* (f.) *will sanctify, we shall sanctify;* (3) *She will sanctify herself, you will sanctify yourselves;* (4) *He will cause to divide,*[1] *they* (m.) *will cause to divide, we shall cause to divide, thou* (f.) *wilt cause to divide, ye* (f.) *shall cause to divide;* (5) *I shall rule, they* (f.) *will cause to rule.*

2. To be translated into Hebrew:—(1) *Thou mayest eat from all the fruit which God has given;* (2) *Thou shalt divide between the good and between the evil;* (3) *Thou mayest not eat from the tree which is in the midst of the garden.*

3. To be translated into English:—(1) שָׁמוֹר (2) אָכֹל תֹּאכֵל; (3) תִּשְׁמֹר; (4) יְקַדֵּשׁ אֱלֹהִים אֶת־הַיּוֹם הַזֶּה עָשָׂה אֱלֹהִים; (5) וַיְצַו אֱלֹהִים אֶת־הָאִישׁ לֵאמֹר לָאָדָם אֶת־הָאָרֶץ תֹּאכֵל פְּרִי.

4. To be written in English letters:—*Verses 15—16 of chapter II., from the pointed text.*

---

[1] Use the root בָּדַל in Hif'il.

5. To be written with points and vowel-signs:—*Verses 15—16 of chapter II., from the unpointed text.*

6. To be written:—(1) The verbs מָלַךְ, מָשַׁל and לָמַד throughout the Imperfect of the Pī'ēl, Hiθpā'ēl and Hif'îl stems.

8. TOPICS FOR STUDY.

(1) Assimilation of לְ. (2) Dif. between the *o* of the Inf. abs. and the *o* of the Inf. const. (3) The Inf. const. before suffixes. (4) The words meaning *being-of*, *to-serve-her*. (5) Peculiarities of laryngeals. (6) Tonal vowels. (7) Mé́θĕğ, Măppîk̄, Râfê and Măk̄k̄êf.

LESSON XXV.—GENESIS II 17-18.

1. NOTE-REVIEW.

(1) וַיְקַדֵּשׁ (221); (2) וַיִּקַּח (158); (3) יָפָּרֵד (205); (4) וַיְכַל (162); (5) תּוֹצֵא (123).

2. NOTES.

227. וּמֵעֵץ—*and-from-tree-of:* וְ, § **49**. 2; מֵ, § **48**. 2.

a. A new disjunctive accent, called rᵉvî(ă)'; § **24**. 5. b.

228. תֹּאכַל—Another spelling of תֹּאכֵל (226).

229. מִמֶּנּוּ כִּי בְיוֹם—*from-him* (= *it*); *for, in-day-of:*

a. מִן takes a special form before suffixes, viz. מִמֶּן; with הוּ, מִמֶּנּוּ = מִמֶּנְהוּ, in which the ה is assim. backwards and represented by D. f. in נ, § **51**. 5. b, and ־ is deflected to ־.

b. D. l. in כ and in ב because of prec. disj. accent, § **12**. 3.

230. אָכְלְךָ—'ɔ̆ŏl-xă—*thy-eating:*

a. The Inf. const. is אֲכֹל, but before ךָ, אָכָל (ŏ), § **71**. 3. *a.* (1).

b. Cf. (1) reg. form קְטֹל, (2) form before ךָ, קָטָל, (3) form before הָ (see Note 223 *f*), קָטְל (ŏ).

Lesson 25.

231. מוֹת תָּמוּת—môθ tâ-mûθ—*dying thou-shalt-die:*
a. The Ḳâl Inf. abs., and Impf. 2 m. sg. of מוּת *to-die.*
b. The explanation of these forms will be given later.

232. הֱיוֹת—hᵉyôθ—*being-of;* cf. עֲשׂוֹת *making-of:*
a. Ḳâl Inf. const. of הָיָה *he-was,* translated as a verbal noun.
b. Under the laryngeal ה appears a compound šᵉwâ.

233. לְבַדּוֹ—*to* or *in-separation-his:* לְ, prep.; בַּד, noun; וֹ, suffix.

234. אֶעֱשֶׂה־לּוֹ—'ĕ-ᵉśĕ(h)l+lô—*I-will-make+for-him:*
a. א indicates the *first* pers. sg.; root is עָשָׂה *he made.*
b. The D. f. in לְ is conjunctive (cf. עֲשֵׂה־פְרִי), § 15. 3.
c. Cf. וַיַּעַשׂ (46), עָשָׂה (71), עֲשׂוֹת, all from עָשָׂה.

235. עֵזֶר—'ê-zĕr—(a)*help* or *helper;* cf. אֶבֶן עֵזֶר *Ebenezer:*
a. Like עֶשֶׂב and עֵדֶן an *i*-class Segolate, § 89. 1. b.

236. כְּנֶגְדּוֹ—*as-over-against-him:* נֶגֶד כְּ, וֹ.

3. GRAMMAR-LESSON.

1. § 65. 1. *a, b.*   The stem and inflection of the Nif'al Impf.
2. § 65. 4.   The stems and inflections of the Pŭ'al and Hŏf'al Impf.

4. WORD-LESSON.

1. Make out a list of the new words in Genesis II 17-18.

5. EXERCISES.

1. To be translated into Hebrew:—(1) *He will be divided,[1] they will be divided, thou* (f.) *shalt be divided, we shall be divided;* (2) *Thou* (f.) *shalt be sanctified, I shall be sanctified, ye shall be sanctified, we shall be sanctified, she will be sanctified;* (3) *Thou* (f.) *shalt be divided,[2] we shall be divided, ye shall be divided;* (4)

---
[1] Use פָּרַד in the Nif'al. [2] Use בָּדַל in Hof'al.

I shall be ruled, thou (m.) *shalt be ruled, we shall be ruled;* (5) *Thou* (f.) *shalt rule thyself, we shall rule ourselves, he will rule himself.*

2. To be translated into Hebrew:—(1) *In that day thou shalt die;* (2) *In the day of thy eating from the tree of fruit thou shalt surely die;* (3) *And the man was not alone in the midst of the garden;* (4) *And there was a helper over-against-him.*

3. To be translated into English:—(1) הִתְקַדֵּשׁ; (2) מוֹת תָּמוּת; (3) בַּיּוֹם הָרְבִיעִי; (4) וַיַּעַשׂ אֱלֹהִים לָאָדָם עֵזֶר; (5) לֹא טוֹב הֱיוֹת הָאָדָם לְבַדּוֹ; פְּרִי לְמִינֵהוּ.

4. To be written in English letters:—*Genesis II, 17-18 from the pointed text.*

5. To be written with points and vowel-signs:—*Genesis II, 17-18 from the unpointed text.*

6. To be written:—The verbs מָשַׁל and קָדַשׁ throughout the Imperfect of the Pi'ēl, Hiθpă'ēl and Hif'îl stems.

8. *TOPICS FOR STUDY.*

(1) The characteristics distinguishing the various Imperfects. (2) The stems of the various Imperfects. (3) The inflection of the various Imperfects. (4) The use of the Infinitive Absolute. (5) The use of the Infinitive Construct.

LESSON XXVI.—GENESIS II. 19-20.

1. *NOTE-REVIEW.*

(1) וַיִּקְרָא (4); הַשָּׂדֶה (171); (3) חַיַּת (128); (2) הָאֲדָמָה (129); (5) בְּהֵמָה (29); (6) עֵזֶר כְּנֶגְדּוֹ (125); (7) וַיִּקַּח (235,236); (221).

2. NOTES.

237. וַיִּצֶר—a defective writing of וַיִּיצֶר (182).

238. וַיָּבֵא—*and-he-caused-to-come;* cf. וַיַּבְדֵּל:

a. Clearly a Hif'îl Impf. 3 m. sg. of the root בוֹא *to-come-in.*

b. Instead of ־ֶ, the preformative וְ has ־ָ in an open syllable.

239. לִרְאוֹת—lĭr-'ôθ—*to-see;* cf. לִמְשֹׁל, לַעֲשׂוֹת:

a. רְאוֹת is the Inf. const. of the verb רָאָה *he-saw.*

b. לְ, before a letter with šᵉwâ, takes ־ִ, § 47. 2.

240. מַה־יִּקְרָא־לוֹ—mă(h)y+yĭḳ-rā'+lô—*what+he-will-call+to-it:*

a. The Interrogative *what?* pointed like the article, § 54. 2. a.

b. לוֹ = *to-him,* just as בוֹ = *in-him.*

241. הוּא—literally *he,* = *is;* cf. Principle 5 (3).

242. שְׁמוֹ ... שֵׁמוֹת—*his-name....names:*

a. Before the suffix וֹ the ־ֵ of שֵׁם becomes ־ְ; but

b. The ־ֵ is retained before the fem. plur. affix ôth.

c. Rᵉvî(ă)‛ (◌֗) over שֵׁמוֹת, §24. 5. b; (cf. 227, and 229).

243. מָצָא—*he-found;* cf. בָּרָא, קָרָא:

a. ־ָ, instead of ־ַ as in שָׁבַת, because א is silent.

b. Lit., *he-found;* here impersonal, = *there-was-found;* cf. French *on dit* = *it is said,* and German *man sagt.*

3. FORMS FOR SPECIAL STUDY.

מִן־הָאֲדָמָה	הָאָדָם	הַשָּׁמַיִם (v. 20)	וַיִּתֵּן
מִתַּחַת	לֹא־מָצָא	וּלְאָדָם (v. 20)	וַיִּפַּח
מֵעַל	הַשָּׂדֶה	שֵׁמוֹת (v. 20)	וַיִּטַּע

4. OBSERVATIONS.

109. The preposition מִן *from* is written separately chiefly before the article; elsewhere it is joined to the following word, the נ suf-

fering assimilation; but, if the following word begins with a laryngeal, the D. f. is rejected and the preceding ־ֽ becomes ־ָ.

110. The syl. standing second before the tone receives Mé̱θĕğ, if it is an *open* syllable.

111. Three accents of high rank are ◌֕ Zâḵēf ḳâṭōn, ◌֕ Zâḵēf gâdôl, ◌֗ Rᵉvî (ă)‛, § **24.** 4, 5. *a*, *b*.

112. Verbs whose first radical is נ assimilate the נ whenever it would stand at the close of a syllable. It is then represented by D. f. in the second radical. Such forms are liable to be confused with Pī‛ēl forms.

5. *GRAMMAR-LESSON.*

1. § **66.** 1. *a—c*,   The *stem* of Imperatives.
2. § **66.** 2. *a*, *b*, and N. 1, The *inflection* of Imperatives.

6. *WORD-LESSON.*

1. In the Word-Lists, under List V., nouns numbered 1—15.
2. Make out a list of the new words in Genesis II., 19-20.

7. *EXERCISES.*

1. To be translated into Hebrew:—(1) *Rule thou* (m.), *keep ye* (f.), *sanctify thou* (f.), *divide ye* (m.), *fill ye, subdue ye, be thou* (f.) *separated, sanctify yourselves, swarm ye.*

2. To be translated into Hebrew:—(1) *What will God call the great luminary?* (2) *Who formed every fowl of the heaven?* (3) *Who gave* (Heb., *called*) *names to the fowl of the heaven, and to the beast of the earth?* (4) *Gold, the gold, to the gold, in the gold, and in the gold;* (5) *He found the fruit in the garden.*

3. To be translated into English :—(1) מַה־שְּׁמִי; (2) מַה־שְּׁמוֹ; (3) יָצַרְתִּי (5) לְמִי זֹאת (4); מַה־יִּקְרָא הָאָדָם לְכָל־הַבְּהֵמָה; (6) אֹתוֹ; (7) יָצַרְתָּ אֹתָהּ; בַּבְּהֵמָה וּבְחַיַּת הָאָרֶץ וּבְדְגַת הַיָּם; וּבְעוֹף הַשָּׁמַיִם לֹא נִמְצָא לְאָדָם עֵזֶר כְּנֶגְדּוֹ.

4. To be written in English letters:—*Verses 19-20 of chapter II., from the pointed text.*

5. To be written with points and vowel-signs:—*Verses 19-20 of chapter II., from the unpointed text.*

6. To be written:—The verbs שָׁמַר, מָשַׁל and פָּקַד in the Imv. of all the stems.

8. TOPICS FOR STUDY.

(1) The Interrogative Pronouns. (2) Verbs with א as their third radical. (3) Verbs with נ as their first radical. (4) Nouns which had originally two short vowels. (5) Preposition מִן. (6) The accents Zâķēf ķāṭon, Zâķēf gâdôl, and R⁽vî(ă)'. (7) The stems and inflection of the various Imperatives.

LESSON XXVII.—GENESIS II. 21, 22.

1. *NOTE-REVIEW.*

(1) אָדָם (131); (2) זָהָב (212); (3) מֵ in מֵאִישׁ (202); (4) וְהָיוּ (80); (5) אֶחָד (37); (6) לֹא (174).

2. *NOTES.*

244. וַיַּפֵּל—wăy-yăp-pēl—*and*(he)-*caused-to-fall:*

a. This form is for וַיַּנְפֵּל, which is, like וַיַּבְדֵּל, in Hif'îl.

b. Root נָפַל, of which נ is assimilated and represented by D. f.

c. נָתַן, נָטַע, נָפַח, נָפַל all have נ for their first radical; the old Jewish paradigm-word was פָּעַל, the first radical of which is פ; hence, technically, these verbs are called פ״ן, i. e., Pē Nûn, § 77. 1.

245. תַּרְדֵּמָה—(a)-*deep-sleep:* on formation see § 98. and R.

246. וַיִּישָׁן—wăy-yî-šăn—*and-he-slept;* cf. וַיִּיצֶר:

a. The ָ is pausal for ַ, § 38. 2.

b. The radical י becomes silent after the preceding ִ.

247. אַחַת—'ă(h)-ḥăθ—*one:* fem. of אֶחָד (37).

a. A d. f. is implied in ח, hence ă is really in a closed syllable.

248. מִצַּלְעֹתָיו—mĭṣ-ṣăl-'ô-θăw—*from-ribs-his:*

a. The מִן with נ assimilated, § 48. 1.

b. צַלְעֹת is plur. const. of צֵלָע (v. 22), a feminine noun.

c. יו_ָ is the same as in אָפָיו, see Note 185. *b.*

249. וַיִּסְגֹּר—wăy-yĭs-gōr—*and-he-closed;* cf. וַיִּשְׁבֹּת.

a. Perfects: הִסְגִּיר, סָגַר, נִסְגַּר, סָגַר.

b. Imperfects: יַסְגִּיר, יִסָּגֵר, יִסְגֹּר.

c. The o is ō, not ŏ; as it always is in Ḳăl Impf.

250. בָּשָׂר—*flesh;* cf. עָפָר, נָהָר, זָהָב, כָּנָף, אָדָם, § 90. 1. *a.*

251. תַּחְתֶּנָּה—tăḥ-tĕn-nă(h)—*instead-of-her:*

a. Prep. תַּחַת, see 49; a connecting syllable, נָ_ ; the fem. suf., ה_ָ.

b. ה is assim. backwards, so that תַּחְתֶּנָה becomes תַּחְתֶּנָּ; then the vowel-letter ה is added, § 6. 1. N. 1.

252. וַיִּבֶן—wăy-yĭ'-vĕn—*and-*(he)*-built;* cf. יֶרֶב:

a. Long form יִבְנֶה (root בָּנָה), as יֶרֶב and יִרְבֶּה (root רָבָה).

b. The ending ה_ָ is *always* lacking in verbal forms with Wăw Conversive; so וַיְהִי, not וַיִּהְיֶה, וַיַּעַשׂ, not וַיַּעֲשֶׂה.

c. יִבְן is difficult to pronounce, so ֶ is inserted under ב, § 82. 5. *b.* (3).

d. From the root בָּנָה *build,* come בֵּן *son,* בַּת *daughter.*

253. הַצֵּלָע—*the-rib;* cf. the form before suf. צַלְעֹת (248).

254. לָקַח—*he-took;* cf. the Ḳăl Impf. יִקַּח (221).

255. לְאִשָּׁה—l°'ĭš-šă(h)—*for-woman;* cf. אִישׁ (v. 23).

256. וַיְבִאֶהָ—wăy-vî-'ĕ'-hă—*and-he-caused-to-come-her:*

a. Root בּוֹא; cf. וַיָּבֵא (238); D. f. omitted from י.

b. The ה is 3 f. sg. suffix *her.*

c. The ֶ is î, though written defectively.

d. In יָבֵא ă has become â before the tone; but in יָבְאָה, this original ă has become ְ , because of the removal of the tone, § 32. 1. c.

e. The connecting element before the suffix is ĕ, a short vowel in an open syl., but under the tone; § 28. 5. Cf. similar forms in 252, 172, 176 and הִשִּׂיאַנִי (330) and אִשְׁתְּךָ (351).

3. FORMS FOR SPECIAL STUDY.

עֶרֶב	מְאֹרֹת but מָאוֹר	יִרְבֶה for יִרֶב
זֶרַע	בִּשְׂרִי but בָּשָׂר	יִבְנֶה for יִבֶן
תַּחַת	יָבְאָה but יָבֵא	יַעֲשֶׂה for יַעַשׂ

4. OBSERVATIONS.

113. The ending ה_ with which all Imperfects of verbs having ה for the third radical end, is lacking with Wâw Conversive.

114. Two consonants with Šᵉwâ seldom stand at the end of a word; a helping vowel (ִ or ֲ) is generally inserted for euphony.

115. A primary short vowel in an open syl. is dependent upon the position of the tone for its form; when pretonic, it modifies its quality (e. g. ă becomes â, ĭ becomes ē, and ŭ becomes ō), but when the tone moves away, it is reduced to Šᵉwâ.

116. Some Seğolates have two Sᵉğôls; others, those with a laryngeal for the third radical, have one Sᵉğôl and one Păθăḥ; still others, those with a laryngeal for the second radical, have two Păθăḥs.

5. PRONOUNS, PERSONAL TERMINATIONS, PRONOMINAL SUFFIXES.

אֹתָנוּ	שָׁמַר	הוּא	He kept or has kept us.
אֹתָךְ	שָׁמְרָה	הִיא	She has kept thee (f.).
אֹתוֹ	שָׁמַרְתָּ	אַתָּה	Thou (m.) has kept him.
אֹתָהּ	שָׁמַרְתְּ	אַתְּ	Thou (f.) has kept her.
אֹתָךְ	שָׁמַרְתִּי	אָנֹכִי	I have kept thee (m.).
אֹתִי	שָׁמְרוּ	הֵם	They (m.) have kept me.
אֶתְכֶן	שָׁמְרוּ	הֵן	They (f.) have kept you (f.).
אֹתָם שְׁמַרְתֶּם		אַתֶּם	Ye (m.) have kept them (m.).
אֹתָן שְׁמַרְתֶּן		אַתֶּן	Ye (f.) have kept them (f.).
אֶתְכֶם שָׁמַרְנוּ		אֲנַחְנוּ	We have kept you (m.).

[**Note.**—Let this exercise be thoroughly mastered; it will be found a most helpful acquisition.]

6. GRAMMAR-LESSON.

1. § 67. 1. *a, b,*   The Infinitive Absolute.
2. § 67. 2. *a, b,*   The Infinitive Construct.
3. § 30. 6. *a,*   The ô that comes by rounding from â.
4. § 30. 7. *c, d,*   The ô that comes by contraction of *au* or *aw*.

7. EXERCISES.

1. To be translated into Hebrew:—(1) *to rule* (abs.), *to cause to rule* (abs.), *to keep* (const.), *to sanctify* (const.), *to sanctify oneself;* (2) *to be kept* (abs.), *to be created* (const.), *to be called* (const.), *to cause a division* (const.), *to rule* (const.), *to be ruled* (abs.).

2. To be translated into Hebrew: (1) *This* (is) *the woman whom God created from the man;* (2) *I will close the flesh;* (3) *God caused*

a deep sleep to fall upon the man; (4) *Rib from his ribs and flesh from the man;* (5) *The waters shall be called seas.*

3. To be translated into English:—(1) הַיּוֹם; (2) אָדָם אֶחָד; (3) לָקַחְתִּי מִן־הַמַּיִם; (4) לָקַח הָאִישׁ מִן־הֶעָפָר; (5) הָאֶחָד; (6) הָאִישׁ הַטּוֹב הַזֶּה; (7) הַנָּהָר יֹצֵא מֵעֵדֶן; (8) לָאוֹר יִקְרָא יוֹם; הָאִשָּׁה הַטּוֹבָה הַזֹּאת.

4. To be written in English letters:—*Verses 21, 22 of chapter II., from the pointed text.*

5. To be written with points and vowel-signs:—*Verses 21, 22 of chapter II., from the unpointed text.*

6. To be written:—(1) The verb פָּקַד in the Infinitive Absol. and Infinitive Construct of all stems; (2) the verb מָשַׁל in the Imperative 2 m. pl. of all stems.

9. *TOPICS FOR STUDY.*

(1) Absence of הַ. (2) Insertion of ָ and ַ. (3) The demonstrative pronoun. (4) The personal pronoun. (5) The pronominal suffixes with the sign of the definite object. (6) The personal terminations of the Perfect. (7) D. f. conjunc. (8) D. f. omitted. (9) Pŭ'al stem. (10) Reduction. (11) The vowels of Seğolates.

LESSON XXVIII.—GENESIS II. 23.

1. *NOTE—REVIEW.*

(1) וַיִּפַּח (244); (2) וַיְבִאֶהָ (256); (3) וַיְצַו (224); (4) וַיַּפֵּל (184); (5) לִמְאוֹרֹת (85).

---

[1] See § 45. 4.

2. NOTES.

257. זֹאת—zô(')θ—*this* (f.); cf. אֵלֶּה (165), § **52.** 1. **c**

a. א is silent here after the vowel ô.

258. הַפַּ֫עַם—hăp-pă'-'ăm—*the-stroke*, = *now:*

a. An *a*-class Seğolate, original ă retained, § **89.** 2. *a.*
b. ־ַ used as a helping-vowel instead of ־ֶ, § **42.** 2. *a.*
c. Article has here its original *demonstrative* force, *this*, i. e., *this stroke* or *time*, meaning *now*.

259. מֵעֲצָמַ֫י—mē-'ăṣă-măy—*from-bones-my:*

a. מֵ for מִן; cf. מֵעַל and מֵאִישׁ (v. 23), § **48.** 2.
b. עֲצָמַי is the form taken by עֶ֫צֶם in the *plural* with the suffix meaning *my;* §§ **108.** 3. *a.* (1); **109.** 4. *c.*

260. מִבְּשָׂרִי—*from-flesh-my;* cf. מְאֹרֹת, גְּדֹלִים:

a. Not בְּשָׂרִי, but בְּשָׂרִי; cf. 256. *d*, § **32.** 1. *c.*
b. A *singular* noun with suffix of 1 person sg.

261. יִקָּרֵא—yĭḳ-ḳă-rē'—*he-* (i. e., *it*)-*shall-be-called:*

a. Nif. Impf. 3 m. sg. of the verb קָרָא *call.*
b. Note the D. f. *in*, and pretonic ־ָ *under* the first radical.

262. לֻקֳחָה־זֹּאת—lŭḳ-ºḥă(h)z+zô(')θ—*was-taken+this:*

a. ־ֻ indicates Pŭ'ăl; comp'd Sᵉwâ under ק, though not a laryngeal.
b. ה ־ָ indicates Perf. 3 fem. sg., cf. הָיְתָה.
c. D. f. conjunctive in זּ, § **15.** 3; Méθěğ before comp'd Sᵉwâ.
d. D. f. omitted from ק and the line *Râfê* placed over ק to call attention to the absence of d. f. §§ **14.** 2; **32.** 3. *b.*
e. Compound Sᵉwâ of the ŭ-class to agree with the preceding ŭ.

3. GRAMMAR-LESSON.

1. § 63. 1. *a*, *c*,   The Ḳăl active and passive Participles.
2. § 63. 2, 3,   The Nĭf'ăl and remaining Participles
3. § 61. 1—3,   Inflection of Ḳăl Perfect Statives.
4. § 64. 1—3 and Notes, Inflection of Ḳăl Imperfect Statives.

Lesson 28.

4. WORD-LESSON.

1. In the Word-Lists, under List V., nouns numbered 16—30.
2. Make out a list of the new words in Genesis II. 23.

4. EXERCISES.

1. To be translated into Hebrew:—(1) *Ruling, ruled, causing to rule, ruling oneself, being caused to rule;* (2) *Resting, causing to to rest, closing, closed, caused to close;* (3) *Eating, causing to rain, finding, serving, sanctifying* (Pī'ēl), *sanctified* (Pŭ'äl), *keeping*.

2. To be translated into Hebrew:—(1) *This woman was taken from this man;* (2) *Thou* (m.) *art old, he is heavy, thou* (f.) *art small, he loves;* (3) *He will be heavy, she will be holy, we shall be old;* (4) *From my flesh, she will keep her, they will keep us;* (5) *We shall keep the garden in the midst of the rivers*.

3. To be translated into English: — (1) בָּרָא אֱלֹהִים אֶת־הָאִישׁ הַזֶּה; (2) הִוֶּה וְאֶת־הָאִשָּׁה הַזֹּאת; (3) לָקְחָה הָאִשָּׁה מִבְּשַׂר הָאָדָם; (4) הַבְּהֵמָה עַל־הָאָרֶץ; (5) וַיְקַדֵּשׁ אֹתוֹ בַּיּוֹם הַהוּא; יִכְבַּד, זָקֵן, קָדַשׁ, קָטֹן, נִכְבַּד.

4. To be written in English letters:—*Genesis II, 23 from the pointed text.*

5. To be written with points and vowel-signs:—*Genesis II, 23 from the unpointed text.*

6. To be written:—(1) The verbs זָקֵן *old* and קָטֹן *small* throughout Ḳăl Perfect; (2) The verbs כָּבֵד *heavy* and גָּדֵל *great* throughout the Ḳăl Imperfect.

5. TOPICS FOR STUDY.

(1) Ḳăl Participles; (2) Other Participles; (3) Stative Verbs; (4) Ḳăl Perfect (stative); (5) Ḳăl Imperfect (stative).

LESSON XXIX.—GENESIS II. 24, 25.

1. *NOTES.*

263. עַל־כֵּן—*upon+so,* = *therefore;* cf. ē of כֵּן and ê of בֵּין.

264. יַעֲזָב־—yă'-ᵃzŏv+—*he-will-forsake*+:

a. For יַעֲזֹב, but before Măḳḳēf ŏ instead of ō; root עָזַב.

b. יַעֲזָב instead of יַעְזָב (cf. יִקְטֹל), because the laryngeal prefers (1) ֲ to ְ, and (2) ַ to ִ, §§ 42. 2. *a.* 3. *b.*

c. Ḳăl Impf. 3 m. sg. of the laryngeal verb עָזַב; synopsis in Ḳăl,
עָזַב, יַעֲזֹב, עֲזֹב, עָזוֹב, עָזוּב.

265. אָבִיו—'ă-vîw—*father-his:*

a. אָב *father;* ִי appears in its construct form and before suffixes.

b. ו is all that is left of הוּ *his* or *him;* cf. ו in אַפָּיו.

266. אִמּוֹ—'ĭm-mô—*mother-his:*

a. אֵם *mother;* וֹ, the suffix of the 3 masc. sg.

b. In אֵם d. f. is lacking from ם, because it is final, and under the tone an original ĭ becomes ē; but in אִמּוֹ d. f. is present and original ĭ is retained in an unaccented syllable before a doubled consonant.

267. וְדָבַק—*and-shall-cleave;* cf. וְהָיוּ:

a. Synopsis in Ḳăl, דָּבַק, יִדְבַּק, דְּבַק, דָּבוֹק, דָּבֵק, דְּבוּק.

b. וְ with the Perf. is Wâw Conversive; cf. וַ with the Imperfect.

268. בְּאִשְׁתּוֹ—bᵉ'ĭš-tô—*in-wife-his:*

a. An irregular form of אִשָּׁה, before the suffix.

269. וַיִּהְיוּ—wăy-yĭh-yû—*and-they-were;* cf. וְהָיוּ:

a. Šᵉwâ under ה is silent.

b. Mé̱θê̱ğ with ִ, to facilitate the pronunciation of the fol. ה.

c. Ḳăl Impf. 3 m. pl. of the verb הָיָה, with Wâw Conversive.

270. שְׁנֵיהֶם—(the) *two-of-them,* = *they-two;* cf. שְׁנֵי, לָהֶם:

a. שְׁנֵי is the construct state of the dual שְׁנַיִם *two.*

b. הֵם is the pronominal suffix of the 3 plur. masc.

271. עֲרוּמִים—ʿărūm-mîm—*naked:*
a. The šᵉwâ under ע, because of distance from the tone.
b. The ו must here be regarded as a short vowel (i. e., an **incorrect** *full* writing of ŭ), on account of the D. f. following.

272. יֵתְבֹּשָׁשׁוּ—yiθ-bô-šā́'-šû—*they-will-be-ashamed:*
a. A formation after the manner of the Hīθpāʿēl.
b. Imperfect 3 masc. plur. of the root בּוֹשׁ.
c. The ָ in pause for ְ.

3. FORMS FOR SPECIAL STUDY.

פָּנִים	שְׁנַיִם	אִם	אֶת	וַיְהִי	יַעֲזֹב־
פְּנֵי	שְׁנֵי	אִמּוֹ	אֶת־	וְהָיוּ	יַעֲלֶה

2. OBSERVATIONS.

117. The ָ which is seen in יִקְטֹל was originally a Păθăḥ; this original Păθăḥ is retained before laryngcals.

118. Wâw Conversive with the Impf. is וַ; with the Perfect, it is וְ.

119. An original ĭ is deflected in a closed unaccented syl. to ָ.

120. An original ĭ is retained unchanged in an unaccented sharpened syllable.

121. The plur. ending ִים becomes in the construct ֵי.

122. The dual ending ַיִם also becomes in the construct ֵי.

3. PRONOUNS, PERSONAL PREFIXES AND TERMINATIONS, PRONOMINAL SUFFIXES.

לָ֫נוּ	יִכְתֹּב	הוּא	He will write to us.
לָךְ	תִּכְתֹּב	הִיא	She will write to thee (f.).
לוֹ	תִּכְתֹּב	אַתָּה	Thou (m.) wilt write to him.
לָהּ	תִּכְתְּבִי	אַתְּ	Thou (f.) wilt write to her.
לְךָ	אֶכְתֹּב	אָנֹכִי	I will write to thee (m.).
לִי	יִכְתְּבוּ	הֵם	They (m.) will write to me.
לָכֶן	תִּכְתֹּ֫בְנָה	הֵן	They (f.) will write to you (f.).
לָהֶם	תִּכְתְּבוּ	אַתֶּם	Ye (m.) will write to them (m.).
לָהֶן	תִּכְתֹּ֫בְנָה	אַתֶּן	Ye (f.) will write to them (f.).
לָכֶם	נִכְתֹּב	אֲנַ֫חְנוּ	We will write to you (m.).

5. GRAMMAR-LESSON.

1. § 72.   General View of the Strong Verb.
2. § 72. R's 1—7,   Characteristics of Stems.

Note 1.—The synopsis of a stem includes (1) the Perf. 3 m. sg., (2) the Impf. 3 m. sg., (3) the Imv. 2 m. sg., (4) the two Infinitives, (5) the Participle or Participles.

Note 2.—In this general review of the strong verb, master the synopsis of each stem, so that it can be pronounced without hesitation, and written with perfect accuracy.

Note 3.—In this work use the following verbs in addition to the paradigm word: (1) מָשַׁל rule, (2) כָּתַב write, (3) לָכַד capture.

6. WORD-LESSON.

1. In the Word-Lists, Lists V. and VI., nouns numbered 31—45.
2. Make out a list of the new words in Genesis II. 24, 25.

7. EXERCISES.

1. To be translated into Hebrew:—(1) *He will rule, he ruled himself, he will be caused to rule, be thou* (m.) *ruled;* (2) *He will be kept, keep thyself* (Nif.), *he caused to keep, to be caused to keep;* (3) *He was holy, he will be sanctified, sanctify thou* (Pi'ēl and Hif'îl), *it will be sanctified;* (4) *To be created, being created, causing to divide, to cause to call, ruled, being caused to keep.*

2. To be translated into Ḥebrew:—(1) *God will not forsake me;* (2) *My mother will write to me;* (3) *The man and the woman became* (Heb., *were for*) *one flesh;* (4) *The man was called Adam;* (5) *The woman forsook her mother, and clave to her husband.*

3. To be translated into English:—(1) לֹא תַעֲזֹב נַפְשִׁי; (2) תַּעֲזֹב אִשְׁתְּךָ; (3) לֹא תַעֲזֹב הָאִשָּׁה אֶת־אִישָׁהּ; (4) הָיוּ שְׁנֵיהֶם; (5) טוֹבִים אָדָם אֵין בְּיוֹם עֲשׂוֹת אֱלֹהִים אֶרֶץ וְשָׁמַיִם.

4. To be written in English letters:—*Genesis II* 24, 25 *from the pointed text.*

5. To be written with points and vowel-signs:—*Genesis II* 24, 25 *from the unpointed text.*

6. Synopses to be written:—(1) *Of* בָּדַל *in* Nĭ. *and* Hĭ.; (2) *of* בָּקַשׁ *in* Pī *and* Pŭ.; (3) *of* בָּשַׁל *in* Ḳăl, Pī., Pŭ. *and* Hĭ.; (4) *of* זָכַר *in* Ḳăl, Nĭ. *and* Hĭ.; (5) *of* פָּקַד *in all seven stems;* (6) *of* כָּבֵד (which has ă in Ḳăl Impf. and Imv.) *in* Ḳăl, Nĭ., Pī., Pŭ., Hĭ., Hiθp.

8. TOPICS FOR STUDY.

(1) Attenuation of ă to ĭ in the preformatives of the Ḳăl Impf. (2) The occurrence of an original ă before laryngeals in the preformatives of the Ḳăl Impf. (3) Wâw Conversive, with the Perf., with the Impf. (4) The words for *man, woman, his-wife, her-husband.* (5) Dual ending in absolute and construct. (6) Changes of the vowel ĭ. (7) Synopses in various stems. (8) Characteristics of various stems. (9) Classes of weak verbs.

LESSON XXX.—REVIEW.

1. *WORD-REVIEW.*

[In this list of words, the superior figures indicate the verse in which the word, or its derivative, is found. In the case of nouns, the singular absolute is given, in the case of verbs, the root. The student is expected to compare with each word as here given, the various forms of that word which occur in the chapter, e. g., with שָׁקָה he will compare הִשְׁקָה *he-caused-to-drink*, לְהַשְׁקוֹת *to-cause-to-drink*.]

1. VERBS.

³קָדַשׁ	²⁴עָזַב	⁷נָפַח	¹⁷מוּת	⁹חָמַד	¹⁶אָכַל
⁸שׂוּם	⁶עָלָה	²¹נָפַל	⁵מָטַר	¹⁹יָדַע	¹⁹בּוֹא
²שָׁבַת	¹⁰פָּרַד	¹¹סָבַב	²⁰מָצָא	⁷יָצַר	²⁵בּוֹשׁ
¹⁵שָׁמַר	¹⁶צִוָּה	²¹סָגַר	¹⁵נוּחַ	²¹יָשֵׁן	²²בָּנָה
⁶שָׁקָה	⁵צָמַח	⁵עָבַד	⁸נָטַע	¹כָּלָה	²⁴דָּבַק
				¹⁵לָקַח	¹⁴הָלַךְ

2. NOUNS, PARTICLES, ETC.

⁵שִׂיחַ	¹צָבָא	¹⁸נֶגֶד	⁷חַיִּים	²²אִשָּׁה	²⁴אָב
²שְׁבִיעִי	²¹צֵלָע	¹⁰נָהָר	⁵טֶרֶם	¹⁸בַּד	¹²אֶבֶן
¹²שֹׁהַם	⁸קֶדֶם	⁷נְשָׁמָה	יְהוָה	¹²בְּדֹלַח	⁶אוּר
⁸שֵׁם	¹⁴קַדְמָה	¹⁸עֵזֶר	⁵לֹא	²¹בָּשָׂר	⁵אַיִן
¹¹שָׁם	¹⁰רֹאשׁ	⁷עָפָר	⁹מַאֲכָל	⁸גַּן	²³אִישׁ
⁴תּוֹלְדָה	⁹רַע	²³עֶצֶם	¹⁹מָה	¹¹הוּא	²⁴אִם
²¹תַּרְדֵּמָה	⁵שָׂדֶה	²⁵עָרוֹם	²מְלָאכָה	⁴זֶה	⁷אַף
		²³פַּעַם	⁹מַרְאֶה	¹¹זָהָב	¹⁰אַרְבָּעָה

2. *VERSE-REVIEW.*

1. Pronounce the pointed text of each verse until it can be read aloud rapidly and without hesitation.

2. Write out on paper the unpointed text, one verse at a time, and then, without the aid of either pointed text or translation, insert the necessary points and vowel-signs. Compare the result with the pointed text, and note the mistakes; repeat the exercise till each verse can be pointed without mistake.

3. Write the Hebrew of the chapter, verse by verse, with only the English translation before the eye. Here also correct the result each time by the pointed text.

4. Write out the transliteration of each verse, referring in doubtful cases to the transliteration of particular words given in the Notes from time to time.

3. *GRAMMAR-REVIEW.*

1. Long ô = â, § **30.** 6.
2. Long ô = *aw*, § **30.** 7.
3. Changes of ă, ĭ, ŭ, § **31.** 2. 3.
4. Reduction, § **36.** 2. *a*, *b*, and N. 1—4.
5. Attenuation, § **36.** 3. *a*, *b*, *c*.
6. Simple verb-stem (Ḳăl), § **58.** 1.
7. Formation and force of the Pī'ēl stem, § **58.** 3. *a*, *b*, *c*.
8. Formation and force of the Pŭ'ăl stem, § **58.** 4. *a*, *b*, *c*.
9. Formation and force of the Hīθpă'ēl stem, § **58.** 7. *a*, *b*, *c*.
10. Formation and force of Hĭf. and Hŏf. stems, § **58.** 5. *a*, *b*, *c*, 6. *a*, *b*, *c*.
11. Formation and force of the Nĭf'ăl stem, § **58.** 2. *a*, *b*, *c*.
12. General view of the verb-stems, § **59.** R's 1—4.
13. Inflection of Ḳăl Perf. (active), § **60.** R's 1—3.
14. Inflection of Ḳăl Perf. (stative), § **61.** 1—3.
15. Inflection of remaining Perfects, § **62.** 1, 2.
16. Inflection of Ḳăl Imperfect (active) § **63.** R's 1—4.
17. Inflection of Ḳăl Imperfect (stative), § **64.** 1—3.
18. Inflection of remaining Imperfects, § **65.** 1—5.
19. Inflection of the various Imperatives, § **66.** 1, 2.
20. The various Infinitives (abs. and const.), § **67.** 1, 2.
21. The various Participles, § **68.** 1—3.
22. General view of the strong verb, § **72.** R's 1—7.
23. Classification of weak verbs, § **77.** 1—6.
24. Seğolate nouns, § **89.** 1.

4. *A REVIEW EXERCISE ON THE STRONG VERB.*

[Supply in each case the vowel-points, etc.; the superior figures denote the number of places in the paradigm represented by the accompanying form, e. g., קְטַלְתֶּן ³ = קְטַלְתֶּן, קְטַלְתֶּן, קְטַלְתֶּן.]

(1) קטלתן³, (2) תתקטלי⁵, (3) קטלנה², (4) נקטלתם,
(5) הקטלו², (6) הקטלת⁴, (7) יקטיל, (8) התקטלנו, (9) התקטלנה,
(10) התקטלת², (11) קטול, (12) הקטלה, (13) אקטיל, (14)
(15) הקטלתם², (16) הקטל⁷, (17) יתקטל, (18) התקטל³,
(19) יקטילו, (20) הקטילה, (21) הקטלי, (22) תתקטלנה¹²,
(23) קטלנו³, (24) תתקטל¹⁰, (25) מקטל³, (26) הקטילו², (27) התקטלה,
(28) נקטיל, (29) תתקטל², (30) תתקטלו, (31) מקטיל,
(32) הקטיל², (33) נקטלה, (34) קטלו⁵, (35) אקטל⁵, (36) אתקטל,
(37) תקטילי, (38) נקטלת², (39) תקטלו⁵, (40) נקטל,
(41) מתקטל, (42) תקטילו, (43) התקטלתם, (44) הקטלנה²,
(45) נקטלו, (46) קטלתי³, (47) יקטל⁵, (48) נקטל⁷, (49) תתקטלנה²,
(50) הקטלנו², (51) נקטלתי, (52) קטלי², (53)
(54) קטלת⁶, (55) יקטלו⁵, (56) הקטילי, (57) הקטלתן²,
(58) נקטלנו, (59) יתקטלו, (60) קטל¹⁰, (61) קטלה³, (62) נקטלתן²,
(63) הקטלתי², (64) קטלתם³, (65) התקטלתי, (66) התקטלי,
(67) התקטלתן², (68) תקטיל².

LESSON XXXI.—GENESIS III. 1-2.

1. *NOTE-REVIEW.*

(1) מָ. (2) כֹּל (49); (3) חַיַּת (108); (4) הַשָּׂדֶה (128); (5) (171);
אִשָּׁה (255); (6) עֵץ (70); (7) הַגָּן (189); (8) בְּתוֹךְ (41); (9) מִמֶּנּוּ
(229).

2. NOTES.

273. וְהַנָּחָשׁ—*and-the-serpent*: §§ **49.** 1; **45.** 1; **90.** 1. *a.*

274. הָיָה—Ḳal Perf. 3 m. sg. of the פ' laryng. and ל"ה verb הָיָה *be*; meaning, *he-was*; corresponding form of the strong verb, קָטַל, § **82.** 1. *a.*

275. עָרוּם—*cunning*: a passive formation, § **91.** 1. *c.*

276. עָשָׂה—Ḳal Perf. 3 m. sg. of the פ' laryng. and ל"ה verb *make*; meaning, *he-made*; corresponding form of the strong verb, קָטַל, § **82.** 1. *a.*

277. אַף—'ăf—*also, even*: an adverb.

278. אָמַר—Ḳal Perf. 3 m. sg. of the פ"א verb אָמַר; meaning, *he-said*; cor. form of strong verb, קָטַל, § **77.** 2.

279. תֹּאכְלוּ—θô'-xᵉlû—*ye-shall-eat*; cf. וַיֹּאמֶר:

a. תּ = *you*, and with the affix וּ (plur.) indicates Impf. 2 pl. m.

b. The א, as in וַיֹּאמֶר, loses its force, and preform. has ô, § **79.** 1.

c. The ־ under כ is for ־ or =, §§ **79.** 2; **63.** R. 3.

280. וַתֹּאמֶר—wăt-tô''-mĕr—*and-she-said*:

a. On the form of Wâw Conversive with Impf. see § **70.** 2. *a.*

b. On the retrocession of the accent, § **70.** 3. *a.* (3).

c. On the vowel after תּ (ô), and the vowel under מ (ĕ), § **79.** 1, 2.

d. Ḳal Impf. 3 f. sg. of the פ"א verb אָמַר *say*; meaning, *she-will-say*; corresponding form of the strong verb, תִּקְטֹל.

281. נֹאכֵל—nô'-xēl—*we-may-eat*; cf. וַיֹּאמֶר:

a. נ, as in נַעֲשֶׂה (130), is connected with אֲנַחְנוּ.

b. א loses its force, and the preformative has ô, § **79.** 1, 2.

c. Ḳal Impf. 1 pl. com., of the פ"א verb אָכַל; meaning, *we-may-eat*; corresponding form of strong verb נִקְטֹל, § **63.** 10.

3. FORMS FOR SPECIAL STUDY.

וַיֹּאמֶר	הָיָה	תֹּאכְלוּ	וַיֹּאמֶר
וַתֹּאמֶר	עָשָׂה	תֹּאמְרוּ	וַתֹּאמֶר
נֹאכַל	בָּרָא	עֵץ־הַגָּן	וַיִּקְרָא
תֹּאכְלוּ	קָרָא	בְּתוֹךְ־הַגָּן	וַיַּבְדֵּל

4. OBSERVATIONS.

123. In verbs פ״א, the א, in Ḳāl Impf., loses its consonantal force, and the preceding vowel is always ô.

124. In verbs ל״ה, where the ה is merely a vowel-letter, and in verbs ל״א, where the א has lost its consonantal force, the ultimate ־ֵ of the root form (cf. קָטֵל) is rounded in the open syllable to ־ָ.

125. The prefix תּ with the affix וּ indicates an Impf. 2 m. pl.

126. Mêθĕğ is found with a long vowel in a closed syllable before Mäḳḳēf, and especially with an unchangeable long vowel.

127. Wâw Conversive with the Imperfect draws the accent from the ultima to the penult, provided the penult is not a *closed* syllable.

5. GRAMMAR-LESSON.

1. § 70. 1. *a. b*,   Use of Impf. and Perf. with **Wâw Conv.**
2. § 70. 2. *a. b*,   The form of the Conjunction.
3. § 70. 3. *a. b*,   The verbal form employed.
   1, 2,
4. § 70. 3. R. and Note.   Special cases.
5. § 73. 1—3. R. and   Laryngeal Verbs.
   Note.
6. § 84. 1, 2,   Bi-literal Verbs.

6. WORD-LESSON.

1. In the Word-Lists, under List VI., nouns numbered 46—60.
2. Make out a list of the new words in Genesis III. 1—2.

7. PRINCIPLES OF SYNTAX.—COMPARISON.

וְהַנָּחָשׁ הָיָה עָרוּם מִכֹּל חַיַּת הַשָּׂדֶה—*And the serpent was cunning from every* (= more cunning than any) *beast of the field.*

Principle 6.—Comparison is expressed by means of the prep. מִן.

8. EXERCISES.

1. To be translated into Hebrew:—(1) *The sun is larger than* (Heb., *great from*) *the moon;* (2) *The man is better than the woman;* (3) *The woman is better than the man;* (4) *We may eat of all good fruit;* (5) *She may eat from the fruit of the tree which is in the midst of the garden;* (6) *We may say, ye* (m.) *may say, she will say, I will say.*

2. To be translated into Hebrew:—(1) *God created the heavens, and made the luminaries;* (2) *He made* (the) *man in the sixth day, and rested in the seventh day;* (3) *He will sanctify the seventh day, and will rest in it;* (4) *The man will give food to the cattle, and to the fowl of the heavens, and will give* (Heb., *call*) *to them names.*

3. To be translated into English:—(1) שָׁבַת; (2) עָשָׂה וַיִּשְׁבֹּת; (3) הָלַכְתִּי וְאֶשְׁבֹּת; (4) יַעֲלֶה וְאָמַר; (5) תִּשְׁבֹּת; (6) וְאָמַרְתָּ; (7) פְּרוּ וּמִלְאוּ; וְיַקְדֵּשׁ הַנָּהָר יִפָּרֵד וְהָיָה לְאַרְבָּעָה רָאשִׁים.

4. To be written in English letters:—*The new words of Genesis III.* 1—2.

5. To be written with points and vowel-signs:—*Genesis III.* 1, 2. *from the unpointed text.*

6. To be described:[1]—The forms שָׁרְצוּ (1:21),[2] יִסְגֹּר (2:21), יִתֵּן (1:17), יִקְרָא (2:23), יַבְדֵּל (1:4), יְקַדֵּשׁ (2:3).

9. *TOPICS FOR STUDY.*

(1) Wâw Conversive with the Impf. (2) Wâw Conversive with the Perfect. (3) First radical of verbs פ"ן. (4) Hif'il Impf. with Wâw Conversive. (5) The ָה of ל"ה Impf's with Wâw Conversive. (6) Change of accent with Wâw Conversive. (7) D. l. after a disjunctive accent. (8) The use of Méθĕğ before Mäḳḳēf.

LESSON XXXII. GENESIS III. 3-5.

1. *NOTE-REVIEW.*

(1) מוֹת (231); (2) תְּמֻתוּן (231); (3) מִמֶּנּוּ (229); (4) וְרָע (199); (5) הוּא (Principle 5).

2. *NOTES.*

282. תִגְּעוּ—θiğ-g^e‘û—*ye-shall-touch*, for תִנְגְּעוּ:

a. תְ, with וּ, indicates Impf. 2 m. pl.
b. נ, the first radical, is assimilated, §§ 78. 2. a.
c. A new disjunctive accent called Tîfḥâ; §§ 22. 10; 24. 6.
d. Ḳăl Impf. 2 m. pl. of the פ"ן and ל' laryng. verb נָגַע *touch;* meaning, *ye-shall-touch;* corresponding form of strong verb, תִּקְטְלוּ.

---

[1] The description of a verb includes a statement of (1) the stem, (2) tense, (3) pers., gen., num., (4) class, (5) root, with its meaning, (6) meaning of the form, (7) corresponding form of קָטַל ; this order is to be followed rigidly.

[2] These figures refer to the chapter and verse of the text in which the form occurs.

Lesson 32.

283. תִּגְּעוּ בּוֹ פֶּן—The D. l. in בְּ and פֶּ, § 12. 3.

284. תְּמָתוּן—tᵉmû-θûn—ye-shall-die; cf. תִּגְּעוּ:

a. ן, with וּ (וּן archaic § 63. R. 3). indicates Impf. 2 m. pl.
b. The root is מוּת die; ־ is defective for וּ, § 6. 4. N. 2.

285. יֹדֵעַ—yô-dē(ă)'—knowing, = knows; cf. זֶרַע:

a. Ḳăl act. part. sg. masc. of the פ״י and ל laryngeal verb יָדַע, know meaning, knowing; corresponding form, קֹטֵל.
b. The ־ under ע is Păθăḥ-furtive, §§ 76. 1. c. (3).

286. אָכָלְכֶם—'ŏχŏl-χĕm—your-eating; cf. אָכְלָה:

a. The ־ under כ is ŏ deflected from original ŭ, § 71. 3. a. (1)
b. Ḳăl Inf. const., with pronominal suffix כֶם.

287. וְנִפְקְחוּ—and-will-be-opened:

a. The וְ is Wâw Conversive with the Perfect, § 70. 2. b.
b. The נ is the characteristic of the Nif‛ăl, § 59. 2.
c. Nif‛ăl Perf. 3 c. plur. of the ל laryng. verb פָּקַח open; meaning, they-were-opened; corresponding form, נִקְטְלוּ.

288. עֵינֵיכֶם—‛ê-nê-χĕm—your eyes:

a. Eye עַיִן [two] eyes עֵינַיִם; [two] eyes-of עֵינֵי, § 107. 6.
b. The grave suffix כֶם, always accented, § 51. 1. a.

289. וִהְיִיתֶם—wĭh-yî-θĕm—and-ye-shall-be:

a. וְ, so written before a consonant with šᵉwâ, is Wâw Conversive.
b. תֶם is the personal termination of the Perf. 2 m. plur.
c. First radical ה, second י, third י; ־ under ה silent.

290. כֵּאלֹהִים—kê'-lô-ḥîm—like-God:

a. For כֵּאלֹהִים according to § 47. 3; but א is weak and loses its consonantal force, and šᵉwâ disappears with it. The vowel under כ then becomes ־ in compensation for the quiescent א, § 47. R. 1.

291. יֹדְעֵי—yô-dᵉ‛ê—knowers-of; cf. יֹדֵעַ (285):

a. The m. plur. const. of יֹדֵעַ; note the ending ־ֵי.

Lesson 32.

3. FORMS FOR SPECIAL STUDY.

עֵינַיִם	יִהְיֶה	נִפְקְחוּ	לֵאמֹר	יֹאכַל	יִתֵּן
עֵינֵיכֶם	וִהְיִיתֶם	נִקְטָל	כֵּאלֹהִים	תֹּאכַל	תִּתֵּן

4. OBSERVATIONS.

128. The ending יִ֑ is the construct ending of *dual* as well as of plural nouns.

129. The letter ה, of הָיָה *be*, always takes simple (silent) Šᵉwâ, unless it is initial.

130. The Nif'äl Perfect and Participle have the prefix נִ.

131. When a consonant is elided after a short vowel, that vowel is strengthened in compensation and becomes unchangeable.

132. Any 3 *masc.* sg. verbal form of the Imperfect may be made 3 *fem.* sg. by change of י to ת.

5. GRAMMAR-LESSON.

1. § **74.** Tabular view, Inflection of עָטַל in Ḳäl, Nif'äl and Hif'îl stems.
2. § **74. 1,** Rejection of D. f. by the laryngeal.
3. § **74. 2.** *a, b,* Preference of laryngeals for *a*-class vowels.
4. § **74. 3.** *a—d,* Preference of laryngeals for comp'd Šᵉwâ.
5. § **42. 1—3,** Peculiarities of laryngeals (*to be read*).

Note 1.—In the study of this class of verbs, (1) examine closely the synopses, noting the variations from the strong verb, (2) analyze exhaustively all forms given under § **74.** with which you are familiar, (3) master thoroughly the sections indicated to be learned, (4) write *without help* a complete paradigm of the Ḳäl, Nif'äl and Hif'îl stems, (5) compare the result with the paradigm given in the grammar.

Note 2.—In the study of פ׳ laryng. verbs use for practice (1) עָמַד *stand*, (2) עָבַד *serve*, (3) חָזַק *be strong*.

6. WORD-LESSON.

1. In the Word-Lists, under List VI., nouns numbered 61-76.
2. Make out a list of the new words in Genesis III. 3—5.

7. PRINCIPLES OF SYNTAX.

כִּי יֹדֵעַ אֱלֹהִים—*For God* (is) *knowing*=For God knows.

בְּיוֹם אֲכָלְכֶם מִמֶּנּוּ וְנִפְקְחוּ עֵינֵיכֶם—*In the day of your eating from it,* THEN *will be opened your eyes.*

Principle 7.—The participle is often used for the present tense.

Principle 8.—The conjunction ו is frequently used "to connect a statement of time with the clause to which it relates."

8. EXERCISES.

1. To be translated into Hebrew:—(1) *She caused to serve;* (2) *He will be strong;* (3) *She was served;* (4) *I caused to stand;* (5) *They will cause to stand;* (6) *Thou* (f.) *wilt be served;* (7) *It will be said;* (8) *She will abandon;* (9) *Ye* (m.) *did abandon;* (10) *I shall be served;* (11) *Be thou served;* (12) *To be abandoned;* (13) *We shall serve;* (14) *Ye* (m.) *shall stand;* (15) *Be strong.*

2. To be translated into Hebrew:—(1) *Serving thou shalt serve God;* (2) *And the man saw the good fruit;* (3) *And the woman saw that the fruit was good;* (4) *Their eyes were opened;* (5) *In the day of your ruling the earth;* (6) *The woman will eat the fruit, and of* (= *from*) *it she will give to her husband, who will eat with her.*

3. To be translated into English:—(1) לָקְחָה הָאִשָּׁה אֶת־הַפְּרִי; (2) וַתִּתֵּן לָאִישׁ; (3) מִי יִתֵּן אֶת־הַפְּרִי הַזֶּה לָאִשָּׁה הַזֹּאת; (4) הָאִישׁ יֹאכַל אֶת־פְּרִי הָעֵץ; (5) וַיַּעֲמֹד הָאִישׁ בַּגַּן; אֱלֹהִים אָמַר יְהִי־אוֹר.

4. To be written in English letters:—*The new words of Genesis III. 3—5*.

5. To be written with points and vowel-signs:—*Genesis III. 3-5, from the unpointed text*.

6. To be described:—The forms עֲשׂוֹת, יַעֲזֹב־, יַעֲלֶה, תֵּרָאֶה, אֶעֱשֶׂה, נַעֲשָׂה, עָבַד.

9. *TOPICS FOR STUDY.*

(1) Dual abs. affix. (2) Dual const. affix. (3) ה with ָ. (4) *And-he-saw, and-she-saw.* (5) Formation of feminine nouns. (6) Synopsis in Hîf. of שָׂכַל. (7) The א of verbs פ״א. (8) The vowel of the Preformative in Ḳăl Impf. of verbs פ״א. (9) The stem-vowel of verbs פ״א in the Ḳăl Impf.

LESSON XXXIII. GENESIS III. 6-8.
1. *NOTE-REVIEW.*

(1) הָיָה (274); (2) תִּגְּעוּ (282); (3) וַיִּהְיוּ (269); (4) וַיַּעַשׂ (87); (5) וַיְבָרֶךְ (114); (6) יַעֲלֶה (179); (7) נִשְׁמַת (186).

2. *NOTES.*

292. וַתֵּרֶא—wăt-tē'-rē'—*and-(she)-saw;* cf. וַיַּרְא *and-(he)-saw:*

a. Full form תֵּרָאֶה (cf. יִהְיֶה), but ה ֶ never stands with Wăw conversive (§ 82. 5. *b*); ֶ standing under the tone, becomes ֵ (§ 82. 5. *b.* (4)); and a helping ֶ is inserted after ר (§ 29. 4. *b.*)

293. תַּאֲוָה—(a) *delight:* a noun formed by prefix ת, § 93.

294. לָעֵינַיִם—*to-the-[two]-eyes:* §§ 45. R. 3; 106. 5. *a.*

295. נֶחְמָד—nĕḥ-mād—*desirable:*

a. Nif. part. of the 'פ laryng. verb חָמַד *desire;* meaning, *desired* or *desirable;* corresponding form נִקְטָל, but the ־ has become ־ִ before ח, § 74. 2. *b.*

b. The strong laryngeal ח has simple (silent) šᵉwâ, § 74. 3. *b.*

296. לְהַשְׂכִּיל—lᵉhăś-kîl—*to-make-wise:*

a. Hîf. Inf. const. of שָׂכַל *be wise;* corresponding form הַקְטִיל.

b. Synopsis: הִשְׂכִּיל, יַשְׂכִּיל, הַשְׂכֵּל, הַשְׂכִּיל, מַשְׂכִּיל;
—note the ־ַ under preformative, except in Perfect.

297. מִפִּרְיוֹ—*from-its-fruit:* (1) וְ, (2) מִן, (3) פְּרִי.

298. וַתִּתֵּן—*and-she-gave:* feminine of וַיִּתֵּן (94).

299. עִמָּהּ—ʾim-mâh—*with-her;* preposition עִם:

c. ־ָהּ, arising from ־ָהָ, is âh, not åh.

300. וַתִּפָּקַחְנָה—*and-*(they, f.)*-were-opened;* cf. יָקוּ:

a. Nifʿăl (note D. f. *in* and ־ַ under פ), Impf. 3 fem. (־נָה) plur. of the לֹ׳ laryngeal root פָּקַח; corresponding form תִּקָּטַלְנָה.

301. עֵינֵי—ʿê-nê—*eyes-of;* cf. עֵינֵיכֶם (288), עֵינַיִם (294).

302. וַיֵּדְעוּ—wăy-yê-ḏᵉʿû—*and-they-knew:*

a. Ḳăl Impf. 3 m. plur. of the פ׳׳י and לֹ׳ laryng. verb יָדַע *know.*

b. Corresponding form, יִקְטְלוּ; the first radical י, being weak, drops out, and ־ִ now standing in an open syl., becomes ־ֵ, § 80. 2. *a.* (1).

c. Méθĕḡ with long vowel before vocal šᵉwâ pretonic, § 18. 2.

303. עֵירֻמִּים—ʿê-rŭm-mîm—*naked:* irregular plural of עֵירֹם.

304. הֵם—hēm—*they* (m.): cf. the other form הֵמָּה, pron. suf. הֶם.

305. וַיִּתְפְּרוּ—wăy-yiθ-pᵉrû—*and-they-sewed:*

a. Ḳăl Impf. 3 m. sg. of תָּפַר *sew;* cor. form, יִקְטְלוּ; 3 m. sg. יִתְפֹּר.

b. Synopsis: תָּפַר, יִתְפֹּר, תְּפֹר, תָּפוֹר, תֹּפֵר, תָּפֻר.

306. עֲלֵה—ᵃlê(h)—*leaf-of:* abs. sg. עָלֶה.

307. תְּאֵנָה—θᵉʾē-nå(h)—*fig-tree:* note the Zåḳēf-ḳåṭōn.

LESSON 33.

308. וַיַּעֲשׂוּ—wăy-yă'-ăśû—and-they-made; cf. וַיַּעַשׂ and-he-made.
309. וַיִּשְׁמְעוּ—and-they-heard; cf. וַיִּתְפְּרוּ (305).
310. קוֹל—kôl—voice; cf. כָּל (kōl) all.
311. מִתְהַלֵּךְ—walking: Hiθpă'ēl participle of הָלַךְ walk.
312. וַיִּתְחַבֵּא—and-(he)-hid-himself; cf. מִתְהַלֵּךְ.

3. FORMS FOR SPECIAL STUDY.

יִשְׁמְעוּ	יֵדְעוּ	יִתְפְּרוּ	יִשְׁמְעוּ

4. OBSERVATIONS.

133. Of two šᵉwâs in the middle of a word the first is silent, the second is vocalized.

134. Where a closed syllable would have ĭ, an open syllable has ē.

5. GRAMMAR-LESSON.

1. § 74. Tabular View, Synopses of עָטַל in Pī'ēl, Pŭ'ăl, Hīθpă'ēl, and Ḥŏf'ăl.
2. § 74. 2. a—b. Preference of the laryngeal for ă.
3. § 74. 3. a—d. Preference of the laryng. for comp'd šᵉwâ.
4. § 42. 1—3, Peculiarities of laryngeals (to be read).

Note 1.—In the study of this class of verbs (1) examine closely the synopses, noting the variations from the strong verb, (2) analyze exhaustively all familiar forms given under § 74. 1-3, (3) master thoroughly the sections indicated to be learned, (4) write *without help* a complete paradigm of the verb, and (5) compare the result with the paradigm given in the grammar.

Note 2.—In this study of 'פ laryng. verbs, use for practice (1) חָמַד *desire*, (2) עָזַב *forsake*, (3) עָלַם *conceal*, (4) הָפַךְ *turn*.

6. WORD-LESSON.

1. In the Word-Lists, under List VII., the nouns numbered 77—84.
2. Make out a list of the new words in Genesis III. 6—8.

7. EXERCISES.

1. To be translated into Hebrew:—(1) *He will desire;* (2) *He was caused to turn;* (3) *She was abandoned* (Pŭ'äl עזב); (4) *She will conceal herself* (Hiθp.); (5) *They will be caused to stand;* (6) *We shall be forsaken* (Nif.); (7) *Thou* (f.) *wilt be desired* (Nif.) (8) *She will be caused to turn;* (9) *Be thou* (f.) *desirable* (Nif.); (10) *Cause ye* (m.) *to forsake;* (11) *Be ye* (m.) *caused to forsake.*

2. To be translated into Hebrew:—(1) *And the woman saw that the fruit was good and she desired it;* (2) *She took the fruit and gave it to the man;* (3) *I caused the man to serve God;* (4) *The man was forsaken in the garden;* (5) *The woman turned herself and saw the man who was standing under the tree.*

3. To be translated into English:—(1) לָקְחָה הָאִשָּׁה מִפְּרִי (2) הָעֵץ וַתֵּרֶא כִּי טוֹב וַתֹּאכַל מִמֶּנּוּ יַעֲזֹב הָאִישׁ אָבִיו; (3) וְאִמּוֹ וְדָבַק בְּאִשְׁתּוֹ; וַיִּתֵּן אֶת הָאִישׁ לַעֲבֹד אֶת־הָאֲדָמָה; (5) נֶחְמָד הַפְּרִי לְהַשְׂכִּיל; (6) מִתְהַלֵּךְ אֱלֹהִים בַּגָּן; (4) וַתִּתְחַבֵּא הָאִשָּׁה וַתַּעַשׂ לָהּ חֲגוֹרָה.

4. To be written in English letters:—*The new words of Genesis III. 6—8.*

5. To be written with points and vowel-signs:—*Genesis III. 6—8.*

6. To be written out:—*Synopses of* עָמַד *and* חָמַד *in all stems.*

7. To be described:—The forms וַתֵּרֶא, יַעֲשֶׂה, נֶחְמָד, יַהֲפֹךְ, יַחְמֹד

8. TOPICS FOR STUDY.

(1) The peculiarities of laryngeals as seen in verbs פ laryng. (2) The meanings of Nīf'äl and Hiθpä'ēl stems. (3) The two ways of vocalizing Imperfect Ḳäl in פ laryng. verbs. (4) The differing grades of strength in the various laryngeals. (5) Compensation for the failure to double a laryngeal. (6) The common element in the Imperfect, Imperative and Infinitive Construct.

LESSON XXXIV. GENESIS III. 9-11.

1. NOTE-REVIEW.

(1) שְׁנֵיהֶם (88,270); (2) רוּחַ (15); (3) אִשְׁתּוֹ (268); (4) פְּנֵי (13);
(5) בְּתוֹךְ (41); (6) הַגָּן (189); (7) וַיִּקְרָא (29); (8) אָדָם (131).

2. NOTES.

313. אַיֶּכָּה—'ăy-yĕ'k-kă(h)—*where-(art)-thou?*:
a. אַי *where*, with union syllable ֶ־, § **71. 2.** *c.* (3).
b. כָה, a fuller writing for ךְ, the pronominal suffix.

314. שָׁמַעְתִּי—*I-heard;* corresponding form קָטַלְתִּי; cf. נָתַתִּי.

315. וָאִירָא—wă-'î-râ'—*and-I-was-afraid:*
a. וָ, the Wâw Convers., before a laryngeal, loses D. f. and becomes וָ.
b. א indicates the first person *I;* the root is יָרֵא *be-afraid.*
c. The accent Tᵉvîr (֛), and that under שָׁמַעְתִּי, Ṭifḥâ (֖), are disjunctives of the third class, § **22.** 10, 11.

316. וָאֵחָבֵא—wă-'ē-ḥâ-vē'—*and-I-hid-myself:*
a. On וָ and א see preceding note (315. *a*).
b. Nifʽâl Impf. 1 c. sg. of the פ' laryng. and ל"א verb חָבָא *hide.*
c. D. f. rejected from ח, and preceding vowel lowered, § **74.** 1.

317. הִגִּיד—(he) *made-known;* cf. הִמְטִיר, יַטֵּעַ, יִפַח:
a. Hiphʽîl (הִ) Perfect 3 sg. m. of the פ"ן verb נָגַד *make known.*
b. Cor. form, הַגִּיד, הַגֵּד, יַגִּיד, הַגֵּד, הַגִּיד; *Synopsis*, הִקְטִיל; מַגִּיד; the D. f. in ג is for the assimilated נ, § **78. 2.** *b.*

318. לְךָ—preposition לְ, with suffix ךָ, § **51.** 3.

319. אָתָּה—pausal for אַתָּה, §§ **50. 2; 38.** 2.

320. הֲמִן—hᵉmin—*?-from,* §§ **46.** 1; **48.**

321. צִוִּיתִךָ—ṣiw-wî-θí'-xă—*I-commanded-thee;* cf. וַיְצַו:
a. Piʽēl Perf. 1 sg. of the ל"י verb צָוָה *command,* § **82.**

b. Cor. form, קְטַלְתִּיךָ; but instead of לְ_ַ, we have יְ_ַ = î; § **82**. 3. *b.*

c. תִי = *I*; ךָ = *thee*; D. f. in ן, characteristic of Pĭ'ēl.

322. לְבִלְתִּי—*to-not*: prep. לְ, and בִלְתִּי, the neg. used with Inf's.

323. אֱכָל־—'ăχŏl+—(to)-*eat:* Ķăl Inf. const. before Măkķēf, § **17.** 2.

3. FORMS FOR SPECIAL STUDY.

יִתְחַבֵּא	שָׁמַעְתִּי בַגָּן	וָאִירָא
אֵחָבֵא	וָאִירָא כִּי	וָאֵחָבֵא

4. OBSERVATIONS.

135. וְ, before the *first* person (א), becomes וָ.

136. A dăğ. l. in an initial spirant will stand even when the preceding word closes with a vowel, if that word carries a disjunctive accent.

137. The Hĭθpă'ēl is generally reflexive; the Nif'ăl was originally reflexive, and in common usage frequently has this force.

5. GRAMMAR-LESSON.

1. § **75.** Tabular View, Synopses of קָאַל in Ķăl, Nĭf'ăl, Hĭf'îl and Hŏf'ăl stems.
2. § **75.** 1. *a, b,* and N. 1-3, Rejection of D. f. by the laryngeal.
3. § **75.** 2. *a-c*, Preference of the laryngeal for ă.
4. § **75.** 3, Preference of the laryngeal for comp'd Š⁽ᵉ⁾wâ.
5. § **42.** 1-3, Peculiarities of laryngeals (*to be read*).

6. WORD-LESSON.

1. Make out a list of the new words in Genesis III. 9—11.

7. PRINCIPLES OF SYNTAX.

בָּרָא אֱלֹהִים אֵת הַשָּׁמַיִם—*God created the heavens.*
וַיְבָרֶךְ אֹתָם אֱלֹהִים—*And God blessed them.*
אֶת־קֹלְךָ שָׁמַעְתִּי בַגָּן—*Thy voice I heard in the garden.*

Principle 9.—The object of the verb generally stands *after* both predicate and subject; but if the object is pronominal it stands between the predicate and subject; or, if the object is to be emphasized, it stands *before* both predicate and subject.

8. EXERCISES.

1. To be translated into Hebrew:—(1) *He will redeem;* (2) *Redeem thou* (f.); (3) *They* (m.) *will redeem;* (4) *Thou* (f.) *wilt be redeemed;* (5) *We were redeemed;* (6) *I shall cause to redeem;* (7) *They caused to redeem;* (8) *He was caused to redeem;* (9) *Being caused to redeem;* (10) *To cause to redeem.*

2. To be translated into Hebrew:—(1) *Thou didst hear the voice of God from the heavens;* (2) *Let us make for ourselves large girdles;* (3) *They will hide themselves* (Nif. or Hiθp.) *in the garden;* (4) *This is the day in which God spoke to the man in the midst of the garden of Eden;* (5) *God will redeem the man and his seed;* (6) *The man will be redeemed in that day.*

3. To be translated into English: — (1) נִשְׁמַע קוֹל אֱלֹהִים (2) עַל־הָאָרֶץ; (3) מִי הִתְחַבֵּא מִפְּנֵי אֱלֹהִים; בָּרוּךְ אֱלֹהַי (4) הַשָּׁמַיִם; (5) בְּכָל־הָאָרֶץ הִמְשַׁל הָאָדָם נֶחְמְדָה הָאָרֶץ בְּעֵינֵי כָּל־הַבָּשָׂר.

4. To be written in English letters:—*The new words of Genesis III., 9—11.*

5. To be written with points and vowel-signs:—*Genesis III., 9—11 from the unpointed text.*

6. To be written out:—Synopses in Ḳăl, Nĭf. Hĭf. and Hŏf. of גָּאַל and שָׁחַת; and of גָּאַל in Pi'ēl, Pŭ'ăl and Hĭθp.

7. To be described:—יִגְאָלוּ, הִגְאִילָה, נִגְאַלְתֶּם, גֹּאֲלִי, יִבְחַר.

9. TOPICS FOR STUDY.

(1) Wâw Conversive before א. (2) Cases of Nĭf. and Hĭθp. stems in Gen. III. 7—11; (3) Synopses of the strong verb קָטַל; (4) The personal pronoun; (5) The inseparable prepositions; (6) Wâw Conversive with Perfect and Imperfect; (7) Synopses of ע״י laryng. verb in Ḳăl, Nĭf. Hĭf. and Ḥŏf. stems.

LESSON XXXV. GENESIS III. 12-14.

1. NOTE-REVIEW.

(1) מִמֶּנּוּ (229); (2) הָאָדָם (131); (3) אִשָּׁה (255); (4) מִן (49); (5) וַתֹּאמֶר (280); (6) הַנָּחָשׁ (273); (7) בְּהֵמָה (125); (8) חַיַּת (128); (9) הַשָּׂדֶה (10) תֹּאכַל (228).

2. NOTES.

324. נָתַתָּה—nâ-θăt-tâ(h)—*thou-gavest;* cf. קָטַלְתָּ:

a. Ḳăl Perf. 2 sg. m. of the פ״נ verb נָתַן, § 78. 2. R. 3.

b. The vowel-letter ה at the end is not usual; the ending is generally תָּ.

325. עִמָּדִי—'ĭm-mâ-dî—*with-me:* note Zâḳēf ḳâṭon, § 24. 4.

326. הִוא נָתְנָה־לִּי—hî' nâ-θᵉnâ(h)l+lî—*she gave+to-me,* § 15. 3:

a. The pronoun used as subject of a verb is expressed whenever, as here, it is emphatic.

Lesson 35.

327. וָאֹכַל—wă-'ô-ẋēl—*and-I-ate;* cf. וָאֲחַבָּא, וָאִירָא:

a. אֹכַל is for אֹאכַל, of which the radical א is lost, § **79**. 1. N.

b. וָ, the form of Wâw Conversive with the Impf., becomes וְ before א, § **70**. 2. a. (3).

328. מַה־זֹּאת—mă(h)z+zô(')θ—*what+this?* §§ **54**. 2. *a*; **52**. 1. *b*.

329. עָשִׂית—*thou-*(f.)*-hast-done;* ת=*thou* (f.); on ◌ִ see § **82**. 3. *b*.

330. הִשִּׁיאַ֫נִי—hĭš-šî-'ă-nî—(he) *deceived-me;* cf. הִגִּיד:

a. נִי is the pron. suf. of 1st pers., ◌ַ the so-called connecting vowel.

b. הִשִּׁיא Hîf. Perf. 3 m. sg. of נָשָׁא, נ being assim., § **78**. 2. *b*.

331. עָשִׂ֫יתָ זֹּאת—'ă-śî-θă-zô(')θ—*thou-*(m.)*-hast-done this:*

a. עָשִׂית=*thou-*(f.)*-hast-done;* עָשִׂ֫יתָ = *thou-*(m.)*-hast-done.*

b. D. f. in זֹ is conj., § **15**. 3; accent over זֹּאת, Sĕḡôltâ, § **24**. 3.

332. אָרוּר—'ă-rûr—*cursed;* Ḳăl Part. Pass. of אָרַר, § **68**. 1. *c.*

333. גְּחֹנְךָ—*thy-belly;* cf. מְאֹרַת, גְּדֹלִים:

a. The absolute form is גָּחוֹן but with suffix גְּחוֹן § **109**. 1. *a.*

b. The ô is here written defectively; the suffix is ךָ with ◌ְ.

334. תֵּלֵךְ—θē-lēẋ—*thou-shalt-go:*

a. The root is הָלַךְ, or יָלַךְ, § **80**. 2. R. 3.

b. The prefix ת = *thou* (m.); cor. form of קָטַל is תִּקְטֹל.

335. יְמֵי—*days-of;* sg. יוֹם, plur. יָמִים, plur. const. יְמֵי.

336. חַיֶּ֫יךָ—ḥăy-yé'-ẋă—*thy-lives;* from the plur. חַיִּים:

a. On the vowel ◌ֶ (ê) see § **30**. 5 and *b*.

3. FORMS FOR SPECIAL STUDY.

הִגִּיד	מִי	עָשִׂ֫יתָ	נְתָנָה־לִי	אָכַ֫לְתְּ	אַתָּה
הִשִּׁיא	מַה־	עָשִׂית	עָשִׂ֫יתָ זֹּאת	נָתַ֫תָּה	אָכַ֫לְתָּ

4. OBSERVATIONS.

138. The radical נ, when it would stand at the end of a syllable, and before a dental consonant is assimilated.

139. The Interrog. pronouns are מִי *who?*, and מָה · *what?*.

140. תָּ = *thou* (m.), תְּ = *thou* (f.), but both have their soft sound (θ) when a vowel precedes.

141. D. f. conj. may or may not be accompanied by Măḳḳēf.

142. The personal termination תָּ *thou* (m.) is generally written without, though sometimes with, the vowel-letter ה .

5. GRAMMAR-LESSON.

1. § **76.** Tabular View, Synopses of קָטַח in Ḳăl, Nĭf. Hĭf. and Hŏf. stems.
2. § **76.** 1. *a, b,* Preference of the laryngeal for ă.
3. § **76.** 1. *c,* Insertion of Păθăḥ-furtive.
4. § **76.** 1. *d,* Insertion of ֵ in Perfects 2 f. sg.
5. § **76.** 2, Preference of the laryng. for comp'd Šᵉwâ.
6. **42.** 1—3, Peculiarities of laryngeals (*to be learned*).

Note 1.—Treat as directed in former Lessons the familiar forms in § **76.** 1, 2.

Note 2.—In the study of לְ laryngeal verbs use for practice (1) מָשַׁח *anoint*, (2) שָׁלַח *send*, (3) שָׁבַע *swear*, (4) שָׁמַע *hear*.

6. WORD-LESSON.

1. In the Word-Lists, under List VII., nouns numbered 85—94.
2. Make out a list of the new words in Genesis III. 12—14.

7. EXERCISES.

1. To be translated into Hebrew:—(1) *I will anoint;* (2) *He will cause to anoint;* (3) *Sending, sent;* (4) *Thou* (f.) *didst hear;* (5) *He will send;* (6) *I swore* (Nĭf.); (7) *I will swear;* (8) *She caused to send;* (9) *To anoint;* (10) *Cause thou* (m.) *to send;* (11) *To be sent.*

2. To be translated into Hebrew:—(1) *He told the man that he was good;* (2) *Hast thou eaten fruit from the tree of lives?* (3) *Who gave the woman to the man?* (4) *He gave me fruit and I ate;* (5) *She gave him fruit and he ate;* (6) *I gave her fruit and we ate.*

3. To be translated into English:—(1) יָמוּת הָאָכֵל מִן־הָעֵץ; (2) מִי עָשָׂה זֹאת; (3) הִשִּׁיא הַנָּחָשׁ אֶת־הָאִשָּׁה וַתֹּאכַל; (4) מַה־נָּתְנָה; (5) הֲמִן־הַמַּיִם לָקַחְתָּ; (6) הֲגָדֵל אַתָּה מִמֶּנּוּ; הָאִשָּׁה לָאִישׁ.

4. To be written in English letters:—*The new words of Genesis III. 12—14.*

5. To be written with points and vowel-signs:—*Genesis III. 12—14 from the unpointed text.*

6. To be written out:—Synopses of מָשַׁח, בָּטַח, and שָׁמַע in Ķăl, Nĭf., Hĭf. and Ḫŏf. stems.

7. To be described:—The forms יִצְמַח, יִפַּח, יִטַּע, יַצְמַח, זֶרַע, הִשְׁבַּעַתְּ, יְדַעַתְּ, שְׂמֹחַ, הַשְׁלַח, מַזְרִיעַ, יֵדַע.

8. *TOPICS FOR STUDY.*

(1) The נ of verbs פ״נ in the Hĭf. (2) Hē Interrogative. (3) The negative used with the Infinitive. (4) The peculiarities of the verb נָתַן. (5) וְ before א. (6) D. f. conjunctive. (7) The Interrogative pronouns. (8) תְּ and תָּה (9) Pāθăḥ-furtive. (10) The helping-vowel ־ֱ in Perfects 2 f. sg. (11) Synopses of the strong verb.

LESSON XXXVI.—GENESIS III. 15-17.

1. *NOTES.*

337. וְאֵיבָה—wᵉ'êvå(h)—*and-enmity:* a fem. noun, from root אָיַב.

338. אָשִׁית—*I-will-put;* א = I, the root being שִׁית (ע״י) *put:*

a. Observe the Rᵉvî(ă)‛, § 24. 5. b.

Lesson 36.

339. זַרְעֲךָ—*thy-seed;* זַרְעָהּ *her-seed;* cf. זַרְעוֹ *his-seed.*

340. יְשׁוּפְךָ—*he-shall-bruise-thee;* תְּשׁוּפֶנּוּ *thou-shalt-bruise-him.*

a. The Ḳal Impf. of שׁוּף is יָשׁוּף (3 m. sg.), תָּשׁוּף (2 m. sg.).

b. When the tone is shifted the â under ו and ת becomes ־ֻ.

c. ךָ with ־ְ = (m.); ־ֶנּוּ is the pron. suffix הוּ *him,* with the connecting syllable ־ֶנ־; § 71. 2. c. (3) and Note 1.

341. רֹאשׁ—*head,* and עָקֵב *heel* are accusative of specification.

342. הַרְבָּה—*causing-to-be-great:* irreg. for הַרְבֵּה, Hif. Inf. Abs. of רָבָה *multiply.*

343. אַרְבֶּה—*I-will-cause-to-be-great:* Hif. Impf. 1 sg. of רָבָה, § 82. 1. b.

344. עִצְּבוֹנֵךְ—'iṣ-ṣᵉvô-nēx—*thy-(f.)-sorrow:*

a. עִצָּבוֹן (root עָצַב, formative addition וֹן, § 103. 3) becomes עִצְּבוֹן when the tone is shifted, as before the pron. suffix, § 109. 1. a.

b. The 2 fem. pron. suf. is ךְ; ־ֵ is the so-called connecting vowel.

345. הֵרֹנֵךְ—*thy-conception:* הֵרוֹן with ךְ and ־ֵ, see 344. b.

a. Note that ־ֵ in the first syl. is away from the tone and in an apparently open syl. In reality, dăḡ. f. has been rejected from ר; hence an original ־ִ has become ־ֵ in compensation for the loss of doubling.

346. עֶצֶב—*sorrow:* an a-class Seġolate, § 89. 1.

347. תֵּלְדִי—tē-lᵉdî—*thou-(f.)-shall-bring-forth:*

a. For תּוֹלְדִי (cf. תִּקְטְלִי), but ו, being weak, drops out and ־ֹ, in an open syllable, becomes ־ֵ, § 80. 2. a.

b. Root יָלַד = וָלַד; Impf. 3 m. sg. יֵלֵד, for יוֹלֵד.

c. ת and ־ִי are fragments of אַתִּי, the older form of אַתְּ, § 50. 3. c.

348. בָּנִים—vă-nîm—*sons:* irreg. plur. of בֵּן *son.*

349. תְּשׁוּקָתֵךְ—tᵉšû-ḳâ-θēx—*thy-*(f.)-*desire:*

a. Abs. תְּשׁוּקָה, a feminine formation, § 98. R.
b. Const. תְּשׁוּקַת, suf. ךְ with ֵ ; cf. הֲרֹנֵךְ (345), עִצְּבוֹנֵךְ (344).
c. Before ךְ, ֵ = in an open syllable becomes ֵ , § 108. 2.

350. יִמְשָׁל־בָּךְ—yĭm-šŏl+bâx—*he-shall-rule+in-thee* (f.):

a. יִמְשָׁל־ for יִמְשֹׁל before Măḳḳēf, § 17. 2; cf. כָּל־, כֹּל.
b. בָּךְ = *in-thee* (f.); cf. בְּךָ *in-thee* (m.), § 51. 3.

351. אִשְׁתֶּךָ—'ĭš-tē'-xâ—*thy-wife;* pausal for אִשְׁתְּךָ, § 38. 1. N.:

a. ת indicates the feminine, here attached to אִישׁ; cf. const אֵשֶׁת.
b. Sᵉġôltâ repeated according to § 23. 6.
c. Another case of a short-vowel (ĕ) in an open syl. under the tone; cf. וַיְבָאֶהָ (256) and הַשִּׂיאַנִי (330).

352. אֲרוּרָה—fem. sg. of אָרוּר (332), Ḳăl Part. pass. of אָרַר *curse.*

353. בַּעֲבוּרֶךָ—bă-ᵃvû-rḗ-xâ—*on-account-of-thee:*

a. A compound preposition, בַּעֲבוּר = *on-account-of, for-the-sake-of.*
b. ךָ with the preceding ֵ changed to ֶ as in אִשְׁתֶּךָ, § 38. 1. N.
c. D. l. in ב because of preceding disjunctive, Ṭîfḥâ (֖), § 22. 10

354. תֹּאכֲלֶנָּה—tô'-xᵃlén-nă(h)—*thou-*(m.)-*shalt-eat-it:*

a. תֹּאכַל is Ḳăl Impf. 2 sg. masc. of אָכַל *eat,* § 79. 1.
b. ‎נָּה is for נָה, just as ‎נּוּ (in תְּשׁוּפֶנּוּ) was for ‎נְהוּ; note carefully § 71. 2. c. (3) and N. 1, 2.

2. FORMS FOR SPECIAL STUDY.

| אָרוּר | אִשְׁתֶּךָ | יִמְשָׁל־בָּךְ | עִצְּבוֹנֵךְ | תְּשׁוּפֶנּוּ |
| אֲרוּרָה | בַּעֲבוּרֶךָ | יַעֲזָב־אִישׁ | תְּשׁוּקָתֵךְ | תֹּאכֲלֶנָּה |

3. OBSERVATIONS.

144. In pausal forms there stands between the verb and the pronominal suffix a syllable, נֶ֫ ; instead of נְהוּ and נְהָ, we find נֶ֫נוּ and נֶ֫הָ.

145. Between the usual form of the noun and the 2 fem. sing. pron. suffix ךְ there stands the vowel ֵ . This may be called a connecting vowel.

146. The o of the Ḳâl Impf. is changeable (ō), and before Mâḳ-ḳēf ŏ appears instead.

147. The ְ which stands before the suffix ךְ is a reduction of an original ֵ, which in pause is restored, and deflected to ĕ.

148. The ֵ which stands directly before the tone is from an original ä; when the tone is shifted with affixes for gender and number, this ă, if in an open syllable, is reduced to Šᵉwâ.

4. GRAMMAR-LESSON.

1. § **78.** Tabular View,   Synopses of נָטַל in various stems.
2. § **78.** 1. *a, b*,   Loss of נ in Ḳâl Inf. const. and Imv.
3. § **78.** 2. *a, b*,   Assimilation of נ.
4. § **78.** 2. N. 1,   The preformative vowel in Hŏf'äl.
5. § **78.** 2. R's 2, 3,   The verbs לָקַח and נָתַן.

Note 1.—In the study of this class of verbs, follow the order indicated in previous Lessons, analyzing exhaustively the familiar forms given under § **78.** 1, 2 and Remarks 1—3.

Note 2.—Use for practice (1) נָגַד in Hif=*make known*, (2) נָפַל *fall*, (3) נָגַשׁ *approach*.

5. WORD-LESSON.

1. In the Word-Lists, under List VII., nouns numbered 95—104.
2. Make out a list of the new words in Genesis III. 15—17.

6. EXERCISES.

1. To be translated into Hebrew:—(1) *Approach thou, to approach;* (2) *She will approach, I shall approach;* (3) *They made known* (Hĭ.)*, thou* (f.) *wilt make known;* (4) *It will be made known;* (5) *I shall take, to take, take thou, taking;* (6) *Thou shalt give, I shall give, to give, give thou* (m.)*;* (7) *He will fall, he will cause to fall.*

2. To be translated into Hebrew:—(1) *Between thee and between me;* (2) *Between him and between her;* (3) *God made known to the woman that the man should rule over her;* (4) *Thou* (f.) *didst hear the voice of thy husband;* (5) *Cursed is the earth because thou didst eat from this tree;* (6) *I will give thee food all the days of thy lives.*

3. To be translated into English:— (1) תְּשׁוּקָתִי אֶל־הָאִישׁ;
(2) בְּעֶצֶב תֵּלֵד הָאִשָּׁה בָנִים; (3) נָתַתִּי לְךָ כֹּל אֲשֶׁר־לִי;
(4) לָתֵת לֵאלֹהִים הוּא טוֹב; (5) גַּשׁ אֶל־יְהוָֹה וּבָרֵךְ שְׁמוֹ.

4. To be written in English letters:—*The new words of Genesis III. 15—17.*

5. To be written with points and vowel-signs:—*Genesis III. 15—17 from the unpointed text.*

6. To be written out:—Synopses of the verb נגר in the Hĭf. and Hŏf., and of נפך in Ķăl, Nĭf., Pĭ'ēl, Hĭf., and Hŏf.

7. To be described:— The forms גֶּשֶׁת, גַּע, יִפַּח, יִטַּע, תִּגְּעוּ, יִקַּח, תֵּן, תֵּת, יִתֵּן, וַיַּפֵּל, הִשִּׂיא, הִגִּיד.

7. TOPICS FOR STUDY.

(1) Form of the pronominal suffix הוּ and of the pron. suf. הָ with נ ָ. (2) The pron. suf. of the 2 f. sg. (3) *Thou* (f.) *shalt bear.* (4) The accent Sᵉğōltâ; its *repetition.* (5) *Cursed* (m.), *Cursed* (f.). (6) Change from ָ to ĕ. (7) הָ and תָ. (8) Loss of נ.

(9) Assimilation of נ. (10) ַ in sharpened syllables. (11) Synopsis and peculiarities of לָקַח; of נָתַן. (12) Synopses of נָטַל in various stems.

LESSON XXXVII.—GENESIS III. 18-21.

1. *NOTES.*

355. תַּצְמִיחַ—*she-will cause-to-spring-forth:* Hîf. of צָמַח § 76. 1. c. (1).

356. לָךְ—pausal for לְךָ *for-thee* (m.); לָךְ = *for-thee* (f.).

357. וְאָכַלְתָּ—Accent on ultima, because of the Wâw Convers. §§ 21. 4; 70. 3. b.

358. בְּזֵעַת—bᵉzê-'âθ—*in-sweat-of;* const. of זֵעָה.

359. אַפֶּיךָ—'ăp-pê'-χå—*thy-nostrils;* from אַף *nose:*

a. Sg. אַף, dual אַפַּיִם, form before ךָ (or ךְ) אַפֵּי; cf. חַיֶּיךָ.
b. The Dåğēš-fŏrtē in פ also serves as Dåğēš-lēnē, § 13. 2. N. 1.
c. On the disjunctive accent Păštâ (֙) see §§ 22. 8; 23. 5, 6.

360. לֶחֶם—*bread;* cf. בֵּית לֶחֶם *Bethlehem.*

361. שׁוּבְךָ—*thy-returning;* Ḳăl Inf. const. with pron. suffix: This is a bi-literal verb, with forms differing from the corresponding triliteral forms; § 55. 3.

362. מִמֶּנָּה—*from-her:* for מִמֶּנָה; cf. מִמֶּנּוּ for מִמֶּנְהוּ, § 51. 5. b.

363. לֻקָּחַתָּ—lŭḳ-ḳå'ḥ-tå—*thou-wast-taken,* § 38. 2.

364. תָּשׁוּב—*thou-shalt-return;* cf. תָּמוּת (231) and שׁוּבְךָ (361):

a. Ḳăl Impf. 2 m. sg. of the biliteral verb שׁוּב *turn.*
b. תָּקְטֹל is for תִּקְטֹל, the ִ being attenuated, and the ְ becoming ō under the tone.

c. Note that ă in תָּשׁוּב has been rounded to â in an open syl. before the tone; and that ֵ has been lengthened to û.

365. חַוָּה—ḥăw-wå̄(h)—*Eve;* cf. חַיָּה *life.*

366. הוּא—*she.* This is an example of the usage of $K^e\theta iv$ and $K^e r\hat{\imath}$; see § 19. The consonants here (i. e., the $K^e\theta iv$) call for the pointing הוּא; the vowel (i. e., the $K^e r\hat{\imath}$) requires the reading הִיא. This is the regular way of writing *she* in the Pentateuch; § 50. 3. a.

367. הָיְתָה—hå-y$^e\theta$å(h)—*she-was:*

a. Ḳăl Perf. 3 f. sg. of the פ׳ laryng., and ל״ה verb הָיָה *be*, § 82. 4.

b. Mĕθĕğ with a long vowel before vocal $\check{s}^e$wå pretonic, § 18. 2.

368. אֵם—but אִמּוֹ (266): אֵם is for אִמְם, § 100. 1. a.

369. חָי—pausal for חַי; an adjective meaning *living.*

370. כָּתְנוֹת—kŏθ-nôθ—*tunics-of;* const. pl. of כְּתֹנֶת.

371. וַיַּלְבִּשֵׁם—wăy-yăl-bî-šēm—*and-he-caused-them-to-put-on:*

a. Hîf. Impf. 3 m. sg. of לָבַשׁ, with suffix ם joined by ִ.

b. The ִ under בּ is î, though written defectively.

2. FORMS FOR SPECIAL STUDY.

1. Verbal Forms:— לָקַחַת, שׁוּבְךָ, תֹּאכַל, וְאָכַלְתָּ, תַּצְמִיחַ, וַיַּלְבִּשֵׁם, וַיַּעַשׂ, הָיְתָה, תָּשׁוּב.

2. Nominal Forms:— עוֹר, קוֹץ, אָדָם, עָפָר, לֶחֶם, עֵשֶׂב.

3. PRINCIPLES OF SYNTAX.

בְּזֵעַת אַפֶּיךָ תֹּאכַל לֶחֶם—*In,* or *at the cost of, the sweat of thy nostrils* (=face) *thou shalt eat bread.*

Principle 10.—The preposition בְּ may denote the condition *in* which, or the cost *at* which a thing may be done, i. e., the manner or the price.

4. GRAMMAR-LESSON.

1. § **79.** 1, 2,   The peculiarities of verbs פ״א.
2. § **83.** Tabular View,   Synopses of קָטַא in various stems.
3. § **83.** 1,   Final א in verbs ל״א.
4. § **83.** 2. *a*, *b*, 3. *a—c*,   Medial א in verbs ל״א.

Note 1.—In the study of verbs פ״א and ל״א, follow the order indicated in previous lessons, analyzing exhaustively the familiar forms given under §§ **79.** 1, 2 and **83.** 1—3, and Remarks.

Note 2.—Use for practice (1) אָמַר *say*, (2) מָצָא *find*, (3) קָרָא *call*.

5. WORD-LESSON.

1. In the Word-Lists, under List VII., nouns numbered 105—115.
2. Make out a list of the new words in Genesis III., 11—21.

6. EXERCISES.

1. To be translated into Hebrew:—(1) *Ye will say, I shall say, she will say, thou* (f.) *wilt say;* (2) *I shall eat, we shall eat, they will eat;* (3) *He will be created, he will cause to call, he was created, he will be caused to call;* (4) *They called, she caused to find, thou* (f.) *wilt find;* (5) *I created, ye were created, thou wast caused to call, we filled* (Pi'ēl); (6) *They* (f.) *will call, ye* (f.) *will be created, call ye* (f.).

2. To be translated into Hebrew:—(1) *The earth caused to sprout forth for man grass and herbs and thorns and thistles;* (2) *We found in the field the fruit which God commanded* (צִוָּה) *not to eat;* (3) *The man shall die, and unto the dust he shall return;* (4) *I shall call the name of my wife Eve;* (5) *I have found my mother;* (6) *Eve was the wife of* (אִישׁ) *Adam, and the mother of all living;* (7) *Adam was Eve's husband.*

3. To be translated into English:—(1) מִי הָיָה אִישׁ חַוָּה ;(2) לָקַח הָאָדָם ;(3) בָּרָא אֱלֹהִים אֶת־הָאָדָם וְאִשְׁתּוֹ וַיַּלְבִּשֵׁם יָמוּת כֹּל אֲשֶׁר (5) עָפָר אָנֹכִי וְאֶל־עָפָר אָשׁוּב (4); מִן־הֶעָפָר בְּאַפָּיו נִשְׁמַת חַיִּים.

4. To be written in English letters:—*The new words of Genesis III. 18—21.*

5. To be written with points and vowel-signs:—*Genesis III. 18—21 from the unpointed text.*

6. To be written out:—Synopses of אָמַר in the Ḳāl and Hīf. stems, of בָּרָא in Ḳāl and Nif., and of מָצָא in Pi'ēl and Hīf.

7. To be described:—The Forms בָּרָא, נֹאכַל, תֹּאכַל, וַיֹּאמֶר, בְּרֵאתָ, מָלֵאת, בְּרָאתִי, נָשָׁאָה, יִקְרָא, תִּדְשָׁא, יִקְרָא, תִּקְרֶאנָה.

7. TOPICS FOR STUDY.

(1) The primary form of קְטֹל. (2) The form שׁוּב. (3) אִם, אִמּוֹ. (4) Peculiarities of verbs פ״א, (5) Inflection of אָטֵל in Ḳāl Impf. (6) Peculiarities of verbs ל״א. (7) Synopses of קָטָא in various stems. (8) Inflection of קָטָא in Ḳāl Perf., in other Perfects, in Impf's and Imv's.

LESSON XXXVIII.—GENESIS III. 22-24.

1. *NOTES.*

372. הֵן—*hēn*—*behold:* same as הִנֵּה (145).

373. כְּאַחַד מִמֶּנּוּ—*like-one-of[from]-us:*

a. אַחַד is the construct of אֶחָד; here followed by a preposition.

b. מִמֶּנּוּ is the form of מִן with נוּ *us*, § **51.** 5. *a;* cf. מִמֶּנּוּ for מִמֶּנְהוּ.

Lesson 38.

374. לָדַ֫עַת—to-know: Ḳăl Inf. const. of יָדַע know, § 80. 2. (3); לְ, § 47. 5.

375. וָחָ֑י—wă-ḥāy—and-(he-should)-live:

a. וָ is Wăw Conversive with Perf., the ָ being pretonic, § 70. 2. b.
b. חָי is Ḳăl Perf. 3 m. sg. of the ע״י verb חָיָה live, § 85. 1.

376. וַֽיְשַׁלְּחֵ֫הוּ — wăy-šăl-lᵉḥē-hû — and-(= therefore)-(he)-sent-him:

a. D. f. of Wăw Convers. omitted from י because it has not a full vowel.
b. Pī‘ēl Impf. 3 m. sg. of the ל׳ laryngeal verb שָׁלַח send; corresponding form, יְקַטְּלֵ֫הוּ
c. The pron. suffix הוּ joined to the verb by the vowel ֵ.

377. לַעֲבֹד—to-till: Ḳăl Inf. const., §§ 74. 3. a; 47. 3.

378. אֲשֶׁר ....מִשָּׁם—which ....from-there, = whence.

379. וַיְגָ֫רֶשׁ—wăy-ğā'-rĕš—and-he-drove-out:

a. This is for וַיְגָרֵשׁ, like וַיְקַדֵּשׁ, or וַיְקַטֵּל: but
b. The י, having only a šᵉwâ, drops its D. f., while ר rejects its D. f., and ֵ under ג becomes ָ in compensation.
c. The accent being drawn to the penult by וַ, ֶ appears instead of ֵ.
d. Pī‘ēl Impf. 3 masc. sg. of the ע׳ laryngeal verb גֵּרֵשׁ drive out, § 75. 1. a.

380. וַיַּשְׁכֵּן—wăy-yăš-kēn—and-he-caused-to-dwell; cf. וַיַּבְדֵּל:

a. Hĭf. Impf. 3 m. sg. (with ֵ, not י) from שָׁכַן dwell, § 70. 3. R.

381. הַכְּרֻבִים—hăk-kᵉrû-vîm—the-cherubim; ְ for וּ; singular כְּרוּב.

382. הַמִּתְהַפֶּ֫כֶת—hăm-mĭṯ-hăp-pĕ-xĕṯ—the-(one)-turning-itself: cf. מְרַחֶ֫פֶת, § 106. 2. b.

383. לִשְׁמֹר—liš-mōr—*to-keep;* cf. לְשָׁמְרָה (223), and לַעֲבֹד (377).

2. FORMS FOR SPECIAL STUDY.

1. Verbal Forms:—לָדַעַת, יִשְׁלַח, וַיְחִי, וַיִּשְׁלָחֵהוּ, לָקַח, וַיְגָרֶשׁ, וַיֵּשֶׁב, מִתְהַפֶּכֶת.

2. Nominal Forms:—אֶחָד, עוֹלָם, עֵדֶן, כְּרֻבִים, לַהַט, חֶרֶב, דֶּרֶךְ.

3. PRINCIPLES OF SYNTAX.

וְעַתָּה פֶּן־יִשְׁלַח יָדוֹ וְלָקַח....וְאָכַל....וָחָי—*And now, lest he put forth his hand and take and eat and live.*

Principle 11.—In the narration of actions which are to occur in the future, or which can be only conditionally realized, the first verb is in the Imperfect while those that follow are in the Perfect and connected with the preceding verb by means of *Wāw Convers.* (§ 70. 1. *b.*)

4. GRAMMAR-LESSON.

1. § 82. Tabular View, Synopses of קָטָה in Ḳăl, Pī'ēl, Hiθp. and Hîf. stems.
2. § 82. 1. *a—f*, Treatment of the 3d radical when *final.*
3. § 82. 2, Treatment of 3d rad. bef. vowel-additions.
4. § 82. 3. *a—e*, Treatment of 3d rad. bef. cons.-additions.
5. § 82. 4, The 3 sg. fem. of Perfects.
6. § 82. 5. *a,b*(1)—(8), Short forms (*to be read*).

Note 1.—In the study of verbs ל״ה, follow the order indicated in previous Lessons, analyzing exhaustively the familiar forms given under § 82. 1—5.

Note 2.—Use for practice (1) גָּלָה *reveal*, (2) בָּנָה *build*, (3) כָּלָה *complete.*

5. WORD-LESSON.

1. In the Word-Lists, under List II., verbs numbered 51—60.
2. Make out a list of the new words in Genesis III. 22—24.

6. EXERCISES.

1. To be translated into Hebrew:—(1) *He built, he will build, building;* (2) *He commanded* (Pīʻēl), *he will command, commanding, command thou;* (3) *To command* (abs.), *to build, to finish* (Pīʻēl); (4) *I commanded* (Pīʻēl), *we built, thou didst cause to reveal;* (5) *We finished* (Pīʻēl), *ye built, they* (f.) *will build;* (6) *They built, they* (m.) *will command, they caused to build;* (7) *She was, she made, she will finish, they will cause to reveal, thou* (f.) *wilt build.*

2. To be translated into Hebrew:—(1) *I shall put forth my hand and take the fruit and eat;* (2) *The man knew good and evil;* (3) *God drove forth* (Pīʻēl) *the man from Eden because he did that which God had commanded him not to do;* (4) *The man will serve the ground whence he was taken;* (5) *Behold the sword turning itself;* (6) *The cherubim and the sword will keep the way of the tree of life.*

3. To be translated into English:— (1) הִשְׁכִּין אֱלֹהִים מִקֶּדֶם (2) הִבְדִיל אֱלֹהִים בֵּין הָרַע וּבֵין הַטּוֹב; לְגַן־עֵדֶן אֶת־הַכְּרֻבִים (3) צִוָּה אֱלֹהִים אֶת־הָאָדָם (4) לֹא טוֹב הֱיוֹת הָאָדָם לְבַדּוֹ (5) גֵּרֵשׁ אֱלֹהִים מֵעֵדֶן אֶת־הָאִישׁ וְאֶת־ לַעֲבֹד אֶת־הָאֲדָמָה אִשְׁתּוֹ.

4. To be written in English letters:—*The new words of Genesis III. 22—24.*

5. To be written with points and vowel-signs:—*Genesis 22—24 from the unpointed text.*

6. To be written out:—Synopses of בָּנָה.

7. To be described:—The Forms הִשְׁקָה, יַעֲלֶה, עָשָׂה, בָּכֹה, עֲשׂוֹת, רְאוֹת, עָשָׂה, יֵרְדוּ, פְּרוּ, הָיוּ, עָשִׂיתָ, תַּעֲשֶׂינָה, הָיְתָה, וַיִּבֶן, וַיְכַל, וַיְצַו.

7. TOPICS FOR STUDY.

(1) The Pī'ēl, Ḥif'īl, and Hiθpa'ēl stems of קָטָה. (2) The defective writing of וֹ. (3) Wâw Conversive with the Perfect. (4) Wâw Conversive with the Imperfect. (5) The form לָדַעַת. (6) The third radical of verbs called ל״ה. (7) The treatment of this radical when final, before vowel-additions, and before consonant-additions. (8) The Perf. 3 sg. fem. (9) Short forms. (10) Synopses of קָטָה in Ḳāl, Pī'ēl, Hiθp. and Hif. stems.

LESSON XXXIX.—GENESIS IV. 1-4.

1. NEW WORDS.*

1. אָח (5), יָסַף (4), אֵת (preposition) (3), קָנָה (2), הָרָה (1), בְּכוֹרָה (6), הֶבֶל (7), רָעָה (8), צֹאן (9), קֵץ (10), מִנְחָה (11), שָׁעָה (13), חֵלֶב (12).

2. NOTES.

V. 1. וַתַּהַר for תָּהֲרָה, §§ 74. 2. *a*; 74. 3. *b*, *d*; 82. 1. *b* and 5. *b*. (5).— וַתֵּלֶד, §§ 80. 2. a (1); 70. 3. *a*. (3).— קָנִיתִי, § 82. 3. *b*.—אֶת־יְ, preposition *with*.

V. 2. וַתֹּסֶף for וַתְּוֹסֶף, §§ 80. 3. *b*; 65. 5. *b*. (1); 70. 3. *a*. (2) and (3).— לָלֶדֶת, §§ 47. 5; 80. 2. *a*. (3).— אָחִיו, §§ 105. 3; 108. 1. *b*. (2); וֹ = הוּ *his*, § 44. 4. *c*.—הֶבֶל, for הָבֶל, § 38. 2.— רֹעֶה, abs. רָעָה, §§ 82. 1. *c*; 107. 3.

V. 3. יָמִים, plur. of יוֹם.—וַיָּבֹא, § 86. 1. d.—לַיהוָֹה, to be read לַאדֹנָי, § 47. R. 2.

V. 4. הֵבִיא, § 86. 1. d, and 3. c.—מִבְּכֹרוֹת, § 48. 1; 106. 3; sg. בְּכוֹרָה, § 91. 1. a, and 2. — וּמֵחֶלְבֵהֶן (û-mē-ḥĕl-vĕ-hĕn), §§ 49. 2; 48. 2; חֵלֶב (ē defective), const. plur. of חָלָב, § 109. 4. e; § 51. 1. c.—וַיִּשַׁע, for יִשְׁעָה, § 82. 5. b. (5).—מִנְחָתוֹ, from מִנְחָה, §§ 106. 2. a. (2); 108. 2.

3. *PRINCIPLES OF SYNTAX.*

V. 2.—וַתֹּסֶף לָלֶדֶת—*And she added to bear*=and again she bore.

Principle 12.—when the second of two verbs expresses the principal idea, the first merely modifying it, the second is often an infinitive depending upon the first.

4. *GRAMMAR-LESSON.*

1. § 82. Tabular View, Synopses of קָטָה in Nîf., Pŭ'ăl and Hîf. stems.
2. Paradigm Ḳ (pp. 204, 205), Inflection of קָטָה in all stems.

Note:—In the study of these forms use for practice, שָׁנָה *change*, פָּנָה *turn*, בָּכָה *weep*.

5. *EXERCISES.*

1. To be translated into Hebrew:—*It* (f.) *was built;* (2) *She was caused to turn;* (3) *They were completed* (Pŭ'ăl); (4) *You* (f.) *were caused to weep;* (5) *Turning, finishing, being built, being caused to turn;* (6) *Turn ye* (f.), *be ye* (m.) *finished, cause ye* (m.) *to build.*

---

* Consult the Hebrew-English Vocabulary, or a Hebrew Lexicon. Be prepared to pronounce, transliterate, describe and define each word. Let this work be done before proceeding further in the study of the Lesson.

2. To be translated into Hebrew:—(1) *The woman conceived and bore a son;* (2) *And the woman spoke again;* (3) *Abel was a shepherd and Cain was a tiller of the ground;* (4) *Cain brought an offering to God;* (5) *Eve was the wife of Adam and the mother of Cain and Abel;* (6) *Abel gave to God from the firstlings of his flock.*

3. To be written with points and vowel-signs:—*Gen. IV.* 1—4 *from the unpointed text.*

4. To be written out:—(1) *Synopses of* בכה *in Ḳăl, Nĭf., Hĭf. and Hŏf. stems, and of* כלה *in Pĭ'ēl and Pŭ'ăl stems.*

5. To be described:—The Forms מִשְׁנֶה, בְּנוֹת, כַּלֵּה, יִבְנוּ, נְשִׁיתָם, and בְּנִיָּה, יִבְנוּ.

6. TOPICS FOR STUDY.

(1) Absence of ה ָ from ל״ה forms. (2) The vowel of the perfect of ל״ה verbs before consonant-additions. (3) The וֹת— of Infin. cst. of verbs ל״ה. (4) The י ִ of אָח before suffixes. (5) The ה ָ and ה ֶ of verbs ל״ה. (6) The preposition ל before אֱלֹהִים and יְהוָה.

LESSON XL.—GENESIS IV. 5-8.

1. NEW WORDS.

(1) חָרָה, (2) לָמָּה, (3) הֲלוֹא, (4) אִם, (5) יָטַב, (6) נָשָׂא, (7) הָרַג, (11) קוּם, (10) רָבֵץ, (9) חַטָּאת, (8) פֶּסַח.

2. NOTES.

V. 5. וַיִּחַר, for יֶחֱרֶה, §§ 82. 5. *b*. (5); 70. 3. (3).—לְקַיִן, on repeated accent, § 23. 6.—וַיִּפְּלוּ, Méθĕğ with a sharpened syllable; on assim. of נ, § 78. 2. a.— פָּנָיו (pā-nāw), § 12. 3; on יו‗ָ, § 108. 3. d; cf. אָפָיו (185).

V. 6. מָה = לָמָה with לְ, the D. f. being *firmative*, § 15. 6.— חָרָה, with accent on penult, § 21. 1.— לָךְ, pausal for לְךָ, § 51. 3 (Tab. View).— פָּנֶיךָ (fā-nê'-Xā), on ‗ֶ (ê), § 108. 3. c.

V. 7. הֲלוֹא (h⁎lô') = *nonne*, § 46. 1; this ô is for â, § 30. 6.— תֵּיטִיב, for תֵּיטִיב (cf. תַּקְטִיל), but ‗ becomes ê (‗ֵ) § 30. 4. b; Hîf. Impf. 2 m. sg. of יָטַב, § 81. 2;— שְׂאֵת, a seemingly irreg. Ḳăl Inf. const. of נָשָׂא, § 78. 1. a.— וְאֵלֶיךָ, § 23. 6; prep. אֶל treated as a noun in plur. before the suffix ךָ, cf. פָּנֶיךָ in v. 6, § 108. 3. c; the ְ becomes ֵ in an open syl.— תְּשׁוּקָתוֹ, §§ 108. 2; 18. footnote.— תִּמְשָׁל־בּוֹ, §§ 17. 2; 51. 3. a.

V. 8. אָחִיו, see in v. 2.— בִּהְיוֹתָם (bĭh-yô-θâm), on ‗ֱ, 47. 2; on Méθĕğ, § 18. 5; on וֹת, § 82. 1. e; ם‗ָ, as in בְּהִבָּרְאָם (167). — וַיָּקָם (wăy-yâ'-ḳŏm), Ḳăl Impf. 3 m. sg. of קוּם; paradigm-form, יָקוּם, but see § 86. 1 e. Rm; the ָ under ק, in an unaccented closed syl., must be ŏ.— וַיַּהַרְגֵהוּ, on ַ under י, § 74. 2. a; on ַ under ה, § 74. 3. d; on ְ, § 71. 2. b (1); on ֵ, 16. 2; on ‗ֵ, § 71. 2. c. (2).

3. *PRINCIPLES OF SYNTAX.*

V. 7.— הֲלוֹא אִם תֵּיטִיב שְׂאֵת:—*Is there not a lifting up, if thou doest well?*

Principle 13.—A question expecting an affirmative answer is introduced by הֲלֹא (= *nonne?*).

4. GRAMMAR-LESSON

1. § 84. Bi-literal verbs.
2. § 85. Tabular View. Synopses of קָטַט in Ḳăl, Nĭf. and Hĭf. stems.
3. § 85. 1—2. The doubling of the 2nd radical.
4. § 85. 3. The separating vowels.
5. § 85. 4. The changes in stem-vowels.
6. § 85. 5. The Preformative vowels.
7. Paradigm M. Inflection of קָטַט in Ḳăl, Nĭf, Hĭf and Hŏf. stems.

Note 1.—Use for practice (1) חָלַל *begin*, (2) סָבַב *encompass*, (3) קָלַל *be light* (i. e. not heavy).

5. EXERCISES.

1. To be translated into Hebrew:—(1) *He began* (Hĭf.), *to begin, beginning;* (2) *Encompassing, he will encompass, he was caused to encompass, he will be encompassed;* (3) *He will be light, he will make light;* (4) *Cause to encompass, encompass thou, he caused to encompass, be thou encompassed.*

2. To be translated into Hebrew:—(1) *The countenance of Cain fell, because God looked not with favor upon his offering;* (2) *Why was Cain angry* (Heb., *why was it kindled to Cain?*); (3) *Did not God say, let there be light?* (4) *Did not Abel bring to God from the firstlings of his flock?* (5) *Did not Cain kill Abel?* (6) *Why did Cain kill Abel?* (7) *God will bless him who shall do well.*

To be written with points and vowel-signs:—*Genesis IV. 5—8 from the unpointed text.*

4. To be written out:—Inflection of the Ḳăl Perf. and Impf. of סבב and ברד; of the Nĭf. Perf. and Impf., of מָרַד, of the Hĭf. Perf., Impf. and Imv. of קלל; of the Hŏf. Perf. and Impf. of חלל.

5. To be described:—The Forms תָּבֹזוּ, הָסֵבִּי, הֶחֱלָה, קְלוּ, גִּלְגַּלְתִּי, סְבִינָה, תְּסֻבֶּינָה, הַסִבּוֹת, נְקַלּוֹתָ, סַבּוֹת.

6. TOPICS FOR STUDY.

(1) Repetition of post-positive accents. (2) The ending ־ִין. (3) D. f. firmative. (4) The ending ־ֶיךָ. (5) הֲלֹא. (6) The ending וֹת in ל״ה Inf. construct. (7) change of ־ִ to ־ָ. (8) ע״י stems before vowel-additions. (9) ע״י stems before consonant-additions.

LESSON XLI.—GENESIS IV. 9—12.

1. NEW WORDS.

(1) דָּם, (2) צְעָק, (3) פְּצָה, (4) פֶּה, (5) יָד, (6) כֹּחַ, (7) נָע (nâ'), (8) נָד (nâd).

2. NOTES.

V. 9. וַיֹּאמֶר, § 79. 2.—אָחִיךָ, § 108. 1. b. (2).—יָדַעְתִּי, a פ״ו and ל״ laryng. verb, cf. קָטַלְתִּי; on the accent ־ֶ, § 24. 4.—הֲשֹׁמֵר, §§ 46. 1; 68. 1. a.

V. 10. מֶה עָשִׂיתָ, §§ 54. d; 82. 3. b.—דְּמֵי, sg. abs., דָּם, const. דַּם, plur. abs. דָּמִים, const. דְּמֵי, §§ 109. 2. b; 106. 4. b.—צֹעֲקִים, §§ 68. 1. a; 109. 3. R. 3; plur. in agreement with דְּמֵי, not קוֹל.—אֵלַי, cf. אֵלֶיךָ in v. 7; really a plural noun.

V. 11. פְּצְתָה, §§ 18. 2; 82. 4. and N.—פִּיהָ, from פֶּה, §§ 105. 3; 108. 1. b. (2).—לָקַחַת, § 47. 5; Ḳâl Inf. const. of לָקַח, § 78. 2. R. 2; on ־ַ under ח instead of ־ֶ, § 89. 2. a, מִיָּדְךָ, pausal for מִיָּדְךָ, §§ 38. 1. N.; 108. 1. R. 2.

V. 12. תַּעֲבֹד, corresponding to הִקְטֵל ; on ⸺ָ, § 74. 2. *a;* on ⸺ַ, § 74. 3. b; on ō, § 64. 1.— תֵּסֶף (ôō-sēf), for תּוֹסֵף; on ô, § 80. 3. *b;* on ⸺ֵ, § 65. 5. *b.* (1)— תָּת־כֹּחָהּ, on Méθĕğ, § 18. 4; on ⸺ַ, lowered from ⸺ֵ, § 78. 2. R. 3. (1); on הַ⸺ָ, § 51. 3. *a.*— נָע וָנָד (nâ' wå-nâḍ,) on the ⸺ָ (â) under נ in each case, § 86. *g;* the roots are נוּעַ and נוּד, and these forms, Kăl Part's act.— תִּהְיֶה, §§ 74. 3. N.; 18. 5; 82. 1. *b.*

3. PRINCIPLES OF SYNTAX.

V. 9.— הֲשֹׁמֵר אָחִי אָנֹכִי —*Am I keeping my brother, or, my brother's keeper?*

Principle 14.—A question asking for information, without necessarily implying the affirmative or negative character of the answer, is introduced by הֲ.

4. GRAMMAR AND WORD-LESSON.

1. § 85. 6 *a—d.*   Intensive stems in ע״י verbs.
2. Paradigm L.   Inflection of Intensive stems in ע״י verbs.
   (p. 206).
3. § 85. 7.   Place of accent in ע״י verbs.
4. Word-Lists,   Verbs numbered 61—70 in Lists II and III.

Note:—After a study of the principles here given, write out a full paradigm of סבב in Kăl, Nĭf., Hĭf. and Pôlēl.

5. EXERCISES.

1. To be translated into Hebrew:—(1) *She encompassed, they caused to encompass, thou* (f.) *wilt encompass, they will be encompassed;* (2) *Thou didst encompass, I caused to encompass, we were encompassed, thou wast caused to encompass;* (3) *Thou wast light, thou shalt encompass, I have encompassed, I shall cause to encompass;* (4) *Cause ye to encompass, they* (f.) *will encompass, ye* (f.) *will cause to encompass, encompass ye* (f.).

2. To be translated into Hebrew:—(1) *I do not know the name of the man;* (2) *Am I a ruler?* (3) *Who did this (f.)?* (4) *Cursed am I from the ground;* (5) *The blood* (pl.) *of thy brother hath cried out to God;* (6) *Thou shalt not till the ground;* (7) *Cain was a wanderer and a fugitive.*

3. To be written with points and vowel-signs:—*Genesis IV. 9—12 from the unpointed text.*

4. To be written out:—Synopses of סָבַב in Ḳāl, Nif. and Hif., of חָקַק in Ḳāl and Pôlēl, and of קָלַל in Nif. and Hif.

5. To be described:—The forms יֵקַל, הֵסֵב, יָמַר, סֹב, יָסוֹב, חַי, נָסַב, הוּחַל, מֵסֵב, הֵחֵל.

6. TOPICS FOR STUDY.

(1) The ô in the Ḳāl Impf. of verbs פ״א. (2) The î of אָח, אָב, and פֶּה before suf. (3) Hē Interrogative. (4) The î of ל״ה Perf's. (5) The Perf. 3 f. sg. of verbs ל״ה. (6) Ḳāl Inf. const. of verbs פ״ן. (7) ־ָ in pause. (8) Ḳāl Impf. of verbs פ laryngeal. (9) The ô of פ״י Hif'ils.

LESSON XLII.—GENESIS IV. 13—17.

1. NEW WORDS.

(1) עָוֹן or עָווֹן, (2) סָתַר, (3) לָכֵן, (4) שִׁבְעָתַיִם, (5) נָקָם, (6) שֵׁם, (7) עִיר, (8) יָשַׁב, (9) נָכָה.

2. NOTES.

V. 13. עֲוֹנִי, גָּדוֹל, pl. גְּדוֹלִים; on formation, § 91. 1. *a.*—עֲוֹנִי, from עָוֹן, of same formation as גָּדוֹל; before יְ־ָ, yields to ־ֵ, § 109. 1. *a.*—מִנְּשֹׂא, the ō being incorrectly written וֹ; מִן indicates comparison.

V. 14. וּמִפָּנֶיךָ, §§ 49. 2; 48.1; on גֵרַשְׁתָּ, for גֵּרַשְׁתָּ, § 75. 1. a; synopsis?—יְ‍ָ, § 108. 3. c.—אֶסָּתֵר, §§ 72. 2; 65. 1. a; synopsis?—וְהָיִיתִי, § 82. 3. b; on וְ, § 70. 2. b.— מֹצְאִי, part. מָצָא with יְ‍ָ; on change of ֹ to ְ, § 109. 3. R. 3.— יַהַרְגֵנִי, composed of יַהֲרֹג‍ and נִי; on change of ō to ֲ, and on ֵ, § 71. 2. b. (1), and c. (2); on change of ֹ to ֵ, § 74. 3. c.

V. 15. יָקֻם, pausal for יָקֻם, on D. f. in ק (for נ), § 78. 2. b; on ֻ in Hŏf., § 78. 2. N. 1.— וַיִּשֶׂם, for וַיָּשֶׂם, § 70. 3. a. (3); ֻ for יְ‍ָ, § 86. 1. d; root, שִׂים (ע״‍י).—הַכּוֹת־אֹתוֹ; on Méθĕǧ, § 18. 4; on D. f. in כ (for נ), § 78. 2. b; on ה, § 58. 5. b; on וֹת, § 82. 1. e; on אֵת, § 51. 2.— מֹצְאוֹ, cf. מֹצְאִי in v. 14.

V. 16. וַיֵּצֵא (wăy-yê-ṣē′); for וַיִּוָּצֵא, but וְ is dropped and ĭ becomes ê, § 80. 2. a. (1); on ֵ under צ, § 64. 3; on Méθĕǧ, § 18. 6; on the accented penult, § 21. 3.—מִלְּפָנֵי, (1) מִן (2) לְ (3) פָּנֵי — וַיֵּשֶׁב, for וַיִּוָּשֵׁב, but וְ is dropped, and ĭ becomes ê, § 80. 2. a. (1); on shifting of tone, § 21. 3.

V. 17. וַיֵּדַע, for וַיִּוָּדַע, but וְ is dropped, and ĭ becomes ê, § 80. 2. a. (1); on ֵ under ע instead of ֵ, § 80. 2. a. (1).—וַתַּהַר, see note on v. 1.—וַתֵּלֶד, for וַתִּוָּלֵד, but וְ is dropped and ĭ becomes ê, § 80. 2. a. (1); on shifting of tone, § 21. 3.— וַיְהִי בֹנֶה עִיר, on the shifting of tone in the case of בֹּנֶה, § 21. 1; on D. l. in ב, § 12. 3.

3. PRINCIPLES OF SYNTAX.

V. 14, גֵּרַשְׁתָּ אֹתִי הַיּוֹם—*thou hast driven me out this day.*

Principle 15.—The article often has its original demonstrative force.

Lesson 42.

V. 15.— כָּל־הֹרֵג קַיִן—*Any one killing Cain.*

Principle 16.— כֹּל is used to make prominent a single one from among a plurality.

4. GRAMMAR-LESSON.

1. § 86. Tabular View.   Synopses of Ḳăl, Nĭf., Hĭf. and Hŏf. stems of Middle-Vowel verb.
2. § 86. 1. *a, b, d, e, g.*   The treatment of the stem-vowel in Middle-Vowel verbs.
3. § 86. 2. *a, b, c,*   The separating vowels.
4. § 86. 3. *a, b, c,* 4.   The Preformative vowels.
5. § 86. 6.   The place of the tone.

Note:—Use for practice, קוּם *to rise,* שׁוּב *to turn,* and כּוּן *to prepare.*

5. EXERCISES.

1. To be translated into Hebrew:—(1) *He will rise, thou shalt turn, turn thou, he will die, we shall die;* (2) *He caused to die, he was caused to turn, he will cause to prepare;* (3) *I caused to rise, ye* (m.) *caused to rise, they caused to rise;* (4) *Thou didst cause to turn, we shall cause to rise, I shall be caused to rise, she rose;* (5) *Ye turned, I rose, they will rise, we shall rise;* (6) *Rise thou* (f.), *rise ye* (f.), *she was risen* (Nĭf.), *they were risen;* (7) *Thou shalt return, she was caused to return.*

2. To be translated into Hebrew:—(1) *God is greater than man;* (2) *I drove him out from the garden of Eden;* (3) *The woman will be hidden from the face of God;* (4) *Any one killing me shall die;* (5) *Any one finding him will kill Cain;* (6) *Cain was avenged seven-fold;* (7) *And Cain went out from Eden, and dwelt in the land of Nod.*

3. To be written with points and vowel-signs:—*Genesis IV.* 13—17 *from the unpointed text.*

4. To be written out:—The inflection in Ḳal of כּוּן, קוּם; in Nif., of מוּג, מוּל; in Hîf. and Hôf., of שׁוּב, רוּם.

5. To be described:—The Forms קָמוּ, יָקוּמוּ, הֲקִימָה, נְקוּמוֹת, תְּשׁוּבֶינָה, שַׁבְתָּ, יְקוּמוּ, אָשִׁיב, תָּשֹׁבְנָה, הֲשִׁיבוֹת.

6. TOPICS FOR STUDY.

(1) Nouns with the original vowels ă—â (= ô). (2) The Pī'ēl of verbs ע׳ laryngeal. (3) The ִ י (= ê) before suffixes ךָ and הָ, and before the plur. fem. נָה. (4) The ִ י of ל״ה Perfects. (5) The change of ־ָ before ־ְ to ־ָ. (6) The Hôf. of verbs פ״ן. (7) The וֹת of ל״ה Inf's const. (8) The הֶ (ê) of ל״ה participles. (9) The Article used as a demonstrative. (10) The separating vowel of Middle-Vowel verbs in Perfect and Imperfect.

LESSON XLIII.—GENESIS IV. 18-22.

1. NEW WORDS.

(5) תֶּפֶשׂ, (4) מִקְנֶה, (3) אֹהֶל, (2) שְׁתֵי (const. שְׁתַיִם (1), בַּרְזֶל (10) נְחֹשֶׁת (9) חָרָשׁ (8) לֹטֵשׁ, (6) עוּגָב, (5) כִּנּוֹר, (11) אָחוֹת.

2. NOTES.

V. 18. וַיִּוָּלֵד, root יָלַד (= וָלַד); on D. f. in וּ, §§ 13. 2; 80. 3. a; on the form, § 65. 1. a; cor. form, יִקָּטֵל.—אֶת־עִירָד, the sign of the def. object with a subject, see Principle 17 (below).

V. 19. וַיִּקַּח, for וַיִּלְקַח; ל assim. like נ, § 78. 2. R. 2; on ־ָ under ק, § 76. 1. a.—שְׁתֵי (štê, not šᵉtê), the šᵉwâ silent; the only case in the language of a syllable beginning with two consonants without an intervening half-vowel; fem. of שְׁנֵי, const. of שְׁנַיִם — נָשִׁים, cf. (1) אִישׁ man, (2) אִשָּׁה woman, (3) אֲנָשִׁים men, (4) אֵשֶׁת wife-of, (5) נְשֵׁי wives-of.— הַשֵּׁנִית .... הָאַחַת, cf. the masc. forms הָאֶחָד .... הַשֵּׁנִי.

V. 20. וַתֵּלֶד, cf. note on v. 17.— אֲבִי, const. of אָב; on יְ, § 108. 1. b. (2); on accent, § 24. 5. a.— יֹשֵׁב, like קְטֵל.— אֹהֶל, a u-class Segolate, cf. בֹּקֶר, § 89. 1 c; here used collectively.— מִקְנֶה (mĭḳnê(h)), meaning *substance, cattle*, and governed by some word understood signifying possession; on form, § 96. 2; on meaning of form, § 97. 2.

V. 21. אָחִיו, see note on v. 2.— תֹּפֵשׂ, like קְטֵל.— כִּנּוֹר, on form, § 93. 4. c.— עוּגָב, on form, § 92. 3.

V. 22. יָלְדָה, § 60. R. 3. b; Synopsis in Ḳal, § 80. 2. a.— לֹטֵשׁ, like קְטֵל. — וַאֲחוֹת, const. of אָחוֹת, and וְחֹרֵשׁ, like קְטֵל with ־ according to § 49. 3.

3. PRINCIPLES OF SYNTAX.

V. 18. — וַיִּוָּלֵד לַחֲנוֹךְ אֶת־עִירָד — *And Irad was born to Enoch.*

Principle 17.—The subject of a passive verb, which would be the *object* of the same verb if it were *active*, is often preceded by אֶת, the sign of the object.

V. 20. — יֹשֵׁב אֹהֶל וּמִקְנֶה — *Dwelling in tent(s) and (possessing) cattle.*

Principle 18.—Two nouns are sometimes connected with a verb, when, strictly speaking, only the former is applicable in meaning (*zeugma*).

4. GRAMMAR- AND WORD-LESSON.

1. Paradigm M.   Inflection of Pôlēl and Pôlăl stems of middle-vowels verbs.
2. § 86. 5. a, b, c, d,   Intensive stems of middle-vowel verbs.
3. § 86. 8.   Interchange of forms between ע״י and middle-vowel verbs.
4. Word-Lists,   Verbs numbered 71—80 in List III.

5. EXERCISES.

1. To be translated into Hebrew:—(1) Inflection of קוּם throughout the Pôlēl stem; (2) Synopsis of רוּם in the Hîf. stem; (3) Inflection of קוּם throughout the Hŏf. stem; (4) Synopsis of שׁוּב in the Ḳăl stem; (5) Synopsis of מוּל in the Nîf. stem.

2. To be translated into Hebrew:—(1) *I will know the name of that city;* (2) *Cain was building the city Enoch;* (3) *Cain and Abel were born to Adam;* (4) *Lamech had* (= *to Lamech were*) *two wives;* (5) *Adam was the father of Cain, and Eve was his mother;* (6) *Abel was the son of Eve, and Tubal Cain was the son of Zillah;* (7) *Father, father-of, mother, son, daughter, husband, wife, wife-of, brother, brother-of, sister, sister-of.*

3. To be written with points and vowel-signs:—*Genesis IV.* 18-22 *from the unpointed text.*

4. To be described.—וַיֵּשֶׁב, הֲשִׁיבוֹת, תִּקְמְנָה, נָכוֹן, נְקוּמוֹת, תְּשׁוּבֶינָה.

6. TOPICS FOR STUDY.

(1) אֵת with the subject. (2) Assim. of לְ. (3) The pronunciation of יִשְׁתְּ. (4) The words meaning *man, men, woman, women, wife-of, wives-of.* (5) Separating vowels in ע״י and middle-vowel verbs. (6) The ô of Ḳăl act. Part's. (7) *U*-class Seğolates. (8) Nouns formed by means of preformative מ. (9) The meanings of nouns with pref. מ.

LESSON XLIV.—GENESIS IV. 23-26.

1. NEW WORDS.

(1) נָשִׁים, irreg. plur. of אִשָּׁה, (2) אָזֵן, (3) אִמְרָה, (4) פֶּצַע,
(5) יֶלֶד, (6) חַבְרָה or חֲבוּרָה, (7) שִׁבְעִים, (8) שִׁבְעָה, (9) עוֹד,
(10) בֵּן, (11) שִׁית, (12) אַחֵר, (13) חָלַל.

2. NOTES.

V. 23. פָּנָיו, אַפָּיו (lᵉnå-šåw); on יו, § 108. 3. d. (cf.
(v. 5)).—שְׁמַעַן, irreg. for שְׁמַעְנָה, ה ָ having been dropped
and inserted, § 37. ·2; Ḳal Imv. 2 f. pl., like קְטֹלְנָה; on under
מְ, § 76. 1. a.—נְשֵׁי, const. of נָשִׁים, cf. נָשָׁיו above.—הַאֲזֵנָּה,
for הַאֲזֵנָּה like הַקְטֵלְנָה; on ה ַ § 58. 5. a. b; on ־ָ, § 74.
3. b; root, אָזֵן.—אִמְרָתִי, cf. מִנְחָתוֹ in v. 4; on formation, § 89.
4; on ־ָת, § 108. 2.—הָרַגְתִּי, from הָרַג; synopsis in Ḳal? on
repetition of accent, § 23. 6.—חַבֻּרָתִי, with ־ֻ for וּ; cf. מִנְחָתוֹ
in v. 4, and אִמְרָתִי above; on formation, § 93. 6.

V. 24. יֻקַּם (for יִנָּקֵם), see on v. 15.—שִׁבְעָה, the sing.
form, is *seven*, while שִׁבְעִים, the plur. form is *seventy*.

V. 25. שֵׁת-לִי, וַיֵּדַע, see on v. 17.—וַתֵּלֶד, see on v. 20,—
(šåθ), on Mêθěğ, § 18. 4; the ־ָ is á, § 86. 1. a;— הָרְגוֹ =
הָרַג + וֹ; in the open syl. *before* the tone an original ă is rounded
to å, but in the open syl. *away* from the tone, ă is reduced to Šᵉwâ,
§ 71. 1. b. (1), (2).

V. 26. גַּם-הוּא, the pronoun inserted thus to emphasize the
preceding noun.—הוּחַל, from the root חָלַל ; § 85. 5. d; what
stem?—לִקְרֹא, cf. לִשְׁמֹר, לִמְשֹׁל; Ḳal Inf. const.

3. PARALLELISM IN HEBREW POETRY.

(1) עָדָה וְצִלָּה שְׁמַעַן קוֹלִי
(2) נְשֵׁי לֶמֶךְ הַאֲזֵנָּה אִמְרָתִי
(3) כִּי אִישׁ הָרַגְתִּי לְפִצְעִי
(4) וְיֶלֶד לְחַבֻּרָתִי׃
(5) כִּי שִׁבְעָתַיִם יֻקַּם־קָיִן
(6) וְלֶמֶךְ שִׁבְעִים וְשִׁבְעָה

Note 1.—The characteristic external feature of Hebrew poetry is parallelism.

Note 2.—In this song there are six lines or members; the second line is, in the main, a repetition of the thought expressed in the first; the fourth, a repetition of the third; hence the parallelism in the case of the first and second, and of the third and fourth members is called *synonymous*.

Note 3.—The same relation, however, does not exist between the fifth and sixth, the latter being necessary to complete the thought of the former; such parallelism is called *synthetic*.

Note 4.—Another kind of parallelism not illustrated in this passage is the *antithetic*, in which the second member is in contrast with the first.

4. GRAMMAR-LESSON.

1. § 80. Tabular View, Synopses of יַטֵל (= וְטַל) in various stems.
2. § 80. 1. The treatment of original ו when initial.
3. § 80. 2. *a, b,* The two treatments in the Ḳăl Impf., Imv., and Inf. const.
4. § 80. 3. *a-c,* The treatment of ו when medial.

Note 1.—In the study of verbs פ״י, follow the order indicated in previous Lessons, analyzing exhaustively the familiar forms given under § 80. 1—3.

Note 2.—Use for practice (1) יָשַׁב sit. dwell, (2) יָלַד bring forth, and (3) יָבֵשׁ (with ă in Ḳāl Impf.) be dry.

5. EXERCISES.

1. To be translated into Hebrew:—(1) *He will dwell,[1] I shall dwell, thou (f.) shalt dwell, dwell thou (f.) to dwell, to bring forth,[1] thou (f.) shalt bring forth;* (2) *He will know,[1] to know, we shall know;* (3) *He will sleep,[2] I shall sleep, we shall sleep;* (4) *He will be brought forth, thou wilt be known, he will be feared;* (5) *He will cause to dwell, I shall cause to know, to cause to bring forth, he was brought forth;* (6) *He was caused to know, she will be caused to bring forth.*

2. To be translated into Hebrew:—(1) *Hear ye (m.) my voice, and give ear to that which* (אֶת־אֲשֶׁר) *I shall say;* (2) *Adah and Zillah were the wives of Lamech;* (3) *Why didst thou kill the man whom I sent to thee?* (4) *Cain was avenged seven-fold;* (5) *He gave him to God;* (6) *They began* (Hĭf.) *to call on the name of God.*

3. To be written with points and vowel-signs:—*Genesis IV. 23-26 from the unpointed text.*

4. To be written out:—Synopses of the verbs יָרַד in Ḳāl, Hĭf. and Hŏf., of יָבַל in Hĭf. and Hŏf., and of יָבֵשׁ in Ḳāl, Pĭ'ēl and Hĭf.

5. To be described:—The forms יִישַׁן, יֵדְעוּ, תֵּלְדִי, יֵשֵׁב, יֵצֵא, הוּרַד, הוֹלִיד, נוֹדַע, יֻלַּד, דַּעַת, לֶדֶת.

6. TOPICS FOR STUDY.

(1) The ending יָ_. (2) The form of the fem.-ending before suffixes. (3) The Hŏf. of verbs פ״ן. (4) The â in the Middle-Vowel Ḳāl Perfects. (5) The Hŏf. of verbs ע״י. (6) Synonymous parallelism. (7) Synthetic parallelism. (8) Antithetic parallelism.

LESSON XLV.—REVIEW.

1. *WORD-REVIEW.*

1. Arrange in alphabetical order the roots of all verbal forms both old and new, occurring in the third and fourth chapters.

2. Arrange in alphabetical order the nominal forms of these chapters, using in each case the form of the absolute state.

3. Arrange in alphabetical order the various particles, prepositions and adverbs occurring in these chapters.

2. *VERSE-REVIEW.*

1. Pronounce the pointed text of each verse until it can be read aloud rapidly and without hesitation.

2. Write out on paper the unpointed text, one verse at a time, and then, without the aid of either pointed text or translation, insert the necessary points and vowel-signs. Compare the result with the pointed text, and note the mistakes; repeat the exercise till each verse can be pointed without mistake.

3. *GRAMMAR-REVIEW.*

1. Compare the forms of the Ḳăl Perf. (3 m. sg.) as they appear in the strong verb and in the various other classes of verbs, § **87.** 1. (Perfect.)

2. Compare the forms of the Ḳăl Impf. stem yăḳ-ṭŭl (3 m. sg.) as they appear in the strong verb and in the various other classes of verbs, § **87.** 1. (Impf. with ō).

3. Compare the same of the stem yăḳ-ṭăl, and of yăḳ-ṭĭl, § **87.** 1.

4. Compare the forms of the Hĭf'îl Perf. and Impf. (3 m. sg.) as they appear in the strong verb, and in the various other classes of verbs, § **87.** 3.

---

[1] This verb forms its Kal as described in § **80.** 2. *a*.
[2] This verb forms its Kal as described in § **80.** 2. *b*.

5. Compare the forms of the Nif'al Perf. and Impf. (3 m. sg.) as they appear in the strong verb and in the various other classes of verbs, § **87.** 4.

Note.—This includes (1) the statement of the forms, and (2) an explanation of the vowel-changes which are seen in each form.

4. *EXERCISES.*

To be translated into Hebrew:—

1. *He made man in the sixth day, and rested in the seventh day.*
2. *He will sanctify the seventh day, and will rest in it.*
3. *The woman will eat the fruit, and of it she will give to her husband who will eat with her.*
4. *In the day of your ruling the earth.*
5. *This is the day in which God spoke to the man.*
6. *Let us make for ourselves large girdles.*
7. *I gave her fruit, and we ate.*
8. *She gave him fruit, and he ate.*
9. *Cursed is the earth, because thou didst eat from this tree.*
10. *God made known to the woman that the man should rule over her.*
11. *I shall call the name of my wife Eve.*
12. *We found in the field the fruit which God commanded not to eat.*
13. *The man will serve the ground whence he was taken.*
14. *I shall put forth my hand and take the fruit and eat.*
15. *The woman conceived and bare a son.*
16. *Did not Abel bring to God from the firstlings of his flock?*
17. *The blood of thy brother hath cried out to God.*
18. *And Cain went out from Eden, and dwelt in the land of Nod.*
19. *Abel was the son of Eve, and Tubal Cain was the son of Zillah.*
20. *Why didst thou kill the man whom I sent to thee?*

LESSON XLVI.—GENESIS V. 1—16.

1. NEW WORDS.

(1) סֵפֶר, (2) חָיָה, (3) שְׁלֹשִׁים, (4) מֵאָה, (5) אַחַר, (6) שְׁמֹנֶה
(12) [1] שְׁתֵּים עֶשְׂרֵה, (11) שֶׁבַע, (10) חָמֵשׁ, (9) תֵּשַׁע, (8) בַּת, (7)
שִׁשִּׁים, (15) עֶשֶׂר, (14) אַרְבָּעִים, (13) תִּשְׁעִים.

2. NOTES.

V. 1. זֶה סֵפֶר *This* (is the) *book-of; this book* would be הַסֵּפֶר הַזֶּה.—תּוֹלְדוֹת (for tāw-lᵉdôṯ), § **98**. 3; used only in pl., from יָלַד—אֱ״² בְּרֹא בְּיוֹם, *in the day of the creating of God;* אֱ״ being definite, בְּרֹא is definite, and consequently יוֹם is definite, Principle 4.—בְּרֹא, Ḳăl Inf. const. of בָּרָא.

V. 2. בְּרָאָם, on ָ, § **71**. 1. *b*. (1); on ְ under ר, § **71**. 1. *b*. (2); on ְ under א, § **71**. 1. *c*. (3.)—וַיְבָרֶךְ, §§ **75**. 1. *a;* **21**. 3; הִבָּרְאָם, the first ְ =Méθĕğ, the second = Sillûk; on D. f. § **72**. 2; the ם ָ, same as in בְּרָאָם.

V. 3. וַיְחִי, for וַיִּחְיֶה from חָיָה *live*, as וַיְהִי for וַיִּהְיֶה from הָיָה *be.*—שְׁלֹשִׁים וּמְאַת שָׁנָה lit., *thirty and a hundred of year;* note that (1) the word for *thirty* is the plural of *three* (שָׁלֹשׁ), (2) the word for *hundred* is const., (3) the word for *year* is sg.—וַיּוֹלֶד, Hîf. of יָלַד (וְלַד), § **80**. 3. *b;* on ֶ for ִ , §§ **21**. 3; **36**. 4. *a;* on ּ for י ִ, § **70**. 3. R.

V. 4. יְמֵי, § **116**. 12.—אַחֲרֵי, noun in plur. const. used as a preposition, § **119**. 3. *a.*—הוֹלִידוֹ. Hîf. Inf. const. (for hăw-lîḏ) with suffix וֹ.—בָּנִים וּבָנוֹת, see the various forms of these words, § **116**. 9, 10.

---

[1] *Twelve*, not given in the Vocabulary in this form.
[2] א״ is the abbreviation of אֱלֹהִים.

Vs. 5, 6. חָי, Ḳāl Perf. 3 m. sg. of the ע״י root חָיָה, § 85.

1.—וַיָּמָת (wăy-yă-mōθ), pausal for וַיָּמָת, § 86. 1. *e*. R.—חָמֵשׁ שָׁנִים, the numeral sg. in form, the subst. plural.

Vs. 8—10. שְׁתֵּים עֶשְׂרֵה lit., *two ten = twelve*; שְׁתֵּים, a contraction of שְׁתַּיִם (cf. שְׁתֵּי, ch. IV. 19), and עֶשְׂרֵה, a form of עֶשֶׂר *ten*.—חֲמֵשׁ עֶשְׂרֵה *nine*.—תֵּשַׁע or תִּשְׁעָה, pl. of תִּשְׁעִים, lit., *five ten = fifteen*, cf. above.

Vs. 13, 16. שִׁשִּׁים, *four*.—אַרְבַּע or אַרְבָּעָה, plur. of אַרְבָּעִים, plur. of שֵׁשׁ or שִׁשָּׁה *six*.

3. PRINCIPLES OF SYNTAX.

V. 4.—אַחֲרֵי הוֹלִידוֹ—*After his begetting = after he had begotten.*

Principle 19.—Where the Hebrew uses a preposition and an Infinitive, the English prefers a conjunction and a finite verb.

V. 6.—עֶשֶׂר שָׁנִים; שֶׁבַע שָׁנִים; חֲמֵשׁ שָׁנִים:
Five years; seven years; ten years.

Principle 20.—With the numerals 3—10 the noun is put in the plural.

Principle 21.—The numerals 3—10 assume the secondary or *masculine* form, when the noun is feminine. [שָׁנִים is feminine, though it has a masculine ending.]

V. 5.—שִׁבְעִים; תִּשְׁעִים שָׁנָה; שְׁלֹשִׁים שָׁנָה,.שָׁנָה—*Thirty years; ninety years; seventy years.*

Principle 22.—The tens, formed by changing ־ָה of the units to ־ִים (except עֶשְׂרִים *twenty*, from עֶשֶׂר *ten*), have the accompanying noun in the *singular*.

4. GRAMMAR- AND WORD-LESSON.

1. § **117.** General view, The numerals 1—10, 11, 12, 20—90, 100, 1,000
2. § **117.** 1—8,   The formation and use of the Cardinals.
3. § **117.** 9—12,   The formation and use of the Ordinals.
4. Word-Lists,   Verbs numbered 81—90 in List III.

5. EXERCISES.

1. To be translated into Hebrew:—(1) *Seven years;* (2) *Nine years;* (3) *Forty years;* (4) *Sixty years;* (5) *Three sons;* (6) *Three daughters;* (7) *Thirty sons and thirty daughters;* (8) *Forty days and forty nights;* (9) *Four heads;* (10) *Fifty days;* (11) *The seven stars;* (12) *Seven of*[1] *the stars;* (13) *Four seasons;* (14) *Twenty-seven days;* (15) *One hundred and fifty-nine years.*

2. To be translated into Hebrew:—(1) *This* (is) *a good book;* (2) *This good book was given to me;* (3) *In his own likeness God created man;* (4) *In the day that God made earth and heaven* (Heb. order, *In day of making of God*); (5) *In the day that God created man* (Heb. order, *In day of creating of God man*); (6) *After he had begotten a son* (Heb., *after his begetting a son*); (7) *And the man lived three hundred and forty-eight years;* (8) *And he begat four sons and three daughters, and he died;* (9) *And all the days of the man which he lived upon the face of the earth after he had begotten sons, were nine hundred and ninety-nine years.*

3. To be written:—A transliteration of verses 1 and 2 of chapter V.

4. To be written:—A verbal form of the Ḳăl Imperfect 3 m. sg. in each of the classes of verbs.

5. To be written:—The numerals 1—10 in English letters.

6. TOPICS FOR STUDY.

(1) Position and agreement of the demonstrative. (2) Nouns formed by prefixing ת. (3) The vowel-changes in קְטָלָם, קָטְלָם. (4) The short form of ל״ה Imperfects (5) Position and agreement of numerals. (6) פ״י Hif'ils. (7) Prep. with plur. form. (8) ע״י Ḳăl Perfect 3 m. sg. (9) ע״י Ḳăl Impf. 3 m. sg. with Wăw convers. in pause. (10) Formation of numerals 20—90. (11) The various forms of the word for *one hundred*. (12) *The form of the numerals* 3—10 with fem. nouns, with masc. nouns.

---

[1] The word *of* after a cardinal must be expressed by מִן.

LESSON XLVII.—GENESIS V. 17-32.

1. NEW WORDS.

(1) נָחַם, (2) מַעֲשֶׂה, (3) יָד.

2. NOTES.

Vs. 17—21. וַיְהִי, on Méθĕğ, § 18. 5; on —, § 74. 2. b. R. 2; on omission of third radical, § 82. 2. חָמֵשׁ, used with a fem. noun; form with masc. noun, חֲמִשָּׁה; ordinal, חֲמִישִׁי.—שְׁתַּיִם, fem. of שְׁנַיִם; cf. שְׁתֵּי, ch. IV. 19.—וּמְאַת שָׁנָה lit., and-(a)-hundred-of year.—מְתוּשָׁלַח (v. 21), pausal for מְתוּשֶׁלַח.

Vs. 22—24. וַיִּתְהַלֵּךְ, form and synopsis? force of Hiθpā'ēl expressed here by the word live.—וַיְהִי כָּל־יְמֵי. D. l. in כָּ after disj. accent; verb in sg. agreeing with כָּל, while in v. 17 it was pl., agreeing with יְמֵי.—וְאֵינֶנּוּ (wᵉê-nĕn-nû); on יְ—, § 111. 2. R. 1; on נֶ—, §§ 118. 2. c; 71. 2. c. (3) and N. 1; on the D. f. in נ, § 71. 2. c. N. 2; four elements, הוּ, נֶ, אֵין, וְ; on ‗, § 24. 5.

V. 29. זֶ֯ה, these accents need not be considered here.—יְנַחֲמֵנוּ, Pī'ēl Impf. 3 m. sg. of the פ"ן and ע"י laryng. root נָחַם comfort, with the suffix נוּ us; on D. f. of Pī'ēl in ח, § 75. 1. b; on —, § 71. 2. c. (2).—מִמַּעֲשֵׂנוּ, made up of מִן, מַעֲשֶׂה (§ 96. 1), and נוּ.—וּמֵעִצְּבוֹן, made up of וְ (§ 49. 2), מִ (§ 48. 2), and the const. state of עִצָּבוֹן, the ָ yielding to šᵉwâ, § 109. 3. a.—יָדֵינוּ, sg. יָד, dual יָדַיִם; before suffixes the old construct ending ay is used; this before נוּ is contr. to ê, § 108. 3. b.—אֵרְרָה ('ē-rᵃrâh), Pī'ēl Perf. 3. m. sg. of the פ' laryng., and ע"ע verb אָרַר curse; for אָרַר, but ר refuses D. f. (§ 75. 1. a), hence אָרַר; הָ‗ becomes ‎הָ‏_, § **71.** 1. c. N.—‎אֲשֶׁר אֲרָרָהּ יְ׳‏ lit., *which cursed-her the Lord* = *which the Lord cursed.*

3. PRINCIPLES OF SYNTAX.

V. 27. ‎וַיִּהְיוּ כָּל־יְמֵי מְתוּשֶׁלַח‏— *And* were *all the days of Methusaleh.*

‎וַיְהִי כָּל־יְמֵי לֶמֶךְ‏—*And* was *all the days of Lamech.*

Principle 23.—The verb in such cases as these may be placed either in the singular or in the plural

V. 31. ‎אֲשֶׁר אֲרָרָהּ יְהוָה‏—*Which the Lord cursed.*

Principle 24.—‎אֲשֶׁר‏ is a particle indicating the subordinate character of the following clause. The subordinate idea may be relative, temporal, causal, etc. In a relative clause having the relative as object of the verb, that object is expressed by a pronominal suffix attached to the verbal form. In a majority of cases, however, the pronominal suffix is not expressed.

4. GRAMMAR- AND WORD-LESSON.

1. § 88. 1—4   What is included in inflection of nouns.
2. § 89. 1,2; **109.** 4. 5.   Strong and weak Seğolates.
3. § 90. 1, 2,   Nouns with two, originally short, vowels.
4. § 91. 1, 2,   Nouns with one short and one long vowel.
5. § 92. 1—3,   Nouns with one long and one short vowel.
6. Word-Lists.   The verbs numbered 91—100 in List III.

Note.—In the study of noun-formation, copy promiscuously, on a slip of paper, nouns of various classes, and then take up each noun and classify it, noting (1) its root with the meaning of the same, (2) the original vowels used in its formation, (3) the changes which these original vowels have suffered, (4) the force of the formation, (5) the meaning of the word.

5. EXERCISES.

1. Form nouns as follows:—(1) From גדל, a *u*-class Seğolate, a noun of the third class (ă—â); (2) from חרש, a *u*-class Seğolate, a noun of the second class, (ă—ă); (3) from חרב, an *a*-class Seğolate, a *u*-class Seğolate (masc. and fem.), a noun of the fourth class (â—ĭ), a noun of the second class (ă—ĭ); (4) from עבד, an *a*-class Seğolate, a fem. noun of the third class (ă—â); (5) from אמן, a *u*-class Seğolate, a fem. noun of the third class (ĭ—û), a noun of the third class (ă—â), two nouns of the second class (ă—ă, ă—ĭ); (6) from מתק, an *i*-class and a *u*-class Seğolate, a noun of the third class (ă—â); (7) from קרב, a noun of the second class (ă—ĭ), a noun of the third class (ă—â).

2. To be translated into Hebrew:— (1) *Will Noah comfort Lamech from the work of his hands?* (2) *God cursed* (Pï'ēl) *the ground which he had created;* (3) *I will walk* (Hĭθpă'ēl) *with God, who created* (Heb., *the one creating*) *the heavens and the earth;* (4) *The sorrow of Cain was exceedingly great;* (5) *The man whom God cursed will die.*

3. To be written:—A transliteration of verses 28 and 29 of chapter V.

4. To be written:—A verbal form of the Hĭf'îl Perf. 3 m. sg. in each of the classes of verbs.

6. TOPICS FOR STUDY.

(1) The Ḳăl Impf's of חָיָה, הָיָה, חָיָה. (2) The word שְׁתַיִם. (3) Various forms of the word for *one hundred*. (4) Particles with verbal suffixes. (5) Synopsis of נָחַם in Pï'ēl. (6) Synopsis of אָרַר in Pï'ēl. (7) Măppîḳ. (8) *A*-class, *I*-class, *U*-class Seğolates. (9) Laryngeal, ע״י, ע״ו, ע״ע, ע״נ and ל״ה Seğolates. (10) Feminine Seğolates. (11) Meaning of Seğolates. (12) Nouns with two short vowels. (13) Nouns with one short and one long vowel. (14) Nouns with one long and one short vowel.

LESSON XLVIII.—GENESIS VI. 1-8.

1. *NEW WORDS.*

(5) שֵׁנַם (in the text. שֵׁנַם) (4) דוּן, (3) בָּחַר, (2) רָכַב (1)
(11) רַק, (6) נְפִלִים (7) גִּבּוֹר, (8) יֵצֶר, (9) מַחֲשָׁבָה, (10) לֵב
נָחַם (in Nif.), (12) עָצַב, (13) מָחָה, (14) חֵן.

V. 1. הַחֵל, from חָלַל, § 85. 1. *a*, 4. *d;* on ‗ under הַ, § 85.
5. *c;* synopsis in Hif.?—לָרֹב, prep. לְ with pretonic ă; רֹב, inf.
const. from רָבַב, § 85. 1. a; synopsis in Ḳǎl?

V. 2. וַיִּרְאוּ, Ḳǎl Impf. 3 m. pl. of רָאָה; on loss of third radical
(י), § 82. 2.—בְּנֵי and בְּנוֹת, constructs of בָּנִים, בָּנוֹת.—טֹבֹת, cf.
טוֹב, טוֹבָה, טוֹבִים, טוֹבוֹת; ô written defectively.—הִנֵּה, D. f.
firmative, §§ 15. 6; 50. 3. *e.*—וַיִּקְחוּ, from לָקַח *take;* on assim.
of לְ, § 78. 2. R. 2; on omission of D. f. and on Râfé, §§ 14. 2;
16. 2; synopsis in Ḳǎl?—נָשִׁים, § 116. 7.—בָּחֲרוּ, pausal for
בָּחֲרוּ.

V. 3. יָדוֹן, Ḳǎl Impf. 3 m. sg. The form looks like that of
יָבוֹא, but it may be from דָּנַן, with ō written like ô as sometimes happens. Nothing certain is known as to either form or
meaning.—בְּשַׁגַּם, rather to be read בְּשַׁגַּם = *in* (their) *wander-
ing;* from שָׁגַג, with ă instead of ŭ in the inf. cst.; the traditional
rendering *in that also* is based on the analysis בְּ *in,* שַׁ = *that*
(§ 53. 2), גַּם *also.*—יָמָיו, cf. אַפָּיו, פָּנָיו, § 108. 3. *d*.

V. 4. אַחֲרֵי־כֵן אֲשֶׁר lit., *after so, when* = *afterwards, when.—*
יָבֹאוּ, cf. the paradigm-form יִקְטְלוּ; the ô is for â, the form corresponding to yăḳ-ṭăl not yăḳ-ṭŭl; § 86. 1. *c;* the Impf. designates
habitual action in past time.—הַגִּבֹּרִים, § 93. 4. *c.*—עוֹלָם, § 92.

1.—אַנְשֵׁי, const. of אֲנָשִׁים, which is plur. of אִישׁ , § 116. 5.

V. 5. רַבָּה, an adj. fem. sg.¹ from רַב, §§ 100. 1. a; 109. 5. b.—רָעַת, const. of רָעָה,—יֵצֶר, § 89. 1. b.—מַחְשֶׁבֶת, const. pl. of מַחֲשָׁבָה.—לִבּוֹ, an ע״ע i-class Segolate; §§ 100. 1. a, 109. 5. b.

Vs. 6—8. וַיִּנָּחֶם, §§ 21. 3; 65. 1. a.— וַיִּתְעַצֵּב , cf. וַיִּתְהַלֵּךְ in ch. V. 22.—אֶמְחֶה, on ־ֶה=e § 82. 1. b.—בְּרֹאתִי, on repeated accent, § 23. 6; on ־ָ under ר, § 83. 1.— נִחַמְתִּי, for נִנְחַמְתִּי, the second נ being assimilated and the D. f. implied in ח; Nif. Perf. 1 c. sg. of נָחַם; Nif. = *repent*, Pi'ēl (ch. V. 29) = *comfort*.— עֲשִׂיתִם, on ־ִ instead of ־ָ, § 71. 1. b. (1); the î with ת, written defectively.—בְּעֵינָי, on first ִי , § 109. 5. a; on second ָי , § 107.

3. PRINCIPLES OF SYNTAX.

V. 4.—בַּיָּמִים הָהֵם.—*In the days the those* = In those days.

Principle 25.—The 3rd personal pronoun is used as the remote demonstrative (*that, those*), and as such stands after its noun, agreeing with it in gender, number and definiteness.

4. GRAMMAR- AND WORD-LESSON.

1. § 93.   Nouns with second radical reduplicated.
2. §§ 96, 97.   Nouns with מ prefixed; their signification.
3. § 98.   Nouns with ת prefixed.
4. § 99.   Nouns formed by means of affixes.
5. Word-Lists,   The verbs numbered 101—110 in List III.

Note.—In the study of noun-formation, copy promiscuously, on a slip of paper, nouns of various classes, and then take up each noun and classify it, noting (1) its root, with the meaning of the same, (2) the original vowels used in its formation, (3) the changes

---

¹ The Kal Perf. 3 f. sg. of רָבַב would be רָבָה.

which these original vowels have suffered, (4) the force of the formation, (5) the meaning of the word.

5. EXERCISES.

1. Form nouns as follows:—(1) from לָמַד, a noun with מְ prefixed (ă—ă), and one with תְ (ă—î); (2) from אָכַל, a fem. u-class Seğolate, a noun with מְ prefixed (ă—ă); (3) from חָשַׁךְ, a u-class Seğolate, a noun with מְ prefixed (ă—ă); (4) from גָבַר, an a-class Seğolate, a noun with second radical doubled (ĭ—â); (5) from זָמַר, an a-class Seğolate, a fem. i-class Seğolate, a noun with מְ prefixed (ĭ—â); (6) from סָפַר, an i-class Seğolate, a noun with מְ prefixed (ĭ—ă).

2. To be translated into Hebrew:—*The daughters of men were exceedingly fair* (טוֹב); (2) *Mankind multiplied;* (3) *We chose wives from all the daughters of men;* (4) *I have found favor in his eyes;* (5) *From eternity unto eternity I am God;* (6) *I grieved in my heart;* (7) *I will not repent that I have made them;* (8) *Those heroes are the men of renown* (*name*).

3. To be written:—A transliteration of verses 1, 2 of chapter VI.

4. To be written:—A verbal form of the Hîf'îl Impf. 2 m. sg. in each of the classes of verbs.

6. TOPICS FOR STUDY.

(1) ע״י Hîf'îls. (2) The absence of י in verbs ל״ה. (3) The various forms of the words for *son*, *daughter*. (4) The personal pronouns. (5) The demonstrative pronouns. (6) The words יָדוֹן and בְּשַׁגַם. (7) The words meaning *his faces*, *his nostrils*, *his days*, *his eyes*. (8) The Impf. of habitual action in past time. (9) ע״י i-class Seğolates. (10) The remote demonstratives. (11) Nouns with second radical reduplicated. (12) Nouns with מְ prefixed. (13) Nouns with תְ prefixed. (14) Nouns with affixes.

LESSON XLIX.—GENESIS VI. 9-15.
1. *NEW WORDS.*

(1) צַדִּיק, (2) תָּמִים, (3) דּוֹר, (4) שַׁחַת, (5) חָמָס, (6) תֵּבָה,
(7) גֹּפֶר, (8) קֵן, (9) כָּפַר, (10) חוּץ, (11) כֹּפֶר, (12) אַמָּה, (13)
אֹרֶךְ, (14) רֹחַב, (15) קוֹמָה.

2. NOTES.

V. 9. (1) = בְּדֹרֹתָיו, § 98. 1.— תּוֹלְדֹת, § 52. 1. *c.*— אֵלֶּה
יָ‍ֽו (cf. אָפָיו); on the pl. ending יָ‍ו (4) וֹת, (3) דּוֹר, (2) בְּ,
after the pl. ending ôθ, § 108. 4 and N.— צַדִּיק, § 93. 5.— תָּמִים,
§ 91. 1. *b.*— אֶת־הָא, here the prep. *with*, not the sign of the def.
object.

Vs. 10, 11. וַיּוֹלֶד, §§ 80. 3. *b;* 70. 3. *a.* (2), (3).— וַתִּשָּׁחֵת,
Synopsis?— וַתִּמָּלֵא, Synopsis?

Vs. 12, 13. נִשְׁחָתָה, pausal for נִשְׁחֲתָה, Nif. Perf. 3 f. of
שָׁחַת; Synopsis?— הִשְׁחִית, Synopsis?— דַּרְכּוֹ, from דֶּרֶךְ; cf.
בָּא (bâ'), either Perf. or Part. — צַלְמוֹ and צֶלֶם and זַרְעוֹ and זֶרַע
in form, § 86. 1. *a, g.*— לְפָנַי, § 108. 3. *a.* (1).— מָלְאָה, Synopsis?
— וְהִנְנִי, the adverbial particle הֵן or הִנֵּה with a verbal suffix,
§ 118. 2. *a.*— מַשְׁחִיתָם Hif. part. of שָׁחַת, with suf. ־ָם.

Vs. 14, 15. עֲשֵׂה ("ⁿśê(h)), § 82. 1. *f.*— תֵּבַת, const. of תֵּבָה,
the ־ being unchangeable.— עֲצֵי, const. of עֵצִים, cf. פְּנֵי from
פָּנִים — קִנִּים, plur. of קֵן, an ע"ע *i*-class Segolate, § 109. 5. *b;*
cf. וְכִפַּרְתָּ — לֵב, with accent on ultima, § 70. 3. *b;* cf. change from
ult. to penult in וַיֹּאמֶר.— מִבַּיִת וּמִחוּץ, *from house and from outside = within and without.*— תַּעֲשֶׂה, cf. נַעֲשֶׂה (ch. I. 26).—
רָחְבָּהּ (rŏḥ-bâh), on ־ָ (ŏ) under ר, § 111. 1. R. 1; on הָ‍ּ,
§ 108. 1. R. 1.

3. PRINCIPLES OF SYNTAX.

V. 10.—שְׁלֹשָׁה בָנִים—*Three sons.*

Principle 26.—When the substantive is *masculine*, the feminine form of the numeral is employed; and when the numeral is a *unit*, the plural form of the substantive is employed.

V. 15.—וְזֶה אֲשֶׁר תַּעֲשֶׂה אֹתָהּ—*And this is how thou shalt make it.*

Principle 27.—The relative particle often introduces subordinate clauses that are not strictly relative clauses.

4. GRAMMAR- AND WORD-LESSON.

1. § 100,   Nouns from bi-literal roots.
2. § 104,   Various ways of forming noun-stems.
3. § 105,   The Formation of Cases.
4. Word-Lists,   Verbs numbered 111—120 in Lists III and IV.

5. EXERCISES.

1. To be translated into Hebrew:—(1) *Noah had (Heb., were to Noah) three sons;* (2) *The sons of Noah were not righteous;* (3) *The earth was corrupt, and it was full of violence;* (4) *The way of all flesh was corrupt;* (5) *God will destroy the earth and all who dwell upon it;* (6) *Thou shalt make a house; its length shall be twenty cubits, its breadth, twelve cubits, its height, twenty-four cubits.*

3. To be written:—A transliteration of verses 14 and 15 of chapter VI.

4. To be written:—A verbal form of the Nifʻâl Perfect 3 m. sg. in each of the classes of verbs.

6. TOPICS FOR STUDY.

(1) The demonstrative pronoun. (2) Nouns formed by reduplication of second radical. (3) אֶת־, a preposition. (4) The ס of פּ״י

Hif'ils. (5) The characteristics of the Nif'äl Impf. (6) Primary form of *u*-class Segolates. (7) Adverbs with verbal suffixes. (8) The ê of ל"ה Imv's. (9) ע"י *i*-class Segolates. (10) Change of accent after Wâw Convers. with Perfect. (11) The form of *u*-class Segolates before pron. suffixes. (12) Relics of the nominative case-ending. (13) The Hē Directive. (14) Other relics of the accusative case-ending.

LESSON L.—GENESIS VI. 16-22.

1. *NEW WORDS.*

(6) שְׁנַיִם, (5) תַּחְתִּי, (4) צַד, (3) מִלְמַעְלָה, (2) צֹהַר (1)
אָסַף (11) בְּרִית, (10) קוּם, (9) גָּוַע, (8) מַבּוּל, (7) שְׁלִישִׁים

2. NOTES.

V. 16. צֹהַר, § 89. 1. *c.*—תֵּעֲשֶׂה (tăʻăśê(h), on ־ under הַ, § 74. 2. *a;* on the ־ under ע, § 74. 3. *b;* on הֶ ָ, § 82. 1. *b.*—תְּכַלֶּנָּה, made up of (1) תְּכַלֶּה, with הָ _ lacking, (2) נֶּה, which is for נְהָ ,__ §§ 72. 3; 71. 2. *c.* (3) and Notes 1, 2; cf. וַיְכַל (ch. II. 2).—מִלְמַעְלָה made up of מִן, לְ, מֵעַל and הָ _ directive; note (1) the Râfê, (2) Zâkēf kâṭōn, (3) simple šᵉwâ under ע; on הָ _, § 105. 2. *a.*—בְּצִדָּהּ (bᵉṣîd-dâh), from צַד with suf. הָ _, the original ־ being attenuated in sharpened syl.—תָּשִׂים Ḳal Impf. 2 m. sg. of the ע"י verb שִׂים put.—תַּעֲשֶׂהָ, same as the word above, with pron. suf. הָ.

V. 17. וַאֲנִי, §§ 49. 3; 50. 3. *d;* here emphatic, being cut off by Rᵉvî(ă)ʻ.—הִנְנִי, a particle with verbal suffix, § 118. 2. *a.*—מֵבִיא Hif. participle from בּוֹא; on preformative ־, § 86. 3. *c;* on stem-vowel, ־, § 86. 1. *d.*—לְשַׁחֵת, Piʻēl Inf. const. of the ע' laryng.

verb שָׁחַת, the D. f. being implied in ה, § 75. 1. b.—יִגְוָע, pausal for יִגְוַע, Ḳäl Impf. of גָּוַע, § 76. 1. a.

V. 18. וַהֲקִמֹתִי, on וְ, §§ 49. 3; 70. 2. b; on הֲ, § 86. 3. a; ־ is î written defectively; ô is separating vowel, § 86. 2. a. אִתָּךְ, pausal for אִתְּךָ, the prep. אֵת with; cf. אֹתְךָ, in which אֵת = אֶת, the sign of the def. object.— וּבָאתָ, Ḳäl Perf. 2 m. sg. of בּוֹא, with Wâw conversive.

Vs. 19, 20. הֲחַי, instead of הַחַי with D. f. implied.— תָּבִיא, Hîf. Impf. 2 m. sg.; § 86. 1. d. and 3. a.— לְהַחֲיוֹת, Hîf. Inf. const. of חָיָה; on וֹת, § 82. 1. e.— יָבֹאוּ, a seemingly irreg. Ḳäl Impf. 3 m. pl. of בּוֹא.

Vs. 21, 22. קַח, Ḳäl Imv. of לָקַח, § 78. 2. R. 2.— מַאֲכָל, §§ 96. 1; 97. 2.— יֵאָכֵל, § 74. 1.— וְאָסַפְתָּ, on the shifting of tone, § 70. 3. b; on Méθěǧ, § 18. 1.— צִוָּה, Pï'ēl Perf. 3 m. sg. of צָוָה command; on ־ָ, § 59. 1. a; on הִ_, § 82. 1. a.

3. PRINCIPLES OF SYNTAX.

V. 17. וַאֲנִי הִנְנִי מֵבִיא—And I, behold I am about to bring.

Principle 28.—The Participle is often used to designate an action which is to take place in the immediate future.

V. 17.—אֶת־הַמַּבּוּל מַיִם—The flood, (that is) water; not the flood of water.

Principle 29.—A noun in the construct state cannot receive the article; hence, in cases like this, the second noun must be in apposition with the first.

4. GRAMMAR- AND WORD-LESSON.

1. § 106. 1, 4,   The masculine singular and plural.
2. § 106. 2. a—c,   The three-fold treatment of the original fem. affix ת.

Lesson 50.

3. § **106**. 3, 5,   The fem. plur. and the dual.
4. Word-Lists,   The verbs numbered 121—130 in List IV.

5. EXERCISES.

1. To be written:—(1) Masc. and fem. sg., masc. and fem. pl. of טוֹב *good*, of גָּדֹל *great;* (2) Fem. pl. of אוֹת *sign*, מָאוֹר *luminary;* (3) Dual of עַיִן *eye*.

2. To be translated into Hebrew:—(1) *Behold, I am about to rain upon the earth;* (2) *I will destroy all flesh in which is the spirit of lives;* (3) *Thou didst establish (= cause to stand) a covenant with me;* (4) *Will he keep the covenant which he established with them?* (5) *Male and female they shall enter the ark, and for them thou shalt take food which may be eaten;* (6) *Noah collected food in order to preserve alive the fowl and the beast(s) and the cattle, and all that was in the ark.*

3. To be written:—A transliteration of verses 18 and 19 of chapter VI.

4. To be written:—The Nif'al Perf. 3 m. sg., and Impf. 3 m. sg. of a verb of each of the classes.

6. TOPICS FOR STUDY.

(1) The ה_ of ל"ה Impfs. (2) The suffix נָה_. (3) Hē directive. (4) Râfê. (5) Zâḳēf ḳâṭōn. (6) The Ḳal Impf. of verbs ע"י. (7) וְ before a laryngeal with Sᵉwâ. (8) The vowel-changes in מֵבִיא. (9) ע' laryng. Pi'ēls. (10) The vowel-points in וַהֲקִמֹתִי. (11) Difference between אֵת *with*, and אֵת sign of def. object. (12) פ' laryng. Nif'als. (13) The retention of the original fem. ת. (14) A later usage of תִ' (15) The origin of ה_ . (16) Affixes for plur. fem. and masc., and for the dual.

LESSON LI.—GENESIS VII. 1-8.

1. *NEW WORDS.*

(1) טָהוֹר, (2) עוֹד, (3) אַרְבָּעִים, (4) מָחָה, (5) יְקוּם.

2. *NOTES.*

V. 1. וַיֹּאמֶר, § 79. 1.—בֹּא, Ķāl Imv. בֵּיתְךָ, on יְ—, § 109. 5. *a;* on ־ָ, § 108. 1. *a.* (2).—רָאִיתִי, the î being attenuated from ĕ, § 82. 3. *b.*—לְפָנַי to my faces, on יְ—, § 108. 3. *a.* (1).—דּוֹר, on ô, § 30. 6. *c.*

Vs. 2, 3. טְהוֹרָה, § 106. 2. *c.*—הוּא, § 50. 3. *a.*—לְחַיּוֹת Pi'ēl Inf. const. of חָיָה; cf. הַחַיּוֹת in ch. VI. 20.

Vs. 4, 5. מַמְטִיר, synopsis in Hif'îl; cf. Principle 28.—אַרְבָּעִים יוֹם, the numeral being plur. in form, the subst. is sg.—וּמָחִיתִי, on יְ—, (cf. רָאִיתִי above), § 82. 3. *b;* from מָחָה.—הַיְקוּם, on omission of D. f. from י, § 14. 2; on formation, § 95. 2.—עָשִׂיתִי, on î, § 82. 3. *b;* cf. מָחִיתִי, and רָאִיתִי, for צִוָּהוּ, צִוָּה אֹתוֹ = הוּ; and צִוָּה (VI. 22).

Vs. 7, 8. וַיָּבֹא, § 86. 1. *c;* the ô is rounded from â—וּבָנָיו, on יָ—, § 108. 3. *d.*—אִתּוֹ with him; cf. אֹתוֹ = (-him.—אֵינֶנָּה, for אֵינֶנָּה; on יְ—, § 109. 5. *a;* on ־ֶ, § 71. 2. *c.* N. 1; on the contraction, ־ֶנָּה, § 71. 2. *c.* N. 2; on particle with suff., § 118. 2. *c.*

3. *PRINCIPLES OF SYNTAX.*

V. 2.—שִׁבְעָה שִׁבְעָה—*Seven, seven* = by sevens.

V. 9.—שְׁנַיִם שְׁנַיִם—*Two, two* = by twos, in pairs.

Principle 30.—Words are often repeated in order to express the *distributive* relation.

Lesson 51.

V. 5.—וְנֹחַ בֶּן־שֵׁשׁ מֵאוֹת שָׁנָה—*And Noah* (was) *the son of six hundred years* = And Noah was six hundred years old.

Principle 31.—The word בֶּן is commonly used to express a characteristic; e. g. a son of wisdom = a wise son.

4. GRAMMAR- AND WORD-LESSON.

1. § 107. 1, 2, The Absolute and Construct states.
2. § 107. 3, Substitution of הָ for ה_ in the construct.
3. § 107. 4, Restoration of original ת_ in the construct.
4. § 107. 6, Substitution of י_ for ים_ and יִם_.
5. § 107. 6. Rm. 3. Explanation of the Construct form.
6. Word-Lists, Verbs numbered 131—140 in List **IV.**

5. EXERCISES.

1. To be written:—The corresponding construct forms of רֹעֶה, מִקְוֶה, חַיָּה, דָּגָה, עֵינַיִם, תֵּבָה, שִׁבְעָה, פָּנִים.

2. To be translated into Hebrew:—(1) *The shepherd of the flock was a good man;* (2) *What did God call the collection of waters?* (3) *The eyes of the man were opened and he saw;* (4) *Noah's ark was made of gopher wood;* (5) *Noah took into the ark of the clean cattle and of the cattle which were not clean;* (6) *The man was forty years old;* (7) *God rained upon the earth forty days and forty nights.*

3. To be written in English letters:—Verses 1, 2 of chapter VII.

4. To be written:—Synopses of the verb אָרַב in Ḳal, Pĭ. and Hĭf., of רָעַשׁ in Ḳal, Nĭf. and Hĭf., and of חָרַב in Ḳal, Nĭf., Pŭ., Hĭf. and Hŏf.

6. TOPICS FOR STUDY.

(1) The ŏ of verbs פ״א. (2) Synopsis in Ḳal of בּוֹא. (3) ע״י Seğolates before suffixes. (4) The î of ל״ה Perf's before consonant terminations. (5) Omission of D. f. (6) The vowels in אִינֶנָּה.

(7) Explanation of the Construct form. (8) The substitution of ה ָ for ה ֶ , of י ִ for ים ִ and ים ָ . (9) The restoration of ת ַ in the construct.

LESSON LII.—GENESIS VII. 9-16.
1. NEW WORDS.

(1) שֵׁשׁ, (2) חֹדֶשׁ, (3) שִׁבְעָה־עָשָׂר, (4) בָּקַע, (5) מַעְיָן, (6) אֲרֻבָּה, (7) פָּתַח, (8) גֶּשֶׁם, (9) צִפּוֹר, (10) בְּעַד.

2. NOTES.

Vs. 9, 10. בָּאוּ, accent, § 36. 6.—כַּאֲשֶׁר, *according as*, the particle introducing a subordinate clause of manner, and the preposition governing that clause.— לְשִׁבְעַת הַיָּמִים lit., *to the heptad of days*, the numeral being in const. relation with the subst.—מֵי, const. of מַיִם.

Vs. 11, 12. בִּשְׁנַת, on ĭ, § 47. 2; abs., שָׁנָה, const., שְׁנַת, the ־ָ being reduced, and ת ַ restored, § 106. 2.— שֵׁשׁ־מֵאוֹת, on Méθĕğ, § 18. 4; cardinal for ordinal, § 117. R. 11.— חַיֵּי, const. of חַיִּים, § 107. 6.— נִבְקְעוּ, Nif. Perf. 3 pl. of בָּקַע.— מַעְיָנוֹת, const. of מַעְיָנוֹת, a denominative from עַיִן, § 103. 2.— רַבָּה, fem. of adj. רַב; on the D. f. 109. 5. b.— נִפְתָּחוּ pausal for נִפְתְּחוּ, § 38. 1.— גֶּשֶׁם an *a*-class Seğolate.

Vs. 13, 14. בְּעֶצֶם הַיּוֹם הַזֶּה *in the bone of this day* = on this very day.—אִתָּם, the original ĭ being found in a sharpened syl.— הֵמָּה, § 50. 1; on D. f. firmative, § 15. 6.— הַחַיָּה, §§ 18. 1; 45. 2.—לְמִינָהּ, §§ 16. 1; 108. 1. *a*. (1) and R. 1.— לְמִינֵהוּ, § 108. 1. *b*. (1).— צִפּוֹר, on formation, § 93. 4. *c*.

Vs. 15, 16. שְׁנַיִם שְׁנַיִם, repetition giving a distributive sense.

הַבָּשָׂר —, cf. מִבְּשָׂרִי (II. 23).— הַבָּאִים, Ḳăl Part. act. pl. of בוֹא; Part. with article = a relative clause: *those that went in.* וַיִּסְגֹּר, with ĭ atten. from ă, and ō lowered from ŭ, § **63**. 1. *a*, and 2. *a*.— בַּעֲדוֹ, prep. בְּעַד *around, behind,* with suff. וֹ *him.*

3. PRINCIPLES OF SYNTAX.

V. 9.—"כַּאֲשֶׁר צִוָּה א׳—*According as God commanded.*

Principle 32.—When אֲשֶׁר follows a preposition, the preposition governs, not the particle, but the clause.

V. 11.—בִּשְׁנַת שֵׁשׁ־מֵאוֹת שָׁנָה—*In* (the) *year of six hundred years* = in the six hundredth year.

Principle 33.—There are no *ordinals* above *ten;* hence the cardinals must serve as ordinals, whenever the context demands.

V. 13.—בָּא נֹחַ וְשֵׁם־וְחָם וָיֶפֶת—*Went in Noah and Shem and Ham and Japhet.*

Principle 34.—The predicate of several subjects united by *and* may stand either in sing. or plur., but it is generally in sing. when it *precedes.*

4. GRAMMAR- AND WORD-LESSON

1. § **108**. *Tabular View,* The noun סוּם with pron. suffixes.
2. § **108**. 1. *a, b,* and R's, Masc. nouns in the sing. with suffixes.
3. § **108**. 2, Fem. nouns in the sing. with suffixes.
4. § **108**. 3. *a—d,* Masc. nouns in the plur. with suffixes.
5. § **108**. 4, Fem. nouns in the plur. with suffixes.
6. Word-Lists, Verbs numbered 141—153 in List IV.

5. EXERCISES.

1. To be translated into Hebrew:—(1) *His day, her day, your* (m.) *day, thy* (f.) *day, our day, their* (m.) *day, thy* (m.) *day;* (2) *Thy lives, her lives, his lives, thy* (f.) *lives, our lives, my lives, your*

lives; (3) *My saying, her saying, your* (m.) *saying, our saying;* (4) *My signs, your signs, our signs, their signs, thy signs;* (5) *My father, thy brother, our father, your father, thy mouth, her mouth.*

2. To be translated into Hebrew:—(1) *Our Father who* (art) *in heaven;* (2) *Take with thee into the ark thy father and thy sons and thy daughters;* (3) *The fowl according to his kind and the beast according to her kind shall enter the ark two by two;* (4) *Everything in which is the spirit of life shall expire;* (5) *I was born in the eighteen hundredth year of our Lord, in the seventh month, on the twenty-fourth day of the month;* (6) *The waters of the flood were upon the earth many days.*

3. To be written:—A transliteration of verses 13 and 14 of chapter VII.

4. To be written:—An exact statement of the origin and force of the following suffixes (including the ending of the stem): (1) ‎יו_ָ, (2) ‎יהָ_ֶ, (3) ‎יךָ_ֶ, (4) ‎ינוּ_ֵ, (5) ‎וֹ, (6) ‎הָ_ָ, (7) ‎ךָ_ְ, (8) ‎ךְ_ֵ, (9) ‎ם_ָ, (10) ‎תִי_ָ.

6. TOPICS FOR STUDY.

(1) A preposition with the Relative particle. (2) Use of cardinals for ordinals. (3) Denominatives formed by prefixing ‎מְ. (4) ‎ע״י stems with affixes. (5) The prep. ‎אֶת with suffixes. (6) The pronominal suffixes. (7) Ḳăl Part's act. of verbs ‎ע״י. (8) The original vowels in ‎יִסְגֹּר. (9) Agreement of predicate. (10) Suffixes attached by the connecting vowel â. (11) Suffixes attached by the connecting vowel ē. (12) Suffixes attached by ‎ְ (13) The various forms assumed by the old construct ending *ay* before suffixes. (14) Plural feminines with pronominal suffixes.

LESSON LIII.—GENESIS VII. 17-24.

1. *NEW WORDS.*

(1) רוּם, (2) גָּבַר, (3) כָּסָה, (4) הַר, (5) גָּבֹהַּ, (6) חָרָבָה, (7) שָׁאַר.

2. *NOTES.*

Vs. 17, 18. וַיִּרְבּוּ, on rejection of the third radical ן or י, § 82. 2.—וַיִּשְׂאוּ, from נָשָׂא; נ assimilated, but D. f. lost, § 14. 2. —וַתָּרָם (wăt-tā'-rŏm), the second ָ being in an unaccented closed syl., must be ŏ; usual form of Middle-Vowel Ķăl Impf., is with ן, e. g., תָּרוּם ; but with Wâw convers. § 86. 1. *e.* R.— יִגְבְּרוּ, (1) י, (2) ן, גָּבַר the root, (3) ן.

Vs. 19, 20. וַיְכַסּוּ, (1) ן, with D. f. lost from י, § 14. 2; (2) י; (3) ֻ = passive; (4) D. f. in ס = intensive; (5) ן = plur.; the root being כָּסָה, cf. וַיְכֻלּוּ (ch. II. 1).—הֶהָרִים, on the ֶ § 45. 4.—גְּבֹהִים, from גָּבֹהַּ, § 109. 1. *a;* but Păθăḥ-furtive disappears when ה ceases to be final, nor is the Măppîķ any longer necessary.—מִלְמַעְלָה, see ch. VI. 16.

Vs. 21, 22. וַיִּגְוַע, § 76. 1. *a.*—נִשְׁמַת, construct of נְשָׁמָה.— אַפָּיו, from אָנְף = אַף, dual, אַפַּיִם; on ־יו, § 108. 3. *d.* — בֶּחָרָבָה, on ֶ § 45. 4; ָ under ח, on account of rejection of D. f. from ר, the formation being according to § 93. 1.—מֵתוּ, on ē under מ, § 86. 1. *a.* R.

Vs. 23, 24. וַיִּמַח, for וַיִּמְחֶה (Ķăl Impf.); ה_ lacking, and a helping vowel ־ inserted, § 82. 5. *b.* (5); Râfé over מ, to show that no D. f. is to be expected.—וַיִּמָּחוּ, Nîf. Impf. 3 plur., of same root as יִמַּח — וַיִּשָּׁאֶר, another Nîf.; tone receding to penult, final vowel is ֶ, not ֵ—אִתּוֹ בַּתֵּבָה, D. l. in בּ, because of preceding disjunctive accent.—יוֹם, sg., although pl. *in sense*.

3. PRINCIPLES OF SYNTAX.

V. 19.—מְאֹד מְאֹד—*Mightily, mightily.*

Principle 34.—Words are often repeated to express *intensity* or *emphasis*.

V. 22.—כֹּל אֲשֶׁר .... בְּאַפָּיו—*All in whose nostrils,* etc.

Principle 35.—The אֲשֶׁר which serves as sign of relation for a following pronominal suffix is generally separated from the word to which the suffix is attached by intervening words.

4. GRAMMAR- AND WORD-LESSON.

1. § 109. 1,   Stem-changes resulting from shifting of tone *one* place.
2. § 109. 2,   Stem-changes resulting from shifting of tone *two* places.
3. § 109. 3,   Stem-changes in the singular construct.
4. § 109. 3. R. 3,   Ḳǎl act. participles, and nouns with ultimate ē.
5. Word-Lists,   Verbs numbered 154—166 in List IV.

5. EXERCISES.

1. In the case of בָּשָׂר *flesh*, עוֹלָם *eternity*, write out (1) the const. sg., (2) the form with suffix for *my*, (3) with suffix for *your* (m.), (4) the plur. abs., (5) the plur. const., (6) the plur. with the suffix for *my*, (7) with the suffix for *your* (m.).

2. To be translated into Hebrew:—(1) *This is my word which I have spoken to you;* (2) *The earth and all which* (is) *in it is God's;* (3) *All the mountains were covered, and the waters prevailed upon the earth;* (4) *Three men were left with him in the ark;* (5) *The man to* (בְּ) *whose word I listened was forty years old;* (6) *And he destroyed man and beast, creeper and cattle from upon the ground.*

3. To be written:—A transliteration of verses 22, 23 of ch. VII.

4. To be written: — Exhaustive analyses of (1) וְהַמַּיִם, (2) מֵאָדָם (5), וּבַבְּהֵמָה (4), מִלְמַעְלָה (3), הֶהָרִים.

6. TOPICS FOR STUDY.

(1) Absence of יו or in verbs ל"ה. (2) Assimilation of נ in verbs פ"ן. (3) The vowels in middle-vowel Ḳâl Imperfects. (4) The artile with ־ָ. (5) The suffix and ending יו ָ. (6) Each vowel in וַיָּ֫מָח and וַיִּמְחוּ. (7) D. l. after a disjunctive accent. (8) When does the tone move *one* place? (9) When does it move *two* places? (10) The vowel-changes in either case. (11) The formation of the singular construct. (12) Nouns with ē in the ultima.

LESSON LIV.—GENESIS VIII. 1-7.

1. NEW WORDS.

(7) חָסַר, (6) כָּלָא, (5) סָכַר, (4) שָׁכַךְ, (3) עָבַר, (2) זָכַר, (1) יָבֵשׁ, (11) עֶרֶב, (10) חַלּוֹן, (9) הַר, (8) קָצֶה.

2. NOTES.

V. 1. וַיִּזְכֹּר, ĭ atten. from ă, ō lowered from ŭ; Ḳâl Impf. 3 m. sg.; synopsis?—וַיַּעֲבֵר, on ־ָ instead of יִ־, § 65. 5. *b*. (1); synopsis?—וַיָּשֹׁכּוּ, from שָׁכַךְ, § 85. 1. *a*, 5. *a;* the ־ָ rounded from orig. ־ַ; the ō with first radical as regularly in ע"ע verbs; the D. f. for strengthening.

Vs. 2, 3. וַיִּסָּכְרוּ, Nĭf. Impf. 3 m. plur. of סָכַר = סָגַר. — וַיִּכָּלֵא, § 72. 2.—וַיָּשֻׁבוּ, for וַיָּשׁוּבוּ: original ŭ is lengthened to û and ă of preformative becomes ā in open syl. § 86. 1. *e*, 3. *a*. —הָלוֹךְ, Inf. abs.; on ô(=â), § 67. 1. *b*. (1).—וָשׁוֹב, on ־ָ, § 49. 4; on שׁוּב, Inf. abs., § 86. 1. *g*.—וַיַּחְסְרוּ, on ־ַ before ח, § 74. 2. *a;* on ־ְ under ח, § 74. 3. *c*.—מִקְצֵה, for מִקְצָה; on omis. of D. f., § 14. 2; on ־ִ under ק, instead of ־ַ, § 109. 6. *b;* on ה ־ֵ (ê), § 107. 3.

Vs. 4, 5. וַתָּנַח, from נוּחַ (cf. וַיַּנִּחֵהוּ ch. II. 15); usual Impf., יָנוּחַ, but the form with Wâw convers. has ŏ, § 86. 1. *e*. R.; but the laryng. prefers ă.— הָרֵי, const. pl. of הָר, which is from הָרַר; hence the ָ is unchangeable, and stands in the const., §§ 109. 5. *b*; 31. 4. N. 2.— חָסוֹר, Inf. abs.; on ô (= â), § 67. 1. *b*. (1)— נִרְאוּ, Nif. of רָאָה — רָאשֵׁי, const. plur.; another case of unchangeable ָ in const.; irreg. plur. of רֹאשׁ, § 116. 17.— הֶהָרִים on the ָ under ה, § 45. 4.

Vs. 6, 7. וַיִּפְתַּח, § 76. 1. *a*.— וַיְשַׁלַּח, on ְ under ל, § 76. 1. *b*.— וַיֵּצֵא, § 80. 2. *a*. (1).— יָצוֹא, § 67. 1. *b*. (1).— יְבֹשֶׁת, a fem. Inf. const., § 80. 2. *b*. R. 1.

3. PRINCIPLES OF SYNTAX.

V. 3.— וַיָּשֻׁבוּ... הָלוֹךְ וָשׁוֹב—*And they returned, going and returning.*

V. 7.— וַיֵּצֵא יָצוֹא וָשׁוֹב—*And it went forth, going forth and returning.*

V. 5.— וְהַמַּיִם הָיוּ הָלוֹךְ וְחָסוֹר—*And the waters were going on and diminishing.*

Principle 36.—The Infinitive absolute, coming after a finite verb from the same root, gives to the latter the force of *continued and lasting action*. This idea of *continuance* is also expressed by the use of the verb הָלַךְ, in which case the principal idea is added in the form of a second Inf. abs. The thought of the phrases given above is: (1) "They went on going backwards"; (2) "It went repeatedly to and fro"; (3) "And the waters were abating continually."

V. 5.— בָּעֲשִׂירִי בְּאֶחָד לַחֹדֶשׁ—*In the tenth* (month), *on the first* (lit., *one*) (day) *of* (lit., *to*) *the month.*

Principle 37.—In dates (1) the words *day* and *month* are often omitted, (2) the cardinals are often used instead of ordinals, and (3) instead of the construct relation, a periphrastic expression by means of לְ is employed.

4. GRAMMAR- AND WORD-LESSON.

1. § **109**. 4. *a—f,* Stem-changes in the inflection of Segŏlates.
2. § **109**. 5. *a, b,* Stem-changes in the inflection of middle-vowel and ע״ע Segŏlates.
3. § **109**. 6. *a, b,* Stem-changes in the inflection of ל״ה nouns.
4. Word-Lists, Verbs numbered 167—180 in List IV.

5. EXERCISES.

1. In the case of קָצֶה, חֹק, זַיִת, מָוֶת, יֶלֶד, write (1) sg. const., (2) sing. form with suffix *your*, (3) plur. abs., (4) plur. const., (5) plur. form with suffix *my*.

2. To be translated into Hebrew:—(1) *Remember thou the days in which God blessed thee;* (2) *God caused the waters to return from upon the earth;* (3) *He died in the sixth year, in the seventh month, on the fifth day of the month;* (4) *The words of God are good;* (5) *He will live unto eternities of eternities;* (6) *The kings of the earth shall return unto their land.*

3. To be written:—A transliteration of verses 2, 3 of ch. VIII.

4. Write a complete analysis of the following forms:—(1) וַיִּשְׁלַח, (5) וּמֵאַת, (4) הַגֶּשֶׁם, (3) לְחָדְשׁ, (2) מַעְיְנֹת.

6. TOPICS FOR STUDY.

(1) Vowels of the Ḳăl Impf. 3 m. sg. of a strong verb. (2) ע״י Ḳăl Impf. (3) Middle-vowel Ḳăl Impf. (4) Nĭf'ăl Impf. 3 m. sg. (5) Form of Inf. abs. (6) The ô of the Inf. abs. (7) The ê of ל״ה nouns. (8) Unchangeable ָ in const. plur. (9) Article with ָ. (10) לְ laryngeal Pĭ'ēl Impf. (11) פ״י Ḳăl Impf. (12) Various forms assumed by Segŏlate stems in inflection. (13) Middle-vowel Segŏlates. (14) ע״ע Segŏlates. (15) ל״ה nouns ending in ָה.

LESSON LV.—GENESIS VIII. 8-14.

1. *NEW WORDS*.

יוֹנָה (1), קָלַל (2), מָנוֹחַ (3), כַּף (4), רֶגֶל (5), חִיל (6), אַחֵר (7),
עֵת (8), זַיִת (9), טָרָף (10), יָחַל (11), רִאשׁוֹן (13), חָרַב (8)
סוּר (14), מִכְסֶה (15).

2. *VERBAL FORMS*.

[In the case of each form, state (1) stem, (2) tense, (3) pers., numb., gen., (4) class, (5) root, (6) meaning of root, (7) corresponding form of קָטַל, (8) the variation, and the section in the "Elements" which explains it. The superior figure indicates the verse in which the word occurs.]

(1) יִשְׁלַח,[8] (2) לִרְאוֹת,[8] (3) קַלּוּ,[8] (4) מָצְאָה,[9] (5) תָּשָׁב,[9] (6)
יִשְׁלַח,[9] (7) יִקָּחֶהָ,[9] (8) יָבֵא,[9] (9) וַיָּחֶל,[10] (10) וַיֹּסֶף,[10] (11) שַׁלַּח,[10]
(12) תָּבֹא,[11] (13) וַיֵּדַע,[11] (14) וַיִּיָּחֶל,[12] (15) שׁוּב,[12] (16) וַיְהִי,[13] (17)
חָרְבוּ,[13] (18) וַיָּסַר,[13] (19) וַיַּרְא,[13] (20) יָבְשָׁה.[14]

3. *NOMINAL FORMS*.

[In the case of each form, state (1) abs. sg., (2) meaning, (3) formation, (4) const. sg., (5) abs. and const. plur., (6) its form with one or more suffixes in sg. and plur.]

(1) אֲדָמָה,[8] (2) רַגְלָהּ,[9] (3) יָדוֹ,[9] (4) יָמִים,[10] (5) עֶרֶב,[11] (6) זַיִת,[11]
(7) חֹדֶשׁ,[13] (8) מִכְסֶה.[13]

4. *PARTICLES, PREPOSITIONS, SUFFIXES, ETC*.

[In the case of each, state all that may be known concerning it.]

(1) אֶת־,[8] (2) מִן,[8] (3) אֵת[8] (with), (4) הָ,[8] (5) הַ־,[8] (6) עַל,[8] (7)
(14) לְ,[11] (13) הָ,[9] (12) וְ,[9] (11) כִּי,[9] (10) אֶל־,[9] (9) לֹא,[9] (8) וְ,[9]
(15) הִנֵּה,[11] ־יו.[12]

5. *GRAMMAR- AND WORD-LESSON.*

1. § **110.** 1—5,   Classification of Noun-stems.
2. § **111.** 1. Tab. View and R's,   Strong and Laryngeal Segolates.
3. § **111.** 2. Tab. View and R's,   ע״ו ,ע״י, ל״ה and ע״ע Segolates.
4. Word-Lists,   Verbs numbered 181—194 in List IV.

6. *EXERCISES.*

1. To be written:—A word-for-word translation of verses 8—14 of Genesis VIII.

2. To be written:—A transliteration of verses 9 and 10 of Genesis VIII.

3. To be written:—Five Hebrew sentences of not less than eight words each, based on the verses constituting this lesson.

LESSON LVI.—GENESIS VIII. 15-22.

1. *NEW WORDS.*

(1) דָּבָר, (2) מִשְׁפָּחָה, (3) מִזְבֵּחַ, (4) עֹלָה, (5) רוּחַ, (6) רֵיחַ, (7) קַיִץ, (8) נִיחֹחַ, (9) נְעוּרִים, (10) קָצִיר, (11) קֹר, (12) חֹם, (13) חֹרֶף.

2. *VERBAL FORMS.*

[In the case of each form, state (1 stem, (2) tense, (3) pers., numb., gen., (4) class, (5) root, (6) meaning of root, (7) corresponding form of קְטֹל (8) the variation from the strong form, the reason for the variation, and the section in the "Elements" which explains it. The superior figure indicates the verse in which the word occurs.]

(1) יְדַבֵּר,[15] (2) לֵאמֹר,[15] (3) צֵא[16] (§ **80.** 2. *a*), (4) הוֹצֵא[17] (acc. to Kᵉrê, הַיְצֵא; usual form would be הוֹצֵא, §§ **19.** 1, 2, 3; **80.** 3. *b*),

(5) וּפָרוּ,[17] (6) וַיֵּצֵא,[18] (7) יָצְאוּ,[19] (8) וַיִּבֶן,[20] (9) וַיִּקַּח,[20] (10) וַיַּעַל,[20]
(13) אָסֹף,[21] (12) וַתָּנַח,[21] (cf. v. 4), (11) וַיִּירַח [21] (in Hîf., not Ḳal),
לְקַלֵּל,[21] (14) לְהָכוּר,[21] (15) עָשִׂיתִי,[21] (16) יִשְׁבֹּתוּ,[22]

3. NOMINAL FORMS.

[In the case of each form, state (1) abs. sg., (2) meaning, (3) formation, (4) const. sg., (5) abs. and const. plur., (6) its form with one or more suffixes in sg. and plur.]

(1) הַחַיָּה,[17] (2) בָּשָׂר,[17] (3) בְּהֵמָה,[17] (4) רֶמֶשׂ,[17] (5) בָּאָרֶץ,[17]
(6) מִשְׁפַּחַת,[19] (7) מִזְבֵּחַ,[20] (8) טָהוֹר,[20] (9) עֹלָה,[20] (10) לִבּוֹ,[21]
(11) יֵצֶר,[21] (12) נְעָרָיו,[21] (13) זֶרַע,[22] (14) קַיִץ,[22] (15) חֹרֶף,[22]

4. PARTICLES, PREPOSITIONS, IRREGULAR FORMS.

[In the case of each, state all that may be known concerning it.]

(1) מִן,[16] (2) אִשְׁתְּךָ,[16] (3) בָּנֶיךָ,[16] (4) נְשֵׁי,[16] (5) אִתָּךְ,[16] (6)
אִתּוֹ,[18] (7) לֹא,[21] (8) בַּעֲבוּר,[21] (9) כַּאֲשֶׁר,[21] (10) יְמֵי,[22]

5. GRAMMAR- AND WORD-LESSON.

1. § **112**. Tab. View and R's, Nouns of the Second Class.
2. § **113**. Tab. View and R's, Nouns of the Third Class.
3. § **114**. Tab. View and R's, Nouns of the Fourth and Fifth Classes.
4. Word-Lists, Verbs numbered 195—208 in List IV.

6. EXERCISES.

1. To be written:—A word-for-word translation of verses 15-22 of Genesis VIII.

2. To be written:—A transliteration of verses 17, 18 of Genesis VIII.

3. To be written:—Five Hebrew sentences of not less than ten words each, based on the verses constituting this Lesson.

MANUAL.

EXPLANATION OF SIGNS

USED IN THE TRANSLATION AND TRANSLITERATION.

---

1. *Parentheses* ( ) enclose words for which there is no equivalent in the Hebrew.
2. *Brackets* [ ] enclose words which are in the Hebrew, but are not to be rendered into English.
3.)(stands for 'ēθ, the sign of the definite object.
4. The *Hyphen* (-) connects those English words which, in Hebrew, form a single word.
5. The sign of *Addition* (+) stands for Măkkēf.
6. The *Asterisk* (*) stands for the 'Aθnâḥ (͞); the *Dagger* (†), for Sᵉġōltâ (͒); the *Period* (.), for Sôf Pâsûḳ (͒͞) preceded by Sillûḳ.

GENESIS I–IV.

THE HEBREW TEXT.

CHAPTER I.

א בְּרֵאשִׁית בָּרָא אֱלֹהִים אֵת הַשָּׁמַיִם וְאֵת הָאָרֶץ׃

2 וְהָאָרֶץ הָיְתָה תֹהוּ וָבֹהוּ וְחֹשֶׁךְ עַל־פְּנֵי תְהוֹם וְרוּחַ אֱלֹהִים מְרַחֶפֶת עַל־פְּנֵי הַמָּיִם׃

3 וַיֹּאמֶר אֱלֹהִים יְהִי־אוֹר וַיְהִי־אוֹר׃

4 וַיַּרְא אֱלֹהִים אֶת־הָאוֹר כִּי־טוֹב וַיַּבְדֵּל אֱלֹהִים בֵּין הָאוֹר וּבֵין הַחֹשֶׁךְ׃

ה וַיִּקְרָא אֱלֹהִים לָאוֹר יוֹם וְלַחֹשֶׁךְ קָרָא לָיְלָה וַיְהִי־עֶרֶב וַיְהִי־בֹקֶר יוֹם אֶחָד׃

6 וַיֹּאמֶר אֱלֹהִים יְהִי רָקִיעַ בְּתוֹךְ הַמָּיִם וִיהִי מַבְדִּיל בֵּין מַיִם לָמָיִם׃

7 וַיַּעַשׂ אֱלֹהִים אֶת־הָרָקִיעַ וַיַּבְדֵּל בֵּין הַמַּיִם אֲשֶׁר מִתַּחַת לָרָקִיעַ וּבֵין הַמַּיִם אֲשֶׁר מֵעַל לָרָקִיעַ וַיְהִי־כֵן׃

8 וַיִּקְרָא אֱלֹהִים לָרָקִיעַ שָׁמָיִם וַיְהִי־עֶרֶב וַיְהִי־בֹקֶר יוֹם שֵׁנִי׃

9 וַיֹּאמֶר אֱלֹהִים יִקָּווּ הַמַּיִם מִתַּחַת הַשָּׁמַיִם אֶל־מָקוֹם אֶחָד וְתֵרָאֶה הַיַּבָּשָׁה וַיְהִי־כֵן׃

י וַיִּקְרָא אֱלֹהִים לַיַּבָּשָׁה אֶרֶץ וּלְמִקְוֵה הַמַּיִם קָרָא יַמִּים וַיַּרְא אֱלֹהִים כִּי־טוֹב׃

11 וַיֹּאמֶר אֱלֹהִים תַּדְשֵׁא הָאָרֶץ דֶּשֶׁא עֵשֶׂב מַזְרִיעַ זֶרַע
עֵץ פְּרִי עֹשֶׂה פְּרִי לְמִינוֹ אֲשֶׁר זַרְעוֹ־בוֹ עַל־הָאָרֶץ
וַיְהִי־כֵן׃

12 וַתּוֹצֵא הָאָרֶץ דֶּשֶׁא עֵשֶׂב מַזְרִיעַ זֶרַע לְמִינֵהוּ וְעֵץ
עֹשֶׂה־פְּרִי אֲשֶׁר זַרְעוֹ־בוֹ לְמִינֵהוּ וַיַּרְא אֱלֹהִים כִּי־טוֹב׃

13 וַיְהִי־עֶרֶב וַיְהִי־בֹקֶר יוֹם שְׁלִישִׁי׃

14 וַיֹּאמֶר אֱלֹהִים יְהִי מְאֹרֹת בִּרְקִיעַ הַשָּׁמַיִם לְהַבְדִּיל
בֵּין הַיּוֹם וּבֵין הַלָּיְלָה וְהָיוּ לְאֹתֹת וּלְמוֹעֲדִים וּלְיָמִים
וְשָׁנִים׃

ט׳ וְהָיוּ לִמְאוֹרֹת בִּרְקִיעַ הַשָּׁמַיִם לְהָאִיר עַל־הָאָרֶץ וַיְהִי־כֵן׃

16 וַיַּעַשׂ אֱלֹהִים אֶת־שְׁנֵי הַמְּאֹרֹת הַגְּדֹלִים אֶת־הַמָּאוֹר
הַגָּדֹל לְמֶמְשֶׁלֶת הַיּוֹם וְאֶת־הַמָּאוֹר הַקָּטֹן לְמֶמְשֶׁלֶת
הַלַּיְלָה וְאֵת הַכּוֹכָבִים׃

17 וַיִּתֵּן אֹתָם אֱלֹהִים בִּרְקִיעַ הַשָּׁמַיִם לְהָאִיר עַל־הָאָרֶץ׃

18 וְלִמְשֹׁל בַּיּוֹם וּבַלַּיְלָה וּלֲהַבְדִּיל בֵּין הָאוֹר וּבֵין הַחֹשֶׁךְ
וַיַּרְא אֱלֹהִים כִּי־טוֹב׃

19 וַיְהִי־עֶרֶב וַיְהִי־בֹקֶר יוֹם רְבִיעִי׃

כ׳ וַיֹּאמֶר אֱלֹהִים יִשְׁרְצוּ הַמַּיִם שֶׁרֶץ נֶפֶשׁ חַיָּה וְעוֹף יְעוֹפֵף
עַל־הָאָרֶץ עַל־פְּנֵי רְקִיעַ הַשָּׁמָיִם׃

21 וַיִּבְרָא אֱלֹהִים אֶת־הַתַּנִּינִם הַגְּדֹלִים וְאֵת כָּל־נֶפֶשׁ הַחַיָּה
הָרֹמֶשֶׂת אֲשֶׁר שָׁרְצוּ הַמַּיִם לְמִינֵהֶם וְאֵת כָּל־עוֹף כָּנָף
לְמִינֵהוּ וַיַּרְא אֱלֹהִים כִּי־טוֹב׃

22 וַיְבָרֶךְ אֹתָם אֱלֹהִים לֵאמֹר פְּרוּ וּרְבוּ וּמִלְאוּ אֶת־הַמַּיִם בַּיַּמִּים וְהָעוֹף יִרֶב בָּאָרֶץ׃

23 וַיְהִי־עֶרֶב וַיְהִי־בֹקֶר יוֹם חֲמִישִׁי׃

24 וַיֹּאמֶר אֱלֹהִים תּוֹצֵא הָאָרֶץ נֶפֶשׁ חַיָּה לְמִינָהּ בְּהֵמָה וָרֶמֶשׂ וְחַיְתוֹ־אֶרֶץ לְמִינָהּ וַיְהִי־כֵן׃

כה וַיַּעַשׂ אֱלֹהִים אֶת־חַיַּת הָאָרֶץ לְמִינָהּ וְאֶת־הַבְּהֵמָה לְמִינָהּ וְאֵת כָּל־רֶמֶשׂ הָאֲדָמָה לְמִינֵהוּ וַיַּרְא אֱלֹהִים כִּי־טוֹב׃

26 וַיֹּאמֶר אֱלֹהִים נַעֲשֶׂה אָדָם בְּצַלְמֵנוּ כִּדְמוּתֵנוּ וְיִרְדּוּ בִדְגַת הַיָּם וּבְעוֹף הַשָּׁמַיִם וּבַבְּהֵמָה וּבְכָל־הָאָרֶץ וּבְכָל־הָרֶמֶשׂ הָרֹמֵשׂ עַל־הָאָרֶץ׃

27 וַיִּבְרָא אֱלֹהִים אֶת־הָאָדָם בְּצַלְמוֹ בְּצֶלֶם אֱלֹהִים בָּרָא אֹתוֹ זָכָר וּנְקֵבָה בָּרָא אֹתָם׃

28 וַיְבָרֶךְ אֹתָם אֱלֹהִים וַיֹּאמֶר לָהֶם אֱלֹהִים פְּרוּ וּרְבוּ וּמִלְאוּ אֶת־הָאָרֶץ וְכִבְשֻׁהָ וּרְדוּ בִּדְגַת הַיָּם וּבְעוֹף הַשָּׁמַיִם וּבְכָל־חַיָּה הָרֹמֶשֶׂת עַל־הָאָרֶץ׃

29 וַיֹּאמֶר אֱלֹהִים הִנֵּה נָתַתִּי לָכֶם אֶת־כָּל־עֵשֶׂב זֹרֵעַ זֶרַע אֲשֶׁר עַל־פְּנֵי כָל־הָאָרֶץ וְאֶת־כָּל־הָעֵץ אֲשֶׁר־בּוֹ פְרִי־עֵץ זֹרֵעַ זָרַע לָכֶם יִהְיֶה לְאָכְלָה׃

ל וּלְכָל־חַיַּת הָאָרֶץ וּלְכָל־עוֹף הַשָּׁמַיִם וּלְכֹל רוֹמֵשׂ עַל־הָאָרֶץ אֲשֶׁר־בּוֹ נֶפֶשׁ חַיָּה אֶת־כָּל־יֶרֶק עֵשֶׂב לְאָכְלָה וַיְהִי־כֵן׃

וַיַּ֤רְא אֱלֹהִים֙ אֶת־כָּל־אֲשֶׁ֣ר עָשָׂ֔ה וְהִנֵּה־ט֖וֹב מְאֹ֑ד וַֽיְהִי־עֶ֥רֶב וַֽיְהִי־בֹ֖קֶר י֥וֹם הַשִּׁשִּֽׁי׃ 31

CHAPTER II.

וַיְכֻלּ֛וּ הַשָּׁמַ֥יִם וְהָאָ֖רֶץ וְכָל־צְבָאָֽם׃ א

וַיְכַ֤ל אֱלֹהִים֙ בַּיּ֣וֹם הַשְּׁבִיעִ֔י מְלַאכְתּ֖וֹ אֲשֶׁ֣ר עָשָׂ֑ה וַיִּשְׁבֹּת֙ בַּיּ֣וֹם הַשְּׁבִיעִ֔י מִכָּל־מְלַאכְתּ֖וֹ אֲשֶׁ֥ר עָשָֽׂה׃ 2

וַיְבָ֤רֶךְ אֱלֹהִים֙ אֶת־י֣וֹם הַשְּׁבִיעִ֔י וַיְקַדֵּ֖שׁ אֹת֑וֹ כִּ֣י ב֤וֹ שָׁבַת֙ מִכָּל־מְלַאכְתּ֔וֹ אֲשֶׁר־בָּרָ֥א אֱלֹהִ֖ים לַעֲשֽׂוֹת׃ 3

אֵ֣לֶּה תוֹלְד֧וֹת הַשָּׁמַ֛יִם וְהָאָ֖רֶץ בְּהִבָּֽרְאָ֑ם בְּי֗וֹם עֲשׂ֛וֹת יְהוָ֥ה אֱלֹהִ֖ים אֶ֥רֶץ וְשָׁמָֽיִם׃ 4

וְכֹ֣ל ׀ שִׂ֣יחַ הַשָּׂדֶ֗ה טֶ֚רֶם יִֽהְיֶ֣ה בָאָ֔רֶץ וְכָל־עֵ֥שֶׂב הַשָּׂדֶ֖ה טֶ֣רֶם יִצְמָ֑ח כִּי֩ לֹ֨א הִמְטִ֜יר יְהוָ֤ה אֱלֹהִים֙ עַל־הָאָ֔רֶץ וְאָדָ֣ם אַ֔יִן לַֽעֲבֹ֖ד אֶת־הָֽאֲדָמָֽה׃ ה

וְאֵ֖ד יַֽעֲלֶ֣ה מִן־הָאָ֑רֶץ וְהִשְׁקָ֖ה אֶֽת־כָּל־פְּנֵֽי־הָֽאֲדָמָֽה׃ 6

וַיִּיצֶר֩ יְהוָ֨ה אֱלֹהִ֜ים אֶת־הָֽאָדָ֗ם עָפָר֙ מִן־הָ֣אֲדָמָ֔ה וַיִּפַּ֥ח בְּאַפָּ֖יו נִשְׁמַ֣ת חַיִּ֑ים וַֽיְהִ֥י הָֽאָדָ֖ם לְנֶ֥פֶשׁ חַיָּֽה׃ 7

וַיִּטַּ֞ע יְהוָ֧ה אֱלֹהִ֛ים גַּן־בְעֵ֖דֶן מִקֶּ֑דֶם וַיָּ֣שֶׂם שָׁ֔ם אֶת־הָֽאָדָ֖ם אֲשֶׁ֥ר יָצָֽר׃ 8

וַיַּצְמַ֞ח יְהוָ֤ה אֱלֹהִים֙ מִן־הָ֣אֲדָמָ֔ה כָּל־עֵ֛ץ נֶחְמָ֥ד לְמַרְאֶ֖ה וְט֣וֹב לְמַאֲכָ֑ל וְעֵ֤ץ הַֽחַיִּים֙ בְּת֣וֹךְ הַגָּ֔ן וְעֵ֕ץ הַדַּ֖עַת ט֥וֹב וָרָֽע׃ 9

ה׳ זעירא ○ v. 4.

ⁱ⁰ וְנָהָר יֹצֵא מֵעֵדֶן לְהַשְׁקוֹת אֶת־הַגָּן וּמִשָּׁם יִפָּרֵד וְהָיָה לְאַרְבָּעָה רָאשִׁים:

¹¹ שֵׁם הָאֶחָד פִּישׁוֹן הוּא הַסֹּבֵב אֵת כָּל־אֶרֶץ הַחֲוִילָה אֲשֶׁר־שָׁם הַזָּהָב:

¹² וּזֲהַב הָאָרֶץ הַהִוא טוֹב שָׁם הַבְּדֹלַח וְאֶבֶן הַשֹּׁהַם:

¹³ וְשֵׁם־הַנָּהָר הַשֵּׁנִי גִּיחוֹן הוּא הַסּוֹבֵב אֵת כָּל־אֶרֶץ כּוּשׁ:

¹⁴ וְשֵׁם הַנָּהָר הַשְּׁלִישִׁי חִדֶּקֶל הוּא הַהֹלֵךְ קִדְמַת אַשּׁוּר וְהַנָּהָר הָרְבִיעִי הוּא פְרָת:

¹⁵ וַיִּקַּח יְהוָה אֱלֹהִים אֶת־הָאָדָם וַיַּנִּחֵהוּ בְגַן־עֵדֶן לְעָבְדָהּ וּלְשָׁמְרָהּ:

¹⁶ וַיְצַו יְהוָה אֱלֹהִים עַל־הָאָדָם לֵאמֹר מִכֹּל עֵץ־הַגָּן אָכֹל תֹּאכֵל:

¹⁷ וּמֵעֵץ הַדַּעַת טוֹב וָרָע לֹא תֹאכַל מִמֶּנּוּ כִּי בְּיוֹם אֲכָלְךָ מִמֶּנּוּ מוֹת תָּמוּת:

¹⁸ וַיֹּאמֶר יְהוָה אֱלֹהִים לֹא־טוֹב הֱיוֹת הָאָדָם לְבַדּוֹ אֶעֱשֶׂה־לּוֹ עֵזֶר כְּנֶגְדּוֹ:

¹⁹ וַיִּצֶר יְהוָה אֱלֹהִים מִן־הָאֲדָמָה כָּל־חַיַּת הַשָּׂדֶה וְאֵת כָּל־עוֹף הַשָּׁמַיִם וַיָּבֵא אֶל־הָאָדָם לִרְאוֹת מַה־יִּקְרָא־לוֹ וְכֹל אֲשֶׁר יִקְרָא־לוֹ הָאָדָם נֶפֶשׁ חַיָּה הוּא שְׁמוֹ:

²⁰ וַיִּקְרָא הָאָדָם שֵׁמוֹת לְכָל־הַבְּהֵמָה וּלְעוֹף הַשָּׁמַיִם וּלְכֹל חַיַּת הַשָּׂדֶה וּלְאָדָם לֹא־מָצָא עֵזֶר כְּנֶגְדּוֹ:

21 וַיַּפֵּל יְהוָֹה אֱלֹהִים תַּרְדֵּמָה עַל־הָאָדָם וַיִּישָׁן וַיִּקַּח אַחַת
מִצַּלְעֹתָיו וַיִּסְגֹּר בָּשָׂר תַּחְתֶּנָּה:
22 וַיִּבֶן יְהוָֹה אֱלֹהִים אֶת־הַצֵּלָע אֲשֶׁר־לָקַח מִן־הָאָדָם
לְאִשָּׁה וַיְבִאֶהָ אֶל־הָאָדָם:
23 וַיֹּאמֶר הָאָדָם זֹאת הַפַּעַם עֶצֶם מֵעֲצָמַי וּבָשָׂר מִבְּשָׂרִי
לְזֹאת יִקָּרֵא אִשָּׁה כִּי מֵאִישׁ לֻקֳחָה־זֹּאת:
24 עַל־כֵּן יַעֲזָב־אִישׁ אֶת־אָבִיו וְאֶת־אִמּוֹ וְדָבַק בְּאִשְׁתּוֹ וְהָיוּ
לְבָשָׂר אֶחָד:
כה וַיִּהְיוּ שְׁנֵיהֶם עֲרוּמִּים הָאָדָם וְאִשְׁתּוֹ וְלֹא יִתְבֹּשָׁשׁוּ:

CHAPTER III.

א וְהַנָּחָשׁ הָיָה עָרוּם מִכֹּל חַיַּת הַשָּׂדֶה אֲשֶׁר עָשָׂה
יְהוָֹה אֱלֹהִים וַיֹּאמֶר אֶל־הָאִשָּׁה אַף כִּי־אָמַר אֱלֹהִים
לֹא תֹאכְלוּ מִכֹּל עֵץ הַגָּן:
2 וַתֹּאמֶר הָאִשָּׁה אֶל־הַנָּחָשׁ מִפְּרִי עֵץ־הַגָּן נֹאכֵל:
3 וּמִפְּרִי הָעֵץ אֲשֶׁר בְּתוֹךְ־הַגָּן אָמַר אֱלֹהִים לֹא תֹאכְלוּ
מִמֶּנּוּ וְלֹא תִגְּעוּ בּוֹ פֶּן תְּמֻתוּן:
4 וַיֹּאמֶר הַנָּחָשׁ אֶל־הָאִשָּׁה לֹא־מוֹת תְּמֻתוּן:
ה כִּי יֹדֵעַ אֱלֹהִים כִּי בְּיוֹם אֲכָלְכֶם מִמֶּנּוּ וְנִפְקְחוּ עֵינֵיכֶם
וִהְיִיתֶם כֵּאלֹהִים יֹדְעֵי טוֹב וָרָע:

מ׳ ברנש ○ v. 25.

6 וַתֵּרֶא הָאִשָּׁה כִּי טוֹב הָעֵץ לְמַאֲכָל וְכִי תַאֲוָה־הוּא
לָעֵינַיִם וְנֶחְמָד הָעֵץ לְהַשְׂכִּיל וַתִּקַּח מִפִּרְיוֹ וַתֹּאכַל
וַתִּתֵּן גַּם־לְאִישָׁהּ עִמָּהּ וַיֹּאכַל:

7 וַתִּפָּקַחְנָה עֵינֵי שְׁנֵיהֶם וַיֵּדְעוּ כִּי עֵירֻמִּם הֵם וַיִּתְפְּרוּ
עֲלֵה תְאֵנָה וַיַּעֲשׂוּ לָהֶם חֲגֹרֹת:

8 וַיִּשְׁמְעוּ אֶת־קוֹל יְהֹוָה אֱלֹהִים מִתְהַלֵּךְ בַּגָּן לְרוּחַ
הַיּוֹם וַיִּתְחַבֵּא הָאָדָם וְאִשְׁתּוֹ מִפְּנֵי יְהֹוָה אֱלֹהִים
בְּתוֹךְ עֵץ הַגָּן:

9 וַיִּקְרָא יְהֹוָה אֱלֹהִים אֶל־הָאָדָם וַיֹּאמֶר לוֹ אַיֶּכָּה:

וַיֹּאמֶר אֶת־קֹלְךָ שָׁמַעְתִּי בַּגָּן וָאִירָא כִּי־עֵירֹם אָנֹכִי
וָאֵחָבֵא:

11 וַיֹּאמֶר מִי הִגִּיד לְךָ כִּי עֵירֹם אָתָּה הֲמִן־הָעֵץ אֲשֶׁר
צִוִּיתִיךָ לְבִלְתִּי אֲכָל־מִמֶּנּוּ אָכָלְתָּ:

12 וַיֹּאמֶר הָאָדָם הָאִשָּׁה אֲשֶׁר נָתַתָּה עִמָּדִי הִוא נָתְנָה־
לִי מִן־הָעֵץ וָאֹכֵל:

13 וַיֹּאמֶר יְהֹוָה אֱלֹהִים לָאִשָּׁה מַה־זֹּאת עָשִׂית וַתֹּאמֶר
הָאִשָּׁה הַנָּחָשׁ הִשִּׁיאַנִי וָאֹכֵל:

14 וַיֹּאמֶר יְהֹוָה אֱלֹהִים אֶל־הַנָּחָשׁ כִּי עָשִׂיתָ זֹּאת אָרוּר
אַתָּה מִכָּל־הַבְּהֵמָה וּמִכֹּל חַיַּת הַשָּׂדֶה עַל־גְּחֹנְךָ תֵלֵךְ
וְעָפָר תֹּאכַל כָּל־יְמֵי חַיֶּיךָ:

---

v. 10. ○ מלעיל

וְאֵיבָה אָשִׁית בֵּינְךָ וּבֵין הָאִשָּׁה וּבֵין זַרְעֲךָ וּבֵין זַרְעָהּ ט׳
הוּא יְשׁוּפְךָ רֹאשׁ וְאַתָּה תְּשׁוּפֶנּוּ עָקֵב׃
אֶל־הָאִשָּׁה אָמַר הַרְבָּה אַרְבֶּה עִצְּבוֹנֵךְ וְהֵרֹנֵךְ בְּעֶצֶב 16
תֵּלְדִי בָנִים וְאֶל־אִישֵׁךְ תְּשׁוּקָתֵךְ וְהוּא יִמְשָׁל־בָּךְ׃
וּלְאָדָם אָמַר כִּי שָׁמַעְתָּ לְקוֹל אִשְׁתֶּךָ וַתֹּאכַל מִן־הָעֵץ 17
אֲשֶׁר צִוִּיתִיךָ לֵאמֹר לֹא תֹאכַל מִמֶּנּוּ אֲרוּרָה הָאֲדָמָה
בַּעֲבוּרֶךָ בְּעִצָּבוֹן תֹּאכֲלֶנָּה כֹּל יְמֵי חַיֶּיךָ׃
וְקוֹץ וְדַרְדַּר תַּצְמִיחַ לָךְ וְאָכַלְתָּ אֶת־עֵשֶׂב הַשָּׂדֶה׃ 18
בְּזֵעַת אַפֶּיךָ תֹּאכַל לֶחֶם עַד שׁוּבְךָ אֶל־הָאֲדָמָה כִּי 19
מִמֶּנָּה לֻקָּחְתָּ כִּי־עָפָר אַתָּה וְאֶל־עָפָר תָּשׁוּב׃
וַיִּקְרָא הָאָדָם שֵׁם אִשְׁתּוֹ חַוָּה כִּי הִוא הָיְתָה אֵם כ׳
כָּל־חָי׃
וַיַּעַשׂ יְהֹוָה אֱלֹהִים לְאָדָם וּלְאִשְׁתּוֹ כָּתְנוֹת עוֹר 21
וַיַּלְבִּשֵׁם׃
וַיֹּאמֶר יְהֹוָה אֱלֹהִים הֵן הָאָדָם הָיָה כְּאַחַד מִמֶּנּוּ 22
לָדַעַת טוֹב וָרָע וְעַתָּה פֶּן־יִשְׁלַח יָדוֹ וְלָקַח גַּם
מֵעֵץ הַחַיִּים וְאָכַל וָחַי לְעֹלָם׃
וַיְשַׁלְּחֵהוּ יְהֹוָה אֱלֹהִים מִגַּן־עֵדֶן לַעֲבֹד אֶת־הָאֲדָמָה 23
אֲשֶׁר לֻקַּח מִשָּׁם׃
וַיְגָרֶשׁ אֶת־הָאָדָם וַיַּשְׁכֵּן מִקֶּדֶם לְגַן־עֵדֶן אֶת־הַכְּרֻבִים 24
וְאֵת לַהַט הַחֶרֶב הַמִּתְהַפֶּכֶת לִשְׁמֹר אֶת־דֶּרֶךְ עֵץ
הַחַיִּים׃

CHAPTER IV.

א וְהָאָדָם יָדַע אֶת־חַוָּה אִשְׁתּוֹ וַתַּהַר וַתֵּלֶד אֶת־קַיִן וַתֹּאמֶר קָנִיתִי אִישׁ אֶת־יְהוָֹה:

2 וַתֹּסֶף לָלֶדֶת אֶת־אָחִיו אֶת־הָבֶל וַיְהִי־הֶבֶל רֹעֵה צֹאן וְקַיִן הָיָה עֹבֵד אֲדָמָה:

3 וַיְהִי מִקֵּץ יָמִים וַיָּבֵא קַיִן מִפְּרִי הָאֲדָמָה מִנְחָה לַיהוָֹה:

4 וְהֶבֶל הֵבִיא גַם־הוּא מִבְּכֹרוֹת צֹאנוֹ וּמֵחֶלְבֵהֶן וַיִּשַׁע יְהוָֹה אֶל־הֶבֶל וְאֶל־מִנְחָתוֹ:

5 וְאֶל־קַיִן וְאֶל־מִנְחָתוֹ לֹא שָׁעָה וַיִּחַר לְקַיִן מְאֹד וַיִּפְּלוּ פָּנָיו:

6 וַיֹּאמֶר יְהוָֹה אֶל־קָיִן לָמָּה חָרָה לָךְ וְלָמָּה נָפְלוּ פָנֶיךָ:

7 הֲלוֹא אִם־תֵּיטִיב שְׂאֵת וְאִם לֹא תֵיטִיב לַפֶּתַח חַטָּאת רֹבֵץ וְאֵלֶיךָ תְּשׁוּקָתוֹ וְאַתָּה הִמְשָׁל־בּוֹ:

8 וַיֹּאמֶר קַיִן אֶל־הֶבֶל אָחִיו וַיְהִי בִּהְיוֹתָם בַּשָּׂדֶה וַיָּקָם קַיִן אֶל־הֶבֶל אָחִיו וַיַּהַרְגֵהוּ:

9 וַיֹּאמֶר יְהוָֹה אֶל־קַיִן אֵי הֶבֶל אָחִיךָ וַיֹּאמֶר לֹא יָדַעְתִּי הֲשֹׁמֵר אָחִי אָנֹכִי:

י וַיֹּאמֶר מֶה עָשִׂיתָ קוֹל דְּמֵי אָחִיךָ צֹעֲקִים אֵלַי מִן־הָאֲדָמָה:

11 וְעַתָּה אָרוּר אָתָּה מִן־הָאֲדָמָה אֲשֶׁר פָּצְתָה אֶת־פִּיהָ לָקַחַת אֶת־דְּמֵי אָחִיךָ מִיָּדֶךָ:

12 כִּי תַעֲבֹד אֶת־הָאֲדָמָה לֹא־תֹסֵף תֵּת־כֹּחָהּ לָךְ נָע וָנָד
תִּהְיֶה בָאָרֶץ׃
13 וַיֹּאמֶר קַיִן אֶל־יְהוָה גָּדוֹל עֲוֺנִי מִנְּשֹׂא׃
14 הֵן גֵּרַשְׁתָּ אֹתִי הַיּוֹם מֵעַל פְּנֵי הָאֲדָמָה וּמִפָּנֶיךָ אֶסָּתֵר
וְהָיִיתִי נָע וָנָד בָּאָרֶץ וְהָיָה כָל־מֹצְאִי יַהַרְגֵנִי׃
טו וַיֹּאמֶר לוֹ יְהוָה לָכֵן כָּל־הֹרֵג קַיִן שִׁבְעָתַיִם יֻקָּם וַיָּשֶׂם
יְהוָה לְקַיִן אוֹת לְבִלְתִּי הַכּוֹת־אֹתוֹ כָּל־מֹצְאוֹ׃
16 וַיֵּצֵא קַיִן מִלִּפְנֵי יְהוָה וַיֵּשֶׁב בְּאֶרֶץ־נוֹד קִדְמַת־עֵדֶן׃
17 וַיֵּדַע קַיִן אֶת־אִשְׁתּוֹ וַתַּהַר וַתֵּלֶד אֶת־חֲנוֹךְ וַיְהִי בֹּנֶה
עִיר וַיִּקְרָא שֵׁם הָעִיר כְּשֵׁם בְּנוֹ חֲנוֹךְ׃
18 וַיִּוָּלֵד לַחֲנוֹךְ אֶת־עִירָד וְעִירָד יָלַד אֶת־מְחוּיָאֵל וּמְחִיָּיאֵל
יָלַד אֶת־מְתוּשָׁאֵל וּמְתוּשָׁאֵל יָלַד אֶת־לָמֶךְ׃
19 וַיִּקַּח־לוֹ לֶמֶךְ שְׁתֵּי נָשִׁים שֵׁם הָאַחַת עָדָה וְשֵׁם הַשֵּׁנִית
צִלָּה׃
כ וַתֵּלֶד עָדָה אֶת־יָבָל הוּא הָיָה אֲבִי יֹשֵׁב אֹהֶל וּמִקְנֶה׃
21 וְשֵׁם אָחִיו יוּבָל הוּא הָיָה אֲבִי כָּל־תֹּפֵשׂ כִּנּוֹר וְעוּגָב׃
22 וְצִלָּה גַם־הִוא יָלְדָה אֶת־תּוּבַל קַיִן לֹטֵשׁ כָּל־חֹרֵשׁ
נְחֹשֶׁת וּבַרְזֶל וַאֲחוֹת תּוּבַל־קַיִן נַעֲמָה׃
23 וַיֹּאמֶר לֶמֶךְ לְנָשָׁיו
עָדָה וְצִלָּה שְׁמַעַן קוֹלִי
נְשֵׁי לֶמֶךְ הַאְזֵנָּה אִמְרָתִי

יתיר י׳ v. 18.

כִּי אִישׁ הָרַגְתִּי לְפִצְעִי
וְיֶלֶד לְחַבֻּרָתִי:
24 כִּי שִׁבְעָתַיִם יֻקַּם־קָיִן
וְלֶמֶךְ שִׁבְעִים וְשִׁבְעָה:
25 וַיֵּדַע אָדָם עוֹד אֶת־אִשְׁתּוֹ וַתֵּלֶד בֵּן וַתִּקְרָא אֶת־שְׁמוֹ שֵׁת כִּי שָׁת־לִי אֱלֹהִים זֶרַע אַחֵר תַּחַת הֶבֶל כִּי הֲרָגוֹ קָיִן:
26 וּלְשֵׁת גַּם־הוּא יֻלַּד־בֵּן וַיִּקְרָא אֶת־שְׁמוֹ אֱנוֹשׁ אָז הוּחַל לִקְרֹא בְּשֵׁם יְהוָה:

GENESIS I—IV.

A LITERAL TRANSLATION.

CHAPTER I.

1. In-beginning created God*)(the-heavens and-)(the-earth.

2. And-the-earth was desolation and-waste; and-darkness (was) upon+faces-of abyss;* and-(the)-spirit-of God (was) brooding upon+faces-of the-waters.

3. And-said God: Shall-be+(or, let-be)+light;* and-(there)-was+light.

4. And-saw God)(+the-light that+good;* and-caused-a-division God between the-light and-between the-darkness.

5. And-called God to-the-light day, and-to-the-darkness called-he night;* and-(it)-was+evening, and-(it)-was+morning, day one.

6. And-said God: Let-be (an) expanse in-(the)-midst-of the-waters;* and-let-it-be dividing between waters to-waters.

7. And-made God)(+the-expanse,†and-caused-a-division between the-waters which (were) from-under to-the-expanse and-between the-waters which (were) from-upon to-the-expanse;* and-(it)-was+so.

8. And-called God to-the-expanse heavens;* and-(it)-was+evening, and-(it)-was+morning, day second.

9. And-said God: Let-be-collected the-waters from-under the-heavens unto+place one, and-let-be-seen the-dry (land);* and-(it)-was+so.

10. And-called God to-the-dry (land) earth, and-to-(the)-collection-of [the]-waters he-called seas;* and-saw God that+good.

11. And-said God: Let-cause-to-spring-forth the-earth grass, herb causing-to-seed seed, tree-of fruit making fruit to-kind-his which seed-his+in-him (*i. e.*, whose seed is in it) upon+the-earth;* and-(it)-was+so.

12. And-caused-to-come-forth the-earth grass; herb causing-to-seed seed to-kind-his, and-tree making+fruit which seed-his+in-him to-kind-his;* and-saw God that+good.

13. And-(it)-was+evening, and-(it)-was+morning, day third.

14. And-said God: Let-be luminaries in-(the)-expanse-of the-heavens, to-cause-a-division between the-day and-between the-night;* and-they-shall-be for-signs, and-for-seasons, and-for-days and-years.

15. And-they-shall-be for-luminaries in-(the)-expanse-of the-heavens to-cause-light upon+the-earth;* and-(it)-was+so.

16. And-made God)(+(the)-two-[of] [the]-luminaries the-great;*)(+the-luminary the-great, for-ruling-of the-day; and-)(+the-luminary the-small, for-ruling-of the-night, and-)(the-stars.

17. And-gave)(-them God in-(the) expanse-of the-heavens;* to-cause-light upon +the-earth[.].

18. And-to-rule in-the-day and-in-the-night, and-to-cause-a-division between the-light and-between the-darkness;* and-saw God that+good.

19. And-(it)-was+evening, and-(it)-was+morning, day fourth.

20. And-said God: Let-swarm the-waters swarm(s), soul-of life;* and-fowl shall-fly upon+the-earth, upon+faces-of (the) expanse-of the-heavens.

21. And-created God)(+the-sea-monsters the-great;* and-)(all+ (the)-soul(s)-of [the]-life the-creeping (*or*, which-creep), (with) which swarmed the-waters to-kinds-their and-)(every+fowl of wing to-kind-his and-saw God that+good.

22. And-blessed)(-them God, to-say (*or*, saying):* Be-ye fruitful and-multiply-ye and-fill-ye)(+the-waters in-the-seas, and-the-fowl let-multiply in-the-earth.

23. And-(it)-was+evening, and-(it)-was+morning, day fifth.

24. And-said God: Shall-cause-to-come-forth the-earth soul-of life to-kind-her, cattle, and-creeper, and-beast-of+(the)-earth to-kind-her;* and-(it)-was+so.

25. And-made God)(+(the)-beast-of the-earth to-kind-her, and-)(+the-cattle to-kind-her, and-)(every+creeper-of the-ground to-kind-his;* and-saw God that+good.

26. And-said God: We-will-(*or*, Let-us)-make man in-image-our, according-to-likeness-our;* and-they-shall-have-dominion in-(the)-fish-of the-sea, and-in-(the)-fowl-of the-heavens, and-in-the-cattle, and-in-all+the-earth, and-in-all+the-creeper(**s**) the-creeping (*or*, which-creep) upon+the-earth.

27. And-created God)(+the-man in-image-his; in-(the)-image-of God created-he)(-him;* male and-female created-he)(-them.

28. And-blessed)(-them God,† and-said to-them God: Be-ye-fruitful and-multiply-ye, and-fill-ye)(+the-earth and-subdue-ye-her;* and-have-ye-dominion in-(the)-fish-of the-sea, and-in-(the)-fowl-of the-heavens, and-in-every+beast the-creeping upon+the-earth.

29. And-said God: Behold! I-have-given to-you)(+every+herb seeding seed which (is) upon+faces-of all+the-earth, and-)(all +the-tree(s) which+in-him (*i. e.*, in-which) (is the) fruit-of +(a)-tree seeding seed;* to-you it-shall-be for-food.

30. And-to-every+beast-of the-earth, and-to-every+fowl-of the-heavens, and-to-every creeping-one upon+the-earth which+in-him (*i. e.*, in-which) (is the) soul-of life, (I have given))(+ every+greenness-of herb for-food;* and-(it)-was+so.

31. And-saw God)(+all+which he-had-done, and-behold+good exceedingly;* and-(it)-was+evening, and-(it)-was+morning, day the sixth.

CHAPTER II.

1. And-were-finished the-heavens and-the-earth and-all+host-their.

2. And-finished God, in-the-day the-seventh, work-his which-he-had-done;* and-he-rested in-the-day the-seventh from-all+work-his which he-had-done.

3. And-blessed God)(+day the-seventh and-sanctified)(-it;* because in-it he-rested from-all+work-his which+created God to-make.

4. These (are) (the) generations-of the-heavens and-the-earth in-being-created-their;* in-(the)-day-of (the) making of Lord God earth and-heavens.

5. And-every shrub-of the-field not-yet had-been (*lit.*, will-be) in-the-earth, and-every+herb-of the-field not-yet had-sprouted-(*lit.*, will-sprout)-forth;* for not had-caused-to-rain Lord God upon+the-earth and-man was-not to-serve)(+the-ground.

6. And-(a)-mist used-to-go-up (*lit.*, will-go-up) from+the-earth,* and-cause-to-drink (*i. e.*, used-to-water))(+all+(the)-faces-of the-ground.

7. And-formed Lord God)(+the-man (out of) dust from+the-ground, and-breathed in-nostrils-his breath-of lives;* and-was the-man for-(a)-soul-of life (*i. e.*, and-became the-man (a) soul-of life).

8. And-planted Lord God (a) garden in-Eden from-east,* and-placed there)(+the-man whom he-formed.

9. And-caused-to-sprout-forth Lord God from+the-ground, every +tree pleasant to-sight and-good for-food,* and-(the)-tree-of [the]-lives in-(the)-midst-of the-garden, and-(the)-tree-of [the]-knowing good and-evil.

10. And-(a)-river goes-forth (*lit.*, going-forth) from-Eden to-water)(+the-garden,* and-from-there it-is-divided and-becomes four heads (*lit.*, and-is for-four heads).

11. (The) name-of the-one (is) Pishon;* it (*lit.*, he) (is) the-(one-encompassing (*or*, which-encompasses))(all+(the)-land-of-[the]-Havilah, which+there (*i. e.*, where) (is) the-gold.

12. And-(the)-gold-of the-land the-that (*lit.*, she) (is) good;* there (is) the-bdellium and-(the)-stone-of [the]-onyx.

13. And-(the)-name-of+the-river the-second (is) Gihon;* it (is) the-(one)-encompassing)(all+(the)-land-of Cush.

14. And-(the)-name-of the-river the-third (is) Tigris; it (is) the-(one)-going eastward-of Assyria;* and-the-river the-fourth is (*lit.*, he) Euphrates.

15. And-took Lord God)(+the-man,* and-caused-to-rest-him (*i. e.*, placed-him) in-garden-of+Eden to-serve-it (*lit.*, her) and-to-keep-it.

16. And-commanded Lord God upon+the-man to-say (*i. e.*, saying):* From-every tree-of+the-garden eating thou-mayest eat[.];

17. But-from-(the)-tree-of [the]-knowing good and-evil, not shalt-thou-eat from-it (*lit.*, him);* for, in-(the)-day-of eating-thy from-it, dying shalt-thou-die.

18. And-said Lord God: Not+good (the)-being-of [the]-man to-separation-his;* I-will-make+for-him (a) help as-over-against-him (*or*, as-his-counterpart).

19. And-formed Lord God from+the-ground every+beast-of the-field and-)(every+fowl-of the-heavens, and-caused-to-come (*i. e.*, brought) unto+the-man to-see what+he-will-call+to-it, (*lit.*, him),* and-all which will-call+to-it the-man, soul-of life, is (*lit.*, he) name-its (*lit.*, his).

20. And-called the-man names to-all+the-cattle, and-to-(the)-fowl-of the-heavens and-to-every beast-of the-field;* and-for-man not +did-he-find (*i. e.*, there was not found) (a) help as-over-against-him.

21. And-caused-to-fall Lord God (a) deep-sleep upon+the-man, and-he-slept,* and-he-took one from-sides-his and-closed (the) flesh instead-of-it.

22. And-built Lord God)(+the-side which+he-took from+the-man for-(a)-woman,* and-caused-to-come-her (*i. e.*, brought her) unto+the-man.

23. And-said the-man † : This, the-tread (*i. e.*, now), bone from-bones-my, and-flesh from-flesh-my;* to-this it-shall-be-called woman, for from-man was-taken+this.

24. Upon+so (*i. e.*, therefore) shall-leave+(a)-man)(+father-his and-)(+mother-his,* and-shall-cleave in-wife-his, and-they-shall-be for-flesh one.

25. And-were (the) two-of-them naked, the-man and-wife-his;* and-not were-(*lit.*, will-be)-they-ashamed.

CHAPTER III.

[In the two remaining chapters, the translation of the pronominal suffix is placed *before* instead of *after* the noun which it limits.]

1. And-the-serpent was crafty from-every beast-of the-field which had-made Lord God;* and-he-said unto+the-woman: (Is it) so that+has-said God, not shall-ye-eat from-every tree-of the-garden[.]?

2. And-said the-woman unto+the-serpent:* From-(the)-fruit-of (the)-tree(s)-of+the-garden we-may-eat[.];

3. But-from-(the)-fruit-of the-tree which (is) in-midst-of+the-garden,† has-said God: Not shall-ye-eat from-it, and-not shall-ye-touch in-it,* lest ye-die.

4. And-said the-serpent unto+the-woman:* Not+dying shall-ye-die.

5. For knowing (is) God that in-(the)-day-of your-eating from-it, then-(*lit.*, and)-shall-be-opened your-eyes,* and-ye-shall-be-like-God, knowers-of good and-evil.

6. And-saw the-woman, that good (was) the-tree for-food, and-that (a) delight-(was)+it to-the-eyes, and-desirable (was) the-tree to-make-wise, and-she-took from-his-fruit and-she-ate;* and-she-gave also+to-her-husband with-her and-he-ate[.];

7. And-were-opened (the) eyes-of (the) two-of-them, and-they-knew that naked (were) they,* and-they-sewed leaf-of fig-tree, and-they-made for-them-(selves) girdles.

8. And-they-heard)(+(the)-voice-of Lord God walking in-the-garden to-(or, at)-(the)-breeze-of the-day;* and-hid-himself the-man and-his-wife from-faces-of Lord God in-midst-of (the) tree(s)-of the-garden.

9. And-called Lord God unto+the-man,* and-said to-him: Where-art-thou[.]?

10. And-he-said:)(+thy-voice I-heard in-the-garden,* and-I-was-afraid, because+naked (was) I; and-I-hid-myself.

11. And-he-said: Who caused-to-know (*i. e.*, made known) to-thee, that naked (wert) thou;* ?-from+the-tree, which I-commanded-thee to-not eat+from it, hast-thou-eaten[.]?

12. And-said the-man:* The-woman whom thou-gave (to be) with-me, she gave+to-me from+the-tree and-I-ate.

13. And-said Lord God to-the-woman: What+(is)+this thou-hast-done?* And-said the-woman: The serpent corrupted-me and-I-ate.

14. And-said Lord God unto+the-serpent: Because thou-hast-done this,† cursed (art) thou from-all+the-cattle, and-from-every beast-of the-field;* upon+thy-belly shalt-thou-go, and-dust shalt-thou-eat all+(the)+days-of thy-lives.

15. And-enmity will-I-put between-thee and-between the-woman, and-between thy-seed and-between her-seed;* it (*lit.*, he) shall-bruise-thee (as to the) head; and-thou shalt-bruise-him (as to the) heel.

16. Unto+-the-woman he-said: Causing-to-be-great I-will-cause-to-be-great (*i. e.*, multiplying I will multiply) thy-sorrow and-thy-conception (*i. e.*, the sorrow of thy conception); in-pain thou-shalt-bring-forth sons,* and-unto+-thy-husband (shall-be) thy-desire and-he shall-rule+-in-(*or*, over)-thee.

17. And-to-man he-said: Because thou hast-hearkened to-(the)-voice-of thy-wife,† and-hast-eaten from+-the-tree which I-commanded-thee, to-say: not shalt-thou-eat from-it,* cursed (is) the-ground for-the-sake-of-thee; in-sorrow shalt-thou-eat-(of)-it all (the) days-of thy-lives.

18. And-thorn and-thistle shall-it-cause-to-spring-forth to-thee;* and-thou-shalt-eat)(+-(the)+-herb-of the-field.

19. In-(the)-sweat-of thy-nostrils, shalt-thou-eat bread, until thy-return unto+-the-ground; for from-it (*lit.*, her) wast-thou-taken;* for+-dust (art) thou, and-unto+-dust thou-shalt-return.

20. And-called the-man (the) name-of his-wife Eve,* for she was mother-of all+-living.

21. And-made Lord God for-man and-for-his-wife tunics-of skin, and-caused-to-put-on-them.

22. And-said Lord God: Behold! the-man has-become like-one-of [from]-us to-know good and-evil;* and-now lest+-he-put-forth his-hand and-take also from-(the)-tree-of [the]-lives, and-eat and-live for-ever.

23. Therefore-(*lit.*, and)-sent-him Lord God from-(the)-garden-of +-Eden,* to-serve)(+-the-ground which he-was-taken from-there.

24. And-he-drove-out)(+-the-man,* and-caused-to-dwell (*i. e.*, placed) from-east to-(the)-garden-of+-Eden,)(+-the-Cherubim, and-)((the) flame-of the-sword (*i. e.*, the flaming sword) the-(one)-turning-itself to-keep)(+-(the)-way-of (the) tree of [the]-lives.

CHAPTER IV.

1. And-the-man knew)(+Eve his-wife;* and-she-conceived, and-she-bore)(+Cain; and-she-said: I-have-gotten (a) man with+ (the) Lord.

2. And-she-added to-bear (*i. e.*, and again she bore))(+his-brother)(+Abel;* and-was+Abel (a) shepherd-of flock(s), and-Cain was (a) tiller-of ground.

3. And-it-was, from-end-of days,* and-caused-to-come (*i. e.*, brought) Cain from-(the)-fruit-of the-ground (an) offering to (the) Lord.

4. And-Abel caused-to-come, also+he, from-(the)-firstlings-of his flock and-from-their-fats;* and-looked-with-favor (the) Lord unto+Abel and-unto+his-offering.

5. And-unto+Cain and-unto+his-offering not did-he-look-with-favor;* and-it-kindled to-Cain (*i. e.*, and Cain was angry), exceedingly, and-fell his-faces (*or*, countenance).

6. And-said (the) Lord unto+Cain: For-what (*or*, why) has-it-kindled to-thee, and-for-what have-fallen thy-faces[.]?

7. (Is there) ?-not, if+thou-makest-(*or*, doest)-good, (a) lifting-up (of the countenance)? and-if not thou-makest-good, at-the-door sin (is) crouching;* and-unto-thee (shall be) his-desire, and-thou shouldst-rule+in-(*or*, over)-him.

8. And-said Cain unto+Abel his-brother;* and-(it)-was in-their-being in-the-field, and-rose Cain unto+Abel his-brother and-killed-him.

9. And-said (the) Lord unto+Cain: Where (is) Abel thy-brother?* And-he-said: Not have-I-known (*i. e.*, do-know); ?-keeper-of my brother (am) I[.]?

10. And-he-said: What hast-thou-done?* (The) voice-of (the) bloods-of thy-brother (are) crying unto-me from+the-ground.

11. And-now cursed (art) thou,* from+the-ground which has-opened)(+her-mouth to-take)(+(the) +bloods-of **thy-brother from-thy-hand.**

12. When thou-shalt-till (*or*, serve))(+the-ground, not+will-it-add to-give+her-strength to-thee;* (a) fugitive and-(a)-vagabond shalt-thou-be in-the-earth.

13. And-said Cain unto+(the) Lord:* Great (is) my-iniquity from-bearing.

14. Behold! thou-hast-driven-out)(-me the-day (*i. e.*, to-day) from-upon (the) faces-of the-ground, and-from-thy-faces shall-I-be-hid;* and-I-shall-be (a) fugitive and-(a)-vagabond in-the-earth, and-it-shall-be (that) any+finding-me will-kill-me.

15. And-said to-him (the) Lord: Therefore (*lit.*, to-so) any+killing Cain, seven-fold shall-he-be-avenged;* and-placed (the) Lord for-Cain (a) sign to-not smite+)(-him any+finding-him.

16. And-went-forth Cain from-to-faces-of (*i. e.*, from the presence of) (the) Lord;* and-he-dwelt in-(the)-land-of+Nod, eastward-of+Eden.

17. And-knew Cain)(+his-wife and-she-conceived, and-bore)(+Enoch;* and-he-was building (a) city, and-he-called (the) name-of the-city according-to-(the)-name-of his-son Enoch.

18. And-there-was-born to-Enoch)(+Irad; and-Irad begat)(+Mehujael;* and-Mehujael begat)(+Methusael; and-Methusael begat)(+Lamech.

19. And-took+to-him Lamech two-[of] wives,* (the) name-of the-one Adah, and-(the)-name-of the-second Zillah.

20. And-bore Adah)(+Jabal;* he was (the) father-of (the) inhabitant-of tent(s) and-(the-possessor-of)-cattle.

21. And-(the)-name-of his-brother (was) Jubal;* he was (the) father-of all+performing-on (the) harp and-(the)-flute.

22. And-Zillah, also+she, bore)(+Tubal Cain, hammerer-of every +cutter-of (*i. e.*, cutting-instrument-of) bronze and-iron;* and-(the)-sister-of Tubal+Cain (was) Naamah.

23. And-said Lamech to-his-wives:—
Adah and-Zillah, hear-ye my-voice,
Wives-of Lamech hearken-unto my-saying;*
For (a) man I-have-killed for-my-wounding;
And-(a)-youth, for-my-hurt.

24. If seven-fold shall-be-avenged+Cain,*
Then-Lamech seventy and-seven.

25. And-knew Adam again)(+his-wife and-she-bare (a) son; and-she-called)(+his-name Seth:* For has-put+to-me God seed another instead-of Abel, for slew-him Cain.

26. And-to-Seth, also+he, was-born+(a)-son; and-he-called)(+his-name Enosh;* then it-was-commenced to-call on-(the)-name-of (the) Lord.

GENESIS I–IV.

THE UNPOINTED HEBREW TEXT.

CHAPTER I.

א בראשית ברא אלהים את השמים ואת הארץ:

2 והארץ היתה תהו ובהו וחשך על פני תהום ורוח אלהים מרחפת על פני המים:

3 ויאמר אלהים יהי אור ויהי אור:

4 וירא אלהים את האור כי טוב ויבדל אלהים בין האור ובין החשך:

ה ויקרא אלהים לאור יום ולחשך קרא לילה ויהי ערב ויהי בקר יום אחד:

6 ויאמר אלהים יהי רקיע בתוך המים ויהי מבדיל בין מים למים:

7 ויעש אלהים את הרקיע ויבדל בין המים אשר מתחת לרקיע ובין המים אשר מעל לרקיע ויהי כן:

8 ויקרא אלהים לרקיע שמים ויהי ערב ויהי בקר יום שני:

9 ויאמר אלהים יקוו המים מתחת השמים אל מקום אחד ותראה היבשה ויהי כן:

י ויקרא אלהים ליבשה ארץ ולמקוה המים קרא ימים וירא אלהים כי טוב:

11 ויאמר אלהים תדשא הארץ דשא עשב מזריע זרע עץ פרי עשה פרי למינו אשר זרעו בו על הארץ ויהי כן:

12 ותוצא הארץ דשא עשב מזריע זרע למינהו ועץ עשה פרי אשר זרעו בו למינהו וירא אלהים כי טוב:
13 ויהי ערב ויהי בקר יום שלישי:
14 ויאמר אלהים יהי מארת ברקיע השמים להבדיל בין היום ובין הלילה והיו לאתת ולמועדים ולימים ושנים:
טו והיו למאורת ברקיע השמים להאיר על הארץ ויהי כן:
16 ויעש אלהים את שני המארת הגדלים את המאור הגדל לממשלת היום ואת המאור הקטן לממשלת הלילה ואת הכוכבים:
17 ויתן אתם אלהים ברקיע השמים להאיר על הארץ:
18 ולמשל ביום ובלילה ולהבדיל בין האור ובין החשך וירא אלהים כי טוב:
19 ויהי ערב ויהי בקר יום רביעי:
כ ויאמר אלהים ישרצו המים שרץ נפש חיה ועוף יעופף על הארץ על פני רקיע השמים:
21 ויברא אלהים את התנינם הגדלים ואת כל נפש החיה הרמשת אשר שרצו המים למינהם ואת כל עוף כנף למינהו וירא אלהים כי טוב:
22 ויברך אתם אלהים לאמר פרו ורבו ומלאו את המים בימים והעוף ירב בארץ:
23 ויהי ערב ויהי בקר יום חמישי:
24 ויאמר אלהים תוצא הארץ נפש חיה למינה בהמה ורמש וחיתו ארץ למינה ויהי כן:

כה ויעש אלהים את חית הארץ למינה ואת הבהמה למינה ואת כל רמש האדמה למינהו וירא אלהים כי טוב:

26 ויאמר אלהים נעשה אדם בצלמנו כדמותנו וירדו בדגת הים ובעוף השמים ובבהמה ובכל הארץ ובכל הרמש הרמש על הארץ:

27 ויברא אלהים את האדם בצלמו בצלם אלהים ברא אתו זכר ונקבה ברא אתם:

28 ויברך אתם אלהים ויאמר להם אלהים פרו ורבו ומלאו את הארץ וכבשה ורדו בדגת הים ובעוף השמים ובכל חיה הרמשת על הארץ:

29 ויאמר אלהים הנה נתתי לכם את כל עשב זרע זרע אשר על פני כל הארץ ואת כל העץ אשר בו פרי עץ זרע זרע לכם יהיה לאכלה:

ל ולכל חית הארץ ולכל עוף השמים ולכל רומש על הארץ אשר בו נפש חיה את כל ירק עשב לאכלה ויהי כן:

31 וירא אלהים את כל אשר עשה והנה טוב מאד ויהי ערב ויהי בקר יום הששי:

CHAPTER II.

א ויכלו השמים והארץ וכל צבאם:

2 ויכל אלהים ביום השביעי מלאכתו אשר עשה וישבת ביום השביעי מכל מלאכתו אשר עשה:

3 ויברך אלהים את יום השביעי ויקדש אתו כי בו שבת מכל מלאכתו אשר ברא אלהים לעשות:

4 אלה תולדות השמים והארץ בהבראם ביום עשות
יהוה אלהים ארץ ושמים:

ה וכל שיח השדה טרם יהיה בארץ וכל עשב השדה
טרם יצמח כי לא המטיר יהוה אלהים על הארץ
ואדם אין לעבד את האדמה:

6 ואד יעלה מן הארץ והשקה את כל פני האדמה:

7 וייצר יהוה אלהים את האדם עפר מן האדמה ויפח
באפיו נשמת חיים ויהי האדם לנפש חיה:

8 ויטע יהוה אלהים גן בעדן מקדם וישם שם את האדם
אשר יצר:

9 ויצמח יהוה אלהים מן האדמה כל עץ נחמד למראה
וטוב למאכל ועץ החיים בתוך הגן ועץ הדעת טוב
ורע:

י ונהר יצא מעדן להשקות את הגן ומשם יפרד והיה
לארבעה ראשים:

11 שם האחד פישון הוא הסבב את כל ארץ החוילה
אשר שם הזהב:

12 וזהב הארץ ההוא טוב שם הבדלח ואבן השהם:

13 ושם הנהר השני גיחון הוא הסובב את כל ארץ
כוש:

14 ושם הנהר השלישי חדקל הוא ההלך קדמת אשור
והנהר הרביעי הוא פרת:

טו ויקח יהוה אלהים את האדם וינחהו בגן עדן לעברה
ולשמרה:

16 ויצו יהוה אלהים על האדם לאמר מכל עץ הגן
אכל תאכל:

17 ומעץ הדעת טוב ורע לא תאכל ממנו כי ביום
אכלך ממנו מות תמות:

18 ויאמר יהוה אלהים לא טוב היות האדם לבדו
אעשה לו עזר כנגדו:

19 ויצר יהוה אלהים מן האדמה כל חית השדה ואת
כל עוף השמים ויבא אל האדם לראות מה יקרא לו
וכל אשר יקרא לו האדם נפש חיה הוא שמו:

כ ויקרא האדם שמות לכל הבהמה ולעוף השמים
ולכל חית השדה ולאדם לא מצא עזר כנגדו:

21 ויפל יהוה אלהים תרדמה על האדם וייׁשן ויקח
אחת מצלעתיו ויסגר בשר תחתנה:

22 ויבן יהוה אלהים את הצלע אשר לקח מן האדם
לאשה ויבאה אל האדם:

23 ויאמר האדם זאת הפעם עצם מעצמי ובשר מבשרי
לזאת יקרא אשה כי מאיש לקחה זאת:

24 על כן יעזב איש את אביו ואת אמו ודבק באשתו
והיו לבשר אחד:

כה ויהיו שניהם ערומים האדם ואשתו ולא יתבששו:

CHAPTER III.

א והנחש היה ערום מכל חית השדה אשר עשה
יהוה אלהים ויאמר אל האשה אף כי אמר אלהים
לא תאכלו מכל עץ הגן:

2 וַתֹּאמֶר הָאִשָּׁה אֶל הַנָּחָשׁ מִפְּרִי עֵץ הַגָּן נֹאכֵל׃
3 וּמִפְּרִי הָעֵץ אֲשֶׁר בְּתוֹךְ הַגָּן אָמַר אֱלֹהִים לֹא תֹאכְלוּ מִמֶּנּוּ וְלֹא תִגְּעוּ בּוֹ פֶּן תְּמֻתוּן׃
4 וַיֹּאמֶר הַנָּחָשׁ אֶל הָאִשָּׁה לֹא מוֹת תְּמֻתוּן׃
ה כִּי יֹדֵעַ אֱלֹהִים כִּי בְּיוֹם אֲכָלְכֶם מִמֶּנּוּ וְנִפְקְחוּ עֵינֵיכֶם וִהְיִיתֶם כֵּאלֹהִים יֹדְעֵי טוֹב וָרָע׃
6 וַתֵּרֶא הָאִשָּׁה כִּי טוֹב הָעֵץ לְמַאֲכָל וְכִי תַאֲוָה הוּא לָעֵינַיִם וְנֶחְמָד הָעֵץ לְהַשְׂכִּיל וַתִּקַּח מִפִּרְיוֹ וַתֹּאכַל וַתִּתֵּן גַּם לְאִישָׁהּ עִמָּהּ וַיֹּאכַל׃
7 וַתִּפָּקַחְנָה עֵינֵי שְׁנֵיהֶם וַיֵּדְעוּ כִּי עֵירֻמִּם הֵם וַיִּתְפְּרוּ עֲלֵה תְאֵנָה וַיַּעֲשׂוּ לָהֶם חֲגֹרֹת׃
8 וַיִּשְׁמְעוּ אֶת קוֹל יְהוָה אֱלֹהִים מִתְהַלֵּךְ בַּגָּן לְרוּחַ הַיּוֹם וַיִּתְחַבֵּא הָאָדָם וְאִשְׁתּוֹ מִפְּנֵי יְהוָה אֱלֹהִים בְּתוֹךְ עֵץ הַגָּן׃
9 וַיִּקְרָא יְהוָה אֱלֹהִים אֶל הָאָדָם וַיֹּאמֶר לוֹ אַיֶּכָּה׃
י וַיֹּאמֶר אֶת קֹלְךָ שָׁמַעְתִּי בַּגָּן וָאִירָא כִּי עֵירֹם אָנֹ֥כִי וָאֵחָבֵא׃
11 וַיֹּאמֶר מִי הִגִּיד לְךָ כִּי עֵירֹם אָתָּה הֲמִן הָעֵץ אֲשֶׁר צִוִּיתִיךָ לְבִלְתִּי אֲכָל מִמֶּנּוּ אָכָלְתָּ׃
12 וַיֹּאמֶר הָאָדָם הָאִשָּׁה אֲשֶׁר נָתַתָּה עִמָּדִי הִוא נָתְנָה לִּי מִן הָעֵץ וָאֹכֵל׃
13 וַיֹּאמֶר יְהוָה אֱלֹהִים לָאִשָּׁה מַה זֹּאת עָשִׂית וַתֹּאמֶר הָאִשָּׁה הַנָּחָשׁ הִשִּׁיאַנִי וָאֹכֵל׃

מִלְעֵיל v. 10, ○

14 וַיֹּאמֶר יהוה אלהים אל הנחש כי עשית זאת ארור
אתה מכל הבהמה ומכל חית השדה על גחנך תלך
ועפר תאכל כל ימי חייך:

טו וְאֵיבָה אשית בינך ובין האשה ובין זרעך ובין
זרעה הוא ישופך ראש ואתה תשופנו עקב:

16 אל האשה אמר הרבה ארבה עצבונך והרנך בעצב
תלדי בנים ואל אישך תשוקתך והוא ימשל בך:

17 ולאדם אמר כי שמעת לקול אשתך ותאכל מן העץ
אשר צויתיך לאמר לא תאכל ממנו ארורה האדמה
בעבורך בעצבון תאכלנה כל ימי חייך:

18 וקוץ ודרדר תצמיח לך ואכלת את עשב השדה:

19 בזעת אפיך תאכל לחם עד שובך אל האדמה כי
ממנה לקחת כי עפר אתה ואל עפר תשוב:

כ ויקרא האדם שם אשתו חוה כי הוא היתה אם
כל חי:

21 ויעש יהוה אלהים לאדם ולאשתו כתנות עור
וילבשם:

22 ויאמר יהוה אלהים הן האדם היה כאחד ממנו
לדעת טוב ורע ועתה פן ישלח ידו ולקח גם מעץ
החיים ואכל וחי לעלם:

23 וישלחהו יהוה אלהים מגן עדן לעבד את האדמה
אשר לקח משם:

24 ויגרש את האדם וישכן מקדם לגן עדן את הכרבים
ואת להט החרב המתהפכת לשמר את דרך עץ
החיים:

CHAPTER IV.

א והאדם ידע את חוה אשתו ותהר ותלד את קין ותאמר קניתי איש את יהוה:

2 ותסף ללדת את אחיו את הבל ויהי הבל רעה צאן וקין היה עבד אדמה:

3 ויהי מקץ ימים ויבא קין מפרי האדמה מנחה ליהוה:

4 והבל הביא גם הוא מבכרות צאנו ומחלבהן וישע יהוה אל הבל ואל מנחתו:

ה ואל קין ואל מנחתו לא שעה ויחר לקין מאד ויפלו פניו:

6 ויאמר יהוה אל קין למה חרה לך ולמה נפלו פניך:

7 הלוא אם תיטיב שאת ואם לא תיטיב לפתח חטאת רבץ ואליך תשוקתו ואתה תמשל בו:

8 ויאמר קין אל הבל אחיו ויהי בהיותם בשדה ויקם קין אל הבל אחיו ויהרגהו:

9 ויאמר יהוה אל קין אי הבל אחיך ויאמר לא ידעתי השמר אחי אנכי:

י ויאמר מה עשית קול דמי אחיך צעקים אלי מן האדמה:

11 ועתה ארור אתה מן האדמה אשר פצתה את פיה לקחת את דמי אחיך מידך:

12 כי תעבד את האדמה לא תסף תת כחה לך נע ונד תהיה בארץ:

13 וַיֹּאמֶר קַיִן אֶל יהוה גָּדוֹל עֲוֹנִי מִנְּשׂוֹא:
14 הֵן גֵּרַשְׁתָּ אֹתִי הַיּוֹם מֵעַל פְּנֵי הָאֲדָמָה וּמִפָּנֶיךָ אֶסָּתֵר וְהָיִיתִי נָע וָנָד בָּאָרֶץ וְהָיָה כָל מֹצְאִי יַהַרְגֵנִי:
15 וַיֹּאמֶר לוֹ יהוה לָכֵן כָּל הֹרֵג קַיִן שִׁבְעָתַיִם יֻקָּם וַיָּשֶׂם יהוה לְקַיִן אוֹת לְבִלְתִּי הַכּוֹת אֹתוֹ כָּל מֹצְאוֹ:
16 וַיֵּצֵא קַיִן מִלִּפְנֵי יהוה וַיֵּשֶׁב בְּאֶרֶץ נוֹד קִדְמַת עֵדֶן:
17 וַיֵּדַע קַיִן אֶת אִשְׁתּוֹ וַתַּהַר וַתֵּלֶד אֶת חֲנוֹךְ וַיְהִי בֹּנֶה עִיר וַיִּקְרָא שֵׁם הָעִיר כְּשֵׁם בְּנוֹ חֲנוֹךְ:
18 וַיִּוָּלֵד לַחֲנוֹךְ אֶת עִירָד וְעִירָד יָלַד אֶת מְחוּיָאֵל וּמְחִיָּיאֵל יָלַד אֶת מְתוּשָׁאֵל וּמְתוּשָׁאֵל יָלַד אֶת לָמֶךְ:
19 וַיִּקַּח לוֹ לֶמֶךְ שְׁתֵּי נָשִׁים שֵׁם הָאַחַת עָדָה וְשֵׁם הַשֵּׁנִית צִלָּה:
20 וַתֵּלֶד עָדָה אֶת יָבָל הוּא הָיָה אֲבִי יֹשֵׁב אֹהֶל וּמִקְנֶה:
21 וְשֵׁם אָחִיו יוּבָל הוּא הָיָה אֲבִי כָּל תֹּפֵשׂ כִּנּוֹר וְעוּגָב:
22 וְצִלָּה גַם הִוא יָלְדָה אֶת תּוּבַל קַיִן לֹטֵשׁ כָּל חֹרֵשׁ נְחֹשֶׁת וּבַרְזֶל וַאֲחוֹת תּוּבַל קַיִן נַעֲמָה:
23 וַיֹּאמֶר לֶמֶךְ לְנָשָׁיו
עָדָה וְצִלָּה שְׁמַעַן קוֹלִי
נְשֵׁי לֶמֶךְ הַאְזֵנָּה אִמְרָתִי
כִּי אִישׁ הָרַגְתִּי לְפִצְעִי
וְיֶלֶד לְחַבֻּרָתִי:

כִּי שִׁבְעָתַיִם יֻקַּם קָיִן 24
וְלֶמֶךְ ,שִׁבְעִים וְשִׁבְעָה:
כה וַיֵּדַע אָדָם עוֹד אֶת אִשְׁתּוֹ וַתֵּלֶד בֵּן וַתִּקְרָא אֶת שְׁמוֹ
שֵׁת כִּי שָׁת לִי אֱלֹהִים זֶרַע אַחֵר תַּחַת הֶבֶל כִּי
הֲרָגוֹ קָיִן:
26 וּלְשֵׁת גַּם הוּא יֻלַּד בֵּן וַיִּקְרָא אֶת שְׁמוֹ אֱנוֹשׁ אָז
הוּחַל לִקְרֹא בְּשֵׁם יהוה:

Transliteration of Genesis I.

1. Bᵉrē'-šîθ bå-rå' 'ᵉlô-hîm* 'ēθ hăš-šå-må-yǐm wᵉ'ēθ hå-'å'-rĕṣ.

2. Wᵉhå-'å'-rĕṣ hå-yᵉθå(h) θṓ-hû wå-vṓ-hû, wᵉḥṓ-šĕχ 'äl+pᵉnê θᵉhôm* wᵉrû(ă)ḥ 'ᵉlô-hîm mᵉrä(ḥ)-ḥĕ-fēθ 'äl+pᵉnê hăm-må'-yǐm.

3. Wăy-yô''-mĕr 'ᵉlô-hîm yᵉhî+'ôr;* wăy-hî+ôr.

4. Wăy-yăr' 'ᵉlô-hîm 'ēθ+hå-'ôr kî+ṭôv;* wăy-yăv-dēl 'ᵉlô-hîm bên hå-'ôr û-vên hä(ḥ)-ḥṓ-šĕχ.

5. Wăy-yǐḳ-rå' 'ᵉlô-hîm lå-'ôr yôm wᵉlä(ḥ)-ḥṓ-šĕχ ḳå'-rå' lå'-yᵉlä(h);* wăy-hî+'é-rĕv wăy-hî+vṓ-ḳĕr yôm 'ĕ(ḥ)-ḥåđ.

6. Wăy-yô''-mĕr ᵉlô-hîm, yᵉhî rå-ḳî(ä)' bᵉθôχ hăm-må'-yǐm;* wî-hî măv-dîl bên må-yǐm lå-må'-yǐm.

7. Wăy-yă-'äs 'ᵉlô-hîm 'ēθ+hå-rå-ḳî(ä)';† wăy-yăv-dēl bên hăm-må-yǐm 'ᵃšĕr мǐt-tå-ḥäθ lå-rå-ḳî(ä)' û-vên hăm-må-yǐm 'ᵃšĕr mē-'äl lå-rå-ḳî(ä)';* wăy-hî+χēn.

8. Wăy-yǐḳ-rå' 'ᵉlô-hîm lå-rå-ḳî(ä)' šå-må'-yǐm;* wăy-hî+'é-rĕv wăy-hî+vṓ-ḳĕr yôm šē-nî.

9. Wăy-yô''-mĕr 'ᵉlô-hîm, yǐḳ-ḳå-wû hăm-må-yǐm mǐt-tå-ḥäθ hăš-šå-må-yǐm 'ĕl+må-ḳôm 'ĕ(ḥ)-ḥåđ, wᵉθē-rå-'é(h) hăy-yăb-bå-šå(h);* wăy-hî+χēn.

10. Wăy-yǐḳ-rå' 'ᵉlô-hîm läy-yăb-bå-šå(h) 'é-rĕṣ, û-lᵉmǐḳ-wê hăm-må-yǐm ḳå-rå' yăm-mîm;* wăy-yăr' 'ᵉlô-hîm kî+ṭôv.

11. Wăy-yô''-mĕr 'ᵉlô-hîm, tăđ-šē' hå-'å'-rĕṣ dé-šē', 'é-sĕv măz-rî(ä)' zé-rä', 'ēṣ pᵉrî 'ô-sé(h) pᵉrî lᵉmî-nô, 'ᵃšĕr zăr-'ô+vô 'äl+hå-'å'-rĕṣ;* wăy-hî+χēn.

12. Wăt-tô-ṣē' hå-'ä'-rĕṣ dé-šĕ, 'é-sĕv măz-rî(ä)' zé-rä' lᵉmî-né-hû, wᵉēṣ 'ô-sé(h)+pᵉrî 'ᵃšĕr zăr-'ô+vô lᵉmî-né-hû;* wăy-yăr' 'ᵉlô-hîm kî+ṭôv.

13. Wăy-hî+'ĕ́-rĕv wăy-hî+vŏ́-ķĕr yôm šᵉlî-šî.

14. Wăy-yô''-mĕr 'ᵉlô-hîm, yᵉhî mᵉ'ô-rôθ bĭr-ķî(ä)' hăš-šå-mắ-yĭm, lᵉhăv-dîl bên hăy-yôm û-vên hăl-lǻ'-yᵉlå(h);* wᵉhå-yû lᵉ'ô-θôθ û-lᵉmô-'ᵃđîm û-lᵉyå-mîm wᵉšå-nîm.

15. Wᵉhå-yû lĭm-'ô-rôθ bĭr-ķî(ä)' hăš-šå-mắ-yĭm, lᵉhå-'îr 'ăl+hå-'ǻ-rĕṣ;* wăy-hî+χēn.

16. Wăy-yắ-'ăs 'ᵉlô-hîm 'ĕθ+šᵉnê hăm-mᵉ'ô-rôθ hăg-gᵉđô-lîm,* 'ĕθ +hăm-må-'ôr hăg-gå-đôl lᵉmĕm-šḗ-lĕθ hăy-yôm, wᵉ'ĕθ+hăm-må-'ôr hăķ-ķå-țōn lᵉmĕm-šḗ-lĕθ hăl-lǻ'-yᵉlå(h), wᵉ'ēθ hăk-kô-χå-vîm.

17. Wăy-yĭt-tēn 'ô-θåm 'ᵉlô-hîm bĭr-ķî(ä)' hăš-šå-mắ'-yĭm,* lᵉhå-'îr 'ăl+hå-'ǻ'-rĕṣ[.],

18. Wᵉlĭm-šōl băy-yôm û-văl-lǻ-yᵉlå(h), û-lᵃhăv-dîl bên hå-'ôr û-vēn hă(h)-h̥ṓ-šĕχ;* wăy-yăr' 'ᵉlô-hîm kî+țôv.

19. Wăy-hî+'ĕ́-rĕv wăy-hî+vŏ́-ķĕr yôm rᵉvî-'î.

20. Wăy-yô''-mĕr 'ᵉlô-hîm, yĭš-rᵉṣû hăm-må-yĭm šḗ-rĕṣ, nĕ-fĕš h̥ăy-yå(h);* wᵉ'ôf yᵉ'ô-fēf 'ăl+hå-'ǻ'-rĕṣ, 'ăl+pᵉnê rᵉķî(ä)' hăš-šå-mắ'-yĭm.

21. Wăy-yĭv-rå' 'ᵉlô-hîm 'ĕθ+hăt-tăn-nî-nîm hăg-gᵉđô-lîm,* wᵉ'ēθ kŏl+nĕ-fĕšhå(h)-h̥ăy-yå(h) hå-rô-mḗ-sĕθ 'ᵃšĕr šå-rᵉṣû hăm-må-yĭm lᵉmî-nē-hĕm, wᵉ'ēθ kŏl-'ôf kå-nåf lᵉmî-nē-hû; wăy-yăr' 'ᵉlô-hîm kî+țôv.

22. Wăy-vǻ-rĕχ 'ô-θåm 'ᵉlô-hîm, lē'-môr,* pᵉrû û-rᵉvû û-mĭl-û 'ĕθ+hăm-må-yĭm băy-yăm-mîm, wᵉhå-'ôf yĭ'-rĕv bå-'ǻ'-rĕṣ.

23. Wăy-hî+'ĕ́-rĕv wăy-hî+vŏ́-ķĕr yôm h̥ᵃmî-šî.

24. Wăy-yô''-mĕr 'ᵉlô-hîm, tô-ṣē' hå-'ǻ'-rĕṣ nĕ-fĕš h̥ăy-yå(h) lᵉmî-nåh, bᵉhē-må(h) wå-rĕ́-mĕś wᵉh̥ăy-θô+'ĕ́-rĕṣ lᵉmî-nåh;* wăy-hî+χēn.

25. Wăy-yắ-'ăs 'ᵉlô-hîm 'ĕθ+h̥ăy-yăθ hå-'ǻ'-rĕṣ lᵉmî-nåh, wᵉ'ĕθ+håb· bᵉhē-må(h) lᵉmî-nåh, wᵉ'ēθ kŏl+rĕ́-mĕś hå-'ᵃđå-må(h) lᵉmî-nē-hû;* wăy-yăr' 'ᵉlô-hîm kî+țôv.

26. Wăy-yô''-mĕr 'ᵉlô-hîm, năʿᵃ-sé(h) 'å-đåm bᵉşăl-mḗ-nû, kĭđ-mû-θé-nû;* wᵉyĭr-dû vĭđ-găθ hăy-yåm û-vᵉʿôf hăš-šå-må-yĭm û-văb-bᵉhē-må(h) û-vᵉχŏl+hå-'å'-rĕş, û-vᵉχŏl+hå-rḗ-mĕś hå-rô-mēś 'äl+hå-'å'-rĕş.

27. Wăy-yĭv-rå' 'ᵉlô-hîm 'ĕθ+hå-'å-đåm bᵉşăl-mô, bᵉşḗ-lĕm 'ᵉlô-hîm bå-rå' 'ô-θô;* zå-χår û-nᵉķē-vå(h) bå-rå' 'ô-θåm.

28. Wăy-vå'-rĕχ 'ô-θåm 'ᵉlô-hîm,† wăy-yô''-mĕr lå-hĕm 'ᵉlô-hîm, pᵉrû û-rᵉvû û-mĭl-'û 'ĕθ+hå-'å'-rĕş wᵉχīv-šû'-hå* û-rᵉđû bĭđ-găθ hăy-yåm û-vᵉʿôf hăš-šå-må-yĭm, û-vᵉχŏl+ḥăy-yå(h) hå-rô-mḗ-śĕθ 'äl+hå-'å'-rĕş.

29. Wăy-yô''-mĕr 'ᵉlô-hîm, hĭn-nē(h) nå-θăt-tî lå-χĕm 'ĕθ+kŏl+'ḗ-sĕv zô-rē(ă)ʿ zḗ-råʿ 'ᵃšĕr 'äl+pᵉnê χŏl+hå-'å'-rĕş, wᵉʿēθ kŏl+hå-ʿēş 'ᵃšĕr+bô fᵉrî+'ēş zô-rē(ă)ʿ zå'-răʿ,* lå-χĕm yĭh-yé(h) lᵉʿŏχ-lå(h).

30. û-lᵉχŏl+ḥăy-yăθ hå-'å'-rĕş û-lᵉχŏl +'ôf hăš-šå-må-yĭm û-lᵉχōl rô-mēś 'äl+hå-'å'-rĕş 'ᵃšĕr+bô nĕ-fĕš ḥăy-yå(h) 'ĕθ+kŏl+ yḗ-rĕķ 'ē-śĕv lᵉʿŏχ-lå(h);* wăy-hî+χēn.

31. Wăy-yăr' 'ᵉlô-hîm 'ĕθ+kŏl+'ᵃšĕr 'å-så(h) wᵉhĭn-nē(h)+ṭôv mᵉ'ôđ;* wăy-hî+ḗ-rĕv wăy-hî+vṓ-ķĕr yôm hăš-šĭš-šî.

GENESIS V–VIII.

THE HEBREW TEXT.

CHAPTER V.

א זֶה סֵפֶר תּוֹלְדֹת אָדָם בְּיוֹם בְּרֹא אֱלֹהִים אָדָם בִּדְמוּת אֱלֹהִים עָשָׂה אֹתוֹ:

2 זָכָר וּנְקֵבָה בְּרָאָם וַיְבָרֶךְ אֹתָם וַיִּקְרָא אֶת־שְׁמָם אָדָם בְּיוֹם הִבָּרְאָם:

3 וַיְחִי אָדָם שְׁלֹשִׁים וּמְאַת שָׁנָה וַיּוֹלֶד בִּדְמוּתוֹ כְּצַלְמוֹ וַיִּקְרָא אֶת־שְׁמוֹ שֵׁת:

4 וַיִּהְיוּ יְמֵי אָדָם אַחֲרֵי הוֹלִידוֹ אֶת־שֵׁת שְׁמֹנֶה מֵאֹת שָׁנָה וַיּוֹלֶד בָּנִים וּבָנוֹת:

ה וַיִּהְיוּ כָּל־יְמֵי אָדָם אֲשֶׁר־חַי תְּשַׁע מֵאוֹת שָׁנָה וּשְׁלֹשִׁים שָׁנָה וַיָּמֹת:

6 וַיְחִי־שֵׁת חָמֵשׁ שָׁנִים וּמְאַת שָׁנָה וַיּוֹלֶד אֶת־אֱנוֹשׁ:

7 וַיְחִי־שֵׁת אַחֲרֵי הוֹלִידוֹ אֶת־אֱנוֹשׁ שֶׁבַע שָׁנִים וּשְׁמֹנֶה מֵאוֹת שָׁנָה וַיּוֹלֶד בָּנִים וּבָנוֹת:

8 וַיִּהְיוּ כָּל־יְמֵי־שֵׁת שְׁתֵּים עֶשְׂרֵה שָׁנָה וּתְשַׁע מֵאוֹת שָׁנָה וַיָּמֹת:

9 וַיְחִי אֱנוֹשׁ תִּשְׁעִים שָׁנָה וַיּוֹלֶד אֶת־קֵינָן:

וַיְחִי אֱנוֹשׁ אַחֲרֵי הוֹלִידוֹ אֶת־קֵינָן חֲמֵשׁ עֶשְׂרֵה שָׁנָה וּשְׁמֹנֶה מֵאוֹת שָׁנָה וַיּוֹלֶד בָּנִים וּבָנוֹת:

11 וַיִּהְיוּ כָּל־יְמֵי אֱנוֹשׁ חָמֵשׁ שָׁנִים וּתְשַׁע מֵאוֹת שָׁנָה וַיָּמֹת:
12 וַיְחִי קֵינָן שִׁבְעִים שָׁנָה וַיּוֹלֶד אֶת־מַהֲלַלְאֵל:
13 וַיְחִי קֵינָן אַחֲרֵי הוֹלִידוֹ אֶת־מַהֲלַלְאֵל אַרְבָּעִים שָׁנָה וּשְׁמֹנֶה מֵאוֹת שָׁנָה וַיּוֹלֶד בָּנִים וּבָנוֹת:
14 וַיִּהְיוּ כָּל־יְמֵי קֵינָן עֶשֶׂר שָׁנִים וּתְשַׁע מֵאוֹת שָׁנָה וַיָּמֹת:
טו וַיְחִי מַהֲלַלְאֵל חָמֵשׁ שָׁנִים וְשִׁשִּׁים שָׁנָה וַיּוֹלֶד אֶת־יָרֶד:
16 וַיְחִי מַהֲלַלְאֵל אַחֲרֵי הוֹלִידוֹ אֶת־יֶרֶד שְׁלֹשִׁים שָׁנָה וּשְׁמֹנֶה מֵאוֹת שָׁנָה וַיּוֹלֶד בָּנִים וּבָנוֹת:
17 וַיִּהְיוּ כָּל־יְמֵי מַהֲלַלְאֵל חָמֵשׁ וְתִשְׁעִים שָׁנָה וּשְׁמֹנֶה מֵאוֹת שָׁנָה וַיָּמֹת:
18 וַיְחִי־יֶרֶד שְׁתַּיִם וְשִׁשִּׁים שָׁנָה וּמְאַת שָׁנָה וַיּוֹלֶד אֶת־חֲנוֹךְ:
19 וַיְחִי־יֶרֶד אַחֲרֵי הוֹלִידוֹ אֶת־חֲנוֹךְ שְׁמֹנֶה מֵאוֹת שָׁנָה וַיּוֹלֶד בָּנִים וּבָנוֹת:
כ וַיִּהְיוּ כָּל־יְמֵי־יֶרֶד שְׁתַּיִם וְשִׁשִּׁים שָׁנָה וּתְשַׁע מֵאוֹת שָׁנָה וַיָּמֹת:
21 וַיְחִי חֲנוֹךְ חָמֵשׁ וְשִׁשִּׁים שָׁנָה וַיּוֹלֶד אֶת־מְתוּשָׁלַח:
22 וַיִּתְהַלֵּךְ חֲנוֹךְ אֶת־הָאֱלֹהִים אַחֲרֵי הוֹלִידוֹ אֶת־מְתוּשֶׁלַח שְׁלֹשׁ מֵאוֹת שָׁנָה וַיּוֹלֶד בָּנִים וּבָנוֹת:
23 וַיְהִי כָּל־יְמֵי חֲנוֹךְ חָמֵשׁ וְשִׁשִּׁים שָׁנָה וּשְׁלֹשׁ מֵאוֹת שָׁנָה:

24 וַיִּתְהַלֵּךְ חֲנוֹךְ אֶת־הָאֱלֹהִים וְאֵינֶנּוּ כִּי־לָקַח אֹתוֹ אֱלֹהִים:

כה וַיְחִי מְתוּשֶׁלַח שֶׁבַע וּשְׁמֹנִים שָׁנָה וּמְאַת שָׁנָה יָוֹלֶד אֶת־לָמֶךְ:

26 וַיְחִי מְתוּשֶׁלַח אַחֲרֵי הוֹלִידוֹ אֶת־לֶמֶךְ שְׁתַּיִם וּשְׁמוֹנִים שָׁנָה וּשְׁבַע מֵאוֹת שָׁנָה וַיּוֹלֶד בָּנִים וּבָנוֹת:

27 וַיִּהְיוּ כָּל־יְמֵי מְתוּשֶׁלַח תֵּשַׁע וְשִׁשִּׁים שָׁנָה וּתְשַׁע מֵאוֹת שָׁנָה וַיָּמֹת:

28 וַיְחִי־לֶמֶךְ שְׁתַּיִם וּשְׁמֹנִים שָׁנָה וּמְאַת שָׁנָה וַיּוֹלֶד בֵּן:

29 וַיִּקְרָא אֶת־שְׁמוֹ נֹחַ לֵאמֹר זֶה ֯ יְנַחֲמֵנוּ מִמַּעֲשֵׂנוּ וּמֵעִצְּבוֹן יָדֵינוּ מִן־הָאֲדָמָה אֲשֶׁר אֵרְרָהּ יְהוָֹה:

ל וַיְחִי־לֶמֶךְ אַחֲרֵי הוֹלִידוֹ אֶת־נֹחַ חָמֵשׁ וְתִשְׁעִים שָׁנָה וַחֲמֵשׁ מֵאֹת שָׁנָה וַיּוֹלֶד בָּנִים וּבָנוֹת:

31 וַיְהִי כָּל־יְמֵי־לֶמֶךְ שֶׁבַע וְשִׁבְעִים שָׁנָה וּשְׁבַע מֵאוֹת שָׁנָה וַיָּמֹת:

32 וַיְהִי־נֹחַ בֶּן־חֲמֵשׁ מֵאוֹת שָׁנָה וַיּוֹלֶד נֹחַ אֶת־שֵׁם אֶת־חָם וְאֶת־יָפֶת:

CHAPTER VI.

א וַיְהִי כִּי־הֵחֵל הָאָדָם לָרֹב עַל־פְּנֵי הָאֲדָמָה וּבָנוֹת יֻלְּדוּ לָהֶם:

2 וַיִּרְאוּ בְנֵי־הָאֱלֹהִים אֶת־בְּנוֹת הָאָדָם כִּי טֹבֹת הֵנָּה וַיִּקְחוּ לָהֶם נָשִׁים מִכֹּל אֲשֶׁר בָּחָרוּ:

○ v. 29. תרי טעמי, והקורא יטעים הגרש קודם התלשא

3 וַיֹּ֣אמֶר יְהֹוָ֗ה לֹא־יָד֨וֹן רוּחִ֤י בָֽאָדָם֙ לְעֹלָ֔ם בְּשַׁגַּ֖ם ה֣וּא בָשָׂ֑ר וְהָי֣וּ יָמָ֔יו מֵאָ֥ה וְעֶשְׂרִ֖ים שָׁנָֽה׃
4 הַנְּפִלִ֞ים הָי֣וּ בָאָרֶץ֮ בַּיָּמִ֣ים הָהֵם֒ וְגַ֣ם אַחֲרֵי־כֵ֗ן אֲשֶׁ֨ר יָבֹ֜אוּ בְּנֵ֤י הָֽאֱלֹהִים֙ אֶל־בְּנ֣וֹת הָֽאָדָ֔ם וְיָלְד֖וּ לָהֶ֑ם הֵ֧מָּה הַגִּבֹּרִ֛ים אֲשֶׁ֥ר מֵעוֹלָ֖ם אַנְשֵׁ֥י הַשֵּֽׁם׃
5 וַיַּ֣רְא יְהֹוָ֔ה כִּ֥י רַבָּ֛ה רָעַ֥ת הָאָדָ֖ם בָּאָ֑רֶץ וְכָל־יֵ֨צֶר֙ מַחְשְׁבֹ֣ת לִבּ֔וֹ רַ֥ק רַ֖ע כָּל־הַיּֽוֹם׃
6 וַיִּנָּ֣חֶם יְהֹוָ֔ה כִּֽי־עָשָׂ֥ה אֶת־הָֽאָדָ֖ם בָּאָ֑רֶץ וַיִּתְעַצֵּ֖ב אֶל־לִבּֽוֹ׃
7 וַיֹּ֣אמֶר יְהֹוָ֗ה אֶמְחֶ֨ה אֶת־הָאָדָ֤ם אֲשֶׁר־בָּרָ֨אתִי֙ מֵעַל֙ פְּנֵ֣י הָֽאֲדָמָ֔ה מֵֽאָדָם֙ עַד־בְּהֵמָ֔ה עַד־רֶ֖מֶשׂ וְעַד־ע֣וֹף הַשָּׁמָ֑יִם כִּ֥י נִחַ֖מְתִּי כִּ֥י עֲשִׂיתִֽם׃
8 וְנֹ֕חַ מָ֥צָא חֵ֖ן בְּעֵינֵ֥י יְהֹוָֽה׃

פרשת נח.

9 אֵ֚לֶּה תּוֹלְדֹ֣ת נֹ֔חַ נֹ֗חַ אִ֥ישׁ צַדִּ֛יק תָּמִ֥ים הָיָ֖ה בְּדֹֽרֹתָ֑יו אֶת־הָֽאֱלֹהִ֖ים הִֽתְהַלֶּךְ־נֹֽחַ׃
10 וַיּ֥וֹלֶד נֹ֖חַ שְׁלֹשָׁ֣ה בָנִ֑ים אֶת־שֵׁ֖ם אֶת־חָ֥ם וְאֶת־יָֽפֶת׃
11 וַתִּשָּׁחֵ֥ת הָאָ֖רֶץ לִפְנֵ֣י הָאֱלֹהִ֑ים וַתִּמָּלֵ֥א הָאָ֖רֶץ חָמָֽס׃
12 וַיַּ֧רְא אֱלֹהִ֛ים אֶת־הָאָ֖רֶץ וְהִנֵּ֣ה נִשְׁחָ֑תָה כִּֽי־הִשְׁחִ֧ית כָּל־בָּשָׂ֛ר אֶת־דַּרְכּ֖וֹ עַל־הָאָֽרֶץ׃

13 וַיֹּ֤אמֶר אֱלֹהִים֙ לְנֹ֔חַ קֵ֥ץ כָּל־בָּשָׂ֖ר בָּ֣א לְפָנַ֑י כִּֽי־מָלְאָ֤ה הָאָ֙רֶץ֙ חָמָ֣ס מִפְּנֵיהֶ֔ם וְהִנְנִ֥י מַשְׁחִיתָ֖ם אֶת־הָאָֽרֶץ:

14 עֲשֵׂ֤ה לְךָ֙ תֵּבַ֣ת עֲצֵי־גֹ֔פֶר קִנִּ֖ים תַּֽעֲשֶׂ֣ה אֶת־הַתֵּבָ֑ה וְכָֽפַרְתָּ֥ אֹתָ֛הּ מִבַּ֥יִת וּמִח֖וּץ בַּכֹּֽפֶר:

15 וְזֶ֕ה אֲשֶׁ֥ר תַּֽעֲשֶׂ֖ה אֹתָ֑הּ שְׁלֹ֧שׁ מֵא֣וֹת אַמָּ֗ה אֹ֚רֶךְ הַתֵּבָ֔ה חֲמִשִּׁ֤ים אַמָּה֙ רָחְבָּ֔הּ וּשְׁלֹשִׁ֥ים אַמָּ֖ה קֽוֹמָתָֽהּ:

16 צֹ֣הַר ׀ תַּֽעֲשֶׂ֣ה לַתֵּבָ֗ה וְאֶל־אַמָּה֙ תְּכַלֶּ֣נָּה מִלְמַ֔עְלָה וּפֶ֥תַח הַתֵּבָ֖ה בְּצִדָּ֣הּ תָּשִׂ֑ים תַּחְתִּיִּ֛ם שְׁנִיִּ֥ם וּשְׁלִשִׁ֖ים תַּֽעֲשֶֽׂהָ:

17 וַֽאֲנִ֗י הִנְנִי֩ מֵבִ֨יא אֶת־הַמַּבּ֥וּל מַ֙יִם֙ עַל־הָאָ֔רֶץ לְשַׁחֵ֣ת כָּל־בָּשָׂ֗ר אֲשֶׁר־בּוֹ֙ ר֣וּחַ חַיִּ֔ים מִתַּ֖חַת הַשָּׁמָ֑יִם כֹּ֥ל אֲשֶׁר־בָּאָ֖רֶץ יִגְוָֽע:

18 וַֽהֲקִֽמֹתִ֥י אֶת־בְּרִיתִ֖י אִתָּ֑ךְ וּבָאתָ֙ אֶל־הַתֵּבָ֔ה אַתָּ֕ה וּבָנֶ֛יךָ וְאִשְׁתְּךָ֥ וּנְשֵֽׁי־בָנֶ֖יךָ אִתָּֽךְ:

19 וּמִכָּל־הָ֠חַי מִֽכָּל־בָּשָׂ֞ר שְׁנַ֧יִם מִכֹּ֛ל תָּבִ֥יא אֶל־הַתֵּבָ֖ה לְהַֽחֲיֹ֣ת אִתָּ֑ךְ זָכָ֥ר וּנְקֵבָ֖ה יִֽהְיֽוּ:

20 מֵהָע֣וֹף לְמִינֵ֗הוּ וּמִן־הַבְּהֵמָה֙ לְמִינָ֔הּ מִכֹּ֛ל רֶ֥מֶשׂ הָֽאֲדָמָ֖ה לְמִינֵ֑הוּ שְׁנַ֧יִם מִכֹּ֛ל יָבֹ֥אוּ אֵלֶ֖יךָ לְהַֽחֲיֽוֹת:

21 וְאַתָּ֣ה קַח־לְךָ֗ מִכָּל־מַֽאֲכָל֙ אֲשֶׁ֣ר יֵֽאָכֵ֔ל וְאָֽסַפְתָּ֖ אֵלֶ֑יךָ וְהָיָ֥ה לְךָ֛ וְלָהֶ֖ם לְאָכְלָֽה:

22 וַיַּ֖עַשׂ נֹ֑חַ כְּ֠כֹל אֲשֶׁ֨ר צִוָּ֥ה אֹת֛וֹ אֱלֹהִ֖ים כֵּ֥ן עָשָֽׂה:

CHAPTER VII.

א וַיֹּאמֶר יְהֹוָה לְנֹחַ בֹּא־אַתָּה וְכָל־בֵּיתְךָ אֶל־הַתֵּבָה כִּי־אֹתְךָ רָאִיתִי צַדִּיק לְפָנַי בַּדּוֹר הַזֶּה:

2 מִכֹּל ׀ הַבְּהֵמָה הַטְּהוֹרָה תִּקַּח־לְךָ שִׁבְעָה שִׁבְעָה אִישׁ וְאִשְׁתּוֹ וּמִן־הַבְּהֵמָה אֲשֶׁר לֹא טְהֹרָה הִוא שְׁנַיִם אִישׁ וְאִשְׁתּוֹ:

3 גַּם מֵעוֹף הַשָּׁמַיִם שִׁבְעָה שִׁבְעָה זָכָר וּנְקֵבָה לְחַיּוֹת זֶרַע עַל־פְּנֵי כָל־הָאָרֶץ:

4 כִּי לְיָמִים עוֹד שִׁבְעָה אָנֹכִי מַמְטִיר עַל־הָאָרֶץ אַרְבָּעִים יוֹם וְאַרְבָּעִים לָיְלָה וּמָחִיתִי אֶת־כָּל־הַיְקוּם אֲשֶׁר עָשִׂיתִי מֵעַל פְּנֵי הָאֲדָמָה:

ה וַיַּעַשׂ נֹחַ כְּכֹל אֲשֶׁר־צִוָּהוּ יְהֹוָה:

6 וְנֹחַ בֶּן־שֵׁשׁ מֵאוֹת שָׁנָה וְהַמַּבּוּל הָיָה מַיִם עַל־הָאָרֶץ:

7 וַיָּבֹא נֹחַ וּבָנָיו וְאִשְׁתּוֹ וּנְשֵׁי־בָנָיו אִתּוֹ אֶל־הַתֵּבָה מִפְּנֵי מֵי הַמַּבּוּל:

8 מִן־הַבְּהֵמָה הַטְּהוֹרָה וּמִן־הַבְּהֵמָה אֲשֶׁר אֵינֶנָּה טְהֹרָה וּמִן־הָעוֹף וְכֹל אֲשֶׁר־רֹמֵשׂ עַל־הָאֲדָמָה:

9 שְׁנַיִם שְׁנַיִם בָּאוּ אֶל־נֹחַ אֶל־הַתֵּבָה זָכָר וּנְקֵבָה כַּאֲשֶׁר צִוָּה אֱלֹהִים אֶת־נֹחַ:

י וַיְהִי לְשִׁבְעַת הַיָּמִים וּמֵי הַמַּבּוּל הָיוּ עַל־הָאָרֶץ:

11 בִּשְׁנַת שֵׁשׁ־מֵאוֹת שָׁנָה לְחַיֵּי־נֹחַ בַּחֹדֶשׁ הַשֵּׁנִי בְּשִׁבְעָה־
עָשָׂר יוֹם לַחֹדֶשׁ בַּיּוֹם הַזֶּה נִבְקְעוּ כָּל־מַעְיְנוֹת תְּהוֹם
רַבָּה וַאֲרֻבֹּת הַשָּׁמַיִם נִפְתָּחוּ:

12 וַיְהִי הַגֶּשֶׁם עַל־הָאָרֶץ אַרְבָּעִים יוֹם וְאַרְבָּעִים לָיְלָה:

13 בְּעֶצֶם הַיּוֹם הַזֶּה בָּא נֹחַ וְשֵׁם־וְחָם וָיֶפֶת בְּנֵי־נֹחַ וְאֵשֶׁת
נֹחַ וּשְׁלֹשֶׁת נְשֵׁי־בָנָיו אִתָּם אֶל־הַתֵּבָה:

14 הֵמָּה וְכָל־הַחַיָּה לְמִינָהּ וְכָל־הַבְּהֵמָה לְמִינָהּ וְכָל־
הָרֶמֶשׂ הָרֹמֵשׂ עַל־הָאָרֶץ לְמִינֵהוּ וְכָל־הָעוֹף לְמִינֵהוּ
כֹּל צִפּוֹר כָּל־כָּנָף:

טו וַיָּבֹאוּ אֶל־נֹחַ אֶל־הַתֵּבָה שְׁנַיִם שְׁנַיִם מִכָּל־הַבָּשָׂר
אֲשֶׁר־בּוֹ רוּחַ חַיִּים:

16 וְהַבָּאִים זָכָר וּנְקֵבָה מִכָּל־בָּשָׂר בָּאוּ כַּאֲשֶׁר צִוָּה אֹתוֹ
אֱלֹהִים וַיִּסְגֹּר יְהוָה בַּעֲדוֹ:

17 וַיְהִי הַמַּבּוּל אַרְבָּעִים יוֹם עַל־הָאָרֶץ וַיִּרְבּוּ הַמַּיִם וַיִּשְׂאוּ
אֶת־הַתֵּבָה וַתָּרָם מֵעַל הָאָרֶץ:

18 וַיִּגְבְּרוּ הַמַּיִם וַיִּרְבּוּ מְאֹד עַל־הָאָרֶץ וַתֵּלֶךְ הַתֵּבָה עַל־
פְּנֵי הַמָּיִם:

19 וְהַמַּיִם גָּבְרוּ מְאֹד מְאֹד עַל־הָאָרֶץ וַיְכֻסּוּ כָּל־הֶהָרִים
הַגְּבֹהִים אֲשֶׁר־תַּחַת כָּל־הַשָּׁמָיִם:

כ חֲמֵשׁ עֶשְׂרֵה אַמָּה מִלְמַעְלָה גָּבְרוּ הַמָּיִם וַיְכֻסּוּ הֶהָרִים:

21 וַיִּגְוַע כָּל־בָּשָׂר ׀ הָרֹמֵשׂ עַל־הָאָרֶץ בָּעוֹף וּבַבְּהֵמָה
וּבַחַיָּה וּבְכָל־הַשֶּׁרֶץ הַשֹּׁרֵץ עַל־הָאָרֶץ וְכֹל הָאָדָם:

22 כֹּל אֲשֶׁר נִשְׁמַת־רוּחַ חַיִּים בְּאַפָּיו מִכֹּל אֲשֶׁר בֶּחָרָבָה מֵתוּ:

23 וַיִּמַח אֶת־כָּל־הַיְקוּם ׀ אֲשֶׁר ׀ עַל־פְּנֵי הָאֲדָמָה מֵאָדָם עַד־בְּהֵמָה עַד־רֶמֶשׂ וְעַד־עוֹף הַשָּׁמַיִם וַיִּמָּחוּ מִן־הָאָרֶץ וַיִּשָּׁאֶר אַךְ־נֹחַ וַאֲשֶׁר אִתּוֹ בַּתֵּבָה:

24 וַיִּגְבְּרוּ הַמַּיִם עַל־הָאָרֶץ חֲמִשִּׁים וּמְאַת יוֹם:

CHAPTER VIII.

א וַיִּזְכֹּר אֱלֹהִים אֶת־נֹחַ וְאֵת כָּל־הַחַיָּה וְאֶת־כָּל־הַבְּהֵמָה אֲשֶׁר אִתּוֹ בַּתֵּבָה וַיַּעֲבֵר אֱלֹהִים רוּחַ עַל־הָאָרֶץ וַיָּשֹׁכּוּ הַמָּיִם:

2 וַיִּסָּכְרוּ מַעְיְנֹת תְּהוֹם וַאֲרֻבֹּת הַשָּׁמָיִם וַיִּכָּלֵא הַגֶּשֶׁם מִן־הַשָּׁמָיִם:

3 וַיָּשֻׁבוּ הַמַּיִם מֵעַל הָאָרֶץ הָלוֹךְ וָשׁוֹב וַיַּחְסְרוּ הַמַּיִם מִקְצֵה חֲמִשִּׁים וּמְאַת יוֹם:

4 וַתָּנַח הַתֵּבָה בַּחֹדֶשׁ הַשְּׁבִיעִי בְּשִׁבְעָה־עָשָׂר יוֹם לַחֹדֶשׁ עַל הָרֵי אֲרָרָט:

ה וְהַמַּיִם הָיוּ הָלוֹךְ וְחָסוֹר עַד הַחֹדֶשׁ הָעֲשִׂירִי בָּעֲשִׂירִי בְּאֶחָד לַחֹדֶשׁ נִרְאוּ רָאשֵׁי הֶהָרִים:

6 וַיְהִי מִקֵּץ אַרְבָּעִים יוֹם וַיִּפְתַּח נֹחַ אֶת־חַלּוֹן הַתֵּבָה אֲשֶׁר עָשָׂה:

7 וַיְשַׁלַּח אֶת־הָעֹרֵב וַיֵּצֵא יָצוֹא וָשׁוֹב עַד־יְבֹשֶׁת הַמַּיִם מֵעַל הָאָרֶץ׃

8 וַיְשַׁלַּח אֶת־הַיּוֹנָה מֵאִתּוֹ לִרְאוֹת הֲקַלּוּ הַמַּיִם מֵעַל פְּנֵי הָאֲדָמָה׃

9 וְלֹא־מָצְאָה הַיּוֹנָה מָנוֹחַ לְכַף־רַגְלָהּ וַתָּשָׁב אֵלָיו אֶל־הַתֵּבָה כִּי־מַיִם עַל־פְּנֵי כָל־הָאָרֶץ וַיִּשְׁלַח יָדוֹ וַיִּקָּחֶהָ וַיָּבֵא אֹתָהּ אֵלָיו אֶל־הַתֵּבָה׃

10 וַיָּחֶל עוֹד שִׁבְעַת יָמִים אֲחֵרִים וַיֹּסֶף שַׁלַּח אֶת־הַיּוֹנָה מִן־הַתֵּבָה׃

11 וַתָּבֹא אֵלָיו הַיּוֹנָה לְעֵת עֶרֶב וְהִנֵּה עֲלֵה־זַיִת טָרָף בְּפִיהָ וַיֵּדַע נֹחַ כִּי־קַלּוּ הַמַּיִם מֵעַל הָאָרֶץ׃

12 וַיִּיָּחֶל עוֹד שִׁבְעַת יָמִים אֲחֵרִים וַיְשַׁלַּח אֶת־הַיּוֹנָה וְלֹא־יָסְפָה שׁוּב־אֵלָיו עוֹד׃

13 וַיְהִי בְּאַחַת וְשֵׁשׁ־מֵאוֹת שָׁנָה בָּרִאשׁוֹן בְּאֶחָד לַחֹדֶשׁ חָרְבוּ הַמַּיִם מֵעַל הָאָרֶץ וַיָּסַר נֹחַ אֶת־מִכְסֵה הַתֵּבָה וַיַּרְא וְהִנֵּה חָרְבוּ פְּנֵי הָאֲדָמָה׃

14 וּבַחֹדֶשׁ הַשֵּׁנִי בְּשִׁבְעָה וְעֶשְׂרִים יוֹם לַחֹדֶשׁ יָבְשָׁה הָאָרֶץ׃

15 וַיְדַבֵּר אֱלֹהִים אֶל־נֹחַ לֵאמֹר׃

16 צֵא מִן־הַתֵּבָה אַתָּה וְאִשְׁתְּךָ וּבָנֶיךָ וּנְשֵׁי־בָנֶיךָ אִתָּךְ׃

17 כָּל־הַחַיָּה אֲשֶׁר־אִתְּךָ מִכָּל־בָּשָׂר בָּעוֹף וּבַבְּהֵמָה וּבְכָל־
הָרֶמֶשׂ הָרֹמֵשׂ עַל־הָאָרֶץ הוֹצֵא אִתָּךְ וְשָׁרְצוּ בָאָרֶץ
וּפָרוּ וְרָבוּ עַל־הָאָרֶץ׃
18 וַיֵּצֵא־נֹחַ וּבָנָיו וְאִשְׁתּוֹ וּנְשֵׁי־בָנָיו אִתּוֹ׃
19 כָּל־הַחַיָּה כָּל־הָרֶמֶשׂ וְכָל־הָעוֹף כֹּל רוֹמֵשׂ עַל־הָאָרֶץ
לְמִשְׁפְּחֹתֵיהֶם יָצְאוּ מִן־הַתֵּבָה׃
כ וַיִּבֶן נֹחַ מִזְבֵּחַ לַיהוָֹה וַיִּקַּח מִכֹּל ׀ הַבְּהֵמָה הַטְּהֹרָה
וּמִכֹּל הָעוֹף הַטָּהוֹר וַיַּעַל עֹלֹת בַּמִּזְבֵּחַ׃
21 וַיָּרַח יְהוָֹה אֶת־רֵיחַ הַנִּיחֹחַ וַיֹּאמֶר יְהוָֹה אֶל־לִבּוֹ לֹא
אֹסִף לְקַלֵּל עוֹד אֶת־הָאֲדָמָה בַּעֲבוּר הָאָדָם כִּי יֵצֶר
לֵב הָאָדָם רַע מִנְּעֻרָיו וְלֹא־אֹסִף עוֹד לְהַכּוֹת אֶת־
כָּל־חַי כַּאֲשֶׁר עָשִׂיתִי׃
22 עֹד כָּל־יְמֵי הָאָרֶץ זֶרַע וְקָצִיר וְקֹר וָחֹם וְקַיִץ וָחֹרֶף
וְיוֹם וָלַיְלָה לֹא יִשְׁבֹּתוּ׃

---

v. 17. הוֹצֵא ק׳

VOCABULARIES.

LIST OF ABBREVIATIONS

USED IN THE VOCABULARIES.

---

act., active.
adv., adverb.
c., common.
cf., compare.
conj., conjunctive.
convers., conversive.
const., construct.
dem., demonstrative.
f., feminine.
Hĭf., Hĭf'îl.
Hĭθp., Hĭθpă'ēl.
Impf., Imperfect.

Imv., Imperative.
Inf., Infinitive.
interrog., interrogative.
lary. laryngeal.
m., masculine.
n., noun.
Nĭf., Nĭf'äl.
Part., Participle.
Perf., Perfect.
pers., personal.
prep., preposition.
pr. n., proper noun.
pron., pronoun.
sg., singular.
suf., suffix.

In the Hebrew-English Vocabulary the numeral immediately following the Hebrew word indicates the number of times it occurs in the Old Testament.

In the English-Hebrew Vocabulary the numeral immediately following each word indicates the number of the corresponding Hebrew word in the Hebrew-English Vocabulary.

HEBREW-ENGLISH VOCABULARY

OF

GENESIS I–VIII.

1. אָב [1155*] ('åv), (const. אֲבִי) m., *father*.
2. אֶבֶן [266] ('ĕvĕn), f., *stone*.
3. אֵד [2] ('ēd), m., *mist, vapor*.
4. אָדָם [560] ('ådåm), m., *man*; cf. אִישׁ.
5. אֲדָמָה [225] ('ᵃdåmå(h)), (const. אַדְמַת) f., *ground, earth*.
6. אֹהֶל [350] ('ōhĕl), m., *tent*.
7. אוֹר [102] ('ôr), *be light, shine*, ('פ Lary.). Hïf., *give light*. Inf. with prep., לְהָאִיר, i. 15, 17, &c.
8. אוֹר [120] ('ôr), m., *light*.
9. אוֹת [76] ('ôθ), f., *sign*, pl. אֹתֹת.
10. אָז ('åz), adv., *then*.
11. אָזַן [42] ('åzăn), Ḳăl not used. ('פ Lary.), Hïf., *listen, give ear*, Imv. 2d pl. הַאֲזִינָה, iv. 23.
12. אָח [688] ('åḥ), (const. אֲחִי) m., *brother*.
13. אָחוֹת [113] ('åḥôθ), (const. אֲחוֹת) f., *sister*.
14. אֶחָד [1000] ('ĕ(ḥ)håd), m., *one*, f. const. אַחַת, iv. 19.
15. אַחֵר [180] ('ă(ḥ)hēr), (const. אַחַר) m., *another*, pl. אֲחֵרִים.
16. אַחַר [770] ('ă(ḥ)hăr), prep. *after*, pl. only in const. אַחֲרֵי.
17. אַי ('ăy), (const. אֵי) interrog. adv. *where?* אַיֶּכָּה *where art thou?* iii. 9.
18. אֵיבָה [5] ('ēvå(h)), (const. אֵיבַת) f., *enmity*.

* The figures in square brackets indicate the number of times the word appears in the Old Testament.

19. אַיִן ('áyĭn), *nothing, there is not*, const. אֵין, with m. suf., אֵינֶנּוּ, v. 24.

20. אִישׁ [1700] ('ĭš), m., *man*, cf. אָדָם.

21. אַךְ ('ăx), *surely, only*.

22. אָכַל [821] ('âxăl), *eat, devour*, (פ"א), Impf. וַיֹּאכַל, iii. 6, וַתֹּאכַל, נֹאכַל, iii. 2, Nĭf. Impf. יֵאָכֵל, vi. 21.

23. אָכְלָה [18] ('ŏxlâ(h)), f., *food*.

24. אֶל ('ĕl), prep. *unto*, with suf., אֵלַי, *unto me*.

25. אֵלֶּה ('ēllê(h)), pron. *these*, cf. זֶה.

26. אֱלֹהִים [2500] ('ĕlôhîm), pl. m., *God* (sing. אֱלוֹהַּ used in poetry).

27. אֵם [220] ('ēm), f., *mother*, with m. suf. אִמּוֹ.

28. אִם ('ĭm), conj. *if*.

29. אַמָּה [240] ('ămmâ(h)), f., *cubit*.

30. אָמַר [5026] ('âmăr), *say*, (פ"א). Inf. const. אֱמֹר, with לֵאמֹר=אֱמֹר לְ, i.

22, v. 29. Impf. with Wâw convers., וַיֹּאמֶר, i. 3, 6, &c., וַתֹּאמֶר, iii. 2, 13, &c.

31. אִמְרָה [35] ('ĭmrâ(h)), (const. אִמְרַת) f., *utterance, song*, iv. 23.

32. אֱנוֹשׁ ('ᵉnôš), pr. n. *Enosh*, (man).

33. אָנֹכִי ('ânôxî), pers. pron. *I*.

34. אָסַף [214] ('âsăf), *gather*, ('פ Lary.), וְאָסַפְתָּ, vi. 21.

35. אַף [282] ('ăf), m., *nose, anger*, pl. with prep. and suf. בְּאַפָּיו, Dual אַפַּיִם.

36. אַף ('ăf), conj. *yea more, but even*, אַף כִּי *is it true that?* iii. 1.

37. אֲרֻבָּה ('ᵃrŭbbâ(h)), f., *lattice, window*, pl. אֲרֻבּוֹת.

38. אַרְבַּע [320] ('ărbă'), (m. אַרְבָּעָה) f., *four*, ord. רְבִיעִי.

39. אֹרֶךְ [96] ('ōrĕx), m., *length*.

40. אֶרֶץ [2000] ('ĕrĕs), f., *earth*.

41. אָרַר [57] ('ărăr), *curse*, (פ' Lary. and ע"ע), Pass. part. אָרוּר, iii. 14, iv. 11. Pï'ēl, אָרֵר, with fem. suf. אֲרָרָה, v. 29.

42. אֲרָרָט ('ᵃrărăṭ), pr. n. *Ararat*.

43. אִשָּׁה [470], ('ïššă(h)), (const. אֵשֶׁת) *woman*, with suf. אִשְׁתּוֹ, vii. 2, pl. נָשִׁים, const. נְשֵׁי, vi. 18.

44. אֲשֶׁר ('ᵃšĕr), rel. particle *who, which*.

45. אֵת ('ēθ), particle placed before *definite* accusative; before Măkḳēf, אֶת־, with suf. אֹתָם, אֹתוֹ, i. 27, 28.

46. אֵת ('ēθ), prep. *with*.

47. אַתָּה ('ăttă(h)), personal pron. *thou*.

48. בְּ (bᵉ), prep. *in, on, among*.

49. בַּד [11] (băd), m., *separation*, לְבַדּוֹ, *to his separation* = *alone*, ii. 18.

50. בָּדַל [42] (bădăl), Ḳăl not used. Hïf. *separate, divide;* Impf. with Wăw conversive וַיַּבְדֵּל, i. 4, 7, &c., Part. מַבְדִּיל, *dividing*, i. 6.

51. בְּדֹלַח [2] (bᵉdŏlăḥ), *bdellium*, ii. 12.

52. בֹּהוּ [3] (bŏhû), m., *emptiness*.

53. בְּהֵמָה [300] (bᵉhēmă(h)), f., *beast, dumb brute*.

54. בּוֹא [2619] (bô'), *go in, come*. Ḳăl Perf. בָּא, vi. 16. Hïf. Perf. הֵבִיא, *bring*, iv. 4. Impf. with Wăw convers. וַיָּבֵא, ii. 19, iv. 3.

55. בּוֹשׁ [109] (bôš), *be ashamed*, Hïθpôlēl Impf. יִתְבֹּשָׁשׁוּ, ii. 25.

56. בָּחַר [102] (băḥăr), *choose*, (ע' Lary.).

57. בֵּין [168] (bên), (*interval*) prep. *between*, for ··· בֵּין ··· לְ, occurs בֵּין ··· בֵּין.

58. בַּיִת [2100] (băyïθ), (const. בֵּית) m., *house, household*, with suf. בֵּיתְךָ, vii. 1, pl. בָּתִּים, (bâtîm).

59. בְּכוֹרָה [120] (bᵉxôrå(h)), f., *first-born*, pl. בְּכֹרוֹת.

60. בִּלְתִּי (biltî), adv. of negation, *lest, not, that not,* iii. 11.

61. בֵּן [4500] (bēn), m., *son.*

62. בָּנָה [380] (bånå(h)), *build,* (ל"ה), Impf. with Wåw convers. וַיִּבֶן, ii. 22. Part. בֹּנֶה, iv. 17.

63. בַּעֲבוּר (baʻavûr), prep. *for, in behalf of,* comp. of בְּ and עֲבוּר from עָבַר, *pass over.*

64. בְּעַד (bᵉʻăd), prep. *behind, after,* with suf. בַּעֲדוֹ, *after him,* vii. 16.

65. בָּקַע [51] (båḳăʻ), *cleave, divide,* (ל'), Nîf. *be broken up,* vii. 11.

66. בֹּקֶר [210] (bṓḳĕr), m., *morning, dawn.*

67. בָּרָא [53] (båråʼ), *form, create,* (ל"א), Impf. with Wåw convers. וַיִּבְרָא.

68. בַּרְזֶל [73] (bărzĕl), m., *iron.*

69. בְּרִית [280] (bᵉrîθ), f., *covenant,* הֵקִים בּ׳, *establish a covenant.*

70. בָּרַךְ [413] (båråx), Piʻēl בֵּרֵךְ, *bless,* Impf. with Wåw convers. וַיְבָרֶךְ, i. 22, v. 2.

71. בָּשָׂר [270] (båśår), m., *flesh.*

72. בַּת [400] (băθ), f., *daughter.*

73. גָּבֹהַּ [35] (gåvô(ă)h), adj. *high,* pl. גְּבֹהִים.

74. גִּבּוֹר [150] (gĭbbôr), m., *hero, man of valor.*

75. גָּבַר [23] (gåvăr), *be strong, be mighty.* (Cf. גִּבּוֹר.)

76. גָּדוֹל [330] (gådôl), m., *great, elder.*

77. גָּוַע [24] (gåwăʻ), *die, expire* (ל'ע Lary.). Impf. יִגְוַע, vi. 17.

78. גָּחוֹן [2] (gåḥôn), m., *belly.* גְּחֹנְךָ, iii. 14.

79. גִּיחוֹן (gîḥôn), pr. n. *Gihon.*

80. גַּם (găm), conj. *also,* גַּם ... גַּם, *both ... and.*

81. גַּן [3] (găn), c. or f. *garden, park.*

82. גֹּפֶר [1] (gŏ́fĕr), m., *pitch, pitch-wood*.

83. גָּרַשׁ [47] (gărăš), *drive, cast out*. Pĭ'ēl, גֵּרֵשׁ *expel*, iv. 14. Impf. with Wāw convers. וַיְגָ֫רֶשׁ, iii. 24.

84. גֶּ֫שֶׁם [35] (gĕ́šĕm), m., *gushing rain, heavy shower*.

85. דָּבַק [54] (dăvăḳ), *cleave, adhere*, ii. 24.

86. דָּגָה [33] (dăgă(h)), (or דָּג m.) f., *fish*, const. דְּגַת, i. 26, 28.

87. דָּנַן, דּוּן [23] (dûn or dănăn), *rule* (?). Impf. יָדוֹן, vi. 3.

88. דּוֹר [170] (dôr), m., *age, generation*, pl. îm and ôθ.

89. דָּם [360] (dăm), m., *blood*, pl. דָּמִים, const. דְּמֵי, iv. 10.

90. דְּמוּת [25] (dᵉmûθ), f., *likeness, image*.

91. דַּרְדַּר [2] (dărdăr), m., *thorny plant, thistle*, iii. 18.

92. דֶּ֫רֶךְ [690] (dĕ́rex), c. *way, journey*.

93. דָּשָׁא [2] (dăšă'), *sprout*. (ל"א), Hĭf. Impf. תַּדְשֵׁא, i. 11.

94. דֶּ֫שֶׁא [14] (dĕ́šĕ'), m., *tender grass*.

95. הַ֗ (hă), Article, *the*, other forms are: הָ֗, הֶ֗, הֶ.

96. הַ (hᵃ), Interrog. particle, same as Latin *ne*, other forms: הָ, הֶ.

97. הֶ֫בֶל (hĕ́vĕl), m., pr. n. *Abel*.

98. הוּא (hû'), pers. pron. *he*.

99. הָיָה (hăyă(h)), *be, happen, come to pass*, (ל"ה), הָיְתָה, i. 2, וְהָיוּ, i. 14, 15, Inf. const. הֱיוֹת with בְּ and suf. בִּהְיוֹתָם, iv. 8, Impf. יִהְיֶה, i. 29, תִּהְיֶה, iv. 12, Jussive יְהִי, i. 3, 6, with Wāw conjunctive וִיהִי, i. 6, with Wāw convers. וַיְהִי, i. 3, 5, &c.

100. הָלַךְ [526] (hălăx), *go*, Part. act. הֹלֵךְ, ii. 14, Hĭθ. *walk, go about*, Impf. with Wāw convers. וַיִּתְהַלֵּךְ, v. 24.

101. הֵן, הִנֵּה (hēn, hĭnnē(h)), adv. *behold, lo!*

102. הֵנָּה (hénnå(h)), pers. pron. f., *they.*

103. הָפַךְ [95] (håfăx), *turn, change into,* ('פ Lary.). Hĭθpăʻēl Part. מִתְהַפֶּכֶת *turning itself,* iii. 24.

104. הַר [560] (hăr), m., *mountain,* pl. הָרִים.

105. הָרַג [170] (hårăğ), *kill, slay,* ('פ Lary.), iv. 23. Impf. with suf. יַהַרְגֵנִי, iv. 14, with Wåw convers. וַיַּהַרְגֵהוּ, iv. 8.

106. הָרָה [43] (hårå(h)), *conceive,* ('פ Lary. and ל"ה). Impf. תֶּהֱרֶה, with Wåw convers. וַתַּהַר, iv. 1, 17, &c.

107. הֵרוֹן [2] (hērôn), m., *conception.*

108. וְ (weʻ), conj. *and,* other forms וָ, וַ, וֶ, וּ, depending on tone and following vowel.

109. זֶה [13] (zê(h)), dem. pron. m., *this,* f. זֹאת, cf. אֵלֶּה.

110. זָהָב [368] (zåhåv), m., *gold.*

111. זַיִת [38] (zăyĭθ), m., *olive-tree.*

112. זָכַר [169] (zåxăr), *remember.*

113. זָכָר [82] (zåxår), m., *male.*

114. זֵעָה [1] (zēʻå(h)), f., *sweat,* const. זֵעַת, iii. 19.

115. זָרַע [55] (zårăʻ), *sow,* ('ל Lary.). Part. זֹרֵעַ, i. 11, Hĭf. *yield seed,* Part. מַזְרִיעַ, i. 11, 12.

116. זֶרַע [220] (zérăʻ), m., *seed,* in pause, זָרַע, i. 29, *seedtime,* viii. 22.

117. חָבָא [33] (håvåʼ), Ḳăl not used. ('פ Lary. and ל"א). Hĭθ. *hide oneself,* Impf. with Wåw convers. וַיִּתְחַבֵּא, iii. 8.

118. חַבּוּרָה [29] (ḥabbûrå(h,)) f., *bruise, wound,* with suf., חַבֻּרָתִי, iv. 23.

119. חֲגוֹרָה [6] (ḥaᵃgôrå(h)), f., *girdle.*

120. חִדֶּקֶל (ḥĭddéḳĕl), pr. n. *Ḥiddekel, Tigris.*

Vocabulary of Genesis I—VIII.

121. חֹדֶשׁ [300] (hṓdĕš), m., new moon, month.

122. חַוָּה (ḥăwwå(h)), f., pr. n. Eve.

123. חוּל [64] (ḥûl) and חִיל (ḥîl), be pained, wait, ('פ Lary. and ע"ו), Ḳăl Impf. 3 m. s. with Wåw convers. וַיָּחֶל, viii. 10.

124. חוּץ [172] (ḥûṣ), m., outside, street, מִבַּיִת מִחוּץ, from within, from without, vi. 14.

125. חַטָּאת [125] (ḥăṭṭå'θ), f., sin.

126. חַי [500] (ḥăy), m., life, pl. חַיִּים.

127. חָיָה [264] (ḥåyå(h)), live, ('פ Lary. and ל"ה), Inf. חֲיוֹת, Impf. יִחְיֶה, Jussive יְחִי, with Wåw convers. וַיְחִי, v. 6, 9.

128. חַיָּה [500] (ḥăyyå(h)), f., living creature, beast, const. חַיַּת, poet. חַיְתוֹ־, i. 24.

129. חָיַי [23] (ḥåyăy), live, ('פ Lary. and ע"ע), חַי, iii. 22, v. 5.

130. חֵלֶב [90] (ḥḗlĕv), m., fat, fatness.

131. חַלּוֹן [31] (ḥăllôn), c., hole, window.

132. חָלַל [139] (ḥålăl), loose, set free, ('פ Lary. and ע"ע), Hĭf. הֵחֵל, begin, vi. 1, Hŏf. הוּחַל, it was begun, iv. 26.

133. חָם [16] (ḥåm), pr. n. Ham.

134. חֹם [14] (ḥōm), m., heat.

135. חָמַד [20] (ḥåmăḋ,) desire, ('פ Lary.), Nĭf. part. נֶחְמָד, iii. 6.

136. חָמָס [60] (ḥåmås), m., violence.

137. חָמֵשׁ [166] (ḥåmēš), f., five, ordinal חֲמִישִׁי, fifth.

138. חֵן [69] (ḥēn), m., favor, grace.

139. חֲנוֹךְ [8] (ḥᵃnôχ), pr. n. Enoch.

140. חָסֵר [22] (ḥåsēr), be diminished, fail, ('פ Lary. mid. e).

141. חָרֵב [40] (ḥårēv), dry up, ('פ Lary., mid. e).

142. חֶרֶב [400] (ḥĕrĕv), f., sword.
143. חָרָבָה [8] (ḥărāvā(h)), f., dryness, dry land.
144. חָרָה [92] (ḥārā(h)), burn, glow (with anger), ('פ Lary. and ה"ל). Impf. with Wâw convers. וַיִּחַר, iv. 5.
145. חֹרֶף [7] (ḥō'rĕf), m., winter.
146. חֶרֶשׁ [1] (ḥôrēš), m., tool, cutting instrument, iv. 22.
147. חֹשֶׁךְ [78] (ḥō'šĕx), m., darkness.
148. טָהוֹר [92] (ṭāhôr), adj., clean, f. טְהוֹרָה, vii. 2.
149. טוֹב [550] (ṭôv), m., good.
150. טֶרֶם (ṭĕrĕm), adv. not yet, before.
151. טָרָף [1] (ṭārāf), adj. fresh, newly plucked.

152. יָבָל (yāvāl), pr. n. Jabal.
153. יָבֵשׁ [60] (yāvēš), be dried up. Ḳăl Inf. const. יְבֹשֶׁת, viii. 7, (פ"י).
154. יַבָּשָׁה [14] (yăbbāšā(h)), f., dry land.
155. יָד [1580] (yāḋ), f., hand.
156. יָדַע [1045] (yāḋă'), know, (פ"ן and ל Lary.), Inf. const. דַּעַת.
157. יְהוָה (yăh-wê(h)) Yahweh, or ('ăḋônāi) = Lord.
158. יוּבָל (yûvăl), pr. n. Jubal.
159. יוֹם [2250] (yôm), day, pl. יָמִים, const. יְמֵי.
160. יוֹנָה [33] (yônā(h)), f., dove.
160a. יָחַל [35] (yāḥăl) wait, not used in Ḳăl. Nĭf. Impf. with Wâw convers. וַיִּיחֶל, viii. 12.
161. יָטַב [23] (yāṭăv), be good, (פ"י), Hĭf. Impf. יֵיטִיב, iv. 7.
162. יָלַד [490] (yālăḋ), bear, bring forth, (פ"ן), Inf. const. לֶדֶת, with ל, לָלֶדֶת, iv. 2, Impf. יֵלֶד, iv. 1, 17, &c., Nĭf. be born, Impf. יִוָּלֵד, iv. 18, Hĭf. beget, הוֹלִיד, v. 4, 7, &c., Impf. יוֹלֶד,

with Wâw convers. וַיּוֹלֶד, v. 3, 7, &c.

163. יֶלֶד [88] (yĕlĕd), m., *child*.
164. יָם [380] (yâm), m., *sea*, pl. יָמִים.
165. יָסַף [210] (yâsăf), *add*, (פּ״וּ), Hîf. Impf. יוֹסִיף, Jussive, יוֹסֵף, with Wâw convers. וַתֹּסֶף, iv. 2.
166. יֶפֶת [11] (yĕ́fĕθ), pr. n. *Japheth*.
167. יָצָא [1075] (yâṣâ'), *go out*, (פּ״וּ and ל״א). Impf. with Wâw convers. וַיֵּצֵא, iv. 16. Hîf. *bring out*. Impf. יוֹצֵא, 3d f. with Wâw convers. וַתּוֹצֵא, i. 12.
168. יָצַר [62] (yâṣăr), *form*, (פּ״וּ), Impf. with Wâw convers. וַיִּיצֶר, ii. 7.
169. יֵצֶר [9] (yḗṣĕr), m., *form, imagination*.
170. יְקוּם [2] (yeqûm), m., *what exists, living being*, (root קוּם).
171. יָרֵא [315] (yârē'), *fear*, (פּ״וּ, and ל״א). Impf.

וַיִּירָא, 1st sing. with Wâw convers. וָאִירָא, iii. 10.

172. יֶרֶד (yĕ́rĕd), (in pause יָרֶד), m., pr. n. *Jared*.
173. יֶרֶק [6] (yĕ́rĕq), m., *greenness*.
174. יָשַׁב [1050] (yâšăv), *sit, dwell*, (פּ״וּ), Impf. יֵשֵׁב, with Wâw convers. וַיֵּשֶׁב, iv. 16, Part. Act. יֹשֵׁב, iv. 20.
175. יָשֵׁן [16] (yâšēn), *sleep*, (פּ״וּ), וַיִּישַׁן, with Wâw convers. וַיִּישָׁן, ii. 21.
176. כְּ (ke), prep. *as, like*.
177. כָּבַשׁ [15] (kâvăš), *tread upon, subdue*, Imv. with fem. suf. כִּבְשָׁהּ, i. 28.
178. כּוֹכָב [36] (kôxâv), (const. כּוֹכַב) m., *star*, pl. כּוֹכָבִים.
179. כֹּחַ [120] (kô(ă)ḥ), m., *strength, might*.
180. כִּי (kî), conj. *that, for*.
181. כֹּל (kōl), m., *totality, all, every*, with Măkkēf כָּל־.

182. כָּלָא [18] (kâlâ'), *hold, restrain*, (ל"א).

183. כָּלָה [206] (kâlâ(h)), *be ended*, (ל"ה), Pī'ēl, *complete, finish*, Impf. וַיְכַלֶּה, with Wâw convers. וַיְכַל, ii. 2. Pŭ'ăl Impf. with Wâw convers. וַיְכֻלּוּ, ii. 1.

184. כֵּן (kēn), adv. *so, thus*, עַל־כֵּן *therefore, on account of this*, ii. 24, לָכֵן, *therefore*.

185. כִּנּוֹר [42] (kĭnnôr), m., *harp, lyre*.

186. כָּנָף [110] (kânâf), (const. כְּנַף) f., *wing*.

187. כָּסָה [149] (kâsâ(h)), *cover*, Pŭ. *be covered*, vii. 19, (ל"ה).

188. כַּף [280] (kăf), m., *palm of hand, sole* of foot; dual כַּפַּיִם.

189. כָּפַר [100] (kâfăr), *cover* (with pitch), vi. 14.

190. כְּרוּב [90] (kᵉrûv), m., *cherub*, pl. כְּרוּבִים.

191. כְּתֹנֶת [28] (kᵉθônĕθ), f., *coat, tunic*.

192. לְ (lᵉ) prep. *to, for*.

193. לֹא (lô'), adv. *not, no*.

194. לֵב [620] (lēv), m., *heart*, with 3d m. suf. לִבּוֹ.

195. לָבַשׁ [116] (lâvăš), *put on* (clothes), Hĭf. *clothe* (another). Impf. with Wâw convers. וַיַּלְבִּישֵׁם, iii. 21.

196. לַהַט [1] (lăhăt), m., *flame, glittering blade* (of a sword), iii. 24.

197. לֶחֶם [300] (lĕḥĕm), c., *food, bread*.

198. לָטַשׁ [5] (lâtăš), *hammer, forge*, Part. act. לֹטֵשׁ, iv. 22.

199. לַיִל [224] (lăyĭl), usually לַיְלָה with Hē of acc., m., *night*.

200. לָמָה (lámmâ(h)), adv. *why?* (מַה, לְ).

201. לֶמֶךְ (lĕmĕx), pr. n. *Lamech*.

202. לָקַח [966] (lâḳăḥ), *take*, ('ל Lary.), Inf. const. קַחַת, Impf. יִקַּח, with

Wâw convers. וַיִּקַּח, ii. 15, iv. 19. Pŭ'ăl, *be taken*, לְקָחָה־, ii. 23.

203. מְאֹד [286] (mᵉ'ôd), adv. *very.*

204. מֵאָה [600] (mē'ā(h)), (const. מְאַת) *hundred.*

205. מָאוֹר [19] (må'ôr), (const. מְאוֹר) m., *light, luminary*, pl. מְאֹרֹת.

206. מַאֲכָל [30] (mă'ᵃχǎl), m., *food.*

207. מַבּוּל [13] (măbbûl), m., *deluge, flood.*

208. מַה (mă(h)), interrog. pron. *what?* Other forms are מֶה־, מַה, מָה.

209. מְהַלַלְאֵל (măhᵃlăl'ēl), pr. n. *Mahalaleel.*

210. מוֹעֵד [200] (mô'ēd), m., *set time, season*, plural מוֹעֲדִים.

211. מוּת [857] (mûθ), *die* (ע״ו), Perf. מֵתוּ, vii. 22, Inf. abs. מוֹת, ii. 17, Impf. יָמוּת, jussive יָמֹת, with Wâw convers. וַיָּמָת, v. 5, 8, &c.

212. מִזְבֵּחַ [310] (mĭzbē(ă)ḥ), m., *altar.*

213. מָחָה [34] (mǎḥǎ(h)), *wipe out, destroy*, ('ע Lary. and ל״ה), Impf. אֶמְחֶה, vi. 7, Ḳǎl Impf. with Wâw convers. וַיִּמַח, vii. 23.

214. מְחוּיָאֵל (mᵉḥûyǎ'ēl), pr. n. *Mehujael.*

215. מַחֲשָׁבָה [53] (măḥᵃšǎvǎ(h)), f., *plan, purpose*, pl. const. מַחְשְׁבֹת, vi. 5.

216. מָטָר [18] (mǎṭǎr), Ḳǎl not used, Hĭf. הִמְטִיר *give rain*, ii. 5.

217. מִי (mî), interrog. pron. *who?*

218. מַיִם [600] (mǎyĭm), (const. מֵי) pl. m., *water.*

219. מִין [31] (mîn), m., *kind, species*, with prep. and m., sg. suf. לְמִינֵהוּ or לְמִינוֹ, i. 11, 12.

220. מִכְסֶה [15] (mĭχsê(h)), (const. מִכְסֵה) m., *covering.*

221. מָלֵא [247] (mâlē'), be full, (ל"א), Imv. 2d pl. מִלְאוּ, i. 22, 28.

222. מְלָאכָה [172] (mᵉlå'-zå(h)), (const. מְלֶאכֶת) f., work.

223. מֶמְשָׁלָה [17] (mĕm-šålå(h)), f., dominion, rule, const. מֶמְשֶׁלֶת, i. 16.

224. מִן (mĭn), prep. from, מִמֶּנּוּ, iii. 3.

225. מָנוֹחַ [7] (mânô(ă)ḥ), m., a resting, resting place.

226. מִנְחָה [200] (mĭnḥå(h)), (const. מִנְחַת) f., an offering, present.

227. מַעְיָן [23] (mă'yån), m., fountain, spring, plural מַעְיָנוֹת and מַעְיָנִים.

228. מַעַל [137] (mă'ăl), adv., above, used only in composition; with הָ locative, מַעְלָה upwards, with לְ and מִן, מִלְמַעְלָה lit. from-to-upwards, vii. 20.

229. מַעֲשֶׂה [240] (mă'ᵃśê(h)), (const. מַעֲשֵׂה) m., work.

230. מָצָא [486] (mâṣâ'), find, (ל"א), ii. 20, Part. act. מֹצֵא, iv. 14.

231. מִקְוֶה [8] (mĭḳwê(h)), (const. מִקְוֵה) m., collection, gathering, i. 10.

232. מָקוֹם [380] (mâḳôm), (const. מְקוֹם) c., place.

233. מִקְנֶה [76] (mĭḳnê(h)), (const. מִקְנֵה) m., substance, wealth.

234. מַרְאֶה [101] (măr'ê(h)), (const. מַרְאֵה) m., appearance, look.

235. מָשַׁל [79] (mâšăl), rule, with בְּ, over, Inf. const. with prep. לְ, לִמְשֹׁל.

236. מִשְׁפָּחָה [270] (mĭš-pâḥå(h)), f., family, pl. מִשְׁפָּחוֹת.

237. מְתוּשָׁאֵל (mᵉθûšå'ēl), pr. n. Methushael.

238. מְתוּשֶׁלַח (mᵉθûšĕlăḥ), pr. n. Methuselah.

239. נָגַד [379] (nâğăd), Ḳăl not used, (פ"ן), Hif. הִגִּיד tell, show, iii. 11.

240. נֶגֶד (nĕğĕd), prep. before, in presence of, with suf. נֶגְדּוֹ, ii. 18.

241. נָגַע [148] (nâğă'), touch, smite, (פ"ן and ל' Lary.), Impf. תִגְּעוּ, iii. 3.

242. נָד [24] (nâd) m., fugitive.

243. נָהָר [123] (nâhâr), m., river.

244. נוֹד (nôd), pr. n. Nod.

245. נוּחַ [64] (nû(ă)ḥ), rest, (ע"ו and ל' Lary.), Hif. הֵנִיחַ, cause to rest, Impf. with suf. and Wâw convers. וַיַּנִּחֵהוּ, ii. 15, Ḳăl Impf. 3 f. sg. with Wâw convers. וַתָּנַח, viii. 4.

246. נֹחַ (nô(ă)ḥ), pr. n. Noah.

247. נָחַם [106] (nâḥăm), Ḳăl not used, (פ"ן and ע' Lary.), Nif. repent, pity, Impf. וַיִּנָּחֶם, vi. 6, Pi'ēl comfort, Impf. יְנַחֲמֵנוּ, v. 29.

248. נָחָשׁ [30] (nâḥâš), m., serpent.

249. נְחֹשֶׁת [135] (nᵉḥōšĕθ), m., bronze.

250. נָטַע [58] (nâṭă'), plant, (פ"ן and ל' Lary.), Impf. with Wâw convers. וַיִּטַּע ii. 8.

251. נִיחֹחַ [43] (nîḥô(ă)ḥ), m., rest, pleasantness.

252. נָכָה [499] (nâxă(h)), Ḳăl not used, (פ"ן and ל"ה), Hif. הִכָּה, smite, strike, Inf. const. הַכּוֹת, iv. 15.

253. נָע [43] (nâ'), m., wanderer.

254. נַעֲמָה (nă'ᵉmâ(h)), pr. n. Naamah.

255. נְעָרִים [46] (nᵉ'ûrîm), (def. writing for נְעוּרִים), used only in pl., m., youth, i. e., time of youth.

256. נָפַח [12] (nâfăḥ), blow, breathe, (פ"ן and ל' Lary.), Impf. with Wâw convers. וַיִּפַּח, ii. 7.

257. נְפִיל [2] (nâfil), m., used only in pl. נְפִילִים, giants.

258. נָפַל [417] (nâfăl), fall, (פ״נ), Hîf. Impf. with Wâw convers. וַיַּפֵּל, ii. 21.

259. נֶפֶשׁ [780] (néfeš), f., breath, soul.

260. נְקֵבָה [22] (nᵉḳēvå(h)), f., female.

261. נָקַם [34] (nåḳăm), avenge, (פ״נ), Hŏf. יֻקַּם, in pause יֻקָּם, iv. 15.

262. נָשָׂא [706] (nåśå'), lift up, (פ״נ and ל״א), Inf. const. שְׂאֵת, iv. 7.

263. נָשָׁא [17] (nåšå'), Ḳăl not used, (פ״נ and ל״א). Hîf. deceive, seduce.

264. נְשָׁמָה [24] (nᵉšåmå(h)), (const. נִשְׁמַת) f., breath, spirit.

265. נָתַן [2090] (nåθăn), give, (פ״נ), Inf. const. תֵּת, iv. 12, Impf. with Wâw convers. וַיִּתֵּן, i. 17.

266. סָבַב [156] (såvăv), turn, encompass, (ע״ע), Part. act. סֹבֵב, ii. 11, 13.

267. סָגַר [90] (sågăr), shut, Impf. with Wâw convers. וַיִּסְגֹּר, ii. 21.

268. סוּר [293] (sûr), turn aside, (middle-vowel).

269. סָכַר [3] (såχăr), (= סָגַר), shut up.

270. סֵפֶר [172] (séfĕr), m., writing, book.

271. סָתַר [83] (såθăr), hide, Nîf. Impf. אֶסָּתֵר, iv. 14.

272. עָבַד [286] ('åvăd), serve, till, ('פ Lary.), Inf. const. with prep. לַעֲבֹד, ii. 5.

273. עָבַר [551] ('åvăr), pass over ('פ Lary.).

274. עַד ('ăd), prep. till, until.

275. עָדָה ('ådå(h)), pr. n. Ada.

276. עֵדֶן [3] ('édĕn), m., Eden.

277. עוּגָב [4] ('ûğåv), m., pipe, reed, organ.

278. עוֹד ('ôd), adv. *still, yet, again*.

279. עוֹלָה [386] ('ôlå(h)), (const. עוֹלַת) f., *burnt-offering*, pl. עוֹלוֹת.

280. עָוֹן [226] ('åwôn), (const. עֲוֹן) m., *guilt, sin*.

281. עוֹלָם [430] ('ôlåm), m., *age, eternity*.

282. עוּף [32] ('ûf), *fly*, (פ' Lary. and mid-vow.), Pôlēl Impf. יְעוֹפֵף, i. 20.

283. עוֹף [70] ('ôf), m., *bird, fowl*, collective.

284. עוֹר [95] ('ôr), m., *skin*.

285. עָזַב [114] ('åzăv), *leave, forsake*, (פ' Lary.), Impf. יַעֲזָב־, ii. 24.

286. עֵזֶר [21] ('ēzĕr), m., *help*.

287. עַיִן [872] ('åyĭn), f., *eye*, pl. with suf. עֵינֵיכֶם, iii. 5.

288. עִיר [1074] ('ĭr), f., *city*, pl. עָרִים.

289. עִירָד ('îråd), pr. n. *Irad*.

290. עֵירֹם [10] ('êrōm), adj. *naked*, pl. עֵירֻמִּם, iii. 7.

291. עַל ('ăl), prep. *upon, with*, מֵעַל, *from upon*.

292. עָלָה [862] ('ålå(h)), *go up*, (פ' Lary. and ל"ה), Impf. יַעֲלֶה, ii. 6, Hĭf. *offer up*.

293. עָלֶה [18] ('ålê(h)), (const. עֲלֵה) m., *leaf*.

294. עִם ('ĭm), prep. *with, along with*.

294a. עִמָּד prep. *with*.

295. עָפָר [108] ('åfår), m., *dust*.

296. עֵץ [326] ('ēṣ), m., *tree*.

297. עָצַב [17] ('åṣăv), *suffer pain*, (פ' Lary.), Hĭθp. w. Wåw convers. וַיִּתְעַצֵּב, *grieve oneself*, vi. 6.

298. עֶצֶב [7] ('ĕṣĕv), m., *pain, grievance*.

299. עִצָּבוֹן [3] (ĭṣṣåvôn), (const. עִצְּבוֹן) m., *labor, pain*.

300. עֶצֶם [120] ('ĕṣĕm), f., *bone*.

301. עָקֵב [14] ('åḳēv), (const. עֲקֵב) m., *heel.*
302. עֶרֶב [132] ('ĕrĕv), m., *evening.*
303. עֹרֵב [10] ('ôrēv), m., *raven.*
304. עָרוֹם and עָרֹם [16] ('årōm), adj. *naked,* pl. עֲרוּמִים, but עֲרֻמִּים ("'rŭmmîm), ii. 25.
305. עָרוּם [11] ('årûm), m., *prudent, crafty.*
306. עֵשֶׂב [33] ('ēśĕv), m., *green herb, plant.*
307. עָשָׂה [2521] ('åśå(h)), *do, make,* ('פ Lary. and ל"ה), Impf. with Wåw convers. וַיַּעַשׂ, i. 7.
308. עֲשִׂירִי [26] ('*a*śîrî), ordinal num. *tenth.*
309. עֶשֶׂר [333] ('åśår), cardinal number *ten,* used only in compounds with units, as in אַחַד עָשָׂר *eleven,* fem. עֶשְׂרֵה ('ĕśrē(h)). v. 8.
310. עֶשֶׂר (m. עֲשָׂרָה) [172] ('ēśĕr), f., *ten.*

311. עֵת [300] ('ēθ), c., *time.*
312. עַתָּה ('ăttå(h)), adv. *now.*
313. פֶּה [480] (pê(h)), *mouth,* with fem. suf. פִּיהָ, iv. 11.
314. פֶּן־ (pĕn +), conj. *lest,* with Impf.
315. פָּנִים [2000] (pånîm), m., *faces,* const. פְּנֵי, i. 2.
316. פַּעַם [110] (pă'ăm), f., *tread* or *step, once.*
317. פָּצָה [15] (påṣå(h)), *rend, open,* (ל"ה) iv. 11.
318. פֶּצַע [7] (pĕṣă'), m., *wounding,* with suf. פִּצְעִי, iv. 23.
319. פָּקַח [20] (påḳăḥ), *open* (the eyes), ('ל Lary.), Nif. נִפְקְחוּ, iii. 5. Impf. with Wåw convers. וַתִּפָּקַחְנָה, iii. 7.
320. פָּרַד [26] (pårăd), *separate* ('ע Lary.), Nif. Impf. יִפָּרֵד, ii. 10.

321. פָּרָה [28] (pårå(h)), bear fruit (ל"ה), Imv. פְּרוּ, i. 22, 28.

322. פְּרִי [115] (pᵉrî), m., fruit.

323. פָּתַח [141] (påθăḥ), open, Nîf. be opened, in pause נִפְתְּחוּ, vii. 11, ('ל Lary.).

324. פֶּתַח [160] (péθăḥ), m., opening, door.

325. צֹאן [268] (ṣô'n), c., sheep, flock, collective.

326. צָבָא [13] (ṣåvå'), m., army, host.

327. צַד [33] (ṣăd), m., side, with prep. and suf. בְּצִדָּהּ, vi. 16.

328. צַדִּיק [203] (ṣăddîḳ), m., just, righteous.

329. צֹהַר [24] (ṣôhăr), f., light, collective, lights, windows.

330. צָוָה [509] (ṣåwå(h)), Ḳăl not used, (ל"ה), Pïēl צִוָּה, command, Impf. with Wåw convers. וַיְצַו.

331. צִלָּה (ṣillå(h)), pr. n. Zillah.

332. צֶלֶם [16] (ṣélĕm), m., image, likeness, i. 26, 27.

333. צֵלָע [42] (ṣēlå'), m., side, rib, pl. צְלָעוֹת.

334. צָמַח [31] (ṣåmăḥ), sprout, ('ל Lary.), Hĭf. make sprout, Impf. with Wåw convers. וַיַּצְמַח, ii. 5.

335. צָעַק [54] (ṣå'ăḳ), cry out ('ע Lary.), Part. act. plur. צֹעֲקִים, iv. 10.

336. צִפּוֹר [39] (ṣĭppôr), c., little bird.

337. קֶדֶם [61] (ḳédĕm), m., front, east, as adv. before.

338. קִדְמָה [4] (ḳĭdmå(h)), f., eastward, const. קִדְמַת, ii. 14.

339. קָדֹשׁ [171] (ḳådăš), be pure, clean, holy, Pïēl consecrate, Impf. with Wåw convers. וַיְקַדֵּשׁ, ii. 3.

340. קָוָה [48] (ḳåwå(h)), hope, (ל"ה), Nif. assemble, gather together, Impf. יִקָּווּ, i. 9.

341. קוֹל [500] (ḳôl), m., voice, sound.

342. קוּם [450] (ḳûm), rise up, (mid-vow.), Impf. with Wâw convers. וַיָּקָם, iv. 8, Hif. הֲקִמֹתִי, vi. 18.

343. קוֹמָה [45] (ḳômå(h)), f., stature, height.

344. קוֹץ [12] (ḳôṣ), m., thorn.

345. קָטֹן [56] (ḳåṭōn), adj. little.

346. קַיִן (ḳáyĭn), pr. n. Cain.

347. קֵינָן (ḳênån), pr. n. Cainan.

348. קַיִץ [20] (ḳáyĭṣ), m., fruit-harvest, summer.

349. קָלַל [82] (ḳålăl), be light in weight, be diminished, (ע"ע), Pĭ'ēl make light of, curse.

350. קֵן [13] (ḳēn), m., cell.

351. קָנָה [81] (ḳånå(h)), get, acquire (ל"ה), iv. 1.

352. קֵץ [65] (ḳēṣ) m., end.

353. קָצֶה [90] (ḳåṣê(h)), (const. קְצֵה) (= קֵץ), m., end.

354. קָצִיר [54] (ḳåṣîr) m., harvest.

355. קֹר [1] (ḳôr), m., cold.

356. קָרָא [855] (ḳårå'), call, (ל"א), Impf. with Wâw convers. וַיִּקְרָא, i. 5. Nif. Impf. יִקָּרֵא, ii. 28.

357. רָאָה [1295] (rå'å(h)), see, look ('ע Lary. and ל"ה), Impf. with Wâw convers. וַיַּרְא, i. 4, vi. 2.

358. רֹאשׁ [600] (rô'š), m., head, pl. רָאשִׁים.

359. רִאשׁוֹן [177] (rĭ'šôn), adj. first.

360. רֵאשִׁית [51] (rē'šîθ), f., denom. from רֹאשׁ, beginning.

361. רַב [466] (răv), m., much, many, fem. רַבָּה.

362. רָבַב [17] (råvăv), multiply, (ע"ע), Inf. const. רֹב, vi. 1.

363. רָבָה [243] (rāvā(h)), *increase* (ל"ה), Impf. Jussive יִרֶב, i. 22, Imv. רְבוּ, i. 22, 28, Hif. הַרְבָּה, Inf. abs. הַרְבָּה, iii. 16, Impf. 1st pers. אַרְבֶּה, iii. 16.

364. רָבַץ [30] (rāvăṣ), *lie down, crouch*, Part. act. רֹבֵץ, iv. 7.

365. רֶגֶל [260] (rĕğĕl), c., *foot*, with suf. רַגְלָהּ, viii. 9.

366. רָדָה [25] (rādā(h)), *have dominion, rule* (ל"ה), Impf. יִרְדּוּ, i. 26, Imv. רְדוּ, i. 28.

367. רוּחַ [11] (rû(ă)ḥ), Ḳăl not used, Hif. *inhale, smell*, 3 m. s. with Wāw convers. וַיָּרַח, viii. 21.

368. רוּחַ [375] (rû(ă)ḥ), f., *breath, spirit, wind*.

369. רוּם [193] (rûm), *be high, become high, rise*, (midvow.) Ḳăl Impf. 3 f. s. with Wāw convers. וַתָּרָם, vii. 17.

370. רֹחַב [21] (rōḥăv), m., *breadth*, with suf. רָחְבָּהּ, vi. 15.

371. רָחַף [3] (rāḥăf.), ('ע Lary.), Ḳăl not used, Pī'ēl רַחֵף, *brood, hover over*, Part. fem. מְרַחֶפֶת, i. 2.

372. רֵיחַ [56] (rê(ă)ḥ), m., *fragrance*.

373. רָמַשׂ [14] (rāmăś), *creep*, Part. act. with art. הָרֹמֵשׂ, i. 26, fem. הָרֹמֶשֶׂת, i. 21.

374. רֶמֶשׂ [17] (rĕmĕś), m., *creeping thing*.

375. רַע (f. רָעָה) [650] (ră'), adj. *bad, evil*.

376. רָעָה (rā'ă(h)), f., *badness, wickedness*.

377. רָעָה [183] (rā'ă(h)), *feed, tend*, ('ע Lary. and ל"ה), Part. act. const. רֹעֵה, iv. 2.

378. רַק (răḳ), adv. *only*.

379. רָקִיעַ [17] (rāḳî(ă)'), m., *expanse*, const. רְקִיעַ, i. 20.

380. שָׁאַר [131] (šâ'ǎr), remain, ('ע Lary.), Nif. be left, vii. 23.

381. שֶׁבַע [96] (šĕvă‘), (m. שִׁבְעָה) f., seven, שְׁבִיעִי seventh, ii. 2, שִׁבְעָתַיִם sevenfold, iv. 15.

382. שָׁבַת [70] (šâvăθ), rest, cease, Impf. with Wâw convers. וַיִּשְׁבֹּת, ii. 2.

383. שַׁגָּם [1] (šaggăm), only in vi. 3, with בְּ, (in their) wandering(?).

384. שֹׁהַם [11] (šōhăm), m., onyx, sardonyx.

385. שׁוּב [1100] (šûv), turn, (mid-vow.), Impf. 2d sg. תָּשׁוּב, iii. 19.

386. שׁוּף [3] (šûf), bruise, crush, (mid-vow.), Impf. יְשׁוּפְךָ, iii. 15.

387. שָׁחַת [151] (šâhăθ), Kăl not used, ('ע Lary.), Pï'ēl destroy, corrupt; Nif. Impf. with Wâw convers. וַתִּשָּׁחֵת, vi. 11.

388. שִׁית [85] (šîθ), put, place, (ע"י), Perf. שָׁת, iv. 25, Impf. 1st. sg. אָשִׁית, iii. 15.

389. שָׁכַךְ [5] (šâxăx), subside, (ע"ע), Impf. 3 m. pl. with Wâw cons. וַיָּשֹׁכּוּ, viii. 1.

390. שָׁכַן [127] (šâxăn), abide, dwell, Hif. Impf. with Wâw convers. וַיִּשְׁכֵּן.

391. שָׁלַח [837] (šâlăḥ), send, put forth ('ל Lary.), Impf. יִשְׁלַח, Pï'ēl Impf. with Wâw convers. and suf. וַיְשַׁלְּחֵהוּ, iii. 23.

392. שָׁלוֹשׁ (šâlôš), (m. שְׁלֹשָׁה) f., three; ordinal שְׁלִישִׁי, third, pl. שְׁלִישִׁים; שְׁלֹשִׁים thirty.

393. שָׁם (šăm), adv. there.

394. שֵׁם [850] (šēm), m., name.

395. שֵׁם (šēm), pr. n. Shem.

396. שָׁמַיִם [400] (šâmăyĭm), m., only in pl. heavens.

397. שְׁמֹנֶה (šᵉmônê(h)), (m. שְׁמֹנָה) f., *eight,* שְׁמֹנִים, *eighty.*

398. שָׁמַע [1104] (šămăʽ), *hear, listen to* (לְ Lary.), Impf. 3 pl. with Wāw convers. וַיִּשְׁמְעוּ, iii. 8, Imv. שְׁמַע, iv. 23.

399. שָׁמַר [460] (šămăr), *keep, watch,* Inf. const. with prep. and suf. לְשָׁמְרָהּ, ii. 15, Part. act. שֹׁמֵר, iv. 9.

400. שָׁנָה [877] (šănâ(h)), f., *year,* pl. שָׁנִים.

401. שֵׁנִי [150] (šēnî), adj. *second,* pl. שָׁנִים, vi. 16.

402. שְׁנַיִם [680] (šᵉnăyĭm), (const. שְׁנֵי) m., *cardinal two,* f. שְׁתַּיִם, const. שְׁתֵּי, iv. 19.

403. שָׁעָה [15] (šăʽâ(h)), *look, regard* ('ע Lary. and ל"ה), Impf. with Wāw convers. וַיִּשַׁע, iv. 4.

404. שָׁקָה [74] (šăḳâ(h)), Ḳăl not used, Hĭf. הִשְׁקָה, *give to drink,* ii. 6.

405. שָׁרַץ [14] (šărăṣ), *swarm, be many* ('ע Lary.), i. 20.

406. שֶׁרֶץ [15] (šĕrĕṣ), m., *swarm,* collective, *reptiles.*

407. שֵׁשׁ [26] (šēš), (m. שִׁשָּׁה) f., *six,* ordinal שִׁשִּׁי, *sixth,* i. 31.

408. שֵׁת (šēθ), pr. n. *Seth.*

409. שָׂדֶה [330] (śădê(h)), m., *field, open country.*

410. שִׂיחַ [4] (śî(ă)ḥ), m., *shrub, bush.*

411. שִׂים [603] (śîm), *put, set, place,* ('ע"י), Impf. יָשִׂים, Jussive. יָשֵׂם, with Wāw convers. וַיָּשֶׂם, ii. 8.

412. שָׂכַל [76] (śăẋăl), *look at, behold,* Hĭf. *make wise,* Inf. const. הַשְׂכִּיל, iii. 6.

413. תַּאֲוָה [26] (tăʼᵃwâ(h)), (const. תַּאֲוַת) f., *desire.*

414. תְּאֵנָה [37] (tᵉʼēnâ(h)), f., *fig, fig-tree.*

415. תֵּבָה [28] (tēvå(h)), f., ark, chest.
416. תֹּהוּ [20] (tốhû), m., wasteness, desolation.
417. תְּהוֹם [35] (tᵉhôm), c., abyss, deep.
418. תּוּבַל קַיִן (tûvăl ḳắyĭn), pr. n. Tubal-cain, iv. 22.
419. תָּוֶךְ [430] (tåwĕx), m., midst, const. תּוֹךְ, i. 6.
420. תּוֹלְדֹת [39] (tôlᵉdôθ), f. pl., generations, history.
421. תַּחַת (tăḥăθ), prep. under.
422. תַּחְתִּי [20] (tăḥtî), m., lowest part, pl. תַּחְתִּים, vi. 16.
423. תָּמִים [90] (tåmîm), (const. תְּמִים) m., perfect, complete.

424. תַּנִּין [1] (tănnîn), m., water-serpent, monster, pl. תַּנִּינִם, i. 21.
425. תָּפַר [4] (tåfăr), sew together, Impf. pl. with Wâw convers. וַיִּתְפְּרוּ, iii. 7.
426. תָּפַשׂ [54] (tåfăś), catch (harp strings), play, Part. act. תֹּפֵשׂ, iv. 21.
427. תַּרְדֵּמָה [7] (tărdēmå(h)), (const. תַּרְדֵּמַת) f., deep sleep, ii. 21.
428. תְּשׁוּקָה [3] (tᵉšûḳå(h)), f., desire, longing.
429. תֵּשַׁע [58] (tēšă‘), (const. תְּשַׁע) (m. תִּשְׁעָה) nine, תִּשְׁעִים, ninety.

ENGLISH-HEBREW VOCABULARY

OF

GENESIS I.–VIII.*

Abel, 97.
abide, 90.
above, 228.
abyss, 417.
acquire, 351.
Ada, 275.
add, 165.
adhere, 85.
after, 16, 64.
again, 278.
age, 88, 281.
all, 181.
alone, 49.
along with, 294.
also, 80.
altar, 212.
among, 48.
and, 108.
anger, 35.
another, 15.
appearance, 234.
Ararat, 42.
ark, 415.
army, 326.
as, 176.
ashamed, be, 55.
aside, turn, 268.
assemble, 340.
avenge, 261.

Bad, 375.
bdellium, 51.
be, 99.
bear, 162.
bear fruit, 321.
beast, 53, 128.
before, 150, 240, 337.
beget, 162.
begin, 132.
beginning, 360.
begun, be, 132.
behind, 64.
behold, v., 412.
behold! 101.
belly, 78.
bend the knee, 70.
between, 57.
bird, 283, 336.
blade, glittering, 196.
bless, 70.
blood, 89.
low, 256.
bone, 300.
book, 270.
born, be, 162.
both..and, 80.
bread, 197.
breadth, 370.
breath, 259, 264, 368.
breathe, 256.
bring, 54.
bring forth, 162.
bring out, 167.

broken up, be, 65.
bronze, 249.
brood, 371.
brother, 12.
bruise, v., 386.
bruise, 118.
brute, dumb, 53.
build, 62.
bush, 410.
burn, 144.
burnt-offering, 279.
but even, 36.

Cain 346.
Cainan, 347.
call, 356.
cast out, 83.
catch, 426.
cast, 382.
cell, 350.
change into, 103.
cherub, 190.
chest, 415.
child, 163.
choose, 56.
city, 288.
clean, 148.
clean, be, 339.
cleave, adhere, 85.
cleave, divide, 65.
clothe, 195.

* See last paragraph on page 228.

coat, 191.
cold, 355.
collection, 231.
come, 54.
come to pass, 99.
comfort, 247.
command, 330.
complete, v., 183.
complete, 423.
conceive, 106.
conception, 107.
consecrate, 339.
corrupt, 387.
country, open, 409.
covenant, 69.
cover, 187.   [189.
cover (with pitch),
covering, 220.
crafty, 304.
create, 67.
creature, living, 128.
creep, 373.
creeping thing, 374.
crouch, 364.
crush, 386.
cry out, 335.
cubit, 29.
curse, 41, 349.
cut, 67.   [146.
cutting instrument,

Darkness, 147.
daughter, 72.
dawn, 66.
day, 159.
deceive, 263.
deep, 417.
deep sleep, 427.
deluge, 207.
desire, v., 135.
desire, 135, 413, 428.
desolation, 416.
destroy, 213, 387.
devour, 22.

die, 77, 211.   [349.
diminished, be, 140.
divide, 50, 65.
dividing, 50.
do, 307.
dominion, 223.
dominion, have, 366.
door, 324.
dove, 160.
dried up, be, 153.
drink, give, 404.
drive, 83.
dry land, 143, 154.
dry up, 141.
dryness, 143.
dust, 295.
dwell, 174, 390.

Ear, give, 11.
earth, 5, 40.
east, 337.
eastward, 338.
eat, 22.
Eden, 276.
eighty, 397.
elder, 76.
emptiness, 52.
encompass, 266.
end, 352, 353.
ended, be, 183.
enmity, 18.
Enoch, 139.
Enosh, 32.
eternity, 281.
Eve, 122.
even, but, 34.
evening, 302.
every, 181.
evil, 375.
existing, being, 170.
expanse, 379.
expel, 83.
expire, 77.

eye, 287.

Faces, 315.
fail, 140.
fall, 258.
family, 236.
fat,-ness, 130.
father, 1.
favor, 138.
fear, 171.
feed, 377.
female, 260.
field, 409.
fifth, 137.
fig,-tree, 414.
find, 230.
finish, 183.
first, 359.
first-born, 59.
fish, 86.
five, 137.
flame, 196.
flesh, 71.
flock, 325.
flood, 207.
fly, v., 282.
food, 23, 197, 206.
foot, 365.
for, 63, 180, 192.
forge, v., 198.
form, v., 67, 168.
form, 169.
forsake, 285.
fountain, 227.
four, 38.
fowl, 283.
fragrance, 372.
free, set, 132.
fresh, 151.
from, 224.
from upon, 291.
front, 337.
fruit, 322.

fruit, bear, 321.
fugitive, 242.
full, be, 221.

Garden, 81.
gather, 34.
gather together, 340.
gathering, 231.
generation, 88, 420.
get, 351.
giants, 257.
Gihon, 79.
girdle, 119.
give, 265.
give rain, 216.
give rest, 245.
glittering, blade, 196.
glow, 144.
go, 100.
go about, 100.
go in, 54.
go out, 167.
go up, 292.
God, 26.
gold, 110.
good, be, 161.
good, 149.
grace, 138.
grass, tender, 94.
great, 76.
green herb, 306.
greenness, 173.
grievance, 298.
grieve oneself, 297.
ground, 5.
guilt, 280.

Ham, 133.
hammer, v., 198.
hand, 155.
happen, 99.
harp, 185.
harvest, 354.

he, 98.
head, 358.
hear, 398.
heart, 194.
heat, 134.
heavens, 396.
heel, 301.
height, 342.
help, 286.
herb, green, 306.
hero, 74.
Hiddekel, 120.
hide, 117, 271.
hide oneself, 103.
high, 73.
high, be, 369.
history, 420.
hold, 182.
hole, 131.
holy, be, 339.
host, 326.
house, 58.
household, 58.
hover over, 371.
hundred, 204.

I, 33.
if, 28.
image, 90, 332.
imagination, 169.
in, 48.
in behalf of, 63.
in, go, 54.
in presence of, 240.
increase, 363.
inhale, 367.
Irad, 289.
iron, 68.

Jabal, 152.
Japheth, 156.
Jared, 172.
journey, 92.

Jubal, 158.
judge, 87.
just, 328.

Keep, 399.
kill, 105.
kind, 219.
knee, bend the, 70.
know, 156.

Labor, 299.
Lamech, 201.
land, dry, 143, 154.
lattice, 37.
leaf, 293.
leave, 285.
left, be, 380.
length, 39.
lest, 60, 314.
lie down, 364.
life, 126.
lift up, 262.
light, 8, 205, 329.
light (not dark), be, 7.
light, be, 349.
light, give, 7.
lights, 329.
like, 176.
likeness, 90, 332.
listen, 11.
listen to, 398.
little, 343.
live, 127, 129. [170.
living creature, 127,
lo! 101.
longing, 428.
look, v., 357, 403.
look, 234.
look at, 412.
loose, 132.
Lord, 157.
lowest part, 422.
luminary, 205.

lyre, 185.

Mahalaleel, 209.
make, 307.
make sprout, 234.
male, 113.
man, 4, 20.
man of valor, 74.
many, 361.
many, be, 406.
Mehujael, 214.
Methushael, 237.
Methuselah, 238.
midst, 419.
might, 179.
mighty, be, 75.
mist, 3.
monster, 424.
month, 121.
moon, new, 121.
more, yea, 36.
morning, 66.
mother, 27.
mountain, 104.
mouth, 313.
much, 361.
multiply, 362.

Naamah, 254.
naked, 290, 304.
name, 394.
newly plucked, 151.
night, 199.
nine, -ty, 429.
no, 193.
Noah, 246.
Nod, 244.
nose, 35.
not, that, 60.
not, there is, 19.
not yet, 150.
nothing, 19
now, 312.

Offering, 226.
offer up, 292.
olive-tree, 111.
on, 48.
on account of; 184.
once, 316.
one, 14.
one tread or step, 316.
only, 21, 378.
onyx, 384.
open, 317, 319, 323.
open country, 409.
opening, 324.
organ, 277.
out, bring, 167.
out, cast, 83.
out, cry, 335.
out, go, 167.
outside, 124.
over, pass, 273.

Pain, 298, 299.
pain, suffer, 123, 297.
palm, 188.
park, 81.
part, lowest, 422.
pass, come to, 99.
pass over, 273.
perfect, 423.
pipe, 277.
pitch, -wood, 82.
pity, 247.
place, v., 388, 411.
place, 232.
plan, 215.
plant, v., 250.
plant, 306.
play, 426.
pleasantness, 251.
present, 226.
prudent, 304.
pure, be, 339.
purpose, 215.

put, 388, 411.
put forth, 391.
put on, 195.

Rain, 84.
rain, give, 216.
raven, 303.
reed, 277.
regard, 403.
remain, 380.
remember, 112.
rend, 317.
repent, 247.
reptiles, 406.
rest, v., 245, 382.
rest, 251.
rest, give, 245.
resting, a, 225.
resting place, 225.
restrain, 182.
rib, 333.
righteous, 328.
rise up, 342, 369.
river, 243.
rule, v., 87, 235, 366.
rule, 223.
rule over, 235.

Sardonyx, 384.
say, 30.
sea, 164.
season, 210.
second, -story, 400.
seduce, 263.
see, 357.
seed, 116.
seed, yield, 115.
seed-time, 116.
send, 391.
separate, 50, 320.
separation, 49.
serpent, 248.
serpent, water-, 424.

serve, 272.
set, 411.
set free, 132.
set time, 210.
Seth, 408.
seven, -th, -fold, 381.
sew together, 425.
sheep, 325.
Shem, 395.
shine, 7.
show, 239.
shower, 84.
shrub, 410.
shut, 67, 269.
side, 327, 333.
sign, 9.
sin, 125, 280.
sister, 13.
sit, 174.
six, -th, 407.
skin, 284.
slay, 105.
sleep, 175.
sleep, deep, 427.
smell, 367.
smite, 241, 252.
so, 184.
sole, 188.
son, 61.
song, 31.
soul, 259.
sound, 341.
sow, 115.
species, 219.
spirit, 264, 368.
spring, 227.
sprout, 93, 334.
sprout, make, 334.
star, 178.
stature, 343.
step, one, 316.
still, 278.
stone, 2.

street, 124.
strength, 179.
strike, 252.
strong, be, 75.
subdue, 177.
subside, 389.
substance, 233.
suffer pain, 297.
summer, 348.
surely, 21.
swarm, v., 405.
swarm, 406.
sweat, 114.
sword, 142.

Take, 202.
taken, be, 202.
tell, 239.
ten, 309, 310.
tend, 377.
tender grass, 94.
tent, 6.
tenth, 308.
that, conj., 180.
that not, 60.
the, 95.
then, 10.
there, 393.
therefore, 184.
these, 25.
they, 102.
third, 392.
thirty, 392.
this, 109.
thistle, 91.
thorn, 344.
thorny plant, 91.
thou, 47.
three, 392.
thus, 184.
Tigris, 120.
till, v., 272.
till, 274.

time, 311.
time set, 210.
to, 192.
tool, 146.
totality, 181.
touch, 241.
tread, one, 316.
tread upon, 177.
tree, 296.
true that? is it, 36.
Tubal-Cain, 418.
tunic, 191.
turn, 102, 266, 385.
turn aside, 268.
turning itself, 103.
two, 402.

Under, 241.
until, 274.
unto, 24.
up, go, 292.
upon, 291.
upon, tread, 177.
upwards, 228.
utterance, 31.

Valor, man of, 74.
vapor, 3.
very, 203.
violence, 136.
voice, 341.

Wait, 123.
walk, 100.
wanderer, 253. (383
wanderings, in their,
wasteness, 416.
watch, 399.
water, 218.
water-serpent, 424.
way, 92.
wealth, 233.
what? 208.

where? 17.
which, 44.
who, 44.
who? 217.
why? 200.
window, 37, 131, 329.
wing, 186.
winter, 145.
wipe out, 213.

wise, make, 412.
with, 46, 294, 294a.
within, from, 124.
without, from, 124.
woman, 43.
work, 221, 229.
wound, 118.
wounding, 318.
writing, 270.

Yahweh, 157.
Yea more, 36.
year, 400.
yet, 278.
youth, time of, 255.

Zillah, 331.

?, 96.
)(, 45.

WORD LISTS—HEBREW.

LIST I.
Verbs occurring 500–5000 times.

1.	אָכַל	8.	יָלַד	15.	עָבַר	22.	רָאָה
2.	אָמַר	9.	יָצָא	16.	עָלָה	23.	שִׂים
3.	בּוֹא	10.	יָשַׁב	17.	עָמַד	24.	שׁוּב
4.	דָּבַר	11.	לָקַח	18.	עָשָׂה	25.	שָׁלַח
5.	הָיָה	12.	מוּת	19.	צִוָּה	26.	שָׁמַע
6.	הָלַךְ	13.	נָשָׂא	20.	קוּם		
7.	יָדַע	14.	נָתַן	21.	קָרָא		

LIST II.
Verbs occurring 200–500 times.

27.	אָהַב	37.	יָסַף	47.	מָלַךְ	57.	פָּקַד
28.	אָסַף	38.	יָרֵא	48.	מָצָא	58.	רָבָה
29.	בָּנָה	39.	יָרַד	49.	נָגַד	59.	רוּם
30.	בָּקַשׁ	40.	יָרַשׁ	50.	נָטָה	60.	שָׁכַב
31.	בָּרַךְ	41.	יָשַׁע	51.	נָכָה	61.	שָׁמַר
32.	זָכַר	42.	כּוּן	52.	נָפַל	62.	שָׁפַט
33.	חָזַק	43.	כָּלָה	53.	נָצַל	63.	שָׁתָה
34.	חָטָא	44.	כָּרַת	54.	סוּר		
35.	חָיָה	45.	כָּתַב	55.	עָבַד		
36.	יָכֹל	46.	מָלֵא	56.	עָנָה		

LIST III.
Verbs occurring 100–200 times.

64.	אָבַד	66.	בּוֹשׁ	68.	בִּין	70.	גָּאַל
65.	אָמֵן	67.	בָּטַח	69.	בָּכָה	71.	גָּדַל

72.	גּוּר	83.	יָטַב	94.	סָבַב	105.	שָׂרַף
73.	גָּלָה	84.	יָתַר	95.	סָפַר	106.	שָׁאַל
74.	דָּרַשׁ	85.	כָּבֵד	96.	עָזַב	107.	שָׁבַע
75.	הָלַל	86.	כָּסָה	97.	פָּנָה	108.	שָׁבַר
76.	הָרַג	87.	כָּפַר	98.	קָבַר	109.	שָׁחָה
77.	זָבַח	88.	לָבַשׁ	99.	קָדַשׁ	110.	שָׁחַת
78.	חָלַל	89.	לָחַם	100.	קָרַב	111.	שָׁכַן
79.	חָנָה	90.	לָכַד	101.	רָדַף	112.	שָׁלַךְ
80.	חָשַׁב	91.	נָגַע	102.	רוּץ	113.	שָׁלֵם
81.	טָמֵא	92.	נָגַשׂ	103.	רָעָה	114.	שָׁרַת
82.	יָדָה	93.	נָסַע	104.	שָׂנֵא		

LIST IV.
Verbs occurring 50–100 times.

115.	אָבָה	130.	חָדַל	145.	יָרָה	160.	נָחַל
116.	אָחַז	131.	חוּל	146.	כָּבַס	161.	נָטַע
117.	אָסַר	132.	חָלָה	147.	כָּעַס	162.	נָכַר
118.	אָרַר	133.	חָלַק	148.	כָּשַׁל	163.	נָצַב
119.	בָּחַר	134.	חָנַן	149.	לוּן	164.	נָצַח
120.	בָּלַע	135.	חָפֵץ	150.	לָמַד	165.	נָצַר
121.	בָּעַר	136.	חָרָה	151.	מָדַד	166.	נָשַׂג
122.	בָּקַע	137.	חָרַשׁ	152.	מָהַר	167.	סָגַר
123.	בָּרָא	138.	חָתַת	153.	מָכַר	168.	סָתַר
124.	בָּרַח	139.	טָהֵר	154.	מָלַט	169.	עוּר
125.	דָּבַק	140.	יָבֵשׁ	155.	מָשַׁח	170.	עָזַר
126.	הָפַךְ	141.	יָכַח	156.	מָשַׁל	171.	עָנָה
127.	זוּר	142.	יָעַץ	157.	נָבַט	172.	עָרַךְ
128.	זָנָה	143.	יָצַק	158.	נָדַח	173.	פָּדָה
129.	זָרַע	144.	יָצַר	159.	נוּחַ	174.	פּוּץ

175.	פָּלָא	184.	קָנָה	193.	רָפָא	201.	שִׁית
176.	פָּלַל	185.	קָרַע	194.	רָצָה	202.	שָׁכַם
177.	פָּעַל	186.	רָחַם	195.	שָׁבַע	203.	שָׁמַר
178.	פָּרַר	187.	רָחַץ	196.	שָׂכַל	204.	שָׁמֵם
179.	פָּרַשׁ	188.	רָחַק	197.	שָׁבַת	205.	שָׁקָה
180.	צָעַק	189.	רִיב	198.	שָׁדַד	206.	תָּמַם
181.	צָפָה	190.	רָכַב	199.	שָׁחַט	207.	תָּפַשׂ
182.	צָרַר	191.	רָנַן	200.	שִׁיר	208.	תָּקַע
183.	קָלַל	192.	רָעַע				

LIST V.

Nouns occurring 500–5000 times.

1.	אָב	11.	בַּיִת	21.	לֵב	31.	קוֹל
2.	אָדָם	12.	בֵּן	22.	מֵאָה	32.	קֹדֶשׁ
3.	אֲדֹנָי	13.	דָּבָר	23.	מַיִם	33.	רֹאשׁ
4.	אָח	14.	דֶּרֶךְ	24.	מֶלֶךְ	34.	שִׁבְעָה
5.	אֶחָד	15.	הַר	25.	נֶפֶשׁ	35.	שֵׁם
6.	אַחַר	16.	חַי	26.	עֶבֶד	36.	שְׁנַיִם
7.	אִישׁ	17.	טוֹב	27.	עַיִן	37.	שָׁנָה
8.	אֱלֹהִים	18.	יָד	28.	עִיר		
9.	אֱנוֹשׁ	19.	יוֹם	29.	עַם		
10.	אֶרֶץ	20.	כֹּהֵן	30.	פָּנִים		

LIST VI.

Nouns occurring 300–500 times.

38.	אָדוֹן	48.	זָהָב	58.	מָקוֹם	68.	פֶּה
39.	אֹהֶל	49.	חֹדֶשׁ	59.	מִשְׁפָּט	69.	רַב
40.	אֶלֶף	50.	חָמֵשׁ	60.	נָבִיא	70.	רוּחַ
41.	אַרְבָּעָה	51.	חֶרֶב	61.	סָבִיב	71.	שָׂדֶה
42.	אִשָּׁה	52.	יָם	62.	עוֹלָה	72.	שַׂר
43.	בְּהֵמָה	53.	כְּלִי	63.	עוֹלָם	73.	שָׁלוֹשׁ
44.	בַּת	54.	כֶּסֶף	64.	עֵץ	74.	שָׁמַיִם
45.	גָּדוֹל	55.	לֶחֶם	65.	עֶשֶׂר	75.	שַׁעַר
46.	גּוֹי	56.	מִזְבֵּחַ	66.	עֶשְׂרִים	76.	תָּוֶךְ
47.	דָּם	57.	מִלְחָמָה	67.	עֵת		

LIST VII.

Nouns occurring 200–300 times.

77.	אֶבֶן	87.	בָּשָׂר	97.	מְאֹד	107.	עָוֹן
78.	אֲדָמָה	88.	גְּבוּל	98.	מוֹעֵד	108.	צֹאן
79.	אַיִל	89.	זֶרַע	99.	מַחֲנֶה	109.	קֶרֶב
80.	אֵל	90.	חַטָּאת	100.	מַטֶּה	110.	רֶגֶל
81.	אָמָה	91.	חַיִל	101.	מַלְאָךְ	111.	רֵעַ
82.	אַף	92.	חֶסֶד	102.	מִנְחָה	112.	רֶשַׁע
83.	אָרוֹן	93.	כָּבוֹד	103.	מַעֲשֶׂה	113.	שָׁלוֹם
84.	בֶּגֶד	94.	כַּף	104.	מִשְׁפָּחָה	114.	שֵׁשׁ
85.	בֹּקֶר	95.	לֵבָב	105.	נַחֲלָה	115.	תּוֹרָה
86.	בְּרִית	96.	לַיְלָה	106.	נַעַר		

LIST VIII.

Nouns occurring 100–200 times.

116.	אֹזֶן	134.	יַיִן	152.	מִשְׁכָּן	169.	צַר
117.	אַרְבָּעִים	135.	יָמִין	153.	נֶגֶב	170.	רִאשׁוֹן
118.	בְּכוֹר	136.	יֵשׁ	154.	נַחַל	171.	רַב
119.	בָּקָר	137.	יָשָׁר	155.	נְחֹשֶׁת	172.	רָחָב
120.	גִּבּוֹר	138.	כָּבַשׁ	156.	נָשִׂיא	173.	רֶכֶב
121.	דּוֹר	139.	כֹּחַ	157.	סוּס	174.	רָעָב
122.	זֶבַח	140.	כָּנָף	158.	סֵפֶר	175.	שָׂפָה
123.	זָקֵן	141.	כִּסֵּא	159.	עֲבוֹדָה	176.	שֵׁבֶט
124.	חוֹמָה	142.	כֶּרֶם	160.	עֵדָה	177.	שַׁבָּת
125.	חוּץ	143.	לָשׁוֹן	161.	עָפָר	178.	שְׁלִישִׁי
126.	חָכָם	144.	מִגְרָשׁ	162.	עֶצֶם	179.	שֶׁמֶן
127.	חָכְמָה	145.	מָוֶת	163.	עֶרֶב	180.	שְׁמֹנָה
128.	חֵמָה	146.	מְלָאכָה	164.	פַּר	181.	שֶׁמֶשׁ
129.	חֲמִשִּׁים	147.	מַמְלָכָה	165.	פְּרִי	182.	שֵׁנִי
130.	חֲצִי	148.	מִסְפָּר	166.	פֶּתַח	183.	שֶׁקֶר
131.	חֹק	149.	מַעַל	167.	צֶדֶק	184.	תּוֹעֵבָה
132.	חֻקָּה	150.	מִצְוָה	168.	צְדָקָה	185.	תָּמִיד
133.	יַחַד	151.	מַרְאֶה				

LIST IX.

Nouns occurring 50–100 times.

186.	אֶבְיוֹן	191.	אֲחֻזָּה	196.	אַלְמָנָה	201.	אֹרַח
187.	אֶרֶז	192.	אַחֲרוֹן	197.	אֱמוּנָה	202.	אֲרִי
188.	אָוֶן	193.	אַחֲרִית	198.	אֵמֶר	203.	אַרְיֵה
189.	אוֹצָר	194.	אֱלוֹהַּ	199.	אֵפוֹד	204.	אֹרֶךְ
190.	אוֹת	195.	אַלּוּף	200.	אֶרֶז	205.	אִשֶּׁה

206.	בֶּטֶן	234.	חֲמוֹר	262.	מַצָּה	290.	פֵּאָה
207.	בָּמָה	235.	חָם	263.	מִקְדָּשׁ	291.	צוּר
208.	בַּעַל	236.	חֵן	264.	מִקְנֶה	292.	צָרָה
209.	בַּרְזֶל	237.	חֵץ	265.	מָרוֹם	293.	קֶדֶם
210.	בְּרָכָה	238.	חֶרְפָּה	266.	מַשָּׂא	294.	קָטוֹן
211.	גָּאוֹן	239.	חֹשֶׁךְ	267.	מָשִׁיחַ	295.	קְטֹרֶת
212.	גְּבוּרָה	240.	טָהוֹר	268.	מִשְׁמֶרֶת	296.	קִיר
213.	גֶּבֶר	241.	טָמֵא	269.	מִשְׁקָל	297.	קָנֶה
214.	גּוֹרָל	242.	יְאוֹר	270.	נֶדֶר	298.	קֵץ
215.	גִּיא	243.	יוֹמָם	271.	נֶסֶךְ	299.	קָצֶה
216.	גָּמָל	244.	יֶלֶד	272.	נַעֲרָה	300.	קָצִיר
217.	גֶּפֶן	245.	יַעַר	273.	סֶלָה	301.	קָרְבָּן
218.	גֵּר	246.	יְרִיעָה	274.	סֶלַע	302.	קָרוֹב
219.	דָּבָר	247.	יְשׁוּעָה	275.	סֹלֶת	303.	קֶרֶן
220.	דְּבַשׁ	248.	כְּסִיל	276.	עֶבֶר	304.	קֶשֶׁת
221.	דֶּלֶת	249.	כְּרוּב	277.	עַד	305.	רֵאשִׁית
222.	דַּעַת	250.	כָּתֵף	278.	עֵדוּת	306.	רָחֹק
223.	הֵיכָל	251.	מִגְדָּל	279.	עוֹר	307.	רִיב
224.	הָמוֹן	252.	מָגֵן	280.	עַז	308.	רֵיחַ
225.	זָכָר	253.	מִדָּה	281.	עֹז	309.	רָצוֹן
226.	זְרוֹעַ	254.	מְדִינָה	282.	עֶלְיוֹן	310.	שְׂמֹאל
227.	חֶבֶל	255.	מוּסָר	283.	עָמָל	311.	שִׂמְחָה
228.	חַג	256.	מִזְמוֹר	284.	עֵמֶק	312.	שָׂעִיר
229.	חָדָשׁ	257.	מִזְרָח	285.	עָנִי	313.	שְׁאוֹל
230.	חִטָּה	258.	מָחָר	286.	עָנָן	314.	שְׁאֵרִית
231.	חָלָב	259.	מַחֲשֶׁבֶת	287.	עֵצָה	315.	שְׁבִיעִי
232.	חֲלוֹם	260.	מַלְכוּת	288.	עֲרָבָה	316.	שִׁבְעִים
233.	חֵלֶק	261.	מְעַט	289.	עֶרְוָה	317.	שׁוֹפָר

318. שׁוֹר	322. שְׁמָמָה	326. שִׁשִׁים	330. תְּפִלָּה
319. שִׁיר	323. שֵׁן	327. תָּמִים	331. תְּרוּמָה
320. שֻׁלְחָן	324. שִׁפְחָה	328. תִּפְאָרָה	332. תִּשְׁעָה
321. שָׁלֵם	325. שֶׁקֶל	329. תִּפְאֶרֶת	

WORD LISTS—TRANSLATION.

LIST I.

Verbs occurring 500—5000 times.

1. Eat
2. Say
3. Go in
4. Speak
5. Be
6. Go
7. Know
8. Bring forth
9. Go out
10. Sit, dwell
11. Take
12. Die
13. Lift up
14. Give
15. Pass over
16. Go up
17. Stand
18. Do, make
19. Command
20. Rise, stand
21. Call, meet
22. See
23. Put
24. Turn
25. Send
26. Hear

LIST II.

Verbs occurring 200—500 times.

27. Love
28. Gather
29. Build
30. Seek
31. Bless
32. Remember
33. Be strong
34. Sin
35. Live
36. Be able
37. Add
38. Be afraid
39. Go down
40. Possess
41. Deliver
42. Prepare
43. Complete
44. Cut
45. Write
46. Be full
47. Be king
48. Find
49. Make known
50. Stretch out
51. Smite
52. Fall
53. Snatch, deliver
54. Turn aside
55. Serve
56. Answer
57. Visit
58. Multiply
59. Be high
60. Lie down
61. Keep
62. Judge
63. Drink

LIST III.

Verbs occurring 100—200 times.

64. Perish
65. Be firm
66. Be ashamed
67. Trust
68. Perceive
69. Weep
70. Redeem
71. Be great
72. Sojourn
73. Reveal
74. Tread, seek
75. Praise
76. Kill
77. Sacrifice
78. Pollute, begin
79. Encamp
80. Impute, think
81. Be unclean

82. Thank
83. Be good
84. Be left
85. Be heavy
86. Conceal
87. Cover
88. Put on
89. Fight
90. Capture
91. Touch
92. Approach

93. Depart
94. Surround
95. Number
96. Abandon
97. Turn about
98. Bury
99. Be holy
100. Draw near
101. Pursue
102. Run
103. Feed

104. Hate
105. Burn
106. Ask
107. Swear
108. Break in pieces
109. Do obeisance
110. Corrupt
111. Dwell
112. Cast
113. Be whole
114. Minister

LIST IV.

Verbs occurring 50—100 times.

115. Be willing
116. Seize
117. Bind
118. Curse
119. Choose
120. Swallow
121. Consume
122. Cleave, split
123. Create
124. Flee
125. Cleave, cling
126. Turn, overthrow
127. Sojourn   [tion
128. Commit fornica-
129. Sow
130. Cease [forth, wait
131. Be pained, bring
132. Be sick
133. Distribute
134. Be gracious
135. Delight
136. Be angry [silent
137. Plow, engrave, be
138. Be dismayed
139. Be clean
140. Be dry
141. Reprove
142. Give counsel

143. Pour out
144. Form
145. Cast, instruct
146. Wash
147. Be provoked
148. Stumble
149. Lodge
150. Learn
151. Measure
152. Hasten
153. Sell
154. Escape
155. Anoint
156. Rule
157. Look, regard
158. Drive away
159. Rest
160. Inherit
161. Plant
162. Know, be ignorant
163. Set
164. Be pre-eminent
165. Keep, watch
166. Reach
167. Shut
168. Conceal
169. Awake
170. Assist

171. Be afflicted
172. Arrange
173. Redeem
174. Scatter
175. Separate, be won-
176. Pray   [derful
177. Do, make
178. Break, fail
179. Spread out
180. Cry out
181. Watch, cover
182. Distress
183. Be light
184. Get, obtain
185. Rend
186. Have mercy
187. Wash
188. Be far off
189. Strive
190. Ride
191. Sing, cry aloud
192. Be evil
193. Heal
194. Be pleased
195. Suffice
196. Act wisely, pros-
197. Cease, rest [per
198. Destroy

199. Kill
200. Sing
201. Put
202. Rise early
203. Destroy
204. Be desolate, as-[tonished]
205. Drink
206. Finish
207. Catch, seize
208. Strike, blow (a [trumpet])

LIST V.

Nouns occurring 500—5000 times.

1. Father
2. Man, mankind
3. Lord
4. Brother
5. One
6. After
7. Man
8. God
9. Man, mankind
10. Earth
11. House
12. Son
13. Word, thing
14. Way
15. Mountain
16. Living, life
17. Good
18. Hand
19. Day
20. Priest
21. Heart
22. Hundred
23. Water
24. King
25. Soul
26. Servant
27. Eye, fountain
28. City
29. People
30. Face
31. Voice
32. Holiness
33. Head
34. Seven
35. Name
36. Two
37. Year

LIST VI.

Nouns occurring 300—500 times.

38. Master
39. Tent
40. Ox, thousand
41. Four
42. Woman
43. Cattle
44. Daughter
45. Great
46. Nation
47. Blood
48. Gold
49. New, month
50. Five
51. Sword
52. Sea
53. Article, vessel
54. Silver
55. Bread
56. Altar
57. War
58. Place
59. Judgment
60. Prophet
61. Around
62. Burnt-offering
63. Age.
64. Tree
65. (Ten)-teen
66. Twenty
67. Time
68. Mouth
69. Many
70. Spirit
71. Field
72. Prince
73. Three
74. Heavens
75. Gate
76. Midst

LIST VII.

Nouns occurring 200—300 times.

77. Stone
78. Ground
79. Ram
80. Mighty one, God
81. Cubit
82. Nose, anger
83. Ark
84. Garment
85. Morning

86. Covenant
87. Flesh
88. Boundary
89. Seed
90. Sin
91. Strength
92. Kindness
93. Honor
94. Palm of hand
95. Heart
96. Night
97. Exceedingly
98. Season
99. Camp
100. Rod, tribe
101. Messenger
102. Offering
103. Work
104. Family
105. Inheritance
106. Boy, servant
107. Iniquity
108. Flock
109. Midst
110. Foot
111. Friend, neigh- [bor
112. Wicked
113. Peace
114. Six
115. Law

LIST VIII.

Nouns occurring 100—200 times.

116. Ear
117. Forty
118. First-born
119. Herd, cattle
120. Hero
121. Generation
122. Sacrifice
123. Old man, elder
124. Wall
125. Abroad
126. Wise
127. Wisdom
128. Heat, fury
129. Fifty
130. Half
131. Statute
132. Statute
133. Together, alike
134. Wine
135. Right hand
136. There is
137. Straight, upright
138. Lamb
139. Strength
140. Wing
141. Throne
142. Vineyard
143. Tongue
144. Pasture
145. Death
146. Work
147. Kingdom
148. Number
149. Above
150. Commandment
151. Appearance
152. Dwelling, [taber-[nacle
153. South country
154. Valley, brook
155. Bronze, copper
156. Prince
157. Horse
158. Book
159. Service
160. Congregation
161. Dust
162. Bone
163. Evening
164. Bullock
165. Fruit
166. Door
167. Righteousness
168. Righteousness
169. Adversary
170. First
171. Abundance
172. Breadth
173. Chariot
174. Famine
175. Lip, shore
176. Rod, tribe
177. Rest, sabbath
178. Third
179. Oil, fat
180. Eight
181. Sun
182. Second
183. Falsehood
184. Abomination
185. Continuity

LIST IX.

Nouns occurring 50—100 times.

186. Needy
187. Socket
188. Iniquity
189. Treasury
190. Sign
191. Possession
192. Last
193. Latter end
194. God
195. Leader, ox
196. Widow
197. Faithfulness
198. Saying
199. Ephod
200. Cedar
201. Way, path
202. Lion
203. Lion
204. Length
205. Fire-offering
206. Belly
207. High-place
208. Master, Baal
209. Iron
210. Blessing
211. Pride
212. Might
213. Mighty one, man
214. Lot
215. Valley
216. Camel
217. Vine
218. Stranger
219. Pestilence
220. Honey
221. Door
222. Knowledge
223. Temple
224. Multitude
225. Male
226. Arm, strength
227. Line, destruction
228. Festival
229. Fresh, new
230. Wheat
231. Fat
232. Dream
233. Portion
234. He-ass
235. Violence
236. Favor, grace
237. Arrow, handle
238. Reproach
239. Darkness
240. Clean
241. Unclean
242. River, Nile
243. Daily
244. Child, youth
245. Forest
246. Curtain
247. Deliverance
248. Fool
249. Cherub
250. Shoulder
251. Tower
252. Shield
253. Measure
254. Province
255. Chastisement,
256. Psalm [warning
257. East
258. To-morrow
259. Thought
260. Kingdom
261. A little
262. Unleavened food
263. Sanctuary
264. Property
265. High place
266. Burden, tribute
267. Anointed one
268. Observance
269. Weight
270. Vow
271. Libation
272. Maiden
273. Pause
274. Rock
275. Fine flour
276. Over, beyond
277. Witness
278. Testimony
279. Skin, leather
280. Goat
281. Strength
282. High
283. Labor, misery
284. Valley
285. Affliction
286. Cloud
287. Counsel

288. Plain	303. Horn	318. Ox
289. Nakedness	304. Bow	319. Song
290. Side	305. Beginning	320. Table
291. Rock	306. Distant	321. Peace-offering
292. Adversity	307. Strife	322. Desolation, waste
293. Before, east	308. Savor	323. Tooth
294. Small	309. Desire	324. Maid-servant
295. Incense	310. Left hand	325. Shekel
296. Wall	311. Rejoicing	326. Sixty
297. Stalk	312. Hairy, goat	327. Perfect
298. End	313. Underworld	328. Glory
299. End	314. Remnant	329. Glory
300. Harvest	315. Seventh	330. Prayer
301. Offering	316. Seventy	331. Heave-offering
302. Near	317. Trumpet	332. Nine

DEC 11 '80
APR 18 '83
MAY 2 8 1985